"If you missed Volumes 1 and 2, you're in luck, since Volume 3 has arrived exactly when educators around the world are adopting a cacophony of blended learning approaches, activities, and analyses."

—Curtis J. Bonk, Professor of Instructional Systems Technology
in the School of Education at University of Indiana, USA

"*Blended Learning: Research Perspectives, Volume 3* promises to set the standard for blended learning research. This is critical reading to advance research and practice of blended learning across educational sectors."

—Peter Shea, Associate Provost for Online Learning and Professor
in the School of Education at University at Albany, USA,
and Editor of *Online Learning Journal*

"This volume, like its two predecessors, is a rich buffet of research reports and insights. But the last entrée is a dessert not to be missed, a concluding chapter that ties together many diverse strands as it speculates about the future."

—George L. Mehaffy, Senior Advisor at Sova

"This book is a culmination of decades of hard work to improve student learning through extensive research and practical application. Its authors are the leading researchers in online and blended learning."

—Jeffrey S. Russell, Vice Provost of Lifelong Learning and
Dean of Continuing Studies at University of Wisconsin-Madison, USA

"Whether you are an academic researcher, an instructor, a technology developer, a learning sciences expert, or an administrator, this book is for you. It provides a wide array of broad and deep insights into the complex subject of blended learning."

—Manoj Kulkarni, CEO of Realizeit

"Central to this work is the importance of student outcomes, faculty engagement, and the appropriate use of technology to support student learning by providing relevant and important research that can serve as a guide for educators and their students."

—Connie Johnson, Chief Academic Officer/Provost at
Colorado Technical University, USA

"This third volume is most welcome and timely. Considering our collective recent experience, blended learning is here to stay, making research into best practices in this area essential to all those involved in post-secondary teaching and learning."

—Malcolm Brown, Consultant for the Horizon Report

"This collection gives details that are most significant and promising, with a conclusion pondering what lies ahead, not just for learning, but all the paths before us, informing our choices and futures. A must-read."

—George Otte, Senior Associate Dean of Academic Affairs at the
CUNY School of Professional Studies, USA

"The first two volumes of *Blended Learning: Research Perspectives* were crucial roadmaps to the future of teaching and learning. This third volume is a beacon of light cutting through the COVID-19 clouds to show us the way forward once again."
—Dale P. Johnson, Director of Digital Innovation in the
University Design Institute at Arizona State University, USA

"A timely and valuable contribution to an increasingly important area by some of the most thorough academic researchers working on blended learning."
—Glenda Morgan, Research Director in Gartner Research

"This is an important work at a critical time in education, providing research for how to make the most effective use of the digital tools that have suddenly become ubiquitous."
—Thomas Cavanagh, Vice Provost for Digital Learning at
University of Central Florida, USA

"This book is a splendid addition to this series. It demonstrates the advancement of the field in the range of methodological approaches to enhance our knowledge of blended learning."
—Tanya Joosten, Senior Scientist and Director of Digital Learning
Research and Development, Academic Affairs, at University of
Wisconsin-Milwaukee, USA

"Comprehensive in its coverage, bracing and eclectic in its approach, the third volume of *Blended Learning: Research Perspectives* empowers the most important learning outcome of all: wisdom."
—Gardner Campbell, Associate Professor of English at
Virginia Commonwealth University, USA

"Volume 3 in this series on blended learning both complements and extends the previous contributions and is essential reading for educators who teach, design, evaluate, and research in contemporary educational environments."
—Gavin Sanderson, SFHEA, Program Director of the
Graduate Diploma in Education Studies (Digital Learning)
at University of South Australia, Australia

"The third volume of *Blended Learning: Research Perspectives* provides a broad depth of knowledge on which to build the core foundation for blended instruction."
—Mary P. Niemiec, Associate Vice President for Digital Education
and Director of University of Nebraska Online
at University of Nebraska, USA

"The variety of topics covered in this book accurately mirrors the complexity facing education. Highly valuable reading for all involved in education."
—Maria Zajac, Editor-in-Chief of *E-Mentor* and Certified Instructional
Designer at SGH Warsaw School of Economics, Poland

"This excellent book, third in a series, captures leading research and practices in the field today, and features a peek into future scenarios. It is a must-read for those wishing to participate in blended education models that ensure quality education."

—Frank Mayadas, Program Director of the Alfred P. Sloan Foundation and Founding President of the Online Learning Consortium

"The third volume of this book is another welcome read for researchers and practitioners trying to sort through the complexity of choice for technologies and pedagogies that support digital and blended learning."

—Karen Vignare, Vice President of Digital Transformation for Student Success and Executive Director of the Personalized Learning Consortium for the Association of Public & Land-Grant Universities

"It's easy to opine about blended learning's usefulness, but much harder to demonstrate it. The authors have done just that, collecting the evidence and presenting it elegantly. You simply must read this book."

—Susan Grajek, Vice President for Partnerships, Communities, and Research at EDUCAUSE

"The third volume of *Blended Learning: Research Perspectives* provides a timely resource for both new and experienced blended learning practitioners and continues in the tradition of the first two volumes."

—John Kane, Professor of Economics and Director of Center for Excellence in Learning and Teaching at State University of New York at Oswego, USA

BLENDED LEARNING

Blended Learning: Research Perspectives, Volume 3 offers new insights into the state of blended learning, an instructional modality that combines face-to-face and digitally mediated experiences. Education has recently seen remarkable advances in instructional technologies such as adaptive and personalized instruction, virtual learning environments, gaming, analytics, and big data software. This book examines how these and other evolving tools are fueling advances in our schools, colleges, and universities. Original scholarship from education's top thinkers will prepare researchers and learning designers to tackle major issues relating to learning effectiveness, diversity, economies of scale, and beyond.

Anthony G. Picciano is Professor of Education Leadership at Hunter College and Professor in the PhD program in Urban Education at the City University of New York Graduate Center, USA.

Charles D. Dziuban is Director of the Research Initiative for Teaching Effectiveness at the University of Central Florida, USA.

Charles R. Graham is Professor of Instructional Psychology and Technology at Brigham Young University, USA.

Patsy D. Moskal is Director of the Digital Learning Impact Evaluation in the Research Initiative for Teaching Effectiveness at the University of Central Florida, USA.

BLENDED LEARNING

Research Perspectives, Volume 3

*Edited by Anthony G. Picciano,
Charles D. Dziuban, Charles R. Graham,
and Patsy D. Moskal*

NEW YORK AND LONDON

First published 2022
by Routledge
605 Third Avenue, New York, NY 10158

and by Routledge
2 Park Square, Milton Park, Abingdon, Oxon, OX14 4RN

Routledge is an imprint of the Taylor & Francis Group, an informa business

© 2022 Taylor & Francis

The right of Anthony G. Picciano, Charles D. Dziuban, Charles R. Graham, and Patsy D. Moskal to be identified as the authors of the editorial material, and of the authors for their individual chapters, has been asserted in accordance with sections 77 and 78 of the Copyright, Designs and Patents Act 1988.

All rights reserved. No part of this book may be reprinted or reproduced or utilised in any form or by any electronic, mechanical, or other means, now known or hereafter invented, including photocopying and recording, or in any information storage or retrieval system, without permission in writing from the publishers.

Trademark notice: Product or corporate names may be trademarks or registered trademarks, and are used only for identification and explanation without intent to infringe.

Library of Congress Cataloging-in-Publication Data
A catalog record for this book has been requested

ISBN: 978-0-367-47678-6 (hbk)
ISBN: 978-0-367-48040-0 (pbk)
ISBN: 978-1-003-03773-6 (ebk)

DOI: 10.4324/9781003037736

Typeset in Bembo
by Apex CoVantage, LLC

To those faculty and students who persevered during the coronavirus pandemic of 2020–2021, finding new ways to teach and new ways to learn.

CONTENTS

About the Editors	*xv*
List of Contributors	*xix*
Preface	*xxii*
Acknowledgements	*xxiv*

SECTION I
Introduction and Foundations   1

1   Introduction   3
Patsy D. Moskal and Anthony G. Picciano

2   Exploring Definitions, Models, Frameworks, and Theory
for Blended Learning Research   10
Charles R. Graham

SECTION II
Student Outcomes   31

3   Neotraditional Students and Online Discussions: What
Do They Really Want?   33
Jeff Renfrow

xii Contents

4 Blended Delivery Modes and Student Success: An In-Depth Exploration of How Different Levels of Online and Blended Course Taking Relate to Student Retention 49
Scott James and Karen Swan

5 Scaling Course Design as a Learning Analytics Variable 73
John Fritz, Thomas Penniston, Mike Sharkey, and John Whitmer

SECTION III
Faculty Issues 95

6 Highly Effective Blended Teaching Practices 97
Cub Kahn and Lynne L. Hindman

7 Blended Faculty Community of Inquiry Transforms Online Teaching Perceptions and Practices 116
Karen Skibba and Maria Widmer

8 Impact Analysis of Ten Years of Blended Learning 131
Concepcion B. Godev and Jaesoon An

SECTION IV
Adaptive Learning Research 145

9 Efficacy of Adaptive Learning in Blended Courses 147
Jeremy Anderson, Heather Bushey, Maura Devlin, and Amanda Gould

10 Adaptive and Active: The Integration of Adaptive Courseware Through the Lens of Blended Learning 163
Janelle D. Voegele and Raiza Dottin

11 A Blended Learning Case Study: Geo Exploration, Adaptive Learning, and Visual Knowledge Acquisition 178
Mark Jack Smith

Contents **xiii**

SECTION V
K–12 Perspectives
191

12 Competencies and Practices for Guiding K–12 Blended
Teacher Readiness 193
*Cecil R. Short, Courtney Hanny, Michelle Jensen, Karen
Arnesen, and Charles R. Graham*

13 Examining Peer-to-Peer Supports in K–12 Blended
Academic Communities of Engagement 214
Jered Borup, Shea Walters, and Rebecca Stimson

14 Intellectual Agency of Linguistically Diverse Students
With Disabilities in a Blended Learning Environment 231
Mary Frances Rice and Mark Stevens

15 Multimodal Blended Learning and English Language Learners 247
Mark Stevens

SECTION VI
International Perspectives
267

16 Negotiating the Blend 269
George R. Bradford and Anders Norberg

17 Blended Learning and Shared Metacognition: What Is
the Connection? 282
Norman D. Vaughan

18 Evidence-Based Blended Learning Design: A Synthesis of
Findings From Four Studies 300
*Ron Owston, Taru Malhotra, Dennis York, and Jirarat
Sitthiworachart*

SECTION VII
Science and Health Research
313

19 Blending Geoscience Laboratory Learning and
Undergraduate Research With Interactive Open
Educational Resources 315
Juhong Christie Liu, Elizabeth Johnson, and Erik Haroldson

xiv Contents

20 Student Experiences Learning Psychomotor Skills in a
Blended Doctor of Physical Therapy Program 333
Timothy Miller and Swapna Kumar

21 Integrative Blended Learning: Theory, Disciplines,
Application, Critical Thinking, and Assessment 349
*Paige L. McDonald, Karen S. Schlumpf, Gregory C. Weaver,
and Mary Corcoran*

The Future 363

22 Education and Blended Learning: Some Possible Futures 365
Charles D. Dziuban and Anthony G. Picciano

Index *403*

ABOUT THE EDITORS

Anthony G. Picciano holds multiple faculty appointments at the City University of New York's Hunter College, Graduate Center; and the School of Professional Studies. He has also held administrative appointments at the City University and State University of New York, including that of vice president and deputy to the president at Hunter College. He assisted in the establishment of the CUNY PhD program in urban education and served as its executive officer for ten years (2007–2018). Dr. Picciano's research interests include education leadership, education policy, online and blended learning, multimedia instructional models, and research methods. He has authored 17 books and numerous articles, including *Educational Leadership and Planning for Technology*, which currently is in its fifth edition (Pearson Education). His latest book is *The Community College in the Post-Recession Reform Era: Aims and Outcomes of a Decade of Experimentation* (Jordan, C., & Picciano, A. G. (2020). Routledge/Taylor & Francis, Publishers).

Dr. Picciano has been involved in major grants from the US Department of Education, the National Science Foundation, IBM, and the Alfred P. Sloan Foundation. He was a member of a research project funded by the US Department of Education-Institute for Education Sciences, the purpose of which was to conduct a meta-analysis on "what works" in postsecondary online education (2017–2019). In 1998, Dr. Picciano co-founded CUNY Online, a multimillion-dollar initiative funded by the Alfred P. Sloan Foundation that provides support services to faculty using the internet for course development. He was a founding member and continues to serve on the board of directors of the Online Learning Consortium (formerly the Sloan Consortium). His blog, started in 2009, has averaged over 600,000 visitors per year. Dr. Picciano has received wide recognition for his

xvi About the Editors

scholarship and research, including being named the 2010 recipient of the Alfred P. Sloan Consortium's (now the Online Learning Consortium) National Award for Outstanding Achievement in Online Education by an Individual.

Visit his website at anthonypicciano.com

Charles D. Dziuban is Director of the Research Initiative for Teaching Effectiveness at the University of Central Florida (UCF), where he has been a faculty member since 1970, teaching research design and statistics and the founding director of the university's Faculty Center for Teaching and Learning. He received his PhD from the University of Wisconsin. Since 1996, he has directed the impact evaluation of UCF's distributed learning initiative, examining student and faculty outcomes as well as gauging the impact of online, blended, and adaptive courses on students and faculty members at the university. Chuck has published in numerous journals, including *Multivariate Behavioral Research, The Psychological Bulletin, Educational and Psychological Measurement,* the *American Education Research Journal, Phi Delta Kappan, The Internet in Higher Education,* the *Journal of Asynchronous Learning Networks* (now *Online Learning*), *EDUCAUSE Review, e-Mentor, The International Journal of Technology in Higher Education, Current Issues in Emerging eLearning, The International Journal of Technology Enhanced Learning,* and the *Sloan-C View.* He has received funding from several government and industrial agencies, including the Ford Foundation, the Centers for Disease Control, the National Science Foundation, and the Alfred P. Sloan Foundation. In 2000, Chuck was named UCF's first-ever Pegasus Professor for extraordinary research, teaching, and service and in 2005 received the honor of Professor Emeritus. In 2005, he received the Sloan Consortium (now the Online Learning Consortium) award for Most Outstanding Achievement in Online Learning by an Individual. In 2007, he was appointed to the National Information and Communication Technology (ICT) Literacy Policy Council. In 2010, Chuck received recognition as the inaugural Online Learning Consortium Fellow. In 2011, UCF established the Chuck D. Dziuban Award for Excellence in Online Teaching for faculty in recognition of Chuck's impact on the field. UCF awarded Dr. Dziuban the inaugural Collective Excellence Award in 2018. Chuck has co-authored, co-edited, or contributed to numerous books and chapters on blended and online learning and is a regular invited speaker at national and international conferences and universities. Currently, he spends most of his time as the university representative to the Rosen Foundation, working on the challenges of educational and economic inequality in the United States.

Charles R. Graham is Professor of Instructional Psychology and Technology at Brigham Young University, with an interest in technology-mediated teaching and learning. Charles studies the design and evaluation of online and blended learning

About the Editors **xvii**

environments and the use of technology to enhance teaching and learning. Charles has authored 50+ articles in over two dozen journals and 20+ chapters related to online and blended learning in edited books. Much of his research is conducted with graduate students, whom he loves to work with and mentor. Charles has co-edited two books on blended learning research (*Handbook of Blended Learning: Global Perspectives, Local Designs* and *Blended Learning: Research Perspectives, Volume 2*) and a book on research methods for young researchers learning to do research in online and blended learning contexts (*Conducting Research in Online and Blended Learning Environments: New Pedagogical Frontiers*). He has also co-authored a free online book for K–12 teachers and administrators, focusing on four key blended teaching competencies (*K–12 Blended Teaching: A Guide to Personalized Learning and Online Integration*) and a book for practitioners interested in designing blended learning environments (*Essentials for Blended Learning: A Standards-based Guide*). In 2015, Charles became a fellow of the Online Learning Consortium "for outstanding achievement in advancing theory, research and effective practice in online and blended learning." He is also a fellow of the Michigan Virtual Learning Research Institute for his work to develop a K–12 blended teaching readiness instrument. Additional details about his scholarly work can be found online at https://sites.google.com/site/charlesrgraham/.

Patsy D. Moskal is Director for the Digital Learning Impact Evaluation in the Research Initiative for Teaching Effectiveness at the University of Central Florida (UCF). Since 1996, she has served as the liaison for faculty research involving digital learning technologies and in support of the scholarship of teaching and learning (SoTL) research at UCF. Her research interests include the use of educational and adaptive learning technologies and learning analytics toward improving student success. Patsy specializes in statistics, graphics, program evaluation, and applied data analysis. She has extensive experience in research methods, including survey development, interviewing, and conducting focus groups and frequently serves as an evaluation consultant to school districts and industry and government organizations. She has served as a co-principal investigator on grants from several government and industrial agencies, including the National Science Foundation, the Alfred P. Sloan Foundation, and the Gates Foundation–funded Next Generation Learning Challenges (NGLC). Patsy frequently serves as a proposal reviewer for conferences and journals and is a frequent special editor of the Online Learning journal, in addition to serving as a reviewer for NSF and DoE proposals.

In 2011, Dr. Moskal was named an Online Learning Consortium Fellow "in recognition of her groundbreaking work in the assessment of the impact and efficacy of online and blended learning." She has co-authored numerous articles and chapters on blended, adaptive, and online learning and is a frequent

xviii About the Editors

presenter at conferences and to other researchers. Patsy is active in both EDU-CAUSE and the Online Learning Consortium (OLC). She serves in the EDUCAUSE Analytics and Research Advisory Group and co-leads the EDU-CAUSE Evidence of Impact Community Group. She currently serves on the OLC board of directors.

CONTRIBUTORS

Jaesoon An, University of North Carolina at Charlotte

Jeremy Anderson, Bay Path University

Karen Arnesen, Brigham Young University

Jered Borup, George Mason University

George R Bradford, Keck Graduate Institute

Heather Bushey, Bay Path University

Mary Corcoran, George Washington University

Maura Devlin, Bay Path University

Raiza Dottin, Portland State University

Charles D. Dziuban, University of Central Florida

John Fritz, University of Maryland, Baltimore County

Concepcion B. Godev, University of North Carolina at Charlotte

Amanda Gould, Bay Path University

Charles R. Graham, Brigham Young University

Courtney Hanny, Brigham Young University

Erik Haroldson, Austin Peay State University

Lynne L. Hindman, Oregon State University

xx Contributors

Scott James, Hobsons

Michelle Jensen, Brigham Young University

Elizabeth Johnson, James Madison University

Cub Kahn, Oregon State University

Swapna Kumar, University of Florida

Juhong Christie Liu, James Madison University

Taru Malhotra, York University

Paige L. McDonald, George Washington University

Timothy Miller, Nova Southeastern University

Patsy D. Moskal, University of Central Florida

Anders Norberg, Umeå University

Ron Owston, York University

Thomas Penniston, University of Maryland, Baltimore County

Anthony G. Picciano, Hunter College and the City University of New York Graduate Center

Jeff Renfrow, Colorado Christian University

Mary Frances Rice, University of New Mexico

Karen S. Schlumpf, George Washington University

Mike Sharkey, Arizona State University

Cecil R. Short, Brigham Young University

Jirarat Sitthiworachart, King Mongkut's Institute of Technology, Ladkrabang

Karen Skibba, University of Wisconsin-Madison

Mark Jack Smith, PGS

Mark Stevens, George Mason University

Rebecca Stimson, Michigan Virtual Learning Research Institute

Karen Swan, University of Illinois Springfield

Norman D. Vaughan, Mount Royal University

Janelle D. Voegele, Portland State University

Shea Walters, George Mason University

Gregory C. Weaver, University of Maryland

John Whitmer, Federation of American Scientists

Maria Widmer, University of Wisconsin-Madison

Dennis York, University of Guelph

PREFACE

In August 2019, Dan Schwartz, our editor at Taylor & Francis, sent an email to us asking if we might be interested in doing a third volume of *Blended Learning: Research Perspectives*. The first volume was published in 2007 and the second in 2014. We have to admit that none of us were thinking about a third volume, but Dan indicated that our second edition had performed well, and, as is always the case, technology continuously changes and evolves, making the time right to revisit the research on blended learning. Blended learning in all its ramifications had surely arrived as the modality of choice at all levels of education with instructors adopting new "blends" to take advantage of developments in mobile technology, adaptive learning, analytics, and more. After a series of phone and video conferences, all of us were in agreement that we could do a third edition, but we had to finish up projects we were already working on, and this book commenced in early 2020.

Because the length of the third edition would be expanded, the three editors of Volume 2 decided to add a fourth in the person of Patsy D. Moskal. Patsy has been a major collaborator of ours on other projects, especially those associated with the Online Learning Consortium (formerly the Alfred P. Sloan Consortium). She has a stellar background in the research of blended learning through her years of association with the Research Initiative for Teaching Effectiveness at the University of Central Florida.

What was most heartening as we began this project was that there was significant interest among researchers in contributing chapters for the new edition. In fact, we had twice as many submissions than we could actually include in the new edition. Selecting the final contributors proved to be a most difficult decision. In total, almost 50 individual researchers contributed material, many of whom worked with modest budgets in pursuing their passion for studying blended learning technology. A glance at the table of contents reveals a span of research issues related to instruction, faculty issues, and adaptive learning. The authors represent a broad spectrum of professionals in the field of educational technology; they are senior and junior faculty, administrators, and graduate students from traditional public and private colleges and universities, K–12 schools and international institutions. The high quality of their work is what has made editing this book a pleasure. Readers might also want to pay attention to the variety of research methods used to study blended learning. Survey research, quasi-experiments, case studies, participatory action research, qualitative approaches, big data analytics, and mixed methods, among other research techniques, are represented in these pages. They provide excellent models for anyone interested in undertaking research in online or blended learning environments.

ACKNOWLEDGEMENTS

The editors owe a debt of gratitude to many people who facilitated this project. First of all, our colleagues at the Online Learning Consortium, both past and present, for bringing our community together into one of theory, research, and practice. They created the environment in which this work was able to take place. Dan Schwartz of Taylor and Francis and his staff provided invaluable design, editorial, and production support for *Blended Learning: Research Perspectives, Volume 3*. It was Dan who suggested it was time for a new edition. We are most grateful to Rachel Griffin and Carissa Hamilton, research assistants at the Research Initiative for Teaching Effectiveness of the University of Central Florida, for their untold hours of editorial work on this book. There is no real way we can properly thank them for their efforts on our behalf. Lastly and most importantly, however, to the authors of the outstanding chapters found herein. This is not our book—it is a celebration of their outstanding research in the blended learning environment. Heartfelt thanks to you all.

Tony, Chuck, Charles, and Patsy

SECTION I
Introduction and Foundations

1

INTRODUCTION

Patsy D. Moskal and Anthony G. Picciano

This project started in January 2020. Anticipation among the four editors was high that we would be starting a third edition of *Blended Research Perspectives* at the invitation of our editor at Routledge/Taylor & Francis. The interest in using the internet for teaching and learning was surely at a peak. Fully one-third of the higher education population, or almost seven million students, were taking one or more fully online courses every year. Mega-universities such as the Southern New Hampshire University and Western Governors University were enrolling more than 100,000 online students every year. In the K–12 sector, tens of millions of students were using Google Chromebooks and Google Classroom, often for blended learning environments. The number of students enrolling in blended courses was and continues to be unknown, but the sense was that more than half—roughly 35 million students, in both higher and K–12 education—were enrolling in some form of blended learning. The exact figure was unknown as no generally accepted definition of blended learning existed in any education sector, and blended learning was increasingly being referred to as a "boundary object," meaning different things to different people.

A call was published in February 2020 for authors to submit chapter proposals for the new edition. Announcements were made at Online Learning Consortium (OLC) events, and emails were sent to various lists of professionals who might be doing research on blended learning. The response was excellent, and it was obvious that a difficult task lay ahead to determine which proposals to accept. Approximately half the proposals were accepted, and invitations were sent in March, with full chapter submissions due in July. At the same time these proposals were being reviewed, news articles began to appear about a new virus that had started in Wuhan, China, and had found its way to Europe, the United States, and most of the world. At first, government leaders were slow to react, and by the time

DOI: 10.4324/9781003037736-2

4 Patsy D. Moskal and Anthony G. Picciano

they did, the coronavirus had evolved into a pandemic that would affect millions of people and claim hundreds of thousands of lives. Hotspots sprang up in major cities in Italy, Spain, France, and the United States. By the end of April 2020, over three million people were diagnosed as having the virus. In the United States, more than one million people were diagnosed, resulting in more than 60,000 deaths. New York City alone had 160,000 cases, with more than 13,000 residents succumbing to the disease. By May, the number of cases in the United States approached two million, with more than 100,000 deaths. By the end of 2020, a projection was made that as many as 400,000 Americans could be victims of this disease. In March, schools and colleges started to close and moved as quickly as possible to remote learning, which had never really been defined. The majority of students began taking substantial parts of their coursework online. Tens of millions of students in primary, secondary, and postsecondary education were now relying on laptops, Chromebooks, iPhones, and other digital devices for instruction. It is not an understatement to conclude that online technology came to the rescue of education during this horrific pandemic (Ubell, 2020). How long this situation would last was completely unknown. In fact, representatives from the United States' Center for Disease Control and Prevention (CDC) were predicting that there likely would be additional waves or phases of the virus into 2021. However, what was becoming apparent as the pandemic stretched from weeks to months was that a "new normal" was emerging in pedagogical practice, based on the plethora of blended learning approaches. There was a sense that when the pandemic subsided, all levels of education would come to embrace blended learning as the model of choice for years to come, allowing some infusion of technology that may replace or supplement face-to-face instruction in the future.

Blended Learning: Research Perspectives (Some History)

In November 2002, a small group of colleagues attending the Annual Sloan-C International Conference on Online Learning in Orlando, Florida had a discussion about what was then a new phenomenon: college faculty were mixing and matching face-to-face and online learning techniques and materials in their courses. This group of colleagues represented institutions such as the University of Illinois, the University of Central Florida, University of Maryland University College, the University of Wisconsin-Milwaukee, and the City University of New York. As the discussion went on, a consensus emerged; they were witnessing a new approach to teaching and learning that was different from either of its basic components. Face-to-face instruction had been around for centuries, and fully online instruction had blossomed in the 1990s with the development and ubiquity of the internet. They observed that there appeared to be no single pattern or model for blending these approaches. Some faculty taught basically a face-to-face course with a small portion of online activities. Others taught essentially online courses with a face-to-face component. In developing online components, various technologies such as interactive and non-interactive media, asynchronous discussion boards, and blogs, as well as synchronous conferencing, were being utilized to meet specific pedagogical goals and objectives. There were also distinctions in the development and scheduling of face-to-face components, some meeting once a week, others every other week, and still others once a month. This discussion resulted in the idea that a group of knowledgeable individuals from around the country be assembled to discuss "blended learning" and its implications for education. Funded by the Alfred P. Sloan Foundation, an invitation-only workshop was held in April 2003 at the University of Illinois-Chicago. About 30 individuals met for two days, and while many ideas were floated, and discussion at times was unwieldy, this group concluded that blended learning was important, needed further investigation, and would likely have significant pedagogical, administrative, and institutional ramifications. A community of professionals was born. This community, under the auspices of the Sloan Consortium, held annual workshops, which in 2012 attracted 665 participants.

In 2006, a dozen scholars who had attended previous workshops were invited to share their work in a book on research perspectives on blended learning. In 2007, *Blended Learning: Research Perspectives* was published. This book received a good deal of critical acclaim as the first book devoted entirely to research in blended learning. A. Frank Mayadas, program officer for the Alfred P. Sloan Foundation, was quoted as saying:

> *Blended Learning: Research Perspectives* was the first major and long-overdue work of research on blended learning. . . . A must read for anyone serious about understanding today's pedagogical practices.
>
> *(Mayadas, 2007)*

Diana Oblinger, president of EDUCAUSE, commented:

> [I]f you are an administrator or faculty member who wants to do blended learning well, this [*Blended Learning: Research Perspectives*] is an important resource that integrates, theory, research and experience.
>
> *(Oblinger, 2007)*

By 2012, the authors of *Blended Learning: Research Perspectives* knew that it was time for a new edition. In the world of technology and digital communications, five years is a lifetime. Many changes had occurred, and new models had evolved that demanded study and research. Digital innovations such as YouTube videos, podcasting, wikis, and mobile technologies had emerged that were adding to the instructional blend. Massive open online courses (MOOCs) radically changed the scale of instruction at a number of colleges and universities. Blended learning had evolved from individual courses to entire academic programs. At the Sloan-C Blended Learning Workshop held in Milwaukee in April 2012, the authors once again reached out to presenters to determine if there was any interest in contributing to a second book. A meeting was held on the afternoon immediately following the conference to discuss ideas and possibilities. More than 30 people attended, signaling much more interest than could be accommodated in the book the authors had in mind. Nevertheless, names and ideas were collected, and invitations were issued for abstracts. In addition to the meeting attendees, the authors contacted colleagues from around the world who were doing important research in blended learning. Again, the response was much more than could be accommodated. And so began the careful work of selecting the best ideas and research on blended learning that comprised *Blended Learning: Research Perspectives, Volume 2*.

In August 2019, Dan Schwartz, our editor at Routledge/Taylor Francis, sent an email to the editors, asking if we might be interested in doing a third edition of *Blended Learning: Research Perspectives*. Dan indicated that our second edition had done well and thought that the time might be right to revisit the research on blended learning. Blended learning, in all its ramifications, had surely arrived as the modality of choice at all levels of education, with instructors adopting new "blends" to take advantage of developments in mobile technology, adaptive learning, analytics, and more.

Definitions, Models, and Frameworks

In discussions with the contributors to this book, it became obvious that finding a single definition, model, or framework for blended learning was impossible. The word *blended* implies a combination or mixture. When a picture is pasted above a paragraph, a presentation is created that may be more informative to the viewer or reader, but the picture and text each remain intact and can be individually discerned. On the other hand, when two cans of different-colored paints are mixed, the new paint will look different from either of the original colors. In fact, if the new paint is mixed well, neither of the original colors will continue to exist. Similar situations exist in blended learning. For instance, in a course that meets for three weekly contact hours, two hours might meet in a traditional classroom while the equivalent of one weekly hour is conducted online. The two modalities for this course are carefully separated, and although they may overlap, they can easily be differentiated. In other forms of blended courses and programs, the modalities are not so easily distinguishable. Consider an online program that offers three online courses in a semester, which all students are required to take. At the same time, students do a collaborative 15-week project that overlaps the courses. The students are expected to maintain regular communication with one another through email, wikis, and group discussion boards. They also are required to meet face to face once a month on weekends, when course materials from the online courses are further presented and discussed, and time is also devoted to group project work. Toward the end of the semester, there are group project presentations. These activities begin to blur the modalities in a new mixture or blend, in which the individual parts are not as discernible as they once were. In this book, the authors have allowed the contributors to define/describe the blended instruction they are studying as they wish without confining them to a rigid definition, model, or framework. Chapter 2 of this book will further examine the issues associated with definitions, models, and frameworks.

Book Outline and Chapters

We structured this book's chapters thematically, according to the focus of each author's research. While there is overlap across some chapter topics, we hope this provides a guide for the reader, who may be occupying a specific space in education and in search of research that can help inform their work. The authors of each chapter are leaders within their own disciplines and share their research and experience using their own implementations of blended learning.

Section I begins with *Introduction and Foundations*, including Charles R. Graham's rich discussion "Exploring Definitions, Models, Frameworks, and Theory for Blended Learning Research." Graham describes the importance of the media, method, and modality intersection in defining blended learning. He examines some concerns with using blended learning as a treatment effect in research, delineating the challenges with this practice. Finally, he provides a useful taxonomy for theoretical blended learning frameworks for future research.

Section II is devoted to works focusing on *Student Outcomes*. In Chapter 3, Jeff Renfrow shares his research at a private, not-for-profit US university, examining student perceptions of asynchronous, text-based discussions versus synchronous, video-based discussion. Scott James and Karen Swan share their research in Chapter 4, examining how students' varying proportions of blended learning courses and programs impact retention and how this differs across various demographics. Chapter 5 presents research by John Fritz, Thomas Penniston, Mike Sharkey, and John Whitmer, examining LMS course design as a learning analytics variable by sharing the results of three different studies on the evolution of their research in the area.

In Section III, we pivot to focus on *Faculty Issues*. In Chapter 6, Cub Kahn and Lynne L. Hindman report on their survey of faculty, identifying 11 highly effective blended teaching practices, and discuss how faculty found these improved their courses. Karen Skibba and Maria Widmer use the community of inquiry in Chapter 7 as a framework to analyze a blended learning program's impact on participants' perceptions and practices. In Chapter 8, Concepcion B. Godev and Jaesoon An focus on a ten-year implementation of blended learning, providing a historical account of this evolution and its impact on their campus.

Section IV is devoted to the relatively new area of *Adaptive Learning Research*. Jeremy Anderson, Heather Bushey, Mara Devlin, and Amanda Gould examine students' performance and perceptions in adaptive blended versus on-ground

8 Patsy D. Moskal and Anthony G. Picciano

courses in Chapter 9. In Chapter 10, Janelle D. Voegele and Raiza Dottin discuss a two-year study of student persistence and perceptions in adaptive learning in blended courses. The use of adaptive learning in industry training is described in Mark Jack Smith's case study in Chapter 11.

We shift to **K–12 Perspectives** on blended learning research in Section V. Cecil R. Short, Courtney Hanny, Michelle Jensen, Karen Arnesen, and Charles R. Graham, in Chapter 12, focus on blended teacher preparation and professional development, examining an extensive collection of blended teaching artifacts with interviews to connect blended teaching practices to competencies. In Chapter 13 Jered Borup, Shea Walters, and Rebecca Stimson report on their focus group study comparing student perceptions regarding their interactions with online versus in-person peers using the Academic Communities of Engagement framework. Mary Frances Rice and Mark Stevens examine intellectual agency for students with disabilities learning English in blended learning courses in Chapter 14—an area with a critical need for more research. Closing out the section on K–12 blended learning, Mark Stevens, in Chapter 15, examines the impact of multimodal blended learning on English language learners (ELLs) in reading, vocabulary, and content knowledge development in a middle-level social studies class.

Section VI presents **International Perspectives** on blended learning research from beyond the US. George R. Bradford and Anders Norberg, in Chapter 16, offer a rich discussion considering new perspectives of blended learning, addressing teaching construct, and discussing blending as integration and time as a blended course design construct and use activity theory to better understand empirical course data. In Chapter 17, Norman D. Vaughan uses a shared metacognition framework and the community of inquiry model to examine how teachers use a blended approach to intentionally design, facilitate, and direct a collaborative, constructive learning environment. Chapter 18 presents work by Ron Owston, Taru Malhotra, Dennis York, and Jirarat Sitthiworachart, discussing their blended learning research across four studies examining students' satisfaction, convenience, engagement, and performance; the relationship between time spent online and time spent face-to-face and student performance and perception; students' perceptions of blended learning across four different blended models; and student perceptions and performance in STEM versus non-STEM blended courses.

Section VI is devoted to **Science and Health Research** with three chapters from experts in the discipline. Juhong Christie Liu, Elizabeth Johnson, and Erik Haroldson in Chapter 19 report on the design and application of blended learning, utilizing open educational resources (OER) for laboratory-based geoscience courses. Chapter 20 presents Timothy Miller and Swapna Kumar's research examining the development and student perceptions of a blended doctor of physical therapy (DPT) program. We end this section with Chapter 21, in which Paige L. McDonald, Karen S. Schlumpf, Gregory C. Weaver, and Mary Corcoran discuss the blended learning model they utilize in a low-residency doctoral program, including the students' perceptions of the program.

In our final section, two of our editors, Charles D. Dziuban and Anthony G. Picciano, in Chapter 22, speculate on **The Future** of blended learning. The complexities of the evolving technological landscape, including the impact of the COVID-19 pandemic on education, will no doubt impact the future of blended learning. While long-term predictions are difficult, they speculate that blended learning and research will play a pivotal role in education across the globe.

References

Mayadas, F. (2007). *Blended learning: Research perspectives.* The Alfred P. Sloan Consortium.

Oblinger, D. F. (2007). *Blended learning: Research perspectives.* The Alfred P. Sloan Consortium.

Ubell, R. (2020, May 13). How online learning kept higher ed open during the coronavirus crisis. *IEEE Spectrum.* Retrieved May 25, 2020, from https://spectrum. ieee.org/tech-talk/at-work/education/how-online-learning-kept-higher-ed-open-during-the-coronavirus-crisis

2

EXPLORING DEFINITIONS, MODELS, FRAMEWORKS, AND THEORY FOR BLENDED LEARNING RESEARCH

Charles R. Graham

Many years ago, I was deeply impressed by an analogy of undertaking research to socializing at a party (David Whetten, personal communication). At the party, there are lots of people standing around in small groups having conversations while they snack on hors d'oeuvres and sip drinks. Interesting conversations are happening in each group. As newcomers arrive at the party, they will get some refreshments and then try to socialize in one of the groups. Experienced partygoers typically draw near to a group, listen to the conversation for a while, and then try to find ways to contribute to the conversation. Socially inexperienced partygoers, on the other hand, might barge in without understanding the conversation that is already happening, or they might not even join a group at all and stand alone, talking to themselves in hope that someone comes over to listen.

Research within a scholarly domain is similar, and some parties have been going for decades. The research conversations around different topics are happening through publications, conference presentations, and other collaborations. Novice researchers might not realize the range of conversations taking place around them, and they might anxiously jump in before carefully listening to the conversations that are already in process. Wiser researchers listen and take note of the conversations that are happening and then contribute their portion to build on these conversations.

The intent of this chapter is to provide background to orient researchers new to blended learning (BL) to key definitions and issues that will help them more quickly become contributing members to the research conversations. Additionally, this chapter will address the important role of theory development in this relatively young research domain. It will also introduce several important areas of inquiry related to BL, highlighting both originary and imported theories that are influencing research conversations (McDonald & Yanchar, 2020).

DOI: 10.4324/9781003037736-3

Nature, Components, and Implications of Blended Learning

The rapid and often informal integration of online practices into traditional in-person classrooms was facilitated by the emergence of the internet beginning in the 1990s. This new phenomenon began to be referred to as hybrid courses and then as BL. Early scholars predicted that this blending would become so ubiquitous that eventually it would not need a distinct name (Cross, 2006) and would just be referred to as "learning." The difficult challenges in defining BL were identified early on by Oliver and Trigwell (2005) in a seminal article titled "Can Blended Learning Be Redeemed?" This article described confusion in the variety of definitions used to describe BL. Several articles from the past decade have been effectively exploring the history and range of definitions with their strengths and limitations (Graham, 2013; Hrastinski, 2019). As the definition of BL has implications for research, novice BL researchers will be more easily able to frame and design their work by understanding BL's relationship to three foundational terms: media, method, and modality. This section will (a) introduce how media, method, and modality relate to the definition of BL; (b) articulate the problem of using BL as a treatment effect in research; and (c) discuss implications for research practice.

Media, Method, Modality

The 3Ms—media, method, and modality—are important dimensions for describing any form of instruction. The modality describes the general physical environment (online or in person) in which instructional tools and technology provide a delivery medium that facilitates learning. Instructors choose instructional methods (strategies and practices) that are influenced and constrained by both the modality and the medium. Table 2.1 contains descriptions and examples of each of the 3Ms. Many of the differences in definitions result from trying to understand BL in terms of combining modalities, instructional methods, and/or delivery media/technology. For example, early work in the Sloan-C BL workshops (now the Online Learning Consortium) defined BL as "courses that integrate online with traditional face-to-face class activities [modality] in a planned, pedagogically valuable manner [method]" (Picciano, 2006, p. 97). Other well-meaning researchers who saw the pedagogically rich possibilities of BL also tried to protect the term by adding pedagogical qualifiers to a definition focused primarily on modality (Garrison & Kanuka, 2004; Vaughan, 2007).

Each blended design might be thought of as having two interwoven layers: (a) a physical (or structural) layer and (b) a pedagogical layer (Graham et al., 2014). The physical layer represents the surface features of a design and may be described using modality and media. For example, a course blend might involve a pattern or rhythm of switching between online and in-person activities (i.e., modalities; Stein &

12 Charles R. Graham

TABLE 2.1 Descriptions and Examples for Media, Method, and Modality

3 Ms	Description	Examples	
Modality	The physical instructional setting or environment	• Online environment • In-person classroom environment • A mix or blend of online and in-person learning	
Media	Physical tools or technology used to deliver or mediate instruction	Digital • Computer • Mobile device • LMS, software	Non-digital • Books • Whiteboard • paper/pencil
Method	Teaching strategies and practices used in instruction	General • Case studies • Class discussion • Simulations • Lecture • Group work	Content specific • Writer's workshop • Primary source • Documentary creation • Scientific inquiry • Math manipulatives

Graham, 2020), and online activities would take place using a particular learning management system or software platform (i.e., medium). The pedagogical layer is described by the methods used, which might involve active learning strategies and/ or teacher lectures, community interactions, and/or online content interaction, etc.

Generally, design elements within the pedagogical layer directly influence student learning, while the physical layer has a direct influence on access and cost (see Figure 2.1). However, the pedagogical layer is not independent of the physical layer. Affordances in the physical layer enable and inhibit pedagogical possibilities. For example, the kind of discussion that can happen in a text-based asynchronous learning environment is different from what can happen in a live in-person classroom, and each has its strengths and limitations (see Table 1.2 in Graham, 2006).

In this chapter (as previously), I make a case for a broad definition of BL that is based entirely on modality (Graham, 2006, 2013, 2019). There is significant evidence that BL is already used commonly as an umbrella term (Hrastinski, 2019) or boundary object (Dziuban et al., 2020; Norberg et al., 2011) that encompasses a wide range of specific practices (methods) and technological tools (media). BL is a term that is

> plastic enough to adapt to local needs and constraints of the several parties employing them, yet robust enough to maintain a common identity across sites . . . weakly structured in common use . . . strongly structured in individual site-use.
>
> *(Star & Griesemer, 1989, p. 393)*

Exploring Definitions, Models, Frameworks   **13**

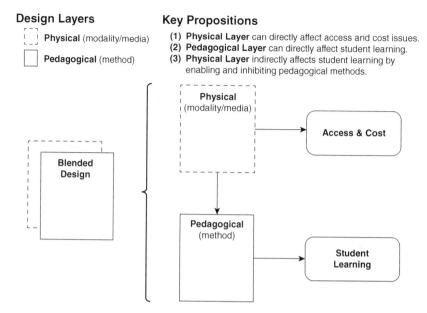

FIGURE 2.1   Design Layers and the Influence of Modality, Media, and Method on Outcomes

Definition: Blended learning is the strategic combination of online and in-person learning.

FIGURE 2.2   Parsimonious Definition of Blended Learning

A practical implication of this definition is that BL is methodologically agnostic. Many different instructional methods can be implemented in a BL environment. You can blend using constructivist, cognitivist, or behaviorist methods. Additionally, there isn't a pedagogical purity litmus test that can be used to tell practitioners whether they are actually blending or not. Thus, the instructional method doesn't indicate whether or not someone is blending; rather, method contributes to the quality of the blend.

A second implication is that BL models differentiate blends based on various factors, including method and media. The importance of this idea was expressed by Ross and Gage (2006): "[W]hat will differentiate institutions from one another will not be whether they have blended learning, but rather how they do the blending and where they fall on the blended learning spectrum" (p. 167). There are many models (hows) of teaching in these environments, and the quality of the learning will depend more on the details of the model and its implementation than on the modality alone. A well-specified blended model would include descriptions of both physical and pedagogical layers.

14 Charles R. Graham

BL as a Treatment Effect

An important question raised by Dziuban et al. (2020) is whether BL should be used as a treatment effect in research. BL has commonly been used as a treatment effect in studies—especially when comparing BL with traditional in-person instruction. A researcher might pose a question like "Do students learn better in a blended or traditional in-person class?" or "Does blended instruction result in X or Y outcome?" A meta-analysis commissioned by the US Department of Education to look at the effectiveness of online learning is an example of this genre of research. Researchers found that students in conditions that used online learning (either fully online or blended) outperformed students in the face-to-face-only condition (Means et al., 2013). The effect size for the fully online versus face-to-face comparison was not statistically significant, while the blended versus face-to-face comparison was statistically significant with an effect size of (g+ = +0.35). The study could not conclusively identify which elements of the blended condition caused the improved outcomes, though blended conditions tended to involve more instructional time, instructional resources, and elements encouraging peer interaction among learners.

Dziuban et al. (2020) took a deeper look into the instructional strategies reported in the individual studies used in the Means et al. (2013) meta-analysis and found a large range of course designs and instructional methods represented. Conventional wisdom from the instructional technology field suggests that the method rather than the media or modality has the greatest impact on learning outcomes.[1] Studies that focus on BL as the treatment effect may risk focusing on surface-level features of the blended design rather than on its core pedagogical features. Graham et al. (2014) summarized in this way:

> Such results are comparable to saying that generally "compact cars" get better gas mileage than "trucks," a claim that does not identify the core attributes that make compact cars more fuel efficient—the weight, shape, or engine size of the vehicle. Significant progress in BL research requires us to "look under the hood" and identify core pedagogical attributes of our BL systems and not maintain focus entirely on the physical attributes of the systems.
>
> *(p. 27)*

In another example of meta-analysis research related to BL, Bernard et al. (2014) compared classroom instruction and BL conditions and found that student achievement in BL was better than with classroom instruction, with an effect size of (g+ = 0.33). He followed up this modality focus by looking at more pedagogically oriented moderating variables related to the purpose for using the technology and to interaction treatments of student-student, student-teacher, and

Exploring Definitions, Models, Frameworks **15**

student-content interactions. For the moderating variables, the strongest effect size was found when the purpose of the technology use was for cognitive support ($g+ = +0.59$). Also, if the treatment condition involved two or three types of interaction (students with peers, teachers, or content) more than the control condition, the effect sizes were $g+ = +0.44$ and $g+ = +0.47$, respectively.

Research that focuses on modality alone is misguided because the instructional methods used in a blend are the active ingredient that influences student learning. The next section will elaborate on some important implications and guidelines for researchers based on these ideas.

Implications for Research

The next three considerations will strengthen how you define and communicate your BL research to others.

1. Definition of blend. Clearly identify what you mean by BL.
2. Quality of blend. Adequately specify the physical and pedagogical elements of your BL model.
3. Quantity/scope of blend. Adequately specify the scope of your blend.
4. Treatment effect. Avoid using BL as a treatment effect.

First, it is important to define what you mean by BL in your research. This chapter provides the definition that I believe is the most widely accepted. However, because there is not a universally accepted definition and many institutions define BL locally, you need to provide a brief description of what you mean by BL.

Second, you must describe elements of both the physical and pedagogical layers of your BL model or implementation. Describing these aspects clearly will let readers better understand the quality elements of your blend and determine how your blend relates to their blended contexts. Because the instructional methods of the blend are essential to the outcomes, what students are doing both online and in person must be included. "This course used a flipped classroom blended model" would be inadequate. You need to share more specific details about the methods.

Third, the scope of your blend should be clear. Blends can occur at the activity or whole-course level (Graham, 2006). For example, a course experimenting with blending a few activities will have different potential outcomes than a course blending across the full semester.

Fourth, BL should be avoided as a treatment effect. As BL is an umbrella term that encompasses many different instructional methods, your particular blended model is better understood if the physical and pedagogical details are specifically identified. You may want to investigate specific elements or outcomes of a model

16   Charles R. Graham

rather than trying to compare it to a traditional in-person context, which might have many practical pedagogical differences.

Contributions and Properties of Theory Development

Theory is crucial in the knowledge-creation process, establishing common terminology and a focus for the activities and conversations that take place in a scholarly community (Dubin, 1978). Without theory, much scholarly conversation would be incoherent: the equivalent of partygoers in the opening analogy talking past each other. Burkhardt and Schoenfeld (2003) noted that "a lack of attention to coherent theory building leaves us looking balkanized and incoherent, the whole . . . being less than the sum of its parts" (p. 13). Burkhardt and Schoenfeld (2003) further claimed that a "reasonably stable theory base . . . allows for a clear focus on important issues and provides sound (though still limited) guidance for the design of improved solutions to important problems" (p. 6).

Theory in Design Fields

Herbert Simon (1999) referred to design fields (e.g., engineering, business, education, architecture, etc.) as "sciences of the artificial." In these fields, primary goals go beyond describing how and why things happen to how to influence or make things happen (Gibbons, 2013; Reigeluth, 2008). BL research as a subdomain of educational research is a design field that has the broad underlying purpose of influencing and improving educational outcomes.

In *Blended Learning Research Perspectives, Volume 2*, Graham et al. (2014) summarized three kinds of theory used in design research.

- Explore. Description—What exists?
- Explain. Prediction—Why does this happen?
- Design. Prescription—How do I achieve this outcome?

Theory in design domains (like BL) often outlines operational principles and the conditions under which they will lead to a particular goal or outcome. Design theories are probabilistic rather than deterministic in that they "increase the chances of attaining the goals rather than ensuring attainment of goals" (Reigeluth, 2008, p. 7). Because the words *model* and *framework* tend to communicate a softer, less deterministic stance than the term *theory*, I assume many researchers in design fields prefer to use these terms to describe their theoretical contributions. The literature shows no current consensus about similarities in and differences between *model*, *framework*, and *theory* (Dickmeyer, 1989; Dubin, 1978; Gregor, 2006; Kaplan, 1964; Merton, 1967; Sutton & Staw, 1995; Whetten, 1989). Thus, in this chapter, the three terms are used interchangeably.

Properties of a Good Theoretical Contribution

Whetten (1989) clearly identified elements of a strong social science theory as

- the *what* (variables/factors)
- the *how* (relationships of variables/factors)
- the *why* (underlying rationale justifying the what and how), and
- the *who, where, when* (context in which the theory is applicable)

As a journal editor with deep experience, Whetten claimed that contributions or changes to the what and how of a theory might lead to important, surprising results that challenge assumptions and stimulate future theorizing. But ultimately attending to the whys is key to meaningful theoretical contributions. Of particular importance to BL researchers is Whetten's (1989) note that "applying an old model to a new setting and showing that it works as expected is not instructive by itself" (p. 493). However, he elaborated that application within new contexts can help theorists learn new things that "improve the tool, not merely reaffirm its utility" (p. 493).

Whetten's perspective is rooted firmly in the explain paradigm of traditional research, described earlier in this chapter. The literature includes less information about what makes a good design theory. Reigeluth (2008) provided some insight into the challenge: "The major concern for people developing and testing descriptive theories is validity, whereas for design theories, it is preferability (i.e., does the method attain your goals for your situation better than any other known method?)" (p. 8). He goes on to elaborate that the desirability is often rooted in tradeoffs between desired outcomes of effectiveness, efficiency, and appeal.

Probably the ultimate test for a theoretical contribution is that it continues to push dialogue about the topic forward. Using the party analogy, this is the equivalent of a discussion topic taking on a life of its own, continuing to generate discussion outside the party, and continuing to evolve and be relevant and exciting at future parties. This usually happens when the contribution provides additional insight or understanding into a phenomenon being studied, as evident in how it continues to be used, modified, and cited in research across time. Within BL research, the community of inquiry (CoI) is a useful example. Since its initial publication in 1999, the framework itself has been cited thousands of times. During its relatively short existence, hundreds if not thousands of studies have used the CoI framework. Some researchers have used the framework as a lens to describe (explore), while others have used it to predict (explain) outcomes, and some have used it as a framework to guide the development (design) of BL environments.

Theoretical Contributions in Important Areas of Blended Learning Inquiry

Well-established scholarly domains have common terminology and widely accepted models and theories that guide inquiry and practice, while researchers in less mature domains struggle to define terms and establish relevant models. Research within the area of BL environments is less than two decades old. Thus, the domain is relatively young and less mature in development of widely accepted models, frameworks, and theories (Graham, 2013; Graham et al., 2014). As might be expected, many of the most frequently used theories within BL research are borrowed from other social science domains (e.g., education, psychology, and business) applied within blended contexts. I refer to these theories as "imported" in contrast to "originary" theories that have been developed specifically for BL design and research (McDonald & Yanchar, 2020). While both imported and originary theories are important for research within a domain, the number and quality of originary theories may be stronger in indicating the maturing of a domain.

This section highlights four broad areas of research within BL, originating from previous literature reviews intended to explore the evolving domain (Drysdale et al., 2013; Graham, 2014, 2019; Halverson et al., 2014). While not comprehensive, they are intended to highlight areas of research in which theories are helping to drive the conversation in productive ways. Within these broad areas, I identify some examples of originary and imported theoretical contributions and indicate what they are intended to accomplish. Coverage is selected to show progress and give examples of places where productive research conversations are happening.

Instructional Design Issues

Research related to BL instructional design or course design issues is prevalent in the literature and important to the field. In 2013, Drysdale et al. analyzed research themes in 205 doctoral dissertations focused on BL. Within the dissertations, the category of instructional design issues was the third most common, addressed in 34.6%, outranked only by dispositions (38.5%) and learner outcomes (51.7%). A year later, Halverson et al. (2014) followed with a study that analyzed research questions in the 85 most cited journal articles and book chapters focusing on BL. Instructional design issues ranked as the top category, represented in 41.2% of analyzed manuscripts. These findings are not surprising, as BL researchers are often concerned with fundamental questions related to design: for example, how to create a blended environment that increases desired learner outcomes, access and flexibility, and cost efficiency (Graham, 2006). Table 2.2 identifies a few of the more prominent frameworks specific to BL and instructional design.

Early models defined and classified types of BL, but unfortunately, they most often focused on the surface physical layer rather than the more important pedagogical design layer (see Figure 2.1). For example, they described BL in terms of physical and temporal variations rather than the unique pedagogical strategies used to blend. This is appropriate for designs focused primarily on improving access/flexibility or cost. HyFlex model, for example, was intended to provide

Exploring Definitions, Models, Frameworks **19**

TABLE 2.2 Examples of Theory/Frameworks/Models for BL Research Related to Course Design

Originary theory	Brief description
Early classification models • K-12 blended (Staker & Horn, 2012) • Higher education (Twigg, 2003) • Corporate training (Rossett & Frazee, 2006)	These models, which appeared early in the development of BL research, are examples of explore research, which sought to categorize and classify types of BL that were emerging in the natural world.
HyFlex model (Beatty, 2014, 2019)	HyFlex model has become more visible recently with challenges due to COVID around the world. It has elements similar to Twigg's (2003) buffet model with greater design guidance.
Time-based blend (Norberg et al., 2011); blended online learning (Power, 2008)	Both of these models focus on the synchronous/asynchronous affordances of a blend as the critical design feature influencing instruction.
Multimodal model (Picciano, 2009, 2017)	This model identifies a range of pedagogical objectives and matches them with instructional approaches available in different modalities.

flexibility (access) through student choice of modality as well as reusability of learning artifacts (cost), while maintaining outcomes equivalent to the traditional in-person model (Beatty, 2014, 2019). More recent models, like the multimodal model (Picciano, 2009, 2017), have begun to focus more on pedagogical elements in a blend. We need more models that attend carefully and deeply to the pedagogical dimensions of BL, not to the physical and temporal dimensions alone.

Institutional Issues

BL practices are being adopted across higher education, K–12, and corporate training landscapes at a pace that has been difficult to document. Early adopters predicted that BL would eventually "emerge as the predominant model of the future" (Watson, 2008, p. 3), and current practitioners have claimed that BL is the "new normal" in higher education (Dziuban et al., 2018, p. 1; Norberg et al., 2011, p. 207). Anecdotal reports and a few large-scale surveys have provided some evidence that this is happening. Graham (2019) summarized our most current understanding of how BL is growing, and yet we know that the data were incomplete because (a) many institutions lack formal mechanisms for labeling and tracking blended courses; (b) the choice to blend is often being made by instructors at a grassroots level without knowledge at the institutional level;

20 Charles R. Graham

and (c) there are many inconsistencies in how BL is defined across institutions. More descriptive (explore) research related to the growth of BL in institutions and across national and international regions is needed. Additionally, research questions about institutional change and adoption, scaling and growth rates, cost efficiencies, and access are among a few that would fit in this category. Questions relating directly to student or faculty issues are considered separately in subsequent sections. Table 2.3 describes some of the originary frameworks currently used for exploring institutional issues.

Most of the existing originary frameworks are descriptive, creating categories or taxonomies for understanding foundational elements related to institutional adoption and/or success with an institutional transition to BL. Research related to institutional issues commonly references imported theory, such as systems theory or Everett Rogers' theory on diffusion of innovations, which describes a four-stage process of adoption: (a) knowledge, (b) persuasion, (c) decision, and (d) confirmation. Additionally, it identifies variables related to characteristics of adopters, the social system for adoption, and

TABLE 2.3 Examples of Theory/Frameworks/Models for BL Research Related to Institutional Issues

Originary theory	Brief description
Framework for institutional adoption of BL (Graham et al., 2013)	This framework identifies three stages of institutional adoption: (a) awareness/exploration, (b) adoption/early implementation, and (c) mature implementation/growth. Indicators for each of the stages related to institutional strategy, structure, and support are described.
Framework of complex adaptive blended learning systems (Wang et al., 2015)	This theoretical framework identifies six interwoven subsystems and their internal driving forces that interact to influence an institutional BL system. The framework adopts a systems approach to characterizing the complex evolving nature of BL at institutions.
Framework for transition to enhanced BL (Adekola et al., 2017)	This framework is intended to help institutions manage effective transitions to BL. It characterizes stakeholder roles, organizational preparedness areas, institutional considerations, and change agents (both internal and external to the institution).
Framework for strategic planning of BL in institutions of higher education (Lim et al., 2019)	This framework was developed in Asia to facilitate strategic planning for BL by institutions in higher education. The framework identifies seven strategic dimensions for institutional consideration and key issues within each dimension.

characteristics of innovations (e.g., complexity, trialability, observability, etc.) that influence adoption.

Student Issues

BL research related to student issues probably includes the largest and broadest range of questions. Issues in this category include questions about student learning effectiveness, engagement, and satisfaction, as well as a large number of student learning issues studied by educational psychologists. Because so much research has been done on student learning and cognition, many of the theories used in this category are imported from other domains and applied in BL contexts. Some common examples of this imported theory include those related to student engagement (Christenson et al., 2012), motivation, and self-regulation (Schunk & Zimmerman, 2012); learning communities; and learning theories. As emphasized previously, mentioning any of these imported psychological or learning theories with BL in general is insufficient without clearly identifying the specific pedagogical and physical dimensions of the blended model being examined.

In this section, I highlight four originary BL frameworks: CoI (Garrison et al., 1999), ACE (Borup et al., 2020), blended learning engagement framework (Halverson et al., 2019), and conceptual framework for learning in blended environments (Shea & Bidjerano, 2010).

Student issues with the body of CoI research are particularly focused in the areas of cognitive presence and social presence. Research related to teaching presence is considered in the Faculty Issues section. The other three theories are specifically for blended and online contexts, but they all build on theories from other domains, examples of evolving theory for more targeted use within the blended context. For example, the ACE framework addresses specific issues related to how personal and course communities can function together to support student academic success. Borrowing from the concept of Vygotsky's zone of proximal development, ACE begins with a zone of independent engagement that is extended through support from actors within the personal and course communities available to the students. Student engagement is measured along dimensions of affective, behavioral, and cognitive (Fredricks et al., 2004), and support elements are identified that can be addressed by a variety of actors in the personal and course support communities.

Faculty Issues

Research and theoretical frameworks for faculty issues have received less attention than the other three areas discussed, possibly due in part to the fact that faculty issues tend to overlap the other categories. Faculty are the actors who often create and implement the blended course designs as well as being implicated, along with students and administrators, in core aspects of institutional adoption. Additionally,

22 Charles R. Graham

TABLE 2.4 Examples of Theory/Frameworks/Models for BL Research Related to Student Issues

Originary theory	Brief description
Community of inquiry (CoI) (Garrison et al., 1999)	This is likely the most referenced theory in BL research. Though technically imported from the domain of distance education, it was strongly and directly applied to blended contexts soon after its development (Garrison & Kanuka, 2004; Garrison & Vaughan, 2008). The theory explains the importance of and relationships involving three types of presence in a learning environment—social, teaching, and cognitive.
Conceptual framework for learning in blended environments (Shea & Bidjerano, 2010)	This framework builds on the how people learn framework (Council National Academies of S. N. R., 2000). It identifies components and influences that impact decisions in a blended environment. It also proposes a grounded process model to bridge theory and practice and to provide design guidance for developing instructional strategies for particular learners in particular contexts.
Blended learning engagement framework (Halverson et al., 2019)	This conceptual framework builds off several imported frameworks for learner engagement. It identifies constructs and indicators for cognitive and emotional engagement of the learner that are appropriate for blended environments.
Academic communities of engagement (ACE) (Borup et al., 2020)	This framework describes a student's affective, behavioral, and cognitive engagement in blended and online environments needed for academic success. It examines how a student's ability to engage is impacted by support from two communities: a personal and a course community. The framework identifies community actors and support elements needed for academic success.

they have a vested interest in student issues, and student success impacts their own feelings of success. Areas of research inquiry that are uniquely related to faculty include their teaching evaluations, workload, competencies and dispositions, and satisfaction with blended approaches. While there is ongoing research related to these issues, few are originary blended frameworks. For example, the conflation of teaching evaluations with course design evaluations is acknowledged (Piña & Bohn, 2014; Thomas & Graham, 2017), but better models are needed to address this issue. Also, some research has showed that existing workload allocation models do not account for issues related to online and blended teaching modalities (Tynan et al., 2015); thus, we need originary models to help us better

Exploring Definitions, Models, Frameworks **23**

TABLE 2.5 Examples of Theory/Frameworks/Models for BL Research Related to Faculty Issues

Originary theory	Brief description
Community of inquiry (CoI) (Garrison et al., 1999)	The CoI framework, also listed in the Student Issues section earlier, includes teaching presence within the framework as an element directly related to faculty work. Sub-elements of teaching presence within the theoretical model include facilitating discourse and delivering direct instruction.
Blended teaching competency framework (Graham et al., 2019)	This framework identifies four foundational blended teaching competency areas: (a) online integration, (b) data practices, (c) personalization, and (d) online interaction. These areas are built on a foundation of technology skills and blended teaching dispositions identified in the framework.

understand blended faculty workload issues. Table 2.5 identifies two originary theories related to faculty teaching competencies.

The teaching presence dimension of the originary theory CoI framework directly addresses skills related to delivering direct instruction and facilitating discourse online. The blended teaching competency framework, which identifies core competency areas for K–12 blended teachers, has contributed by leading to the development and validation of a Blended Teaching Readiness Instrument (Archibald et al., 2021 in press; see instrument at http://bit.ly/K12-BTR). Research related specifically to faculty adoption of BL has applied the framework for institutional adoption of BL (Porter & Graham, 2016), as well as imported frameworks such as the technology acceptance model (Davis, 1989).

Future Directions

The global pandemic beginning in 2019 will likely change the landscape of blended and online learning practice and research for the foreseeable future. Many faculty and students who had no interest and lacked the dispositions and skills to teach or learn online are having to explore online options out of necessity. Much of the pandemic online instruction is weak pedagogically, but this is to be expected when teachers are learning new skills that have significant differences from the traditional in-person teaching they have observed and practiced for most of their careers (Barbour, 2012; Pulham et al., 2018). The ultimate outcome will be greater numbers of teachers and students who have developed new perspectives about what is possible. When educational institutions return to normal, many, if not most, will return to in-person education but will want to augment that experience with what they consider the best of the online learning possibilities for their students. This will be a world where BL truly is the norm.

Teachers and students will then develop their blended teaching and learning skills, not to meet the immediate demands of pandemic emergency remote instruction, but because these opportunities are in the best long-term interests of students. At that time, there will be an even more important need for solid research related to blended instructional design issues to help with navigating the wide range of available blended models and pedagogical strategies. A major claim of this chapter is that future blended models need to focus on the pedagogical layer in addition to the physical/structural layer. Some of those models will likely include

1. adaptive instruction (with machines making some instructional decisions)
2. personalized instruction (with students making significant decisions about the time, place, goals, pace, and/or path of their learning)
3. differentiated instruction (with teachers customizing instruction to individual student needs) and
4. domain-specific blends designed for particular signature pedagogies (Shulman, 2005) used in different disciplinary contexts (e.g., models varied pedagogically for students in nursing, art, engineering, science, and humanities)

Increased blended research may also be required for institutional issues. The number and range of global institutions interested in blended education is vast, with some similarities but many differences in needs. Some differences are obvious, as needs are quite different for institutions serving K–12 students and those targeted to higher education or corporate training interests. Even within those categories, broad differences will impact the kinds of blended models that need to be developed. For example, in recent exposure to BL in Asia, the Middle East, and South America, I have discovered that these areas have unique institutional challenges and much to offer in localized blended solutions to these challenges (Lim et al., 2019). While much of the current blended research has come out of the US and Canada, I have learned that researchers in partnership across the globe can learn much from each other (Spring & Graham, 2016, 2017; Spring et al., 2016).

Finally, blended research related to faculty and student issues will continue to be important. Factors that influence student learning and satisfaction have a long research history, and BL researchers have drawn upon many working theories from broader social science domains. The unique situations and challenges that come with mixing online and in-person modalities provide rich opportunities for BL researchers to gain new insights that can, in turn, contribute to further development of the existing theoretical frameworks.

Note

1. In the 1980s and early 1990s, researchers debated whether or not media influenced learning. See articles from the media/method debates (Clark, 1983, 1986, 1994a, 1994b; Cunningham, 1986; Kozma, 1991; Kozma, 1994).

References

Adekola, J., Dale, V. H. M., & Gardiner, K. (2017). Development of an institutional framework to guide transitions into enhanced blended learning in higher education. *Research in Learning Technology, 25*(1063519), 1–16. https://doi.org/10.25304/rlt.v25.1973

Archibald, D. E., Graham, C. R., & Larsen, R. (2021, in press). Validating a blended teaching readiness instrument for primary/secondary preservice teachers. *British Journal of Educational Technology.*

Barbour, M. K. (2012). Training teachers for a virtual school system: A call to action. In D. Polly, C. Mims, & K. A. Persichitte (Eds.), *Creating technology-rich teacher education programs: Key issues* (pp. 499–517). IGI Global. https://doi.org/10.4018/978-1-4666-4502-8.ch081

Beatty, B. J. (2014). Hybrid courses with flexible participation—the HyFlex course design. In L. Kyei-Blankson & E. Ntuli (Eds.), *Practical applications and experiences in K–20 blended learning environments* (pp. 153–177). IGI Global.

Beatty, B. J. (Ed.). (2019). *Hybrid-flexible course design: Implementing student-directed hybrid classes.* EdTech Books. https://edtechbooks.org/hyflex

Bernard, R. M., Borokhovski, E., Schmid, R. F., Tamim, R. M., & Abrami, P. C. (2014). A meta-analysis of blended learning and technology use in higher education: From the general to the applied. *Journal of Computing in Higher Education, 26*(1), 87–122. https://doi.org/10.1007/s12528-013-9077-3

Borup, J., Graham, C. R., West, R. E., Archambault, L., & Spring, K. J. (2020). Academic communities of engagement: An expansive lens for examining support structures in blended and online learning. *Educational Technology Research and Development, 68*(2), 807–832. https://doi.org/10.1007/s11423-020-09744-x

Burkhardt, H., & Schoenfeld, A. H. (2003). Improving educational research: Toward a more useful, more influential, and better-funded enterprise. *Educational Researcher, 32*(9), 3–14. https://doi.org/10.3102/0013189X032009003

Christenson, S. L., Reschly, A. L., & Wylie, C. (Eds.). (2012). *Handbook of research on student engagement.* Springer.

Clark, R. E. (1983). Reconsidering research on learning from media. *Review of Educational Research, 53*(4), 445–459.

Clark, R. E. (1986). Absolutes and angst in educational technology research: A reply to Don Cunningham. *Educational Communication and Technology Journal, 34*(1), 8–10.

Clark, R. E. (1994a). Media will never influence learning. *Educational Technology Research & Development, 42*(2), 21–29.

Clark, R. E. (1994b). Media and method. *Educational Technology Research & Development, 42*(3), 7–10.

Council National Academies of S. N. R. (2000). *How people learn: Brain, mind, experience, and school* (J. D. Bransford, A. L. Brown, R. R. Cocking, M. S. Donovan, & J. W. Pellegrino, Eds., expanded ed.). National Academies Press.

Cross, J. (2006). Forward. In C. J. Bonk & C. R. Graham (Eds.), *The handbook of blended learning: Global perspectives, local designs* (pp. xvii–xxiii). Pfeiffer Publishing.

Cunningham, D. J. (1986). Good guys and bad guys. *Educational Communication and Technology Journal, 34*(1), 3–7.

Davis, F. D. (1989). Perceived usefulness, perceived ease of use, and user acceptance of information technology. *MIS Quarterly: Management Information Systems, 13*(3), 319–339. https://doi.org/10.2307/249008

Dickmeyer, N. (1989). Metaphor, model, and theory in education research. *Teachers College Record, 91*(2), 151–160.

Drysdale, J. S., Graham, C. R., Spring, K. J., & Halverson, L. R. (2013). An analysis of research trends in dissertations and theses studying blended learning. *The Internet and Higher Education, 17*(1), 90–100. https://doi.org/10.1016/j.bbr.2011.03.031

Dubin, R. (1978). *Theory building* (revised ed.). The Free Press.

Dziuban, C., Graham, C. R., Moskal, P., Norberg, A., & Sicilia, N. (2018). Blended learning: The new normal and emerging technologies. *International Journal of Educational Technology in Higher Education, 15*(3). https://doi.org/10.1186/s41239-017-0087-5

Dziuban, C., Shea, P., & Moskal, P. (2020). A question of blended learning: Treatment effect or boundary object? *EDUCAUSE Review*, 1–9. https://er.educause.edu/articles/2020/4/a-question-of-blended-learning-treatment-effect-or-boundary-object

Fredricks, J. A., Blumenfeld, P. C., & Paris, A. H. (2004). School engagement: Potential of the concept, state of the evidence. *Review of Educational Research, 74*(1), 59–109.

Garrison, D. R., Anderson, T., & Archer, W. (1999). Critical inquiry in a text-based environment: Computer conferencing in higher education. *The Internet and Higher Education, 2*(2–3), 87–105. https://doi.org/10.1016/S1096-7516(00)00016-6

Garrison, D. R., & Kanuka, H. (2004). Blended learning: Uncovering its transformative potential in higher education. *The Internet and Higher Education, 7*(2), 95–105. https://doi.org/10.1016/j.iheduc.2004.02.001

Garrison, D. R., & Vaughan, N. D. (2008). *Blended learning in higher education: Framework, principles, and guidelines.* Jossey-Bass.

Gibbons, A. S. (2013). Instructional design and theory. In *An architectural approach to instructional design.* Routledge.

Graham, C. R. (2006). Blended learning systems: Definition, current trends, and future directions. In C. J. Bonk & C. R. Graham (Eds.), *Handbook of blended learning: Global perspectives, local designs* (pp. 3–21). Pfeiffer Publishing.

Graham, C. R. (2013). Emerging practice and research in blended learning. In M. G. Moore (Ed.), *Handbook of distance education* (3rd ed., pp. 333–350). Routledge.

Graham, C. R. (2019). Current research in blended learning. In M. G. Moore & W. C. Diehl (Eds.), *Handbook of distance education* (4th ed., pp. 173–188). Routledge.

Graham, C. R., Borup, J., Short, C. R., & Archambault, L. (2019). *K–12 blended teaching: A guide to personalized learning and online integration.* EdTechBooks.org. http://edtechbooks.org/k12blended

Graham, C. R., Henrie, C. R., & Gibbons, A. S. (2014). Developing models and theory for blended learning research. In A. G. Picciano, C. D. Dziuban, & C. R. Graham (Eds.), *Blended learning: Research perspectives* (Vol. 2, pp. 13–33). Routledge.

Graham, C. R., Woodfield, W., & Harrison, J. B. (2013). A framework for institutional adoption and implementation of blended learning in higher education. *Internet and Higher Education, 18*, 4–14. https://doi.org/10.1016/j.iheduc.2012.09.003

Gregor, S., & Gregor, B. S. (2006). The nature of theory in information systems. *MIS Quarterly, 30*(3), 611–642.

Halverson, L. R., & Graham, C. R. (2019). Learner engagement in blended learning environments: A conceptual framework. *Online Learning, 23*(2), 145–178. https://doi.org/10.24059/olj.v23i2.1481

Halverson, L. R., Graham, C. R., Spring, K. J., Drysdale, J. S., & Henrie, C. R. (2014). A thematic analysis of the most highly cited scholarship in the first decade of blended learning research. *Internet and Higher Education, 20*, 20–34. https://doi.org/10.1016/j.iheduc.2013.09.004

Hrastinski, S. (2019). What do we mean by blended learning? *TechTrends, 63*(5), 564–569. https://doi.org/10.1007/s11528-019-00375-5

Kaplan, A. (1964). *The conduct of inquiry: Methodology for behavioral science.* Chandler.

Kozma, R. (1991). Learning with media. *Review of Educational Research, 61*(2), 179–211.

Kozma, R. (1994). Will media influence learning? Reframing the debate. *Educational Technology Research & Development, 42*(2), 21–29.

Lim, C. P., Wang, T., & Graham, C. (2019). Driving, sustaining and scaling up blended learning practices in higher education institutions: A proposed framework. *Innovation and Education, 1*(1), 1–12. https://doi.org/10.1186/s42862-019-0002-0

McDonald, J. K., & Yanchar, S. C. (2020). Towards a view of originary theory in instructional design. *Educational Technology Research and Development, 68*(2), 633–651. https://doi.org/10.1007/s11423-019-09734-8

Means, B., Toyama, Y., Murphy, R., & Baki, M. (2013). The effectiveness of online and blended learning: A meta-analysis of the empirical literature [pdf]. *Teachers College Record, 115*(3), 1–47. www.tcrecord.org/library/content.asp?contentid=16882

Merton, R. K. (1967). *Social theory and social structure: Five essays, old and new.* Free Press.

Norberg, A., Dziuban, C. D., & Moskal, P. D. (2011). A time-based blended learning model. *On the Horizon, 19*(3), 207–216. https://doi.org/10.1108/10748121111163913

Oliver, M., & Trigwell, K. (2005). Can "blended learning" be redeemed? *E-Learning, 2*(1), 17–26. https://doi.org/10.2304/elea.2005.2.1.2

Picciano, A. G. (2006). Blended learning: Implications for growth and access. *Journal of Asynchronous Learning Networks, 10*(3), 95–102.

Picciano, A. G. (2009). Blending with purpose: The mutimodal model. *Journal of Asynchronous Learning Networks, 13*(1), 7–18. www.rcetj.org/index.php/rcetj/article/view/11/14

Picciano, A. G. (2017). Theories and frameworks for online education: Seeking an integrated model. *Online Learning Journal, 21*(3), 166–190. https://doi.org/10.24059/olj.v21i3.1225

Piña, A. A., & Bohn, L. (2014). Assessing online faculty: More than student surveys and design rubrics. *The Quarterly Review of Distance Education, 15*(3), 25–34.

Porter, W. W., & Graham, C. R. (2016). Institutional drivers and barriers to faculty adoption of blended learning in higher education. *British Journal of Educational Technology, 47*(4), 748–762. https://doi.org/10.1111/bjet.12269

Power, M. (2008). The emergence of a blended online learning environment. *Journal of Online Learning and Teaching, 4*(4), 503–514.

Pulham, E., Graham, C. R., & Short, C. R. (2018). Generic vs. modality-specific competencies for K–12 online and blended teaching. *Journal of Online Learning Research, 4*(1), 33–52. www.learntechlib.org/j/JOLR/v/4/n/1/

Reigeluth, C. (2008). What is instructional-design theory and how is it changing? In C. M. Reigeluth & A. A. Carr-Chellman (Eds.), *Instructional-design theories and models* (Vol. III, pp. 5–29). Routledge.

Ross, B., & Gage, K. (2006). Global perspectives on blended learning: Insight from WebCT and our customers in higher education. In C. J. Bonk & C. R. Graham (Eds.), *The handbook of blended learning: Global perspectives, local designs* (pp. 155–168). Pfeiffer Publishing.

Rossett, A., & Frazee, R. V. (2006). *Blended learning opportunities.* American Management Association.

Schunk, D. H., & Zimmerman, B. J. (Eds.). (2012). *Motivation and self-regulated learning: Theory, research, and applications.* Routledge.

Shea, P., & Bidjerano, T. (2010). Learning presence: Towards a theory of self-efficacy, self-regulation, and the development of a communities of inquiry in online and blended learning environments. *Computers and Education, 55*(4), 1721–1731. https://doi.org/10.1016/j.compedu.2010.07.017

Shulman, L. S. (2005). Signature pedagogies in the professions. *Daedalus, 134*(2), 52–59.

Simon, H. A. (1999). *The sciences of the artificial* (3rd ed.). MIT Press.

Spring, K. J., & Graham, C. R. (2016). Blended learning citation patterns and publication across seven worldwide regions. *Australasian Journal of Educational Technology, 33*(2), 24–50. https://doi.org/10.14742/ajet.2632

Spring, K. J., & Graham, C. R. (2017). Thematic patterns in international blended learning literature, research, practices, and terminology. *Online Learning, 21*(4), 337–361. https://doi.org/10.24059/olj.v21i4.998

Spring, K. J., Graham, C. R., & Hadlock, C. (2016). The current landscape of international blended learning. *International Journal of Technology Enhanced Learning, 8*(1), 84–102. https://doi.org/10.1504/IJTEL.2016.075961

Staker, H., & Horn, M. B. (2012). *Classifying K–12 blended learning.* www.innosightinstitute.org/innosight/wp-content/uploads/2012/05/Classifying-K-12-blended-learning2.pdf

Star, S. L., & Griesemer, J. R. (1989). Institutional ecology, "translations" and boundary objects: Amateurs and professionals in Berkeley's Museum of Vertebrate Zoology, 1907–39. *Social Studies of Science, 19*(3), 387–420. https://doi.org/10.1177/030631289019003001

Stein, J., & Graham, C. R. (2020). *Essentials for blended learning: A standards-based guide* (2nd ed.). Routledge.

Sutton, R. I., & Staw, B. M. (1995). What theory is not. *Administrative Science Quarterly, 40*(3), 371–384. http://links.jstor.org/sici?sici=0001-8392%28199509%2940%3A3%3C371%3AWTIN%3E2.0.CO%3B2-FAdministrative

Thomas, J. E., & Graham, C. R. (2017). Common practices for evaluating post-secondary online instructors. *Online Journal of Distance Learning Administration, 20*(4). www.westga.edu/~distance/ojdla/winter204/thomas_graham204.html

Twigg, C. A. (2003). Improving learning and reducing costs: New models for online learning. *EDUCAUSE Review, 38*(5), 28–38.

Tynan, B., Ryan, Y., & Lamont-Mills, A. (2015). Examining workload models in online and blended teaching. *British Journal of Educational Technology, 46*(1), 5–15. https://doi.org/10.1111/bjet.12111

Vaughan, N. (2007). Perspectives on blended learning in higher education. *International Journal on E-Learning, 6*(1), 81–94.

Wang, Y., Han, X., & Yang, J. (2015). International forum of educational technology & society revisiting the blended learning literature: Using a complex adaptive systems framework. *Source: Journal of Educational Technology & Society, 18*(2), 380–393. https://doi.org/10.2307/jeductechsoci.18.2.380

Watson, J. (2008). *Blended learning: The convergence of online and face-to-face education.* www.inacol.org/cms/wp-content/uploads/2012/09/NACOL_PP-BlendedLearning-lr.pdf

Whetten, D. A. (1989). What constitutes a theoretical contribution? *The Academy of Management Review, 14*(4), 490–495. https://doi.org/10.2307/258554

SECTION II
Student Outcomes

3

NEOTRADITIONAL STUDENTS AND ONLINE DISCUSSIONS

What Do They Really Want?

Jeff Renfrow

Introduction

For much of recorded human history, formal education has been structured within the contexts of teacher-directed, face-to-face synchronous experiences in physical classroom spaces. The advent of the internet in the late twentieth century presented newfound opportunities to redefine long-held notions of what teaching and learning could look like in the dawning of the twenty-first century (Gomes, 2008). The digitization of learning resources presented something of an educational tabula rasa that promised to liberate students and teachers from the traditional classroom bounds of time and space, literally adding new dimensions of possibility to the academic options of higher education. Flashing forward to 2009, we find a private, not-for-profit university in the Western United States (henceforth referred to in pseudonym as Western Region University, or WRU) that is just beginning its journey of developing and offering fully online programs that could leverage these new opportunities to benefit their adult student population.

When entering the online higher education marketspace in the late 2000s, WRU chose to develop their online courses using almost entirely asynchronous learning elements. This decision was based on institutional anecdotal evidence and the otherwise reasonable assumption that adult learners would choose *not* to enroll in courses that included any synchronous requirement, even if those requirements could be satisfied online. Additionally, WRU was reluctant to include synchronous elements due to the cost and accessibility restraints of synchronous learning technologies available at that time. These decisions and their implications for instructional design were held for nearly ten years as WRU enjoyed a decade of healthy enrollment growth in their adult online division.

DOI: 10.4324/9781003037736-5

As adult demand for online learning options continues to grow, it is important for institutions of higher education (IHEs) to more fully understand how instructional design decisions impact these students and their outcomes within the unique contexts of the online teaching and learning paradigm. One context that is unique to online learning, but ubiquitous within online learning, is the virtual discussion experience. The traditional text-based, asynchronous, whole-group discussion experience has been used as something of the "low-hanging fruit" of online learning engagement strategies for many years. While it has certainly provided opportunities for students to interact in an online course, this model presents limits on students' social presence, which research shows is related to perceptions of learning and satisfaction in an online course. Perhaps even more important is research showing that social presence, perception of learning, and satisfaction are related to increased rates of persistence for adult learners (Yang et al., 2017).

In consideration of this emerging research, WRU commissioned a study that would seek to measure their online adult division students' perceptions of social presence, learning, and satisfaction as related to the infamous online discussion. This study compared student experiences with a treatment discussion model and the control model used by WRU for over a decade. The control model utilized text-based, asynchronous, whole-group discussion elements, while the treatment model utilized video-based, synchronous, small-group discussion elements that are supported by social constructivist learning theory and blended learning literature. The study hypothesized that the treatment model would result in higher levels of student perceptions of social presence, learning, and satisfaction than the control. If the hypothesis was shown to be correct, WRU would have a clearer understanding of their rapidly growing student body and their response to synchronous course elements. This understanding could then lead to the addition of new, research-supported teaching and learning design tools in their online course development toolbox. Following is a review of this design study, which begins with a discussion of important study concepts and terms; then moves into an explanation of the study constructs, methods, and results; and concludes with a discussion of the implications and future considerations arising from the study.

The Neotraditional Student

Online learning has made postsecondary education more accessible to adults (Kascus, 1997), who, in 2003, became the majority postsecondary learning population (Ausburn, 2004). This group has continued to be the fastest growing market segment for online learning in higher education (NCES, 2015; Shea, 2002; Symonds, 2003). Some estimates show that so-called "traditional" full-time, residential college students between 18 and 21 years old represent only 20% of total enrollments in higher education (Picciano, 2016). This data suggests that adult students, historically referred to as "non-traditional students," have been the majority postsecondary student population for nearly two decades following 2003, which raises the question: When do we stop referring to them as non-traditional students? In response to the data and the question it prompts, the author will refer to the adult online, postsecondary student as the "neotraditional" student, honoring that this majority demographic presents itself as a new adaptation of education that once had a different majority tradition. The author has chosen to further define neotraditional students as those who are independent for the purposes of financial aid and perform adult roles such as full- or part-time worker, participating citizen, spouse, parent, etc.

On the topic of technology innovations for teaching and learning, Hastie et al. (2007, p. 1) said it well: "We have the machine, but we are still waiting for the teaching manuals to be written." This could also be said about our understanding of neotraditional students. While online programs have significantly increased higher education access opportunities, this group is showing significantly lower persistence and completion rates than to their traditional peers (U.S. News and World Report, 2015). It seems that there is something unique and as yet not fully understood about how to effectively help the neotraditional student achieve their formal learning goals.

Toward Writing the Manual

Numerous studies in both face-to-face and online courses show that increases in student perceptions of social presence, learning, and satisfaction are related to increases in persistence and completion rates (Baturay, 2011; Kuo & Belland, 2016). A question that naturally follows is, Where and how can we increase these important persistence and completion factors within our online programs? For the purposes of the present study, it was decided that primary consideration of any learning design changes would be informed by the social constructivism theories of Dewey (1910), Piaget (1953), Vygotsky (1979), and Bruner (1991) and adult learning theory, including Knowles' (1984) andragogy, Tough's (1967) self-directed learning, and Kolb's (1984) experiential learning. Additional consideration was given to Moore's (1993) transactional distance framework, which asserts that instructional design decisions can either increase or decrease the psychological and communication space between the learner, content, and instructor, leading to potential increases or decreases in misunderstanding and sense of connection.

Also given consideration was the social presence theory of Short et al. (1976), who posit that different communication media will allow different ways for people to interact, resulting in differing degrees of social presence. Finally, but not least among these, the community of inquiry (CoI) framework of Garrison et al. (2001) was given consideration; more specifically, attention was given to finding a way to positively impact the intersection between CoI's social presence and cognitive presence in an area called "supporting discourse." It is noted by

Armstrong and Thornton (2012) that the CoI framework presents an information gap at this intersection (see Figure 3.1). They assert that "there is no discussion of the instructional strategies needed to create a specific environment that encourages and supports the use of discourse and discussion" (2012, p. 3). This study attempted to contribute to filling this alleged knowledge gap by offering a strategy that is shown to effectively promote discourse and discussion between neotraditional students.

Considering the broad and important research base and various frameworks, we were compelled to wonder if the decision so many years ago to eliminate synchronous interactions in our courses might be contributing to lower satisfaction, learning, and social presence and, perhaps more importantly, to lower retention and completion rates of our neotraditional students. It was decided the study would introduce a synchronous course element grounded in the previously mentioned theories and frameworks so we could study how this might affect the outcomes of social presence, learning, and satisfaction in our historically asynchronous courses.

The online discussion forum presented itself as the greatest opportunity to leverage the learning theories discussed earlier. Consequently, our long-used, text-based, whole-group asynchronous discussion (henceforth referred to as TAWD) model was flipped on its head, resulting in a video-based, small-group synchronous discussion (henceforth referred to as VSSD) model used as the

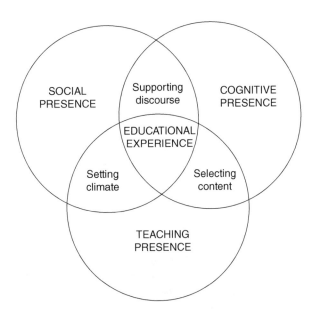

FIGURE 3.1 Community of Inquiry Framework

Source: (CoI Framework, 2019)

treatment in the study. By default, this design study examining the impact of a novel synchronous discussion protocol was simultaneously examining the impact of transitioning our completely asynchronous courses into the realm of blended learning.

Although there is yet to be a commonly accepted definition of blended learning, much of the literature tends to describe it in terms of combining the best elements of in-seat, or "face-to-face," learning with the best elements of online learning (Norberg et al., 2011, as cited in Picciano et al., 2014). As the conceptualization of blended learning evolves, the author suggests that the definition of "face-to-face" course elements should extend beyond that of the physical "in-seat" realm to include those experiences in which learning communities interact synchronously via web-enabled meeting platforms. This study, using such a platform, reveals a statistically significant difference between the measured outcomes of the TAWD and the VSSD, thereby providing support for this suggestion. Further analysis of the outcomes is provided in the Study Results section. Following is a discussion of the three primary study variables, why they are important, and how learning theory informed their inclusion in the VSSD.

Social Presence, Learning, and Satisfaction

It is difficult to discuss social presence, learning, and satisfaction in isolation as an examination of one is inevitably linked to the others in learning research literature. For example, Baturay (2011) discusses how student sense of belonging to the learning community is strongly related to student satisfaction, regardless of whether the learning experience is situated online or in seat. Lowenthal et al. (2017) explain that social presence and satisfaction are related to students' perceptions of learning, while Garrison et al. (2001) and Rovai (2002) assert that social presence enhances measured student learning outcomes.

Social Presence

While research methodologies and contexts have varied, many studies indicate that social presence is a predictor of student satisfaction (Lowenthal et al., 2017), learner motivation, persistence, and completion (McKinney et al., 2006; Rovai, 2002). Much of the social constructivism literature considers the social aspect of the learning experience to be a means to the end of cognitive outcomes. While research does support that student learning outcomes (real and perceived) are related to higher rates of persistence and retention (Beachboard et al., 2011), research also suggests that learning outcomes and persistence are inter-related with social presence and satisfaction (Baturay, 2011).

One of the most common ways instructional designers and instructors attempt to develop social presence in their online courses is through the discussion board. Discussion boards can apply many combinations of design elements such as

38 Jeff Renfrow

small group, large/whole group, synchronous, asynchronous, text based, video based, etc. WRU students have almost exclusively experienced online discussions through the commonly used text-based, asynchronous whole-group model. However, there are limits to the amount of deep, socially connected learning that can occur in this model (Oztok, 2014). Short et al.'s (1976) social presence theory offers robust support for this conclusion. Originally developed to explain how communication is affected by telecommunications media, social presence in this theory is defined as the degree to which a person is perceived to be "real" in mediated communication. The researchers posit that different communication media will allow different ways for people to interact, resulting in differing degrees of social presence. For example, they argue that people perceive that audio-mediated communication allows for a higher degree of social presence than text-based communication, and video-mediated communication allows for a higher degree of social presence than audio-mediated communication (Lowenthal, 2012).

The VSSD treatment discussion included video-based (V) and synchronous (S) elements, which the literature shows could result in greater student perceptions of social presence compared to students in the TAWD control model. Joksimović et al. (2015) state that in addition to increased levels of motivation, satisfaction, and retention, a sense of belonging (i.e., social presence) might also be related to the degree of perceived learning. This is a second variable in the study and will be discussed next.

Perceived Learning

Several studies have shown the academic benefits associated with engaging students with each other. In a 2011 study of online students, Baturay found that sense of community and course satisfaction are strongly related to each other and that students' perceived cognitive learning is highly related to their course satisfaction. Again, all these variables are shown to be related to increased persistence and completion rates and are therefore worthy of consideration when developing online courses.

Jung and Associates (2002) studied the effects of academic, collaborative, and social interaction on student learning, satisfaction, and participation. The study showed that the social interaction group outperformed the other groups on achievement, potentially demonstrating the positive effect of socially constructed learning in adult online higher education. This effect was also noted by Rovai and Barnum (2003), who suggest that immediacy behaviors (e.g., interaction, engagement, presence) could be associated with student learning in online courses. Another study by Zirkin and Sumler (1995) reported that, in an online education environment, increased student involvement by immediate interaction resulted in increased learning as reflected by test performance, grades, and student satisfaction.

It is commonly understood that instructional practices influence student learning. However, one might wonder why the present study would choose to examine perceptions of learning rather than actual or measured learning. For decades, instructor grading of assignments, projects, and assessments has been the standard method to document and communicate student learning. However, this practice is fraught with problems, particularly in higher education, where it is not uncommon to see final course grades with very small percentage ranges, usually showing superior achievement (i.e., the *A*) for nearly all students. Also, grades may not accurately reflect what the student has learned during the class. It is possible that the student already knew the material, therefore potentially exiting the class with no new knowledge or skills. Grading authentic performance assessments, particularly those designed with constructivist notions, is also challenging because different teachers are unlikely to grade the work with consistency (Rovai & Barnum, 2003). For all these reasons, using grades to measure and report learning can be problematic.

Research supports that self-reports of perceived learning can be used as valid measures of learning. Richmond et al. (1987) argued that because college students are adults with significant experience in education, they are able to accurately estimate the amount they learned in a given course. In fact, they go so far as to argue that "it is likely that their estimate is at least as good as subjective grades provided by teachers in many classes or by tests administered in classes not based on clear behavioral objectives" (1987, p. 581, as cited in Rovai et al., 2009). For this reason, the present study operationalizes the construct of learning through the lens of adult student perceptions of their learning within the VSSD or TSWD experience.

The video-based (V), synchronous (S), and small-group (S) elements of the VSSD can support social presence, discourse, and immediacy of feedback, which are all shown to increase learning in online courses. As noted earlier, social presence, perception of learning, and satisfaction are variables that are often correlated in research. As a result, satisfaction is a third variable in the study and will be explored in the next section.

Satisfaction

Satisfaction is an outcome that reflects affective domains of an experience such as learning. Baturay (2011) found that higher student satisfaction can lead to higher retention and completion, as well as increased academic performance. This same study also found that dissatisfaction is reported to be a major factor in student decisions to withdraw from online courses.

Woods (2002) suggests that quantity and quality of interaction with peers and instructors are perhaps more important to student satisfaction in online courses than in traditional courses. Presenting a slightly different finding, Kuo and Belland (2016) explain that learner-to-instructor and learner-to-content interactions are

40 Jeff Renfrow

more influential than learner-to-learner factors in student satisfaction. However, they note that "[i]nteraction among learners [does] not usually have a significant effect on student satisfaction in fully online settings unless specific group work or projects are assigned to online students" (p. 664). The VSSD model intended to leverage this finding by including synchronous, video-based, small-group elements with intentional and clearly articulated group-based discussion activities. It was hypothesized that when compared to the TAWD model, the inclusion of these elements in the VSSD model would result in greater perceptions of satisfaction as a result of greater perceptions of social presence and learning.

Context, Sample, and Methods

This quasi-experimental design study took place at a mid-size online, private, faith-based IHE in the Western United States. Participants included a non-purposive random sample of 138 globally dispersed neotraditional students enrolled in either a business, psychology, leadership, or teacher education course. The sample was generally representative of the greater population of WRU. There were 68 students in the TAWD/control group and 70 students the VSSD/treatment group. Other key demographic variables were equally represented in both groups (see Table 3.1).

In this study, WRU administration sought to determine if their neotraditional students would tolerate and benefit from participation in synchronous course elements. The following formal research questions guided the research:

- Will neotraditional students perceive greater social presence, learning, and satisfaction when participating in a VSSD compared to students participating in a TAWD?

TABLE 3.1 Participant Demographics by Sample, Treatment, and Course

Measure	Sample	VSSD	TAWD	Business 100	Education 400	Leadership 500	Counseling 600
N	138	70	68	31	28	14	65
Male	23	12	11	8	1	3	11
Female	115	58	57	23	27	11	54
Age in Years (M)	38	37	38	40	35	36	38
Age (Range/SD)	53/12	41/11	53/13	52/11	31/9	38/14	52/13
Race							
AK/AM Native	1	0	1				
Two or More	3	3	0				
Black	14	7	7				
Hispanic	26	13	13				
White	94	47	47				

- Are student perceptions of social presence, learning, or satisfaction impacted by participation in the VSSD when accounting for other factors such as age, GPA, or tech efficacy?

The discussion board tool in the Blackboard™ learning management system was used for the TAWD, while institutional Pro ZOOM accounts were used by students to facilitate the VSSD. In order to reduce the effect of selection bias, students did not know which discussion format was being used in which course sections at the time of course registration.

The VSSD protocol requires a user level of technology sophistication beyond that of the TAWD. Technology efficacy is a variable shown to possibly introduce confounding effects on learning (Arbaugh et al., 2008) and social capital (Kim et al., 2012) in the online context. This kind of technological efficacy refers to a person's judgment of their confidence in organizing, managing, and performing computer- and internet-related activities to complete certain tasks. Consequently, participants completed a voluntary pre-course survey called the Computer Attitudes Scale, or "CAS" (Loyd & Loyd, 1985), which was shown to be significantly correlated to the World Wide Web Attitude Scale ($r = .092$, $P < 0.000$) in a 2004 study by Horvat, Petric, and Mikrut. Data collected from the CAS and extant data available through WRU's student management system enabled the study to control for the possible effect of tech efficacy and was used to inform study results.

Participants engaged in weekly discussions exclusively using their respective model (see Figure 3.2). Courses were five to seven weeks long. Both groups were given the prompt for the week on Mondays. The TAWD groups were directed to make their initial posts by Wednesday and engage with at least two other classmates in the forum by Sunday evening. Discussion participation was evaluated by the instructor using a rubric. The TAWD instructors were directed to interact in the discussions but to assume a "guide on the side" role.

The VSSD students were randomly assigned by the instructor before the first day of class into discussion groups of four to six students, who remained in the same group during the course. By keeping the groups small and unchanging throughout the course, the study hoped to nurture rapid progression through

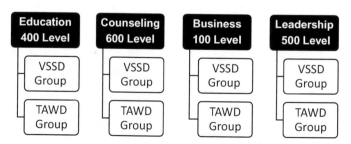

FIGURE 3.2 Participant Groupings

42 Jeff Renfrow

Tuckman's stages of group development (1965), thereby engaging in more meaningful, productive (i.e., "performing") discussions. It was predicted that this element of the VSSD would contribute to greater perceptions of social presence, learning, and satisfaction. The instructor was directed not to attend the live student discussions. This student-led approach leverages adult learning principles described earlier and is shown to be the most popular collaboration design for online students in a 2007 study by Correia and Davis.

VSSD groups were provided the following additional guidance and direction:

- Use the instructor-provided Google form to coordinate a 45-minute time to hold your small group's discussion by Sunday afternoon.
- Use a webcam when meeting.
- Identify a weekly discussion facilitator. (Additional guidance was provided to student facilitators to help them guide a productive discussion.)
- Individual students record and submit a three- to five-minute ZOOM audio or video reflection that summarizes their learning.
- Instructors evaluate the reflection using a VSSD reflection rubric and provide individualized video, audio, or text-based feedback.

During the final week of the course, the students took a voluntary online survey, which gathered participant perceptions of learning, satisfaction, and social presence as related specifically to their experience in the course discussions. The survey comprised a selection of modified indicators from the Classroom Community Scale (Rovai et al., 2009) to collect social presence and perceived learning data. It also included items from a 2013 satisfaction survey by Kuo et al.

It is worth noting that research shows asynchronous discussions are better suited for topics requiring significant reflection and introspection prior to engaging and replying to others (Oztok & Brett, 2011). The same literature notes that synchronous discussions lend themselves to topics that can be immediately processed in groups without fear of reprisal or judgement. In other words, a discussion topic that works well in the TAWD model may not work well in the VSSD model, and vice versa. Considering this, the study used instructor-provided weekly discussion prompts in the VSSD that were at times different in content and context from the instructor-provided TAWD discussion prompts in the same course.

The Results

Independent t-tests were used to determine the significant differences between group overall scores of perceived social presence, learning, and satisfaction. A regression analysis was used to determine if certain student demographic variables, such as age, gender, GPA, and tech efficacy, might introduce mediating effects on student perceptions. Finally, a Cohen's d calculation was used to determine effect size. Following is a summary of the findings based on this analysis.

The data revealed a statistically significant difference between VSSD students (higher) and TAWD students (lower) in regard to their perceptions of social presence, learning, and satisfaction in their respective online discussion experience (see Table 3.2). These differences continued to be significant, even after accounting for the effects of student technology efficacy. Regression analysis showed that age, gender, GPA, and academic level did not significantly predict perceptions of social presence, learning, or satisfaction in either the TAWD or the VSSD model. However, technology efficacy was shown to be positively and significantly correlated to all three variables in both groups. This finding is consistent with other research (Gangadharbatla, 2008), showing a link between student understanding of course hardware, software, information searching, and trouble shooting and the student's ability to successfully complete the required tasks and activities of an online or blended course. There was no correlation shown between a student's age and their self-report of technology efficacy.

To further interpret the results, the researcher calculated a Cohen effect size for each variable. Using Cohen's (1988) recommendations for effect size rankings of small, medium, and large, the VSSD was shown to have a medium effect on social presence perceptions ($d = 0.57$), a small to medium effect on learning perceptions ($d = 0.47$), and a small to medium effect on satisfaction perceptions ($d = 0.39$). Hattie and Yates (2014) suggest that in social science and education research, an effect size of .4 or greater is worth noting as a finding that may have important practical significance. Considering there is an effect "worth noting" in the study results, the following section offers an illumination of the practical implications and additional considerations prompted by the study outcomes. Discussion will focus on the domains of course design and student experience within blended learning environments.

TABLE 3.2 Study Results

	n	Mean (sd)	Mean difference	t	d
Social Presence					
VSSD	70	6.0 (.97)			
TAWD	68	5.5 (.78)	0.50	3.57**	.57
Learning					
VSSD	70	6.1 (.93)			
TAWD	68	5.7 (.78)	0.40	2.70**	.47
Satisfaction					
VSSD	70	6.1 (1.0)			
TAWD	68	5.7 (.78)	0.40	2.05*	.39

* $p < .05$; ** $p < .01$

44 Jeff Renfrow

Implications and Considerations

With the exception of a student's technology efficacy, the TAWD and the VSSD present accessible and equitable online discussion models across varying demographics, including student age, gender, race, and academic level (graduate vs. undergraduate). Stated another way, these critical demographic variables did not significantly affect student perceptions of social presence, learning, or satisfaction in either discussion model. Students who reported lower technology efficacy also reported lower satisfaction, social presence, and learning. However, perceptions of tech efficacy were not related to any of the student demographics, including age. This finding supports a 2009 study by Ke and Xie, who found that older students do not necessarily perceive themselves as less tech savvy than their younger peers and that age alone is not a predictor of online and blended learning outcomes. Additionally, this finding supports a robust body of research showing that intentional efforts to train and support learning technology tool use is important in any online learning program and for any online learner, regardless of age (McBrien et al., 2009; Giesbers et al., 2013).

From the unchanging, student-led small groups of four to six students to the Google form for organizing the discussion groups to the individual video-based discussion summaries, careful, research-based considerations were given to every element of the VSSD in an effort to optimize perceptions of social presence, learning, and satisfaction. If one intends to implement the VSSD in a course or program, it is important to consider that changes to any aspect of the VSSD protocol, or significant variances from the study sample, may produce different results. This study did not examine how much of an effect any particular element of the VSSD might be having on the results. For example, what if we replaced the video-based element with a text-based element, effectively using a "TSSD"? Or what if we replaced the small group with a whole group (i.e., VSWD)? Would these changes result in different perceptions of social presence, learning, or satisfaction? Considering the research and theory noted earlier in this chapter, the author would hypothesize that there would be lower average ratings for all three variables by applying either of these changes to the VSSD protocol.

You may recall that the WRU administration had two driving questions that prompted this study:

1. Will our students *benefit* from participation in blended course activities?
2. Will our students *tolerate* a requirement to participate in a synchronous blended course element?

The results clearly answer the first question in the affirmative. However, the answer to the second question is not yet so clear. In the context of this study, satisfaction and toleration are closely related constructs. Therefore, it is reasonable to conclude that the higher reports of satisfaction in the VSSD indicate that

WRU's students will tolerate this blended learning strategy more than they tolerate the TAWD. While this is a promising conclusion from the satisfaction survey data, there is a particular survey item that perhaps speaks to the second question better than any other data point. Item five states, "In the future, I would be willing to take a course that uses this kind of discussion model." The mean score on this question for the VSSD group was in the "Agree" range, while the TAWD group's mean score was in the "Slightly Agree" range. Although this item does not attempt to explain *why* the VSSD students were more inclined to take another course that uses the VSSD protocol, the results do suggest that the VSSD is a slightly more preferred (read: tolerated) blended discussion model. This finding suggests an opportunity for future research into why students were more likely to enroll in a course with VSSD elements than a course with TAWD elements.

TAWD or VSSD?

While it is true that the VSSD produced higher student ratings of social presence, learning, and satisfaction than the TAWD model, this result should not be interpreted to mean that the TAWD no longer has a place on the menu of instructional design options. The real question of TAWD or VSSD isn't a question of winner and loser; it's a question of which one should be used when considering the intended outcomes of the learning experience. This perspective is supported by Moallem et al. (2011), who demonstrated that blending synchronous and asynchronous video interactions may result in greater outcomes than using only one format. The important idea here is that the intended learning outcomes should drive the pedagogy and its supporting technologies and not the other way around. This is not a new idea, but it is an idea that was recently elaborated on in the context of blended learning by researcher Anthony G. Picciano, who explains that in the fourth wave (of five) of online education, "pedagogy drives technology in a comprehensive and sophisticated blended learning environment" (2016, p. 151).

If the desired outcome of a given discussion requires personal reflection time, deep content exploration, and increased cognitive engagement, then, pedagogically, this would suggest choosing an asynchronous discussion model such as the TAWD. If problem solving, team strategy development, group production tasks, developing social presence, and immediate feedback are important elements of the discussion outcome, then a synchronous discussion model such as the VSSD would be recommended. Consistent with Picciano's (2016) "fourth wave" condition, it is recommended by the author that a prioritization of the learning goals should occur first. Those that rise to the top should then inform the pedagogical strategies, which should lastly inform the use (or not) of particular technologies.

In closing, this study has demonstrated the efficacy of a research-supported synchronous discussion protocol that produced increased neotraditional student perceptions of social presence, learning, and satisfaction as compared to the traditional text-based, whole-group discussion model. It also showed that institutions like WRU can reconsider notions that their neotraditional students will not tolerate synchronous course elements, thereby improving student outcomes through the use of this research-supported blended learning strategy.

References

Arbaugh, J., Cleveland-Innes, M., Diaz, S., Garrison, D., Ice, P., Richardson, J., & Swan, K. (2008). Developing a community of inquiry instrument: Testing a measure of the community of inquiry framework using a multi-institutional sample. *The Internet and Higher Education, 11*(3–4), 133–136.

Armstrong, A., & Thornton, N. (2012). Incorporating Brookfield's discussion techniques synchronously into asynchronous online courses. *The Quarterly Review of Distance Education, 13*(1), 1–9.

Ausburn, L. (2004). Course design elements most valued by adult learners in blended online education environments: An American perspective. *Educational Media International, 41*(4), 327–337.

Baturay, M. (2011). Relationships among sense of classroom community, perceived cognitive learning and satisfaction of students at an e-learning course. *Interactive Learning Environments, 19*(5), 563–575.

Beachboard, M., Beachboard, J., Li, W., & Adkison, S. (2011). Cohorts and relatedness: Self-determination theory as an explanation of how learning communities affect educational outcomes. *Research in Higher Education, 52*(8), 853–874.

Bruner, J. (1991). The narrative construction of reality. *Critical Inquiry, 18*(1), 1–21. https://doi.org/10.1086/448619

Cohen, J. (1988). *Statistical power analysis for the behavioral sciences*. Routledge, Academic.

CoI Framework (2019). www.coi.athabascau.ca

Correia, A. P., & Davis, N. E. (2007). The design of collaboration in the virtual classroom. In M. Simonson (Ed.), *30th annual proceedings of selected papers on the practice of educational communications and technology* (Vol. 2, pp. 84–87). AECT.

Dewey, J. (1910). *The school and society*. University of Chicago Press.

Gangadharbatla, H. (2008). Facebook me: Collective self-esteem, need to belong, and Internet self-efficacy as predictors of the Igeneration's attitudes toward social networking sites. *Journal of Interactive Advertising, 8*(2), 5–15.

Garrison, D. R., Anderson, T., & Archer, W. (2001). Critical thinking, cognitive presence, and computer conferencing in distance education. *American Journal of Distance Education, 15*(1), 7–23.

Giesbers, B., Rienties, B., Tempelaar, D., & Gijselaers, W. (2013). A dynamic analysis of the interplay between asynchronous and synchronous communication in online learning: The impact of motivation. *Journal of Computer Assisted Learning, 30*(1), 30–50.

Gomes, M. (2008). Reflections on the institutional adoption of e-learning: New challenges, new opportunities. *e-Curriculum Journal, 3*(2), 1809–3876.

Hastie, M., Chen, N. S., & Kuo, Y. H. (2007). Instructional design for best practice in the synchronous cyber classroom. *Educational Technology & Society, 10*(4), 281–294.

Hattie, J., & Yates, G. (2014). *Visible learning and the science of how we learn*. Routledge, Taylor & Francis Group.

Horvat, J., Petrič, G., & Mikrut, M. (2004). Measuring computer and web attitudes using CAS and WAS measurement instruments. *Proceedings of the International Conference on Information Technology Interfaces, ITI, 1,* 441–446. https://doi.org/10.1109/ITI.2004.242078

Joksimović, S., Gašević, D., Kovanović, V., Riecke, B., & Hatala, M. (2015). Social presence in online discussions as a process predictor of academic performance. *Journal of Computer Assisted Learning, 31*(6), 638–654.

Jung, I., Choi, S., Lim, C., & Leem, J. (2002). Effects of different types of interaction on learning achievement, satisfaction and participation in web-based instruction. *Innovations in Education and Teaching International, 39*(2), 153–162.

Kascus, M. (1997). Converging visions of library services for off-campus distance education. *Journal of Library Services for Distance Education, 1*(1), 32–41.

Ke, F., & Xie, K. (2009). Toward deep learning for adult students in online courses. *The Internet and Higher Education, 12*(3–4), 136–145.

Kim, K., Oh, I., Chiaburu, D., & Brown, K. (2012). Does positive perception of oneself boost learning motivation and performance? *International Journal of Selection and Assessment, 20*(3), 257–271.

Knowles, M. (1984). *The adult learner: A neglected species* (3rd ed.). Gulf Publishing.

Kolb, D. A. (1984). *Experiential learning: Experience as the source of learning and development* (Vol. 1). Prentice-Hall.

Kuo, Y., & Belland, B. (2016). An exploratory study of adult learners' perceptions of online learning: Minority students in continuing education. *Educational Technology Research and Development, 64*(4), 661–680.

Lowenthal, P. (2012). *Social presence: What is it? How do we measure it?* [PhD.]. University of Colorado.

Lowenthal, P., Dunlap, J., & Snelson, C. (2017). Live synchronous web meetings in asynchronous online courses: Reconceptualizing virtual office hours. *Online Learning, 21*(4), 177–194.

Loyd, B. H., & Loyd, B. E. (1985). The reliability and validity of instruments for the assessment of computer attitudes, *Educational and Psychological Measurement, 45,* 903–908.

McBrien, J. L., Jones, P., & Cheng, R. (2009). Virtual spaces: Employing a synchronous online classroom to facilitate student engagement in online learning. *The International Review of Research in Open and Distributed Learning, 10*(3).

McKinney, J., McKinney, K., Franiuk, R., & Schweitzer, J. (2006). The college classroom as a community: Impact on student attitudes and learning. *College Teaching, 54*(3), 281–284.

Moallem, M., Pastore, R., & Martin, F. (2011). A comparative study on the impact of various communication tools on student learning, motivation, self-regulation, and satisfaction. In C. Ho & M. Lin (Eds.), *Proceedings of E-Learn 2011—world conference on e-learning in corporate, government, healthcare, and higher education* (pp. 1519–1534). Association for the Advancement of Computing in Education (AACE).

Moore, M. G. (1993). Theory of transactional distance. In D. Keegan (Ed.), *Theoretical principles of distance education* (pp. 22–29). Routledge.

NCES (2015). *Nces.ed.gov* [PDF file]. https://nces.ed.gov/pubs2015/2015025.pdf

Norberg, A., Dzubian, C., & Moskal, P. (2011). A time-based blended learning model. *On the Horizon, 19*(3), 207–216.

Oztok, M., & Brett, C. (2011). Social presence and online learning: A review of research. *Journal of Distance Education, 25*(3).

Oztok, M., Wilton, L., Lee, K., Zingaro, D., Mackinnon, K., & Makos, A. (2014). Polysynchronous: Dialogic construction of time in online learning. *E-Learning and Digital Media, 11*(2), 154–161.

Piaget, J. (1953). *The origin of intelligence in the child.* Routledge & Kegan Paul.

Picciano, A. (2016). *Online education policy and practice.* Taylor and Francis.

Picciano, A., Dziuban, C., & Graham, C. (2014). *Blended learning research perspectives* (Vol. 2). Taylor and Francis.

Richmond, V. P., Gorham, J. S., & McCroskey, J. C. (1987). The relationship between selected immediacy behaviors and cognitive learning. In M. A. McLaughlin (Ed.), *Communication yearbook* (Vol. 10, pp. 574 – 590). Sage.

Rovai, A. P. (2002). Sense of community perceived cognitive learning, and persistence in asynchronous learning networks. *Internet and Higher Education, 5*(4), 319–332.

Rovai, A. P., & Barnum, K. T. (2003). On-line course effectiveness: An analysis of student interactions and perceptions of learning. *Journal of Distance Education, 18*(1), 57–73.

Rovai, A. P., Wighting, M., Baker, J., & Grooms, L. (2009). Development of an instrument to measure perceived cognitive, affective, and psychomotor learning in traditional and virtual classroom higher education settings. *The Internet and Higher Education, 12*(1), 7–13.

Shea, R. H. (2002, October 28). E-learning today. *U.S. News & World Report,* 54–56.

Short, J., Williams, E., & Christie, B. (1976). *The social psychology of telecommunication.* John Wiley & Sons.

Symonds, W. (2003, November 17). Cash-cow universities. *Business Week,* 71–74.

Tough, A. (1967). *Learning without a teacher.* Educational Research Series, No. 3. Institute for Studies in Education.

Tuckman, B. W. (1965). Developmental sequence in small groups. *Psychological Bulletin, 63*(6), 384–399.

U.S. News and World Report (2015, January 30). *Experts debate graduation rates for online students.* U.S. News and World Report.

Vygotsky, L., Cole, M., John-Steiner, V., Scribner, S., Souberman, E., & Wertsch, J. (1979). Mind in society: The development of higher psychological processes. *The American Journal of Psychology, 92*(1).

Woods, R. H. (2002). How much communication is enough in online courses? Exploring the relationship between frequency of instructor-initiated personal email and learners' perceptions of and participation in online learning. *International Journal of Instructional Media, 29,* 377–394.

Yang, D., Baldwin, S., & Snelson, C. (2017). Persistence factors revealed: Students' reflections on completing a fully online program. *Distance Education, 38*(1), 23–36.

Zirkin, B., & Sumler, D. (1995). Interactive or non-interactive? That is the question! An annotated bibliography. *Journal of Distance Education, 10*(1), 95.

4

BLENDED DELIVERY MODES AND STUDENT SUCCESS

An In-Depth Exploration of How Different Levels of Online and Blended Course Taking Relate to Student Retention

Scott James and Karen Swan

Although a class in which time is split between online and face-to-face instruction is the primary definition of "blended learning," a common and alternate blend occurs at the program level, when students take some classes face to face and other online (Bloemer & Swan, 2014). For several years, we have been investigating this form of blending and its relationship to retention and other student outcomes when compared with taking classes solely face to face or solely online. We found that students blending their classes had significantly better outcomes than students taking only online classes and that they often did comparably to students taking only face-to-face classes (James et al., 2016; Swan & James, 2017; James & Swan, 2019).

Just as comparing outcomes between students who take only face-to-face classes and those of students who take any online classes obscures important differences among the latter, so there are likely important outcome differences among students who are blending their classes in different proportions (Shea & Bidjerano, 2018). This chapter explores those differences for both students blending classes and students taking differing proportions of blended and face-to-face classes. In the sections that follow, we review research on the effects of blending classes as well as our own findings in this area and present our methodology. Then we review our findings for bachelor's students blending their classes, bachelor's students taking blended classes, and finally for associate's students blending their classes and taking blended classes. We conclude with a discussion of the findings.

Background

For as long as there have been online and blended classes, researchers have been comparing them with the face-to-face modality. While there is general agreement

DOI: 10.4324/9781003037736-6

that students learn as much if not more in online classes (Bernard et al., 2014), there is considerable debate about the effects of online and blended learning on student retention.

In particular, a series of studies utilizing large data sets exploring the effects of online delivery on undergraduate student retention (Jaggars et al., 2013; Johnson et al., 2015; Shea & Bidjerano, 2018) has raised issues about the efficacy of online classes, most especially at the community college level. Findings were mixed across the studies. Some researchers found that community college students were more likely to withdraw or fail in online classes, that online class completers had lower grades than on-ground students, and that these negative effects were more pronounced for males, African Americans, younger students, and students with lower GPAs (Hart et al., 2016; Jaggers & Xu, 2010; Johnson et al., 2015).

However, other findings confound these results. For example, Wladis and colleagues (2016) found that, while students enrolled in online classes were more likely to drop them, taking online classes had no direct effect on college persistence; rather, other characteristics seemed to make students simultaneously both more likely to enroll in online classes and more likely to drop out of college. Researchers in both California (Johnson et al., 2015) and New York State (Shea & Bidjerano, 2014, 2016) found that community college students who took at least some classes online were more likely to earn an associate's degree or transfer to a four-year institution than those who did not. However, Shea and Bidjerano (2018) also found that community college students taking more than 40% of their classes online began to lose those benefits.

Beginning in 2016, our own research compared retention outcomes between three groups of students—students taking face-to-face classes only, students taking classes only online, and students taking some classes online and some classes face to face. Our first study (James et al., 2016) compared students in these groups at five primarily on-ground community colleges, five primarily on ground four-year universities, and four primarily online institutions. Controlling for factors related to retention and progression including GPA, we found that only students taking solely online classes at community colleges had lower odds of retention.

Our second study (Swan & James, 2017) explored the effects of online class enrollment for students at seven universities. The findings were similar to and support those of Wladis and colleagues (2016), in that we found that differences in retention rates had more to do with learner characteristics than with delivery mode per se. We also found that full-time students taking online classes had slightly greater odds of dropping out than full-time students taking all classes on ground. However, this result was reversed for part-time students at two of the colleges studied, and at four others, there was no difference in retention between delivery modes for part-time students.

Our third study (James & Swan, 2019) built on our earlier work and examined relationships between online course participation and a variety of academic outcomes—GPA, course withdrawals, retention, and degree completion—in a new sample of students seeking certificate, associate's, and bachelor's degrees. We found that taking online courses had a minimal effect on the outcome variables for bachelor's degree students after adjusting for learner characteristics. There was, however, a small negative effect on outcomes for associate's students, and a small-to-medium negative effect on outcomes for certificate students. We also found that outcome gaps between students taking exclusively in-person classes, some online classes, and only online classes were amplified at all levels for minority students.

Methodology

Subjects and Setting

Two data sets were used for analysis in this study, one comprising bachelor's-degree-seeking students attending four-year universities (Sample 1) and the other comprising associate's-degree-seeking students primarily attending community colleges (Sample 2). Both samples included students who began courses at their institutions between Fall 2015 and Spring 2018. Sample 1 totaled 68,869 students from eleven universities, six public and five private, located in the Midwest, Northeast, and West. Sample 2 totaled 66,222 students from thirteen public community colleges located in the Midwest and Northeast and one public university that offers associate degrees located in the West.

The primary outcome of the study, retention to a second year, is defined as being actively enrolled or having earned a credential between 12 and 18 months after initial enrollment. The primary variables of interest were the percentage of credits taken online (online attempt ratio) and the percentage of credits taken in blended classes (hybrid attempt ratio) during a student's first six months at their institution. This corresponds closely to a student's first fall or spring term at traditional institutions and is flexible enough to include institutions that have shorter, more frequent terms. We included the following covariates to adjust for potential differences in student characteristics:

- age at entry
- cohort
- credits attempted during the first six months
- developmental education ratio[1]
- gender
- institution
- Pell recipient
- prior college credits
- general program area
- race

As non-traditional students tend to have a higher propensity to take online courses (and possibly blended courses as well), it followed that factors related to non-traditional students include more "career-oriented" program areas. Prior studies have shown relationships between race, gender, and Pell status and online course taking (Jaggers & Xu, 2010; Johnson et al., 2015; Hart et al., 2016; James & Swan, 2019), and we hypothesized that more recent cohorts might have had a higher inclination for taking online courses. We suspected online and blended class availability would vary by institution as well. Moreover, each of the factors listed could influence student retention. We were careful not to include any covariates that might themselves be impacted by differences in delivery mode choices (for example, GPA).

Methods

Our previous work has shown the importance of separating students who are "blending" their classes and those who are taking solely online classes for identifying the relationship between class participation and student outcomes. In this chapter, we attempt to better understand how different levels and types of "blended learning" might relate to the likelihood of retention. To do this, we consider students blending classes and students taking blended (hybrid) classes separately (whereas previously, students taking blended classes were included with the "blended" group). Further, we examine both the online attempt ratio and the hybrid attempt ratio as continuous variables rather than binning them into a reduced set of categories. The object of this approach is to impose as few restrictions as possible on the associations between different levels of the two delivery modes and retention. We examine the relationships using a random forest classifier and partial dependence plots. While linear models would limit us to fitting a linear or polynomial (likely quadratic or cubic) relationship, partial dependence plots allow for more complex patterns (Greenwell, 2017). This reduces the influence of researcher decisions on the results and maximizes the possibility of uncovering a more complex dynamic between delivery mode ratios and student retention. One model was built for each of the two samples that included the background variables listed earlier, online credit attempt ratio, and hybrid credit attempt ratio as the primary predictor variables with retention to a second year as the outcome.

Random forests are tree-based ensemble methods, leveraging many individual decision trees to generate predictions and estimate the probability of a given outcome. Each tree that makes up the random forest is built using a random sample of the available data along with a random sample of the variables included and contributes a "vote" toward the model's prediction for a given observation (Breiman, 2001). Because random forests are not limited by parametric assumptions, nonlinear patterns and interactions can be uncovered easily and are naturally incorporated into the model. However, unlike general linear models, the random forest on its own does not provide directionality to the relationship between predictors and outcomes of interest or any insight into such relationships beyond the predictive strength of a given variable. By applying partial dependence plots to a random forest model, those relationships can be clarified (Greenwell, 2017).

Partial dependence plots show the marginal effect of a given variable on the model's predictions by estimating the relationship between the variable and the predictions after parsing out the effects of the other covariates (Friedman, 2001). Essentially, partial dependence plots reveal the "partial effect" a variable has on the probability of an outcome within the model. A major limitation of partial dependence plots is the assumption that the predictor variables considered in a model are not highly correlated. Because previous research has shown that the covariates in our study interact with course delivery mode, we show two-way partial dependence plots for the variables age, credit attempts, race, and Pell status (in each case, other variables included in the model are still assumed to not be correlated with online/hybrid attempt ratios).

We also show the variable importance of each predictor in the models to identify the predictive strength for both the online and hybrid credit attempt ratios compared to the background variables considered. Variable importance was assessed using the importance function in the random forest package in R. This measure shows the mean decrease in accuracy obtained by deriving the difference in prediction error when the actual values of the variable are used and when the values of the variable are permuted for each tree, averaging the differences over all trees, and normalizing the results (Liaw & Wiener, 2002).

Results

Bachelor's Students—Online Credit Attempt Ratio

We start by examining the distributions of online credit attempt ratios to get a sense of what levels of online course taking are most common. In our sample of bachelor's degree students (Sample 1), we find that 78% of students took no online courses, 6% took exclusively online courses, and 16% took at least one online course and at least one course in person during their first six months. The 16% (those considered to be blending course delivery modes) are the focus of this study, although results will include those who are 0% and 100% online as well. Figure 4.1 shows the distribution of the percentage of credit attempts taken online, excluding those who took 0% to better visualize the distribution among blended students.

The highest concentrations of students blending online and face-to-face courses in Sample 1 occurred at the lower levels of online credit attempt ratios. We found that many students attempted around 5% to 7% of their course credits online, which, for students taking a fifteen-credit course load, would correspond to having a one-credit online course. Another group of students were

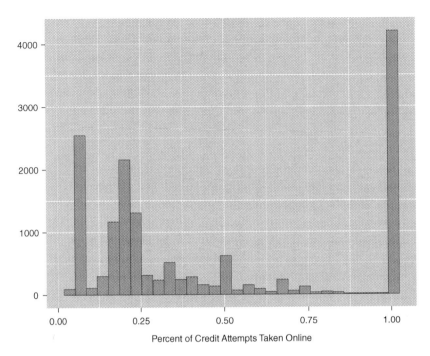

FIGURE 4.1 Distribution of Online Credit Attempt Ratio Excluding Students Who Took No Online Courses (Bachelor's Students)

concentrated between 15% and 25% of course credits online, approximately corresponding to a single three-credit course for a student attempting fifteen credits. There are over 500 students attempting 50% of their credits online but very few students attempting more than 50% and fewer than 100% of credits online.

The online credit attempt ratio had some influence on the model's predictions, ranking fifth in variable importance behind total credits attempted, institution, age, and prior credits. The online credit attempt ratio carried more predictive power than race, Pell status, gender, and the hybrid credit attempt ratio. Full results for variable importance are shown in Table 4.1.

Next, we examine the partial dependence plot (Figure 4.2) revealing the marginal effect of online credit attempt ratio split by five different levels of credit attempts (6, 9, 12, 15, and 18). Note that these plots begin at 0% online, or fully face to face. Among students with 6 and 9 credit attempts, we see very little association between the online credit attempt ratio and the probability of retention among common levels of blending classes (5%–50% of credits attempted online) as these curves are relatively flat. For students attempting 12, 15, and 18 credits, there is more evidence of increased risk, although it remains low for students attempting 15% to 35% of their credits online. This is most noticeable for students attempting 15 credits, for whom the average probability of retention drops from

TABLE 4.1 Variable Importance—Bachelor's Students

Variable	Mean Decrease Accuracy (Standardized)
Credits Attempted During First Six Months	145.70
Institution	128.07
Age at Entry	117.38
Prior College Credits	96.59
Online Credit Attempt Ratio	79.95
Major/Program	77.51
Pell Recipient	67.35
Race	62.21
Hybrid Credit Attempt Ratio	47.21
Cohort Year	24.38
Gender	20.54

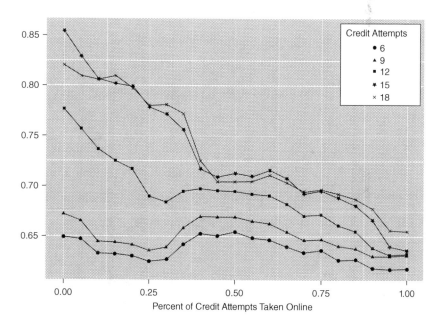

FIGURE 4.2 Partial Dependence Plot: Retention Probability by Online Percentage and Credit Attempts (Bachelor's Students)

85% at 0% online to 78% at 25% online, then further to around 70% for students attempting half their courses online.

In the next plot, we consider how the relationship between the online credit attempt ratio and retention might further depend on age. We focus on students attempting 15 credits both because 15 credits represents a typical course load for a full-time student and because we did not observe strong relationships between the online credit attempt ratio and retention for part-time students. We selected age groups at four-year intervals among common age ranges observed in the data for better visualization. Figure 4.3 reveals that for 22-, 26-, 30-, and 34-year-old students, there is little marginal effect of the online credit attempt ratio when going from 0% to 25%, as the probability of retention drops at most two to three percentage points for these students. However, we do observe a drop of five to eight percentage points moving from 0% to 50% online and a larger decline still for going from 50% to 100% online. For 18-year-old students, the marginal effect of going from 0% to 25% online is much stronger, however, resulting in a drop of seven percentage points in average retention probability.

Additionally, we examined how this relationship varied by both race (Figure 4.4) and Pell status (Figure 4.5). While predicted equity gaps are present across all levels of online course taking, going from 0% to 25% online appears to have a more negative marginal effect for white students than for minority students. This could relate to the greater percentages of white students being younger (and so more likely to negatively affected by taking online courses—see Figure 4.3). Higher online course taking (50% and 100%) is associated with notably lower probability of retention for all three racial groups. The relationship between the online credit attempt ratio and retention is also less negative for Pell recipients, though this is partly a result of Pell recipients being more at risk of dropping out when taking all classes face to face.

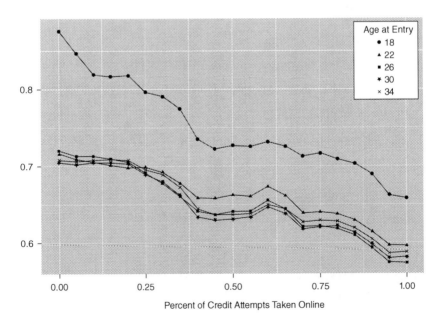

FIGURE 4.3 Partial Dependence Plot: Retention Probability by Online Percentage and Age Among Students Attempting 15 Credits (Bachelor's Students)

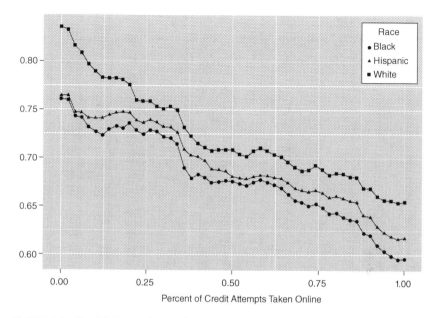

FIGURE 4.4 Partial Dependence Plot: Retention Probability by Online Percentage and Race (Bachelor's Students)

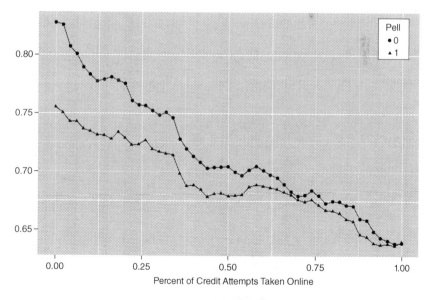

FIGURE 4.5 Partial Dependence Plot: Retention Probability by Online Percentage and Pell Status (Bachelor's Students)

Bachelor's Students—Hybrid Credit Attempt Ratio

Overall, 79% of students did not take a single hybrid class, <1% took all classes, and 21% took at least one but not all classes in a hybrid delivery mode. Figure 4.6 reveals a high concentration of students attempting between 15% and 30% of credits in hybrid classes (approximately corresponding to one three-credit class for a typical full-time student). As with the online credit attempt ratio, few students took more than 50% of their courses in blended sections, though unlike the online credit attempt ratio, very few students took 100% of their courses in blended sections.

The hybrid attempt ratio had the ninth highest variable importance in the model, ahead of only cohort year and gender, indicating less predictive power compared than the online attempt ratio. Figure 4.7 shows the partial dependence plot for the marginal effect of the hybrid credit attempt ratio on retention probability, split out by the same total credit attempt levels as for the online credit attempt ratio. As with online ratio, going from 0% blended classes to 25% was associated with little change in the probability of retention for students attempting only six or nine credits. While we do observe a slight decrease for students taking larger course loads, the change in probability associated with going from

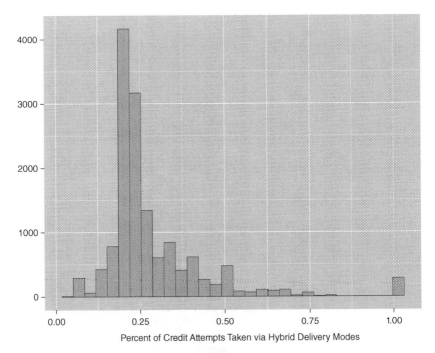

FIGURE 4.6 Distribution of Hybrid Credit Attempt Ratio Excluding Students Who Took No Hybrid Courses (Bachelor's Students)

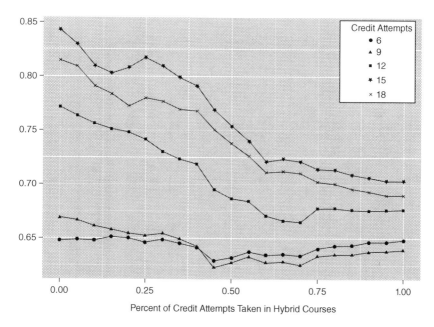

FIGURE 4.7 Partial Dependence Plot: Retention Probability by Hybrid Percentage and Credit Attempts (Bachelor's Students)

0% to 25% was still small. Attempting 50% of credits in blended courses was associated with increased risk.

After isolating students who attempted 15 credits and splitting by age, we find that 22-, 26-, 30-, and 34-year-old students had virtually no increased risk of dropping out taking as many as 40% of their classes in a blended format. At higher levels, retention probabilities did begin to decrease for these same students. For 18-year-old students, there was some risk associated with taking 40% of their courses in a blended format, with retention probability falling approximately five percentage points. At more common levels of blended class taking (25% credit attempts), little risk was observed. The partial dependence plot for the hybrid credit attempt ratio and retention split by age is shown in Figure 4.8.

Figures 4.9 and 4.10 show the partial dependence plots for the relationship between the hybrid credit attempt ratio and retention split by race and Pell status, respectively. For black and Hispanic students, we find essentially no increase in risk going from taking no blended classes to taking 25% of their classes in a blended format, while there was a four-percentage-point decrease in the probability of being retained for white students. For all three racial groups, retention probability decreases slightly and linearly between 25% and 60% hybrid credit attempts. Changes in retention probability going from 0% hybrid to 25% hybrid similarly decreased five to six percentage points for Pell recipients and non–Pell recipients.

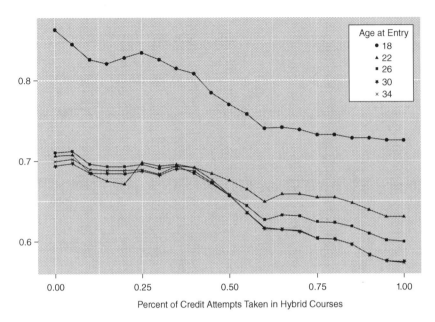

FIGURE 4.8 Partial Dependence Plot: Retention Probability by Hybrid Percentage and Age Among Students Attempting 15 Credits (Bachelor's Students)

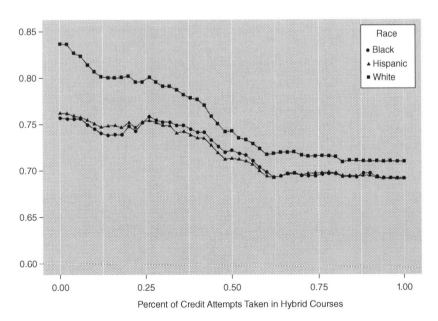

FIGURE 4.9 Partial Dependence Plot: Retention Probability by Hybrid Percentage and Race (Bachelor's Students)

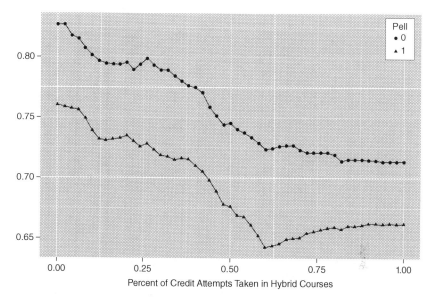

FIGURE 4.10 Partial Dependence Plot: Retention Probability by Hybrid Percentage and Pell Status (Bachelor's Students)

Associate's Students—Online Credit Attempt Ratio

In examining the sample for associate's-seeking students, we find that 75% of students did not take any online courses, 8% took exclusively online courses, and 17% took at least one but fewer than 100% of courses online during their first six months (Figure 4.11). The distribution of online credit attempt ratios among associate's students differs from that of bachelor's students in that there is not a concentration of students attempting ~5% of credits online. The distributions are similar to those for bachelor's degree students in that many students are concentrated around the 20% to 25% range of online credit attempts, and few students attempted more than 50% but fewer than 100% of credits online.

The online credit attempt ratio had the sixth highest variable importance in the model for associate's students, behind institution, credit attempts, age, race, and prior credits (Table 4.2). Figure 4.12 shows the partial dependence plot for the relationship between the online credit attempt ratio and retention probability, split out by common levels of credit attempts. The plots show that retention probability generally decreases as the online credit attempt ratio increases, decreasing more sharply as it approaches 100%. At the most common level of online course taking for students blending classes (25%), the decrease in retention probability was small. For example, going from 0% to 25% online was associated with a five-percentage point decrease in probability of retention for students attempting 15 credits.

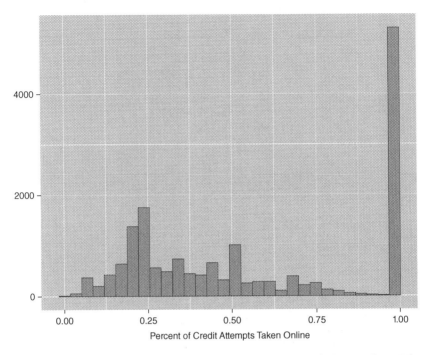

FIGURE 4.11 Distribution of Online Credit Attempt Ratio Excluding Students Who Took No Online Courses (Associate's Students)

TABLE 4.2 Variable Importance—Associate's Students

Variable	Mean Decrease Accuracy (Standardized)
Institution	116.37
Age at Entry	104.56
Credits Attempted During First Six Months	89.68
Race	75.00
Prior College Credits	65.90
Online Credit Attempt Ratio	60.22
Major/Program	53.88
Developmental Education Credit Attempt Ratio	53.25
Pell Grant	52.11
Hybrid Credit Attempt Ratio	31.04
Gender	25.13
Cohort	12.75

As with bachelor's degree students, we next isolated students attempting 15 credits and split the results by different age levels (Figure 4.13). For 22-, 26-, 30-, and 34-year-old students, the lines are mostly flat through common levels of online course taking, although we do see reduced likelihood of retention for

Blended Delivery Modes and Student Success 63

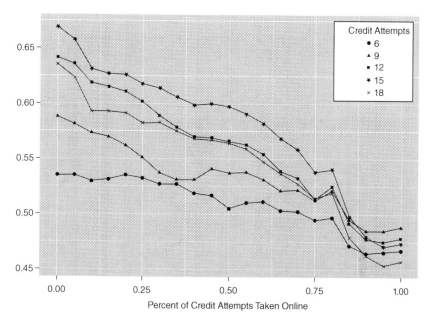

FIGURE 4.12 Partial Dependence Plot: Retention Probability by Online Percentage and Credit Attempts (Associate's Students)

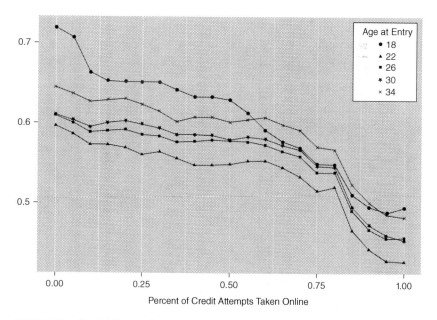

FIGURE 4.13 Partial Dependence Plot: Retention Probability by Online Percentage and Age Among Students Attempting 15 Credits (Associate's Students)

students attempting a majority (or all) of their courses online. For 18-year-old students, going from 0% to 25% online credit attempts was associated with a six-point drop in retention probability.

Splitting results by race showed very little marginal effect moving from 0% to 25% credit attempts online for all three racial groups (Figure 4.14). Although Pell recipients who were not taking any online classes had a slightly higher probability of retention than students who were not Pell recipients, the partial dependence plots for Pell and non-Pell students track almost perfectly across varying degrees of online course taking (Figure 4.15).

Associate's Students—Hybrid Credit Attempt Ratio

Associate's students were less likely to take blended classes, with 85% not taking any at all. Just 1.4% of associate's degree students took exclusively blended classes, and 13% took at least one but not all classes in a blended format (Figure 4.16). As with online attempt ratio, many students were concentrated around 20% to 25% of credit attempts taken in a blended format, and most students taking blended classes took between 15% and 50% of their credits in a blended format. Associate's students, however, were more likely than bachelor's degree students to take all their classes in a blended format.

The hybrid credit attempt ratio had the third lowest variable importance in the model, ahead of only gender and cohort year (Table 4.2). Analyzing the

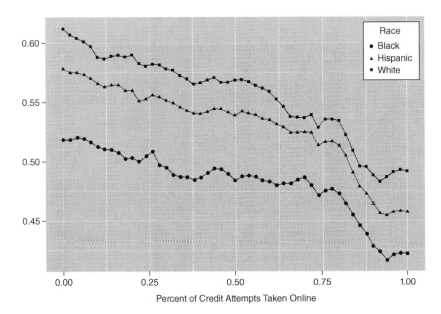

FIGURE 4.14 Partial Dependence Plot: Retention Probability by Online Percentage and Race (Associate's Students)

Blended Delivery Modes and Student Success **65**

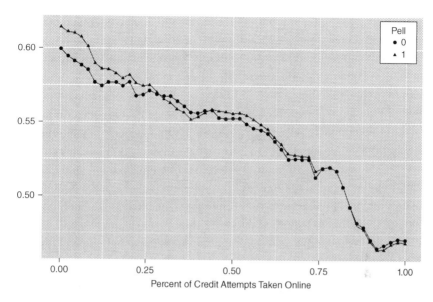

FIGURE 4.15 Partial Dependence Plot: Retention Probability by Online Percentage and Pell Status (Associate's Students)

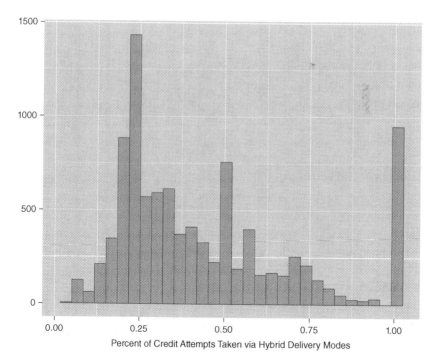

FIGURE 4.16 Distribution of Hybrid Credit Attempt Ratio Excluding Students Who Took No Blended Classes (Associate's Students)

partial dependence plot for the hybrid attempt ratio and retention, split by varying levels of credit attempts, we find that retention probability decreases as the hybrid attempt ratio increases at most levels of credit attempts (Figure 4.17). The slopes of these lines are small, however, as going from 0% to 25% blended classes is associated with a decrease in just five percentage points for students attempting fifteen credits. For students attempting nine credits, the decrease is lower still.

Isolating students attempting 15 credits then grouping them by age reveals that the marginal effect of going from 0% to 25% hybrid credit attempts is larger for 18-year-old students than for older students. For all age groups, retention probability was lowest for students taking 100% of their courses in a blended delivery mode, as shown in Figure 4.18.

Figures 4.19 and 4.20 show the partial dependence plots for the hybrid credit attempt ratio and retention probability splitting by race and Pell status, respectively. We observe little risk associated with hybrid credit attempts of 25% across all three racial groups and for both Pell and non-Pell recipients. Moving from a 0% to a 50% hybrid credit attempt ratio was associated with a decrease in retention probability of about five percentage points for Pell and non-Pell recipients, although there was little change in retention probability between those same levels when splitting by race.

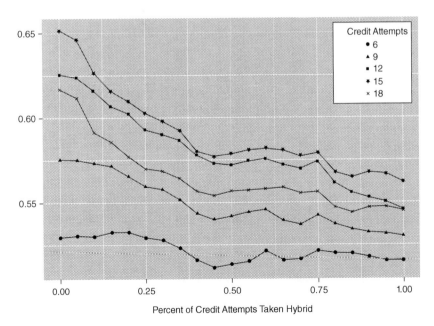

FIGURE 4.17 Partial Dependence Plot: Retention Probability by Hybrid Percentage and Credit Attempts (Associate's Students)

Blended Delivery Modes and Student Success 67

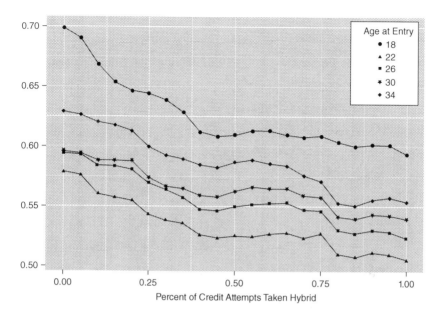

FIGURE 4.18 Partial Dependence Plot: Retention Probability by Hybrid Percentage and Age Among Students Attempting 15 Credits (Associate's Students)

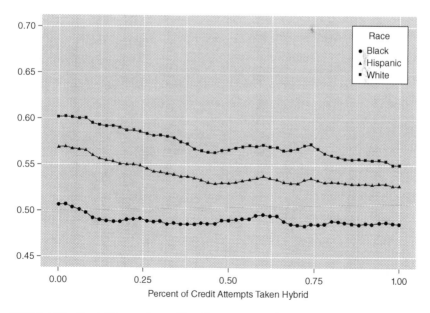

FIGURE 4.19 Partial Dependence Plot: Retention Probability by Hybrid Percentage and Race (Associate's Students)

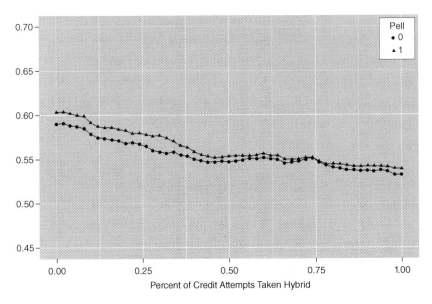

FIGURE 4.20 Partial Dependence Plot: Retention Probability by Hybrid Percentage and Pell Status (Associate's Students)

Discussion

The findings here produce five major takeaways:

1. The probability of retention was never greater for students taking online or blended classes compared to those taking no such classes.
2. Taking low levels of online or blended classes (25% or less) was associated with low risk at most.
3. Taking blended classes generally had a lesser effect on predicted retention than blending online and face-to-face classes.
4. Blending classes, whether online and in person or blended and in person, resulted in higher retention probabilities than taking courses exclusively online or exclusively in blended formats.
5. Generally, students who were more at risk (most notably part-time students and adult learners, but in some cases, also racial minorities) appear less affected by taking low levels of online/blended classes than their less at-risk counterparts (e.g., full-time, 18-year-old, and in some cases white students).

That students attempting low levels of online/blended classes were never associated with a higher probability of retention than taking exclusively in-person courses runs counter to some previous research (Shea & Bidjerano, 2018). We should note that this study is based on a very different sample of students and that our previous research has shown mildly conflicting results for students blending their classes in different data samples.

Moreover, taking up to 25% of classes online or in a blended format was associated with low levels of increased risk, corresponding to our own previous findings (James et al., 2016; Swan & James, 2017). In many cases, we found a decrease of just five percentage points related to taking some online or blended classes. This is small enough that it could easily be explained by other unobserved variables (such as work or family obligations) but still large enough to indicate noticeable risk for institutions. While identifying best practices for teaching online and blended classes goes beyond the scope of this chapter, thoughtful implementation of non-traditional delivery modes may be key to eliminating such risk.

The overall variable importance was lower for the hybrid credit attempt ratio than for the online credit attempt ratio in both samples, and the slopes of the partial dependence plots were generally less steep when examining the hybrid credit attempt ratio as well. This could have implications for institutions looking to expand the delivery modes by which they offer classes, as blended classes may be a slightly safer bet for the average student.

Perhaps the most interesting finding was that full-time 18-year-old students had the most risk associated with taking online and blended classes across all levels. For students attempting fewer credits and for students older than 18, a nonlinear pattern emerged in which little if any risk was associated with going from 0% to 25% of classes offered online or in a blended format (in some cases, this extended to 50% or 60%), although retention probability did decline for these students at higher levels (although still less so compared than full-time 18-year-old students). Again, this corresponds to our previous research, indicating that much of the differences in outcomes across delivery modes disappears after adjusting for variables such as course load and age (Swan & James, 2017). That taking lower levels of online/or blended classes was, in some cases, associated with less risk for minority students does run counter to some prior research (James & Swan, 2019).

Aside from sample differences, this study also differs in its approach by treating online and hybrid credit attempt ratios as continuous predictors and not categorical indicators and by using a random forest with partial dependence plots rather than general linear models. More research is needed to determine how risk varies for different demographic groups. It is also noteworthy that many of the students who had little risk associated with low levels of online and blended class taking were students who tended to be more at risk overall. Retention probabilities were still generally highest for full-time, 18-year-old students and higher for white students as well. However, part-time students, adult learners, and racial minorities, while still at greater risk of dropping out, were little affected by taking some online or blended classes. As it is vital for institutions to ensure these students are well supported, it makes sense for them to consider non-traditional delivery formats for non-traditional students.

Limitations

As with many observational studies, the data used here does not represent a random sample of American universities and colleges, and the results found here will not necessarily hold across all institutions of higher learning. Additionally, our study did not determine whether there are differences in the implementation of blended or online courses across (or even within) institutions that might lead to different outcomes. There are also very few students attempting more than 50% but fewer than 100% of credits online or in blended classes in this sample. Because of this, the results observed in partial dependence plots between 50% and 99% online/blended are likely to be noisier. It is for this reason that we focused most of this chapter on more common levels of online and blended course taking (e.g., 25% or 50%). Most notably, it is not clear how unobserved variables might be influencing the results. For instance, if work and family obligations are more common among students taking online or blended courses, negatively impact retention, and are not adjusted out of the results through differences in credit attempts, age, etc., then some of the negative associations observed here might reflect those factors rather than the delivery mode itself.

Implications

This study is among the largest to examine the effect of online and blended course taking on student retention, and it leverages very recent data to do so. At low levels of online and blended course taking, we find evidence of little to no increased risk for part-time students; for students 22 through 36; and/or for blended-course-taking, black, and Hispanic students. We do find small levels of risk at low levels of online course taking for full-time 18-year-old students. This suggests that either full-time 18-year-old students attempting higher percentages of online or blended classes have unobserved characteristics that place them at risk or that younger students may be more at risk when taking courses online than when taking them in person. In either case, retention probabilities remain highest for full-time students and for 18-year-old students. This suggests that at lower levels of online/blended course taking, older and part-time students are more likely to need supports unrelated to course delivery mode, while full-time 18-year-old students may need supports that directly address the increased risk of taking classes in an online or blended environment. Further, the possibility exists that there are "balancing factors" for part-time and older students when taking online and blended classes that do not exist at the same level for younger full-time students. For example, adult students may benefit from the flexibility of taking some courses online as they can more easily navigate family and work responsibilities while learning at their own pace. There may be some increased risk associated with taking online (or, to a lesser extent, blended) classes that is mitigated by the increased flexibility for adult students, while 18-year-old students do not benefit from increased flexibility or are perhaps even hindered by it. Across the board, we do observe increased risk at higher levels of online/blended course taking indicating additional supports may be needed to ensure students taking half or all their courses in such settings are able to learn effectively and maintain a close tie with their classmates and their institution.

Online and blended classes can offer increased flexibility in learning, making higher education more accessible to many non-traditional learners. It is promising that for many students, there is little risk associated with low levels of online and blended credit attempts, though more research is needed to better understand how to mitigate the risks that do exist and ensure all students are adequately supported. Most importantly, the findings suggest digging deeper into data to better serve one's students.

Note

1. This variable was only used in the models for associate's students as very few bachelor's-seeking students take any developmental education courses.

References

Bernard, R. M., Borokhovski, E., Schmid, R. F., Tamim, R. M., & Abrami, P. C. (2014). A meta-analysis of blended learning and technology use in higher education: From the general to the applied. *Journal of Computing in Higher Education, 26*(1), 87–122.

Bloemer, W., & Swan, K. (2014). Investigating informal blending at the University of Illinois Springfield. In A. G. Picciano, C. D. Dziuban, & C. R. Graham (Eds), *Blended learning research perspectives* (Vol. 2, pp. 52–70). Routledge.

Breiman, L. (2001). Random forests. *Machine Learning, 45*(1), 5–32.

Friedman, J. H. (2001). Greedy function approximation: A gradient boosting machine. *Annals of Statistics*, 1189–1232.

Greenwell, B. M. (2017). PDP: An R package for constructing partial dependence plots. *The R Journal, 9*(1), 421–436. https://journal.r-project.org/archive/2017/RJ-2017-016/index.html

Hart, C. M. D., Friedmann, E., & Hill, M. (2016). *Online course-taking and student outcomes in California community colleges*. http://education.ucdavis.edu/sites/main/files/hart_friedmann_hill_03232016_0.pdf

Jaggars, S. S., Edgecombe, N., & Stacey, G. W. (2013, April). *What we know about online course outcomes*. Community College Research Center, Teachers College, Columbia University.

Jaggers, S. S., & Xu, D. (2010, September). *Online learning in the Virginia community college system*. Community College Research Center, Teachers College, Columbia University.

James, S., & Swan, K. (2019). A closer look at online course taking and student success. In S. Whalen & T. Bennett (Eds.), *Proceedings of the 15th National Symposium on Student Retention* (pp. 12–29). University of Oklahoma.

James, S., Swan, K., & Daston, C. (2016). Retention, progression, and the taking of online courses. *Online Learning, 20*(2), 75–96.

Johnson, H., Cuellar Mejia, M., & Cook, K. (2015). *Successful online courses in California's community colleges.* Public Policy Institute of California.

Liaw, A., & Wiener, M. (2002). Classification and regression by random forest. *R News, 2*(3), 18–22.

Shea, P., & Bidjerano, T. (2014). Does online learning impede degree completion? A national study of community college students. *Computers & Education, 75,* 103–111.

Shea, P., & Bidjerano, T. (2016). A national study of differences between distance and non-distance community college students in time to first associate degree attainment, transfer, and dropout. *Online Learning, 20*(3), 7–19.

Shea, P., & Bidjerano, T. (2018). Online course enrollment in community college and degree completion: The tipping point. *International Review of Research in Open and Distributed Learning, 19*(2), 283–293.

Swan, K., & James, S. (2017). Online learning gets a passing grade: How online course taking impacts retention for university students. In S. Whalen (Ed.), *Proceedings of the 13th National Symposium on Student Retention, Destin, Florida.* The University of Oklahoma.

Wladis, C., Conway, K. M., & Hachey, A. C. (2016). Assessing readiness for online learning: Research models for identifying students at risk. *Online Learning, 20*(3), 97–109.

5

SCALING COURSE DESIGN AS A LEARNING ANALYTICS VARIABLE

John Fritz, Thomas Penniston, Mike Sharkey, and John Whitmer

Introduction

Over the past decade, there have been many studies analyzing student usage data from learning management systems (LMS) and other academic technologies that might serve as a plausible proxy for student engagement (Campbell, 2007; Whitmer, 2012; Fritz, 2016). Others have also identified differences in predictive analytics for course grade and data regarding the design of particular courses (Bakharia et al., 2016; Fritz, 2016; Fritz & Whitmer, 2017a). However, given variation in student learning (Gašević et al., 2015) and instructor "pedagogical intent" (Macfadyen & Dawson, 2010, p. 598), many learning analytics researchers and practitioners have focused on specific contexts and typically examine a relatively small number of courses. The title of one study (Gašević et al., 2016), which examined nine courses, even cautioned "Learning analytics should not promote one size fits all: The effects of instructional conditions in predicting academic success."

Still, given the potential, scalable impact on student success, key questions remain about faculty LMS course design as a learning analytics variable. For example, is LMS course design a discernable attribute? If so, how do academic outcomes relate to student use of the LMS? This raises the question of whether LMS course design can scale when not centrally coordinated by instructional designers in a center for teaching and learning. Finally, for the purposes of this chapter on blended learning, how does the delivery of a course (e.g., face to face, blended/hybrid, or fully online) relate to its designed versus actual use by students?

In this chapter, we will explore these questions through a case study spanning three academic years and more than 6,000 courses at the University of Maryland,

DOI: 10.4324/9781003037736-7

Background

In 2018, Blackboard (Bb) released a "course archetype" system administrator's tool that allows institutions to categorize courses in the LMS based on how students use the course. The "course archetype" sysadmin tool was informed by Blackboard's own research on clients it hosts (Whitmer et al., 2016), including UMBC since 2014.[1] Blackboard's research framework established five archetypes ranging from "supplemental" to "holistic" courses (described next):

1. supplemental (content heavy, low interaction)
2. complementary (one-way communication via content, announcements, and gradebook)
3. social (high peer-to-peer interaction through discussion board)
4. evaluative (heavy use of assessments)
5. holistic (high LMS activity; balanced use of assessments, content, and discussion)

As illustrated in Table 5.1, Blackboard's course archetypes echo prior research on faculty use of the LMS:

In 2018, the primary reason UMBC's Division of Information Technology (DoIT) was interested in the "course archetype" sysadmin tool was to better understand the depth and complexity of current campus Bb usage as it gauged the effort required to move to the latest version of Bb's LMS software, called Learn Ultra (see umbc.edu/go/ultra). We knew that faculty used the LMS in different ways but wanted to better understand how, so we could determine the fit gap between the current and new Bb Learn platforms and the level of IT support needed to migrate the campus. We also recognized an opportunity to advance higher education's understanding of how the design of online courses relates to student use of them.

Methods and Analysis

A few observations about Blackboard's 2016 "archetype research"—and UMBC's 2018 analysis using the sysadmin tool it is based on ("UMBC Blackboard Use Differs from Most Schools," 2018)—are noteworthy. First, Blackboard created its five archetypes based on analysis of more than 3,374,462 unique students in 70,000 courses from 927 institutions hosted by Blackboard in North America in spring of 2016. This data set was filtered to identify courses with substantive usage, given that a large number of all courses were archived courses, course shells used for student services, or simply empty course shells.

To identify pedagogically relevant use of the LMS, the filters Blackboard used included shells with between 10 and 500 students, average student use of at least

TABLE 5.1 How Faculty Use an LMS
(See tinyurl.com/blrpvol3ch5, slide 2, or QR code for larger version)

Learning Analytics Research & Practice[2]	Blackboard Course Archetypes[3]
User & Document Management • *Auto course creation and enrollment* • *Password-protected class & group space* • *Post documents, perhaps w/expiration dates* Interactive Tools • *Announcements* • *Email, messages* • *Discussion & chat* Assessments • *Electronic assignment delivery & collection* • *Quizzing, surveys, online grade center* • *Adaptive release of content based on prior action or grades*	Supplemental • *Content heavy* • *Low interaction* Complementary • *One-way communication via content, announcements, and gradebook* Social • *High peer-to-peer interaction through discussion board* Evaluative • *Heavy use of assessments* Holistic • *High LMS activity* • *Balanced use of assessments, content, and discussion*

60 minutes, and faculty use of the gradebook. This resulted in a data set for analysis that included 601,544 learners (17.82%) in 18,810 courses (26.87%) (Fritz, 2016b, p. 2). When UMBC's DoIT ran the course archetype tool on the university's 1,469 active Fall 2018 Bb courses, only 464 (31%) did not meet the same enrollment size and usage criteria compared with 51,190 (73%) of the 70,000 courses hosted by Blackboard but were also filtered out of the study, as the vendor had done.

Second, Blackboard found the vast majority of courses it studied were "supplemental" (content-heavy, low interaction) or "complementary" (one-way, instructor-led, minimal communication) courses, or 53% and 24%, respectively (77% total). By contrast, DoIT found nearly 40% of UMBC's remaining 991 Fall 2018 courses were characterized at the top end of Blackboard's course design archetype: "evaluative" (heavy use of assessments) and "holistic" (high LMS activity with balanced use of assessments, content, and discussion), or 21% and 18%, respectively (39% total).

Finally, in the LMS vendor's analysis, researchers did not find a systematic relationship between course archetype and student grade. Initially, DoIT did not look at how UMBC students' activity is associated with outcomes because Fall 2018 final grades had not yet been submitted when the analysis was completed and published at the end of the term. This was completed the following term and is reported later in the chapter. In short, we found that a greater percentage of UMBC's courses were at the higher end of interactivity than in Blackboard's original study. However, we also found a negative correlation between student final grades in courses with a higher course design archetype, which was unexpected. One possible explanation is that the courses with more complex designs were more difficult courses as this analysis did not control for variation in grade.

From a learning-analytics perspective, this is both important and challenging due to what we think we know but cannot yet prove. For example, we know that (a) LMS course design is related to higher student LMS usage, which (b) is related to better student outcomes. However, we cannot yet establish that (c) LMS course design (as an intervention) is related to better student outcomes. While we did not want to over analyze the data to yield evidence that does not exist, the conundrum resulting from our initial analysis prompted a different look at outcomes or dependent variables. Specifically, instead of looking only at final grades, we assessed the strength of the relationship between student activity and final grades by its LMS course design archetype. This allowed us to move beyond looking at course averages and examine the relationship of individual learner activity with their outcomes.

Consequently, in the section that follows, we will first report findings from our analysis of final grades in three successive terms (Fall 17, Spring 18, and Fall 18), completed about a year before the first draft of this chapter was written. Then we will share our analysis of the activity/grade relationship in the three terms (Spring 19, Fall 19, and Spring 20) we just completed. Why not combine all terms? We considered that, but apart from the fact that we were migrating to two different data warehouses, we also thought this case study could show how our thinking has evolved over time to introduce a new frame of reference for scaling course design as a learning-analytics variable.

Findings

Final Grades by Course Design: Fall 17, Spring 18, and Fall 18

Beyond applying Blackboard's new "archetype" system administrator's tool to analyze Fall 2018 courses, UMBC also looked at student final grades in courses by course design archetype for the Fall 2017 and Spring 2018 semesters. Similar to Blackboard's 2016 research mentioned earlier, UMBC courses with enrollments of fewer than ten students were removed from the original course set (i.e., ≤ 1%), leaving 3,323 total courses, of which approximately one-third were from each term, and cases with no course activity are excluded from the reporting.

Figure 5.1 illustrates the distribution of course archetypes across all three terms. The most prevalent archetype is supplemental, followed closely by complementary. These two classifications account for two-thirds of all courses offered during these terms. Notably, UMBC has a far greater percentage of courses designated as holistic and lower rate of those defined as social than Whitmer and colleagues' original research findings (2016), even after removing courses with no Blackboard activity.

To evaluate the relationship between archetypes and DFW rates, a number of variables were generated to account for variance in the models created by factors related to the course pedagogy and broader design. These variables include whether the course was upper or lower division, the academic discipline, and the student enrollment.[4] Table 5.2 illustrates the most relevant of the associated findings. Higher-level courses were operationally defined as having a course number above or equal to the 300 level. The median enrollment for all courses was 26 students; the 90th percentile was 80 students.

As illustrated by Table 5.2, the results tell a complicated story. Holistic courses, overall, have the highest DFW rates. However, the rates for supplemental and complementary courses are all in the same general range. Course level proves

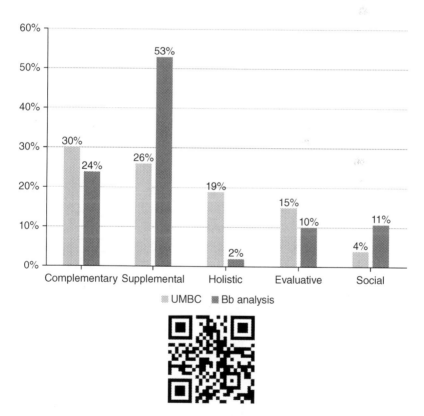

FIGURE 5.1 UMBC Archetype Distribution (FA17, SP18, & FA18) vs. Bb Study (2016)

(See tinyurl.com/blrpvol3ch5, slide 5 or QR code for color version)

TABLE 5.2 UMBC Mean DFW Rates and Counts by Archetype (FA17, SP18, FA18) (See tinyurl.com/blrpvol3ch5, slide 3, or QR code for larger version)

Archetype	All Courses	Upper Division	>Median Enrollment	>90% Enrollment
Complementary	11.15 (1,004)	8.76 (607)	11.56 (534)	15.51 (107)
Supplemental	11.01 (852)	9.48 (522)	11.85 (425)	15.17 (60)
Holistic	12.83 (645)	8.84 (348)	14.10 (374)	17.50 (119)
Evaluative	8.93 (508)	7.89 (329)	9.66 (238)	12.77 (38)
Social	9.26 (147)	6.73 (110)	8.62 (12)	NA

to be a much more impactful variable. Lower-level courses have more than 5% higher DFW rate than higher-level courses (14% vs. 8.75%).

We can also see that the course size has a positive relationship with DFW rates. An increase above the median is associated with a rise in DFWs (9.96% vs. 11.74%). The impact of course size gets more pronounced as the number of student enrollments increase, to the extent that there is a 5.5% difference in DFW rates between courses above the 90th percentile and those at or below it (10.30% vs. 15.82%).

UMBC used OLS regressions and included controls for archetypes, some basic demographics, interactions, and department. We see that the statistically significant variables increasing DFW rates across models are course enrollments, the percentage of males in the course, and the percentage of white students ($p < .001$).[5]

The Table 5.3 column intersections illustrate the archetype as the comparison group in the given model. As an example interpretation, supplemental courses demonstrate slightly lower DFW rates than complementary courses ($p < .01$). Changing the state of the course from the supplemental to the complementary archetype demonstrates a reduction in DFW rates ($p < .01$), and both supplemental ($p < .001$) and evaluative ($p < .01$) show reductions compared with the holistic archetype.

In general, there are some trends in DFW rates when comparing individual archetypes, but these differences are minimal and less influential than the impacts associated with other variables, including class size and higher-level course status. Additionally, this assessment does not take into consideration academic rigor. An important follow-up question to consider is how students who successfully complete these classes fare in their course progression compared with students

TABLE 5.3 Comparing UMBC DFW Rates by Course Archetype
(See tinyurl.com/blrpvol3ch5, slide 4, or QR code for larger version)

	Supplemental	Complementary	Social	Evaluative	Holistic
Supplemental	—	-1.32**	-.99	-.56	-2.45***
		(.47)	(.92)	(.60)	(.66)
Complementary	1.32**	—	.33	.75	-1.14
	(.47)		(.89)	(.55)	(.59)
Social	.99	-.33	—	.43	-1.46
	(.92)	(.89)		(.93)	(.94)
Evaluative	.56	-.75	-.43	—	-1.89**
	(.60)	(.55)	(.93)		(.63)
Holistic	2.45	1.14	1.46	1.89**	—
	(.66)	(.59)	(.94)	(.63)	
% Male	.11***	.11***	0.11***	.11***	.11***
	(.01)	(.01)	(.01)	(.01)	(.01)
% White	.02	.02	0.02	.016	.016
	(.01)	(.01)	(.01)	(.01)	(.01)
Average Interactions	.24	.24	0.24	.24	.24
	(.17)	(.17)	(.17)	(.17)	(.17)
Upper Division Course	-3.57***	-3.57***	-3.57***	-3.56**	-3.57***
	(.42)	(.42)	(.42)	(.42)	(.42)
Enrollment	.02***	.02***	.02***	.02***	.021***
	(.00)	(.00)	(.00)	(.00)	(.00)
Adj R-squared	0.31	0.31	0.31	0.31	0.32

who experienced alternative archetypes or a traditional face-to-face course. Is the content equally salient? Another unaddressed consideration is the potential benefit of the data exhaust from high-interaction courses, which could be used to identify risk patterns at increasingly earlier points in the semester, given valid and robust LMS data that could inform interventions such as behavioral nudging to promote student persistence.

Activity and Final Grades by Course Design: Spring 19, Fall 19, and Spring 20

As stated earlier, given our unexpected findings that UMBC's holistic and evaluative course design archetypes actually had higher DFW rates than supplemental and complimentary courses, we needed to reevaluate why this might be and if/how we could justify continuing to look at the relationship between course design and student outcomes.

Around this same time, just prior to the start of Fall 18, Blackboard announced results from another study (Forteza et al., 2018) involving seven "gateway" UMBC courses (four in STEM disciplines with enrollments over 100 students) and VitalSource (UMBC's e-textbook provider), to see if multiple data sources might improve a predictive model of student outcomes. The results were compelling and reinforced what we thought we knew about student LMS usage and outcomes, which made the subsequent analysis by course design archetype all the more puzzling. Specific results from the 2018 UMBC, Blackboard, and Vital-Source study included the following:

1. Early activity in the LMS was a strong predictor of student success.
2. Student activity patterns differed from course to course. (See Figure 5.2.)
3. Student LMS data—as proxy for engagement—was a more powerful predictor of student achievement than demographic or educational background.
4. Combining student activity data from multiple digital sources improved prediction accuracy.
5. Students who actively used multiple online resources were more likely to pass the class.

Figure 5.2 illustrates what we refer to as a waterfall chart, patterned after a debut prototype by David Wiley (2011), then of Brigham Young University (BYU) and now chief academic officer of Lumen Learning. Specifically, in Wiley's waterfall visualization of a local high school's LMS he was working with,[6] each row is a student, each column is a day, and the density of the color is the number of times a student logged in that day. From top to bottom, Wiley also organized students by average grade or GPA. We did the same, but in Figure 5.2, we looked at student activity by weeks (not days), which were organized by final grade earned in a course (not GPA), as we could not fit UMBC's 14,000 distinct students (rows) across the entire LMS onto one chart.

Notice that in both the math and physics courses, there are striking similarities and differences. For example, in both courses, there is virtually no difference (by final grade) in how active students are in the first week of the semester. By week 2 (second column), less successful students begin to evaporate in terms of activity, but this is also where we see differences that appear to be related to the design of the course. Specifically, across all final grades in the math course, students are relatively more active in the early weeks of the term overall than students in the physics course. In fact, the math course has a fairly regular pattern of overall student activity across the term, except for the Thanksgiving break, which appears in both courses. By contrast, the physics course displays a pattern of activity that one might associate with the typical "two midterms and a final." Which course

Scaling Course Design as a Variable 81

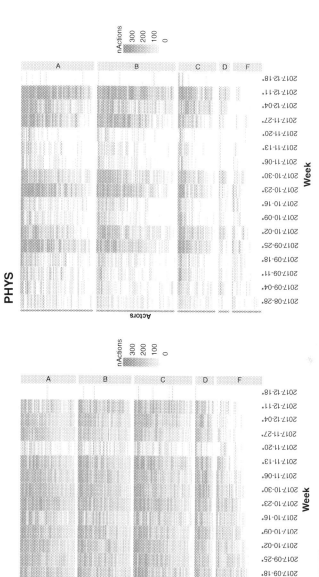

FIGURE 5.2 UMBC LMS Waterfall of a Math and Physics Course (Fall 18)

(See tinyurl.com/blrpvol3ch5, slide 6, or QR code for color version)

pattern would more easily provide students with regular feedback to promote self-assessment and identify at-risk students or possible early interventions?

With this in mind, UMBC recently began working with Mike Sharkey, Founder of Dataandgraphs.com and former VP of analytics at Blackboard, to prototype an interactive application designed to show and rank (from high to low) all courses' strength of relationship between student LMS activity and outcomes. Specifically, we sorted all courses by "fit" (e.g., how well or poorly a course's activity correlates to final grade). Essentially, this is the slope of a line (covariance divided by variance of independent variables) from A to B to C to D to F. If the slope is zero, there's little to no difference in activity by grade. If the slope is large, then As are more active than Bs, which are more active than Cs and so on. (See Figure 5.3.)

A similar, tabular view of the data (see Figure 5.4) ranks courses (from high to low) by aggregate slope across all final grades, with color density for enrollment size (the darker the color, the higher the enrollment).

It should be noted that every semester for many years now, Blackboard LMS courses in UMBC's College of Natural and Mathematical Sciences (CNMS) are typically more active than other colleges' due to a higher use of assessments, which generate higher levels of student activity, even though there are fewer courses at the college overall ("Why CNMS Student Bb Use Is So High," 2019). Consequently, notice also how many of the courses listed in Figure 5.4 have evaluative or holistic Bb course design archetypes. To be sure, online or hybrid courses may use the LMS more than "in-person" or face-to-face courses, but by focusing on a course's strength of relationship between student activity and grade, one can still filter by delivery mode, course type (e.g., lecture, lab, discussion, etc.), and course design archetype, to better understand how a course may be designed for and actually used by students. Additionally, one can drill into any course's waterfall to examine student activity over time, grade distribution, or enrollment size, all of which can factor into the course's strength of relationship or slope. As a result, it is now easier to find effective course design "needles" in the schedule of courses "haystack," which can be examined more closely to identify effective practices to be "reverse engineered" and possibly applied to other courses. Instructors can also be interviewed to understand, qualitatively, why and how they designed their LMS courses to be used, a "mixed methods" approach to faculty development that we have used for years.

For example, consider the LMS waterfall for CHEM 102 in Figure 5.5. Though the course's 282 aggregate slope "strength of relationship" for activity and grades ranked 21st in CNMS for Spring 20 ($r2 = .919$, $p < .01$), this is understandable, given it is typically the largest course taught on campus every term ($n = 480$). Additionally, in a joint study between UMBC, VitalSource, and ACT (Whitmer et al., 2019), the Spring 19 version of CHEM 102 emerged as a very strong course in terms of facilitating students' social and emotional learning, which was also related to predicting student outcomes. Still, unlike

Scaling Course Design as a Variable   83

FIGURE 5.3 Visual Scan of UMBC CNMS Slope (Spring 20)

(See tinyurl.com/blrpvol3ch5, slide 7, or QR code for color version)

84 Fritz, Penniston, Sharkey, and Whitmer

FIGURE 5.4 Tabular Scan of UMBC CNMS Slope (Spring 20)

(See tinyurl.com/blrpvol3ch5, slide 8, or QR code for color version)

Scaling Course Design as a Variable **85**

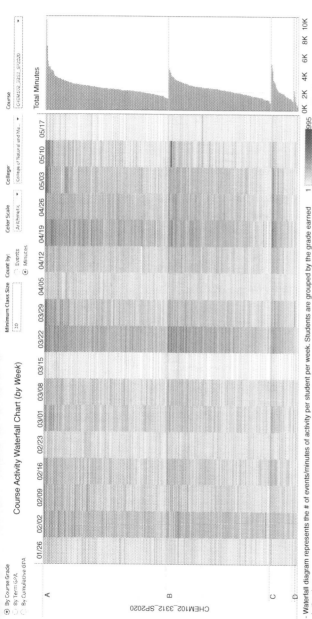

FIGURE 5.5 UMBC LMS Waterfall for CHEM102 (Spring 20)

(See tinyurl.com/blrpvol3ch5, slide 9, or QR code for color version)

Figure 5.2 from the 2018 Blackboard, VitalSource, and UMBC study, the LMS waterfall for CHEM 102 in Figure 5.5 doesn't show as stark a contrast in engagement (measured in minutes) between the majority of students earning As and Bs and other students earning lower grades. However, notice what happens after the coronavirus global pandemic forced this and all other UMBC courses into "remote instruction" during the week of March 15, 2020: across the entire grade distribution, all students spent considerably more time in the course. Unfortunately, the differences in engagement also became more pronounced from midterm on. There also appears to have been more assessments or assigned work, perhaps to make up for the lost week of March 15th to prepare for remote instruction.

Finally, Figure 5.6 shows the entire distribution of courses by archetype and activity-to-grade relationship by Spring 19, Fall 19, and Spring 20 terms.[7] Notice that unlike the previous three terms illustrated in Figure 5.1, evaluative and holistic courses design archetypes accounted for a higher number of all course designs, with Spring 20 evaluative courses showing the highest "activity-to-grade" aggregate slope (143.3) for all three terms. Curiously, Spring 20 saw the largest increase in holistic course design types but also an aggregate slope (73) of barely half what similar course designs had been a year earlier (140.8). However, like the relatively lower aggregate slope for CHEM 102, this may likely just be the law of large numbers in effect.

Implications

In terms of the initial questions posed in the introduction, UMBC's case study helps us better understand how faculty LMS course design may relate to student use of the same tool, as a proxy for both their engagement and eventual academic outcomes. First, LMS course design does appear to be a broadly discernable and relevant attribute that can help identify and investigate effective practices. This does not preclude overlap, but from a bird's eye view of the LMS, it can be helpful to observe—more specifically than delivery mode alone—how faculty are using course tools and how their use by students is distributed across the system by college, department/discipline, undergrad/grad level, and enrollment size and even among prerequisite or "gateway" courses.

Second, by focusing on course design as a control or interaction variable that meters or even regulates the core relationship between student LMS course activity and grades, the UMBC case study may help colleges and universities—and their faculty—better understand the nuances of teaching and learning that are expressed in a digital learning environment like an LMS. In the end, we believe students earn their grades; the role of time, attention, and the effort students do (or do not) bring to their studies is of critical importance. At the same time, instructors do vary in how they think of and use the LMS to express their pedagogical intent.

Scaling Course Design as a Variable **87**

FIGURE 5.6 UMBC Activity-to-Grade Relationship by Course Archetype and Term

(See tinyurl.com/blrpvol3ch5, slide 10, or QR code for color version)

Indeed, Robertson's (1999) classic model of faculty beliefs about their teaching shows they can, indeed, evolve over time, principally in three stages:

1. egocentrism: focusing on their role as teachers
2. aliocentrism: focusing on the role of learners
3. systemocentrism: focusing on the shared role of teachers and learners in community

If this evolution of belief and practice occurs among teachers, Robertson identifies telltale signs of the transformation. First, as faculty move from one stage to the next, they bring the benefits and biases of the previous stage. Second, they typically change their beliefs and practices only when confronted by the limitations of a current stage, which is brought about by "teaching failures." Finally, their desire for certainty, stability, and confidence either keeps faculty frozen in a status quo framework or drives their evolution into the next stage in an effort to avoid a paralyzing and stagnant neutral zone consisting of "a familiar teaching routine that they have deemed inappropriate and with nothing to replace it" (p. 279).

As the old adage goes, nobody learns from a position of comfort. It is not until we find our current knowledge, skills, and abilities to be wanting—perhaps especially if compared to peers, role models, or exemplars we wish to emulate—that we can begin the necessary first step of wanting to change our status quo. By extension, institutional technology systems that support teaching and learning can be designed to accentuate this process of self-awareness through peer and exemplar comparison. We have been leveraging this kind of subtle "peer pressure" among students for years by showing them how their LMS usage compares to an anonymous summary of course peers (Fritz, 2013, 2017).[8] We have also seen faculty keenly interested in what their colleagues and peers are doing in the LMS as well.

Admittedly, all this makes course design a challenging learning analytics variable to parse and interpret, let alone scale. But by focusing on the digital footprints of time and attention students leave in an LMS course shell, we can make reasonable inferences about course design that might have facilitated it. We may also be able to intervene with at-risk students before they earn final grades, which are certainly definitive but not particularly actionable during a term, when they might have more runway to avert a projected outcome. At its best, student and faculty use of an LMS can help shine light on a symbiotic relationship, in which awareness of each party's behavior might be informative to and influential on one's own conception and use of the tool.

Third, if judged only by the increasing proportion of evaluative and holistic Bb course archetypes from Fall 17 to Spring 20, UMBC's case study suggests that LMS course design can indeed scale when not centrally coordinated by

Scaling Course Design as a Variable **89**

instructional designers in a center for teaching and learning or instructional technology. As of Fall 19, UMBC had 555 full-time and 376 part-time instructional faculty (UMBC Common Data Set, n.d.). Collectively, between the campus Faculty Development Center and DoIT's instructional technology team, UMBC has 12 full-time staff providing pedagogical and student learning outcome, instructional design, or instructional technology support (or a 46-to-1 ratio of full-time faculty to FTE support staff). Like nearly all public institutions, we simply never have had enough instructional designers to touch all courses, nor will we.

Instead, we have always relied on and even tried to foster that faculty learn best from each other. To help, we have used analytics to identify, learn from, support, promote, and connect effective practitioners and practices among the faculty. For years, we have published our most active Blackboard courses. (See doit.umbc.edu/most-active-bb-courses.)[9] We also encourage faculty to use existing analytics reports inside their courses (see https://wiki.umbc.edu/x/doEpB) and outside their departments or colleges ("REX [Analytics] Tools for Teaching Available to Instructors," 2017), to gain a "bird's-eye view" of LMS use and grade distribution, as well as student retention, persistence, and graduation. As UMBC president Freeman Hrabowski frequently says, "If you want to change the culture, shine light on success, not failure." But this means you need to have a plausible, working definition of success and, more importantly, actually show where it is achieved.

Finally, for the purposes of this chapter on blended learning, the UMBC case study shows how the design of a course is different from and (we think) more important than its face-to-face, blended/hybrid, or fully online delivery. If the coronavirus global pandemic has taught us anything, it's that even when all instruction is delivered remotely, not all online courses are the same. The same has always been true of traditional face-to-face courses, but somehow, we seem more willing to treat online learning as a stock, two-dimensional caricature without pedagogical nuance. If good teaching is good teaching, regardless of how a course is delivered, we need to focus on if and how it is designed to help students take responsibility for their own learning.

In fact, in *Leaving College*, Vincent Tinto (1993) cautioned institutions from absolving students of at least partial responsibility for their own education.

> To do so denies both the right of the individual to refuse education and the right of the institution to be selective in its judgements as to who should be further educated. More importantly, it runs counter to the essential notion that effective education requires that individuals take responsibility for their own learning.
>
> *(p. 144)*

Nearly 30 years later, we can leverage technology and analytics to nudge student responsibility for learning and identify course designs that help.

Limitations and Future Work

To some, the biggest limitation of the UMBC case study—for a chapter on blended learning—may be that the vast majority of our LMS courses have been delivered in traditional face-to-face courses, up until the coronavirus pandemic in 2020. This is true particularly at the undergraduate level, which has no online degree programs and no online-only undergraduate courses during the major fall and spring terms. We do have a handful of applied master's online graduate degree programs, but no more than 5% of all university course credits are offered through online, hybrid, or blended delivery each fall and spring. Also, there is no consensus definition of hybrid/blended learning, though we've found this is common in higher education generally.

Historically, though, more than half of all summer and two-thirds of all winter special session courses are offered through some form of "alternate delivery," thanks largely to student demand as well as the Division of Professional Studies (DPS) sponsoring DoIT's alternate delivery program (ADP)[10] since 2006. Also, the ADP's "lessons learned" informed a new DoIT program called PIVOT (planning instructional variety in online teaching),[11] which was scaled to respond to the coronavirus pandemic and adopted by more than half of all faculty to date (Hansen, 2020).

In terms of next steps, part of the change in data warehouse strategy is to afford a deeper analysis of course, program, and university student learning outcomes (not just final grades that attempt to summarize course-level learning). Just as course design archetypes afford a deeper level of analysis than a focus on course delivery, we're hoping to combine this granularity with more direct measures of assessing of student learning. Typically, student learning outcomes get scant mention except just before and maybe briefly after an institution's accreditation site visit every five to ten years. But in the past few years, this conversation has started to "stick" at UMBC, thanks largely to the work of UMBC's Faculty Development Center and college deans and a growing commitment to active learning across the disciplines. This is difficult learning analytics work to operationalize because it requires broad consensus on direct measures of assessment of what students ought to be able to know, understand, or do after completing a course, program, or general education program. We're not there yet, but we can see how marrying data on student learning with behavioral engagement data like student LMS activity and course design could afford a deeper, richer, and maybe even real-time understanding of teaching and learning across campus.

Conclusion

While UMBC's Blackboard courses may represent a different profile from most Bb clients hosted by the company, it is unclear if or how other institutions have leveraged the company's own "course archetype" sysadmin tools or research in this way. We have tried to leverage and extend Blackboard's research to help us identify and promote design of effective courses that engage students early and often; encourage time on task; afford timely, regular feedback without an undue grading burden on faculty; identify at-risk students sooner than later in a term; and help more students perform better than we might otherwise expect based on incoming factors they might not be able to change. In short, we believe understanding how course design influences student responsibility for learning could help make course redesign one of the most scalable student success interventions any institution can pursue.

Notes

1. Before moving to Bb's managed hosting in 2014, UMBC had self-hosted its own Bb server since 2000. Note: UMBC has always had high adoption—typically 95% of all students, 87% of all instructors, and 82% of all sections use Bb during any given term.
2. Campbell, 2007; Macfadyen & Dawson, 2010; Whitmer, 2012; Fritz, 2013; Fritz & Whitmer, 2017. Full citation of these sources is available in the reference list.
3. Whitmer et al., 2016. Full citation of this source is available in the reference list.
4. Including standard demographics, whether a course was upper divisional, enrollment count, interactions, and academic department.
5. Accounting for 31% of the variance.
6. A brief (four-minute), blurry, but still compelling copy of the recorded video of Wiley's remarks about his LMS waterfall during his keynote presentation at the 2011 ELI annual meeting is available at https://umbc.box.com/davidwileylmswaterfall.
7. In Spring 18, UMBC began developing a learning record store (LRS) to supplement our institutional data warehouse (rex.umbc.edu). However, some Blackboard data were missing from Fall 18 and could not be included in our interactive application pictured in Figures 5.3 through 5.6.
8. For a brief (five-minute) demo of UMBC's Check My Activity (CMA) feedback tool for students, see https://youtu.be/rpU1GdvS_yc.
9. To avoid prematurely and needlessly raising faculty hackles, we call it a ranking of activity not quality.
10. See https://doit.umbc.edu/itnm/adp/.
11. See https://doit.umbc.edu/itnm/training/pivot/.

References

Bakharia, A., Corrin, L., de Barba, P., Kennedy, G., Gašević, D., Mulder, R., Williams, D., Dawson, S., & Lockyer, L. (2016). A conceptual framework linking learning design with learning analytics. *Proceedings of the Sixth International Conference on Learning Analytics & Knowledge*, 329–338. https://doi.org/10.1145/2883851.2883944

Campbell, J. (2007). *Utilizing student data within the course management system to determine undergraduate student academic success: An exploratory study*. http://proquest.umi.com/pqd web?did=1417816411&Fmt=7&clientId=11430&RQT=309&VName=PQD

Common Data Set (2019–2020) (n.d.). *Institutional research*. University of Maryland (UMBC). Retrieved October 13, 2020, from https://oir.umbc.edu/university-data/common-data-set-cds/

Forteza, D., Whitmer, J., Fritz, J., & Green, D. (2018). Improving risk predictions: Blackboard analytics [case study]. *Blackboard*. www.blackboard.com/education-analytics/improving-risk-predictions.html

Fritz, J. (2013). *Using analytics at UMBC: Encouraging student responsibility and identifying effective course designs* (p. 11) [Research Bulletin]. Educause Center for Applied Research. www.educause.edu/library/resources/using-analytics-umbc-encouraging-student-responsibility-and-identifying-effective-course-designs

Fritz, J. (2016a). LMS course design as learning analytics variable. *Proceedings of the 1st Learning Analytics for Curriculum and Program Quality Improvement Workshop*, 15–19. https://pdfs.semanticscholar.org/be7e/8fe65384513355467e56cc84b368296 69482.pdf

Fritz, J. (2016b). *Using analytics to encourage student responsibility for learning and identify course designs that help* [PhD]. University of Maryland. http://search.proquest.com.proxy-bc. researchport.umd.edu/pqdtlocal1005865/docview/1795528531/abstract/8BFCC74B 55A94651PQ/1

Fritz, J. (2017). Using analytics to nudge student responsibility for learning. *New Directions for Higher Education*, *179*, 65–75. https://doi.org/10.1002/he.20244

Fritz, J., & Whitmer, J. (2017, February 27). Learning analytics research for LMS course design: Two studies. *EDUCAUSE Review Online*. http://er.educause.edu/articles/2017/2/learning-analytics-research-for-lms-course-design-two-studies

Gašević, D., Dawson, S., Rogers, T., & Gasevic, D. (2016). Learning analytics should not promote one size fits all: The effects of instructional conditions in predicting academic success. *The Internet and Higher Education*, *28*, 68–84. https://doi.org/10.1016/j.iheduc.2015.10.002

Gašević, D., Dawson, S., & Siemens, G. (2015). Let's not forget: Learning analytics are about learning. *TechTrends*, *59*(1), 64–71. https://doi.org/10.1007/s11528-014-0822-x

Hansen, S. (2020, July 9). UMBC faculty on a mission to prepare robust, high-quality online classes for fall semester. *UMBC News*. https://news.umbc.edu/umbc-faculty-on-a-mission-to-prepare-robust-high-quality-online-classes-for-fall-semester/

Macfadyen, L. P., & Dawson, S. (2010). Mining LMS data to develop an "early warning system" for educators: A proof of concept. *Computers & Education*, *54*(2), 588–599. https://doi.org/10.1016/j.compedu.2009.09.008

REX [Analytics] Tools for Teaching Available to Instructors (2017, March 28). *UMBC DoIT News*. https://doit.umbc.edu/news/?id=66749

Robertson, D. L. (1999). Professors' perspectives on their teaching: A new construct and developmental model. *Innovative Higher Education*, *23*(4), 271–294. https://doi.org/10.1023/A:1022982907040

Tinto, V. (1993). *Leaving college: Rethinking the causes and cures of student attrition* (2nd ed.). University of Chicago Press.

UMBC Blackboard Use Differs from Most Schools (2018, December 11). *UMBC DoIT News*. https://doit.umbc.edu/news/?id=80996

Whitmer, J. (2012). *Logging on to improve achievement: Evaluating the relationship between use of the learning management system, student characteristics, and academic achievement in a hybrid large enrollment undergraduate course*. University of California. http://johnwhitmer.net/dissertation-study/

Whitmer, J., Nuñez, N., Harfield, T., & Forteza, D. (2016, October 27). Patterns in blackboard learn tool use: How instructors actually use the LMS. *Blackboard Blog*. https://blog.blackboard.com/patterns-in-course-design-how-instructors-actually-use-the-lms/

Whitmer, J., Walton, K. E., Moore, J. L., & Lotero, A. A. (2019). The constructs behind the clicks. *ACT Research Report, 26*. https://actnext.org/wp-content/uploads/R1803-la-sel-2019-11.pdf

Why CNMS Student Bb Use Is So High (2019, November 25). *UMBC DoIT News*. https://doit.umbc.edu/news/?id=88786

Wiley, D. (2011, February 15). *Openness, learning analytics, and continuous quality improvement*. Educause Learning Initiative. https://events.educause.edu/eli/annual-meeting/2011/proceedings/openness-learning-analytics-and-continuous-quality-improvement

SECTION III
Faculty Issues

6

HIGHLY EFFECTIVE BLENDED TEACHING PRACTICES

Cub Kahn and Lynne L. Hindman

Blended learning has become a widely used and accepted teaching modality in higher education during the past two decades, and research strongly supports the efficacy of hybrid approaches, but research specifically identifying highly effective blended teaching practices from the viewpoint of instructors is lacking. This study surveyed hybrid course instructors in 2016 and 2019 for their perspectives on highly effective teaching practices. Secondarily, this research examined differences in the perspectives of faculty who had participated in a ten-week hybrid faculty learning community (hybrid FLC) and those who had not.

Institutional Context

Hybrid instruction has been an officially recognized course modality at Oregon State University (OSU) since 2012 and is defined as including both regularly scheduled on-site classroom meetings and significant online components that replace regularly scheduled class meeting time. Thus, these courses are reduced-seat-time courses. The reduction in class meeting time ranges from 25% to 80%. For the purposes of this chapter, *hybrid* and *blended* are used interchangeably.

OSU does not mandate faculty training prior to designing or teaching a hybrid course based on the Corvallis (main) or Cascades campus. (OSU Ecampus does mandate training for faculty developing or teaching Ecampus hybrid courses that meet at various off-campus sites, but this study only considers Corvallis and Cascades campus hybrid courses and faculty.) The Center for Teaching and Learning has facilitated optional ten-week hybrid faculty learning communities (hybrid FLCs) since 2012. These hybrid FLCs consist of cross-disciplinary cohorts of 6 to 12 faculty; each FLC participant is involved in the process of redesigning a traditional classroom course as a reduced-seat-time hybrid. These learning

DOI: 10.4324/9781003037736-9

communities, which are open to faculty in all 11 academic colleges, have been conducted in a hybrid format and focus on professional development pertaining to blended course design, technology, and pedagogy. The curriculum of the hybrid FLCs includes study of recognized effective practices in the design and delivery of blended learning. Each participant also works individually with the FLC facilitator on the design of their hybrid course.

Background

Much of the understanding of best practices in blended teaching is based on evidence-based best practices in fully online teaching. But as Stein and Graham (2020) note, while design and delivery of hybrid and online courses have strong similarities, they also have fundamental differences. McGee and Reis (2012) stated, "If the blended delivery model continues to expand and become a mainstay for higher education [which it has], then more clearly vetted models, examples of effective course designs, and well-substantiated effective practices are needed" (p. 12).

The authors of this chapter aimed to rise to this challenge by helping substantiate effective practices for delivering blended learning. To set the stage for the 2016 survey, a thorough review of the literature revealed McGee and Reis's meta-analysis of best practices for hybrid teaching to be the largest compendium of this sort available at that time. While McGee and Reis's meta-analysis served as the backbone for the present study, their findings were supported by many other sources. Altogether, the authors extracted from the literature 22 best practices for hybrid teaching that are listed and referenced in Appendix A.

The purpose of this research was to examine OSU instructors' perceptions of highly effective hybrid teaching practices The study employed the following research questions: What do OSU hybrid faculty identify as highly effective hybrid teaching practices, and, secondarily, in regards to identifying highly effective teaching practices, do differences exist between faculty who have participated in hybrid FLCs and faculty who have not participated?

Methods

The researchers developed and administered to OSU hybrid faculty a 22-item online survey (see Appendix B) regarding their use and perceptions of effective hybrid teaching practices as identified from the literature. This survey included both closed- and open-ended questions. To streamline the user experience, the survey incorporated skip logic elements that directed respondents to efficiently jump to questions based on their prior responses.

As of the date of each survey—October 2016 and October 2019—all current OSU faculty who had been instructors of record for at least one completed hybrid course on the Corvallis (main) or the Cascades campus were invited to participate via email in the study. Seventy-five faculty members were invited to participate in the 2016 survey, and, due to substantial growth in the number of hybrid courses offered, 224 faculty were invited to complete the identical 2019 survey. To encourage participation, two follow-up reminder emails were also sent, two weeks apart.

The first page of the email that potential participants received displayed a thorough explanation of the research that included the survey's first question, which asked participants if they desired to participate. Those who clicked "no" received a message of thanks, while those who clicked "yes" gave their consent and were directed to the next page of the survey.

Descriptive analyses were conducted on the quantitative and qualitative data obtained from the survey. Content and inductive analysis were used to interpret qualitative survey data (Kyngäs, 2020). Additional sub-group comparative analyses were conducted for those who had participated in a hybrid FLC versus those who had not.

Results and Analysis

Demographics of Survey Respondents

Twenty-eight faculty members responded to the 2016 survey (a 37% response rate), and 65 responded to the 2019 survey (29% response). Both surveys invited participation from faculty in all eleven of the university's academic colleges. The 2016 survey received responses from faculty in seven academic colleges; the 2019 survey respondents included faculty in ten colleges. Since the surveys were designed for anonymity, it is unknown how many instructors may have participated in both surveys.

The average (mean) level of teaching experience in higher education was 10.8 years for 2016 respondents and increased to 14.5 for 2019 respondents. Tenured/tenure-track faculty comprised 25% of the 2016 respondents; that proportion rose to 43% in 2019. Non-tenure-track instructors and senior instructors made up 70% of the 2016 respondents but dropped to 49% of respondents in 2019. The remainder of the respondents were graduate students and administrative staff who had served as hybrid instructors of record.

Comparing the 2016 and 2019 surveys, the portion of respondents who had taught two or fewer hybrid courses increased from 19% to 44%, even while the percentage who had taught five or more hybrid courses increased from 33% to 41%. In both surveys, slightly more than one-fourth of the respondents (29% in 2016 and 28% in 2019) had taught large-enrollment hybrid courses with more than 80 students.

Seventy-three percent of the 2016 survey respondents had previously participated in a ten-week hybrid faculty learning community; 66% of the 2019 respondents had done so.

Faculty Perceptions of Highly Effective Blended Teaching Practices

What do OSU hybrid faculty recognize as highly effective hybrid teaching practices? Survey participants were first asked about their use of 22 effective blended teaching practices identified from the literature. Seventeen of the 22 practices had been used in teaching hybrid courses by more than 80% of the 2016 respondents; among the 2019 respondents, 18 of the 22 practices had been used by more than 80% of the respondents as indicated in Table 6.1.

Participants were then asked to rate the efficacy of each of the 22 effective teaching practices that they had used. The five possible ratings of each practice were as follows: not effective at all, slightly effective, moderately effective, very effective or extremely effective. In both surveys, 11 of the 22 teaching practices were identified by at least two-thirds of faculty as very effective or extremely

TABLE 6.1 Use of 22 Effective Hybrid Teaching Practices by Hybrid Course Faculty

Teaching Practices Used by More Than 80% in Both 2016 and 2019

Integration between classroom and online learning environments
Student-to-instructor interaction in both the classroom and online environments
Lectures of less than 15 minutes interspersed with other class activities
Active learning (e.g., think-pair-share, problem-solving exercises, group work)
Classroom discussions
Real-world applications to connect theory to practice
Clear statement of learning outcomes in syllabus
Alignment of learning outcomes with course content, assignments, and assessments
Students encouraged to take responsibility for their learning
Technology supports learning outcomes
Prompt and specific feedback given on assessments (e.g., quizzes, papers, projects)
Frequent low-stakes quizzes/formative assessment used to assess/guide progress
Some assessments conducted online
Clear instructions re: course comprises both online and face-to-face components
Online content/learning activities referred to during face-to-face meetings to reinforce
Learning activities outside class prepare students to participate in class meetings
Sense of community nurtured among students in the course

Teaching Practices Used by More Than 80% in 2019 but Not in 2016

Student-to-student interaction in both classroom and online environments

Teaching Practices Used by Fewer Than 80% in Both 2016 and 2019

Online discussions
Students oriented to any requisite technical skills
Group activities that have both an in-class and out-of-class component
Peer review of student work

effective. In order of their rating across both surveys, these 11 "highly effective" hybrid teaching practices are:

1. Real-world applications to connect theory to practice
2. Student-to-instructor interaction in both the classroom and online environment
3. Lectures of less than 15 minutes interspersed with other class activities
4. Student-to-student interaction in both classroom and online environments
5. Integration between classroom and online learning environments
6. Active learning (for example, think-pair-share, problem-solving exercises, group work)
7. Online content/learning activities referred to during face-to-face meetings to reinforce
8. Learning activities outside class prepare students to participate in class meetings
9. Group activities that have both an in-class and out-of-class component
10. Prompt and specific feedback given on assessments (e.g., quizzes, papers, projects)
11. Classroom discussions

Respondents in the first survey (2016) rated two additional practices at this high level of effectiveness: clear instructions provided that the course comprises both online and face-to-face components and frequent low-stakes quizzes or other forms of formative assessment used to assess understanding and guide student progress.

Faculty Response Differences Related to Learning Community Participation

In regards to identifying highly effective teaching practices, do differences exist between faculty who have participated in a hybrid FLC and faculty who have not participated? As noted earlier, the majority of participants in both surveys had previously participated in a ten-week hybrid FLC, and the learning community curriculum includes study of recognized effective practices in blended course design and teaching.

In the 2016 survey, respondents who had participated in hybrid FLCs reported that 15 of the teaching practices they had used were "highly effective" (once again defined as two-thirds of the users of the teaching practice classifying it as very effective or extremely effective). Learning community non-participants reported that only 11 of the teaching practices were highly effective. This situation was reversed in the 2019 survey, in which the non-participants in hybrid FLCs identified 16 highly effective practices, but the hybrid FLC participants only identified 11 as shown in Table 6.2.

TABLE 6.2 Highly Effective Hybrid Teaching Practices* Identified by Hybrid FLC Participants (FLC) and Learning Community Non-Participants (Non)

2016		2019		*Teaching Practices*
FLC	*Non*	*FLC*	*Non*	
H		H	H	Group activities that have an in-class and out-of-class component
H	H	H	H	Integration between classroom and online learning environments
H	H		H	Student-to-student interaction in classroom & online environments
H	H	H	H	Student-to-instructor interaction in classroom & online environments
H	H	H	H	Lectures of <15 minutes interspersed with other class activities
H	H	H	H	Active learning (e.g., think-pair-share, problem-solving, group work)
H	H	H	H	Classroom discussions
H				Peer review of student work
H	H	H	H	Real-world applications to connect theory to practice
	H		H	Alignment of outcomes with content, assignments, & assessments
H			H	Students encouraged to take responsibility for their learning
		H	]	Technology supports learning outcomes
H		H	H	Prompt and specific feedback given on assessments (quizzes, papers, projects)
H			H	Frequent low-stakes quizzes/formative assessment used to assess understanding and guide student progress
	H			Some assessments conducted online
H			H	Clear instructions provided that the course comprises both online and face-to-face components
			H	Students oriented to any requisite technical skills
H	H	H	H	Online content and learning activities referred to during face-to-face meetings to reinforce
H	H	H	H	Learning activities outside class prepare students to participate in class meetings

* H indicates a highly effective practice, defined as one rated "very effective" or "extremely effective" by at least two-thirds of instructors who have used that practice.

Despite these apparent differences, the strong rating of the efficacy of the 11 highly effective practices identified earlier was largely consistent among survey respondents regardless of whether respondents had participated in hybrid faculty learning communities. In fact, 8 of the 11 highly effective practices were rated as such by both hybrid FLC participants and non-participants in both the 2016 and 2019 surveys. The only exceptions were lower ratings of efficacy by learning community non-participants in the 2016 survey of "group activities that have both an in-class and out-of-class component" and "prompt and specific feedback given on assessments," and by hybrid FLC participants in the 2019 survey of "Student-to-student interaction in both classroom and online environments."

Discussion

Effective Practices

The number of faculty who had taught hybrid courses at Oregon State tripled between the 2016 survey and the 2019 survey, reflecting extremely rapid growth of the modality. Starting with only a handful of official hybrid courses in 2012, the number of hybrid-identified courses grew to 725 by September 2020. The number of hybrid course sections offered on the main (Corvallis) campus increased by more than 20% annually every year from the 2012 inception of official hybrid courses through 2019. Much of this growth of hybrids was at the impetus of individual instructors in the absence of a strong institutional mandate to hybridize.

Demographically, compared to the 2016 survey respondents, the 2019 survey respondents had more teaching experience and were more likely to be tenured/tenure-track. For instance, no full professors responded to the 2016 survey, but eight did in 2019. The 2019 respondents were also more likely to be either rather new to teaching in this modality, having taught no more than two hybrids, or quite experienced, having taught five or more hybrids.

Despite shifts in hybrid faculty demographics, both surveys revealed a high prevalence of use of the majority of the 22 effective blended teaching practices identified in the literature and a strong consensus around the high efficacy of 11 highly effective practices. Though the motivations of faculty to use various teaching methods were not identified, many of these practices are widely used, irrespective of modality. For example, the use of active learning and the use of real-world applications to connect theory to practice are known to increase student success (Brame, 2016).

Five of the highly effective teaching practices identified in this study are more specifically related to blended/hybrid or flipped teaching:

- Student-to-instructor interaction in both the classroom and online environment
- Student-to-student interaction in both classroom and online environments
- Integration between classroom and online learning environments
- Online content/learning activities referred to during face-to-face meetings to reinforce
- Learning activities outside class prepare students to participate in class meetings

In each case, these teaching practices involve explicit linking of classroom and online learning activities, and they are to a large degree "baked into" the blended course design. Anecdotally, from the authors' experience supporting teaching faculty at a land-grant university, with each passing year, these practices appear to be a bigger part of mainstream on-campus teaching and learning.

As noted earlier, during the three-year interval between the first and second surveys, hybrid courses became much more widespread within the institution, and many more faculty became hybrid course instructors. Compared to the 2016 survey, the 2019 survey revealed wider use of 15 of the 22 effective teaching practices identified from the literature. For example, the percentage of instructors who used online discussions and the percentage who used frequent low-stakes quizzes or other types of formative assessment both rose by 10%. This increased use is promising in terms of improvement of instruction.

The identification of highly effective blended teaching methods by hybrid instructors is potentially useful in designing faculty development programs and sharing what works, according to hybrid instructors, with faculty moving into hybrid course design and teaching for the first time. As Ginsberg and Ciabocchi (2014) noted in their national study of blended faculty development practices, successful faculty development programs are rooted in best practices. The 11 highly effective practices identified across both surveys are widely applicable across the curriculum and would be at the heart of a blended pedagogy checklist in many disciplines regardless of class size or course level. These practices provide a focus for the OSU Center for Teaching and Learning's support of new and continuing hybrid course faculty, as well as support of faculty teaching in the COVID-era remote modality that blends synchronous Zoom sessions with asynchronous online learning activities.

Overall, there was significant similarity in the identification of highly effective teaching practices by faculty who had participated in hybrid FLCs and faculty who had not participated in these learning communities. As noted previously, in the 2016 survey, hybrid FLC participants identified more highly effective practices than non-participants, while in the 2019 survey, the non-participants identified more highly effective practices than the hybrid FLC participants. The reasons for this seeming reversal are unclear, but confounding factors include the unknown motivations of faculty to participate or to not participate in a hybrid FLC, the varying teaching skills and experience of the instructors, and the diverse nature of the hybrid courses they teach (e.g., large general ed survey courses versus small graduate courses). Additionally, only six learning community non-participants responded to the 2016 survey; this small number of responses may not accurately represent these faculty perspectives.

Effects of Blended Teaching on Instructional Practice

The surveys produced one other notable finding beyond the two central research questions. In both surveys, approximately four out of five respondents (82% in

2016; 79% in 2019) reported that their teaching practices in other classes had changed as a result of teaching hybrid courses. As a follow-up to this question, participants were asked to "explain how your teaching practices have changed." Responses from both surveys clustered around five common themes:

- greater use of active learning
- better class organization
- more application of flipped learning
- increased integration of classroom and online learning
- improved Canvas/online tool use

Two other themes emerged in the responses to this question in the 2019 survey:

- increased community building/engagement
- placing more responsibility for learning on students

A 2019 survey respondent reported, "I have learned in my on-campus classes how to become more daring in online exercises, which means that we can use class time more effectively. Online, I have learned how important it is to set up intentional community-building exercises." This comment is indicative of the way in which many faculty members describe the growth of their teaching skills as a consequence of teaching blended courses.

As faculty are increasingly called upon to teach in multiple modalities (on campus, blended and fully online)—in addition to synchronous remote teaching and HyFlex teaching in response to the COVID-19 crisis—the capacity for teaching faculty to be adaptable and to teach effectively in multiple modalities is a necessity for successful teaching careers in higher education.

The findings of this study suggest that teaching in a blended format is in itself a form of professional development for educators. The survey respondents reported overwhelmingly that teaching hybrid courses led to the adoption of such useful evidence-based teaching practices as improved class organization, more use of active learning and flipped learning, integration of classroom and online learning, and improved LMS/online tool use. Effective hybrid teaching may improve the student experience as course delivery continues to evolve.

Future Research

Future research directions potentially include delving into the student side of the blended teaching-and-learning equation and looking at the "why" of faculty application of effective hybrid teaching practices:

- What blended teaching practices do students identify as highly effective? In particular, what blended teaching practices can best support diversity, equity, and inclusion in the learner-centered, part-synchronous/part-asynchronous, part-virtual/part-physical classrooms of today and tomorrow? What instructional practices in blended courses contribute to the success of all learners?

- How do hybrid course faculty select the blended teaching practices they use, including practices they rate as highly effective? To what degree are these choices the result of participation in professional development, of collaboration with instructional designers and instructional technologists, of adoption of teaching practices successfully modeled by peers, or of other factors?

Conclusions

In summary, two hybrid faculty surveys, conducted three years apart, identified 11 blended teaching practices that are widely used and are also perceived as highly effective by faculty teaching hybrid courses. Research supports the effectiveness of these practices. This study indicates that from a faculty perspective, these 11 practices are widely used and therefore valuable in their hybrid teaching.

The vast majority of hybrid course faculty in both surveys reported that blended teaching had changed their teaching practices in other courses as well, citing areas such as improved course organization, greater use of active learning, and better integration of classroom and online learning. As more faculty teach in a hybrid format, a trend greatly accelerated by COVID-19, the benefits found here bode well for the future of teaching and learning in all modalities.

References

Alberts, P. P., Murray, L. A., & Stephenson, J. E. (2010). Eight educational considerations for hybrid learning. In *Handbook of research on hybrid learning models: Advanced tools, technologies, and applications* (pp. 185–202). IGI Global.

Allen, I. E., Seaman, J., & Garrett, R. (2007). *Blending in: The extent and promise of blended education in the United States*. Sloan Consortium.

Aycock, A., Garnham, C., & Kaleta, R. (2002). Lessons learned from the hybrid course project. *Teaching with Technology Today*, 8(6), 9–21.

Beatty, B. J. (2006). *Designing the HyFlex world—hybrid, flexible classes for all students*. Association for Educational Communication and Technology International Conference.

Beatty, B. J. (2010). *Connecting online and on-ground learners with HyFlex courses*. Invited Plenary Session, EDUCAUSE Learning Initiative (ELI).

Brame, C. (2016). *Active learning*. Vanderbilt University Center for Teaching. Retrieved September 21, 2020, from https://cft.vanderbilt.edu/active-learning/

Collins-Brown, E. (2011, March). *Quality by design: Course design for optimal blending*. Presentation at the 8th Annual Sloan Consortium Blended Learning Conference and Workshop.

Crummett, C., Mazoue, J., Anderson, R., Daughtrey, T., Love, W., MacDonald, S., Stoloff, M., Wilcox, D., & Zemliansky, P. (2010). *Best practices for online and hybrid course delivery*. James Madison University. www.jmu.edu/dl/wm_library/JMU_Best_Practices.pdf

Eke, K., & Bell, M. (2010). *Blended course design made easy: 3 simple steps.* Presentation at the 16th annual Sloan Consortium International Conference on Online Learning.

Elliott, D., Gamino, M., & Jenkins, J. J. (2016). Creating community in the college classroom: Best practices for increased student success. *International Journal of Education and Social Science, 3*(6).

Garnham, C., & Kaleta, R. (2002). Introduction to hybrid courses. *Teaching with Technology Today, 8*(6), 5.

Gerbic, P. (2009). Including online discussions within campus-based students' learning environments. In *Effective blended learning practices: Evidence-based perspectives in ICT-facilitated education* (pp. 21–38). IGI Global.

Ginsberg, A. P., & Ciabocchi, E. (2014). Growing your own blended faculty: A review of current faculty development practices in traditional, not-for-profit higher education institutions. *Blended Learning: Research Perspectives, 2,* 190–202.

Hall, O. P., & Mooney, J. G. (2010, August). Hybrid learning systems: Meeting the challenges of graduate management education. In *International conference on hybrid learning* (pp. 35–48). Springer.

Hofmann, J. (2003). *Managing the synchronous blend.* American Society for Training and Development (ASTD).

Jiang, M., & Ting, E. (2000). A study of factors influencing students' perceived learning in a web-based course environment. *International Journal of Educational Telecommunications, 6*(4), 317–338.

Kaleta, R., Garnham, C., & Aycock, A. (2005). Hybrid courses: Obstacles and solutions for faculty and students. In *19th annual conference on distance teaching and learning.* The Board of Regents of the University of Wisconsin System.

Kelly, R. (2008, October 29). Nine tips for creating a hybrid course. *Faculty Focus.* www.facultyfocus.com/articles/online-education/nine-tips-for-creating-a-hybrid-course

Kim, K. J., Bonk, C. J., & Oh, E. (2008). The present and future state of blended learning in workplace learning settings in the United States. *Performance Improvement, 47*(8), 5–16.

Kyngäs, H. (2020). Inductive content analysis. In *The application of content analysis in nursing science research* (pp. 13–21). Springer.

Martyn, M. (2003). The hybrid online model: Good practice. *EDUCAUSE Quarterly, 26*(1), 18–23.

McGee, P., & Reis, A. (2012). Blended course design: A synthesis of best practices. *Journal of Asynchronous Learning Networks, 16*(4), 7–22.

Picciano, A. G. (2009). Blending with purpose: The multimodal model. *Journal of Asynchronous Learning Networks, 13*(1), 7–18.

Poirier, S. (2010). A hybrid course design: The best of both educational worlds. *Techniques: Connecting Education and Careers (J1), 85*(6), 28–30.

Pouyioutas, P. (2010, August). Hybrid learning curriculum development using the ReProTool—lessons from ancient philosophy. In *International conference on hybrid learning* (pp. 160–170). Springer.

Rossett, A., Douglis, F., & Frazee, R. V. (2003). Strategies for building blended learning. *Learning Circuits, 4*(7), 1–8.

Shibley, I. (2009). *Blended course design.* Magna Publications.

Shibley, I. (2011, February 21). Putting the learning in blended learning. *Faculty Focus.* www.facultyfocus.com/articles/blended-flipped-learning/putting-the-learning-in-blended-learning/

Siu-Man, R. T., & Gonzalez, L. M. (2013). Quality of interactions in face-to-face and hybrid career development courses: An exploration of students' perceptions. *Journal of Online Learning and Teaching, 9*(3), 316.

Staley, L., Van Noord, R., Gutsche, B., Hillman, B., Kellison, E., & Musselman, D. (2007). *Blended learning guide.* OCLC Online Computer Library Center. http://web.junc tion.org/content/dam/WebJunction/Documents/webJunction/Blended-Learning-Guide.pdf

Stein, J., & Graham, C. R. (2020). *Essentials for blended learning: A standards-based guide* (2nd ed.). Routledge.

Strait, J. R., & Nordyke, K. (Eds.). (2015). *eService-learning: Creating experiential learning and civic engagement through online and hybrid courses.* Stylus.

Sun, J. R. (2004). *Turning a regular (face-to-face) course into a more engaging blended (hybrid) course.* www.oln.org/conferences/OCDE2004/papers/Regular_to_Hybrid_Course.pdf

Swan, K. (2004). Relationships between interactions and learning in online environments. *The Sloan Consortium,* 1–6.

Tan, L., Wang, M., & Xiao, J. (2010, August). Best practices in teaching online or hybrid courses: A synthesis of principles. In P. Tsang, S. K. S. Cheung, V. S. K. Lee, & R. Huang (Eds.), *Hybrid learning* (Vol. 6248). ICHL 2010, Lecture Notes in Computer Science, Springer.

Troha, F. J. (2002). Bulletproof instructional design [R]: A model for blended learning. *USDLA Journal, 16*(5), n5.

Twigg, C. A. (2003). Models for online learning. *EDUCAUSE Review, 38,* 28–38.

Yukawa, J. (2010). Communities of practice for blended learning: Toward an integrated model for LIS education. *Journal of Education for Library and Information Science,* 54–75.

APPENDIX A

Hybrid Teaching Best Practices Identified in the Literature

1. Group activities that have both an in-class and out-of-class component (Hall & Mooney, 2010; McGee & Reis, 2012; Picciano, 2009; Yukawa, 2010; Shibley, 2009)
2. Integration between classroom and online learning environments (Alberts et al., 2010; Allen et al., 2007; Crummett et al., 2010; Hall & Mooney, 2010; Hofmann, 2003; Kaleta et al., 2005; Kim et al., 2008; Martyn, 2003; Shibley, 2009; McGee & Reis, 2012; Staley et al., 2007; Sun, 2004)
3. Student-to-student interaction in both classroom and online environments (Alberts et al., 2010; Crummett et al., 2010; Hall & Mooney, 2010; McGee & Reis, 2012; Swan, 2004; Tan et al., 2010)
4. Student-to-instructor interaction in both classroom and online environments (Alberts et al., 2010; Crummett et al., 2010; Hall & Mooney, 2010; Jiang & Ting, 2000; McGee & Reis, 2012; Siu-Man & Gonzalez, 2013; Swan, 2004; Tan et al., 2010)
5. Lectures of less than 15 minutes interspersed with other class activities (Hofmann, 2003; Kelly, 2008; McGee & Reis, 2012; Rossett et al., 2003; Shibley, 2009)
6. Active learning: for example, think-pair-share, problem-solving exercises, and group work (Alberts et al., 2010; Beatty, 2010; Collins-Brown, 2011; Crummett et al., 2010; Hall & Mooney, 2010; Hofmann, 2003; Kaleta et al., 2005; Kim et al., 2008; McGee & Reis, 2012; Poirier, 2010; Pouyioutas, 2010; Shibley, 2009; Staley et al., 2007; Swan, 2004; Yukawa, 2010)
7. Classroom discussions (Hofmann, 2003; Shibley, 2009; Martyn, 2003; McGee & Reis, 2012)
8. Online discussions (Gerbic, 2009; Hofmann, 2003; Martyn, 2003; McGee & Reis, 2012; Shibley, 2009; Swan, 2004)

9. Peer review of student work (McGee & Reis, 2012)
10. Real-world applications to connect theory to practice (McGee & Reis, 2012; Strait & Nordyke, 2015)
11. Clear statement of learning outcomes in syllabus (Beatty, 2006, 2010; Collins-Brown, 2011; Eke & Bell, 2010; McGee & Reis, 2012; Tan et al., 2010; Yukawa, 2010)
12. Alignment of learning outcomes with course content, assignments, and assessments (Beatty, 2006, 2010; Collins-Brown, 2011; Eke & Bell, 2010; McGee & Reis, 2012; Poirier, 2010; Shibley, 2011)
13. Students encouraged to take responsibility for their learning (Collins-Brown, 2011; Hofmann, 2003; Kaleta et al., 2005; Kim et al., 2008; McGee & Reis, 2012; Pouyioutas, 2010, Rossett et al., 2003; Sun, 2004; Twigg, 2003)
14. Technology supports learning outcomes (Alberts et al., 2010; Crummett et al., 2010; Kim et al., 2008; McGee & Reis, 2012)
15. Prompt and specific feedback given on assessments: for example, quizzes, papers, projects (Alberts et al., 2010; Crummett et al., 2010; Kim et al., 2008; McGee & Reis, 2012)
16. Frequent low-stakes quizzes or other forms of formative assessment used to assess understanding and guide student progress (Martyn, 2003; McGee & Reis, 2012; Shibley, 2009; Swan, 2004; Twigg, 2003)
17. Some assessments conducted online (Hofmann, 2003; Martyn, 2003; McGee & Reis, 2012; Shibley, 2009)
18. Clear instructions provided that the course comprises both online and face-to-face components (Eke & Bell, 2010; McGee & Reis, 2012; Yukawa, 2010)
19. Students oriented to any requisite technical skills (Alberts et al., 2010; Collins-Brown, 2011; Crummett et al., 2010; Garnham & Kaleta, 2002; Hofmann, 2003; Kaleta et al., 2005; Kelly, 2008; Kim et al., 2008; Martyn, 2003; McGee & Reis, 2012; Poirier, 2010; Staley et al., 2007; Sun, 2004; Tan et al., 2010; Troha, 2002; Yukawa, 2010)
20. Online content/learning activities referred to during face-to-face meetings to reinforce (Aycock et al., 2002; McGee & Reis, 2012; Rossett et al., 2003; Staley et al., 2007)
21. Learning activities outside class prepare students to participate in class meetings (Alberts et al., 2010; Collins-Brown, 2011; Crummett et al., 2010; Hofmann, 2003; Kaleta et al., 2005; Martyn, 2003; McGee & Reis, 2012; Poirier, 2010; Rossett et al., 2003; Shibley, 2011; Staley et al., 2007; Sun, 2004; Twigg, 2003; Yukawa, 2010)
22. Sense of community nurtured among students in the course (Elliott et al., 2016; Martyn, 2003; McGee & Reis, 2012; Poirier, 2010; Staley et al., 2007; Swan, 2004; Tan et al., 2010; Yukawa, 2010)

APPENDIX B

Survey

Which of the following practices have you used when teaching a hybrid course?

[If yes for a particular practice.] From your perspective, how effective is this practice in fostering student learning in a hybrid course on a scale of 1 to 5? (1 = not effective at all, 2 = slightly effective, 3 = moderately effective, 4 = very effective, 5 = extremely effective)

- Group activities that have both an in-class and out-of-class component
- Integration between classroom and online learning environments
- Student-to-student interaction in both classroom and online environments
- Student-to-instructor interaction in both the classroom and online environments
- Lectures of less than 15 minutes interspersed with other class activities
- Active learning (for example, think-pair-share, problem-solving exercises, group work)
- Classroom discussions
- Online discussions
- Peer review of student work
- Real-world applications to connect theory to practice
- Clear statement of learning outcomes in syllabus
- Alignment of learning outcomes with course content, assignments, and assessments
- Students encouraged to take responsibility for their learning
- Technology supports learning outcomes

112 Cub Kahn and Lynne L. Hindman

- Prompt and specific feedback given on assessments (for example, quizzes, papers, projects)
- Frequent low-stakes quizzes or other forms of formative assessment used to assess understanding and guide student progress
- Some assessments conducted online
- Clear instructions provided that the course comprises both online and face-to-face components
- Students oriented to any requisite technical skills
- Online content/learning activities referred to during face-to-face meetings to reinforce
- Learning activities outside class prepare students to participate in class meetings
- Sense of community nurtured among students in the course

Please describe additional practices that you have found effective in fostering student learning in a hybrid course? _____

Please rate yourself on a scale of 1 (completely unable) to 5 (extremely able) on each item:

- I can describe recognized effective practices for design and delivery of a hybrid course, for example, methods to foster student engagement in a blended learning environment.
- I can design a hybrid course syllabus and develop course content that employs effective practices for blended learning, such as techniques to integrate online and face-to-face learning activities and materials.
- I can identify OSU resources—including the Center for Teaching and Learning, Technology Across the Curriculum—and other online resources—such as the Online Learning Consortium and MERLOT—to support hybrid course development and delivery.
- I can recognize and apply policies and procedures applicable to hybrid course development and delivery, such as standards for online course site functionality.
- I can employ fundamental features of the Canvas learning management system for course delivery, for example, posting announcements and facilitating online discussions.

Overall, as a result of teaching hybrid courses, my teaching practices in other classes have changed:

- Yes
- No

Highly Effective Blended Teaching **113**

If yes; please explain how your teaching practices have changed: _____

Total number of OSU-designated hybrid course sections taught (including this term):

- 1 to 2
- 3 to 4
- 5 or more

What year did you first teach an OSU-designated hybrid course here at OSU? (OSU first officially recognized and scheduled hybrid courses in 2012.)

- 2012
- 2013
- 2014
- 2015
- 2016
- 2017
- 2018
- 2019

What is the *maximum* enrollment of any hybrid course you have taught?

- 1–40
- 41–80
- 81–120
- 121–200
- 201+

What is the *minimum* enrollment of any hybrid course you have taught?

- 1–40
- 41–80
- 81–120
- 121–200
- 201+

Have you participated in a *Center for Teaching & Learning* Hybrid Faculty Learning Community?

- Yes
- No

114 Cub Kahn and Lynne L. Hindman

Within OSU, have you participated in other professional development, training, or coursework that prepared you to teach hybrid courses?

- Yes
- No

If yes, please describe: _____

Outside OSU, have you participated in professional development, training, or coursework that prepared you to teach hybrid courses?

- Yes
- No

If yes, please describe: _____

In the future, which of the following professional development activities focusing on hybrid teaching would you be likely to participate in? (Check all that apply)

- An advanced 10-week Hybrid Faculty Learning Community for faculty who have already taught hybrid courses
- A series of monthly brown-bag seminars in which hybrid instructors present about their teaching techniques
- A series of monthly brown-bag seminars in which instructional designers present hybrid teaching tools and techniques
- A workshop on how to facilitate more online interaction in hybrid courses
- A workshop on how to create and edit mini-lecture videos
- Other (please specify): _____

Would you be interested in mentoring faculty who are developing hybrid courses for the first time?

- Yes
- Maybe
- No

Total number of years teaching in higher education:

- _____ [Pull-down menu: 1 to 30+]

In which college are you located?

- Agricultural Sciences
- Business

- Earth, Ocean, and Atmospheric Sciences
- Education
- Engineering
- Forestry
- Graduate School
- Honors
- Liberal Arts
- Pharmacy
- Public Health and Human Sciences

Academic Rank (check one):

- Instructor
- Senior Instructor
- Assistant Professor
- Associate Professor
- Professor
- Other: _____

7

BLENDED FACULTY COMMUNITY OF INQUIRY TRANSFORMS ONLINE TEACHING PERCEPTIONS AND PRACTICES

Karen Skibba and Maria Widmer

Introduction

Overall enrollment growth in online postsecondary education in the United States remains positive year over year. Online education is now "common enough and significant enough" to be considered part of mainstream academic programming at many institutions (Garrett et al., 2020, p. 36). Therefore, it is important to ensure that instructors are prepared. The skills needed to effectively teach and ensure student success in online courses can be difficult for instructors to learn on their own (Skibba, 2012). This chapter identifies the features of a blended faculty learning community that contribute to change in participants' perceptions of and practices for online course design and teaching.

Garrison (2017) articulates the challenges that instructors and faculty developers face when applying active learning strategies shown to be effective in online and blended education. Garrison presents the community of inquiry (CoI) theoretical framework as being "enormously useful in structuring workshops and guiding faculty through the complexities of designing online and blended learning courses" (p. 150). The CoI framework represents a process for creating collaborative-constructivist learning experiences through the development of three interdependent elements: teaching, social, and cognitive presence (Garrison et al., 2001). This framework provides a model of instructional design for online and blended learning, including teacher professional development (Vaughan & Garrison, 2016; Garrison, 2017).

In the two decades following its introduction, the CoI framework has found broad empirical support in the literature on online and blended teaching and, in turn, has informed practitioners' approaches to designing and facilitating learning

DOI: 10.4324/9781003037736-10

experiences (Garrison, 2017). Despite the widespread use of CoI as a theoretical framework, its application in the literature on faculty development has been limited. Further research into implementation of the CoI framework in professional development could support faculty developers with evidence-based strategies for teaching transformation. Faculty learning communities are one form of teacher professional development in which, with the guidance of knowledgeable facilitators, participants support each other in exploring new teaching practices (Wicks et al., 2015).

This chapter shares a case study of a large, blended faculty learning community analyzed using the CoI framework to determine which methods had the most impact on participants' perceptions and practices of online education and why those methods had significant impact. The first section of this chapter provides a brief overview of a blended faculty learning program and its component characteristics categorized with the CoI framework. Next, the methods and results of a mixed-methods case study are presented. The chapter concludes with a discussion of findings and potential implications for future research. Practical techniques can establish teaching, social, and cognitive presence in a holistic educational experience that supports teaching transformation.

Research Questions and Methodology

The primary focus of this chapter is an exploration of the impact of a blended faculty learning community on instructors' perceptions of and practices for online education. The research questions are: Which methods utilized in a blended faculty learning community, categorized by the presences of the community of inquiry framework, had the most impact on participants' perceptions and practices of online course design and teaching? Why were these methods impactful?

A mixed-method, descriptive case study (Merriam, 1998) was conducted in order to answer these questions. Data sources included program evaluations and interviews with learning community participants. Program evaluations comprised surveys asking participants to evaluate the impact of the learning community after they had taught online and a thematic analysis of the program's asynchronous components. The thematic content analysis examined online discussions in which participants shared challenges, concerns, lessons learned, and strategies they planned to implement in their own courses.

Eleven instructors (six men, five women) participated in the in-depth interviews. These instructors were selected because they had completed the learning community program and taught an online course within one year of the interview date. They came from diverse disciplines and held both tenure track and non–tenure track positions.

Case Study

A blended faculty learning community at a large Midwestern public research university served as the site of the case study. Developed by a cross-campus committee of instructional designers in 2015, the learning community has been offered for six years. To date, 383 unique participants completed one or both courses; 66% (252) of participants completed both courses, for a total of 640 enrollments. The primary objective of the faculty learning community is to advance high-quality online education by preparing instructors for the course development and teaching process. To achieve this objective, participants experience and share online course design and teaching practices.

The learning community is divided into two blended courses: Plan & Design and Facilitation & Management. In Plan & Design, instructors make applied progress on planning an online course. In Facilitation & Management, instructors explore techniques to connect with students, manage course activities, and facilitate discussion.

Online modules modeled effective online course design and facilitation practices. These modules were followed by in-person lunch sessions or synchronous webinars that engaged participants in further exploration of the online content, providing a blended learning experience (Laster et al., 2005). According to Cox (2004), a faculty learning community is "an active, collaborative, yearlong program with a curriculum about enhancing teaching and learning" (p. 8). While Cox (2004) recommends a cross-disciplinary group of 6 to 15 members, the learning community discussed in this chapter had cohorts of 20 to 80 members due to institutional demand. Participants were divided into smaller groups during online discussions, webinars, and in-person meetings.

Data Analysis

The constant comparative method was used to analyze the case study data (Lincoln & Guba, 1985). An inductive category coding approach was combined with

TABLE 7.1 Blended Faculty Learning Community Curriculum

Module	Plan & Design Course	Facilitation & Management Course
0	Orientation	Orientation
1	Course Design	Online Instructor Roles
2	Objectives & Alignment	Supporting eLearners
3	Assessment	Online Discussions
4	Instructional Materials	Communication & Participation
5	Learner Interaction	Course Management Strategies
6	Putting It All Together	Lessons Learned

Listed are the online modules that comprise the blended faculty learning community: "Plan & Design" and "Facilitation & Management."

simultaneous comparison of all units of meaning and then subsequently grouped. The units of meaning used for this analysis were the teaching presence, social presence, and cognitive presence elements of the CoI framework (Garrison, 2017). The coding scheme categorized qualitative data by instructors' perspectives and practices before participating in the learning community, at the end of the learning community, and after having taught their own online courses. The authors assured credibility through triangulation and peer debriefing (Lincoln & Guba, 1985).

Analysis

The primary focus of the research addressed in this chapter is an analysis of the impact of a blended faculty learning community on online course planning and teaching practices. The analytic approach categorized features of the learning community with the CoI framework to identify the methods that most impacted participants' perceptions of and practices for online education.

Teaching Presence

Teaching presence is the "design, facilitation, and direction of cognitive and social processes for the purpose of realizing personally meaningful and educationally worthwhile learning outcomes" (Anderson et al., 2001, p. 5). Teaching presence is manifested in everything the instructor does to guide, support, and shape a learner's experience.

The following analysis comprises the key teaching presence strategies used in the faculty learning community that were cited most often by the participants as having impacted their ideas of and practices for teaching online. Results are organized by the three roles of an educator explained in the CoI coding scheme (Table 7.2): Design and Organization, Direct Instruction, and Facilitating Discourse.

Design and Organization

Design and organization involves developing and implementing curriculum, assessments, content, course design, deadlines, and expectations (Garrison, 2017). Design and organization represents both the course curriculum and the synchronous activities in the learning community. The online courses in the learning community showcased Quality Matters standards; a variety of technologies; and research-based content, assessments, and activities. Instructional content included activity templates and techniques to chunk, align, and present course elements.

Participants were able to browse course examples provided by other online instructors and adapt those models for their own courses. One participant noted that "the content and tools provided were very practical and easy to use, they

120 Karen Skibba and Maria Widmer

TABLE 7.2 Community of Inquiry Coding Scheme

Elements and Categories	Select Indicators
Teaching Presence	
Design & Organization	Setting curriculum and methods
Facilitating Discourse	Shaping constructive exchange, prompting discussion
Direct Instruction	Resolving issues, presenting content, sharing knowledge, confirming understanding, providing feedback
Social Presence	
Personal/Affective	Expressing emotions, projecting personality
Open Communication	Communicating with risk-free expression
Group Cohesion	Encouraging collaboration
Cognitive Presence	
Triggering Event	Recognizing problems, sense of puzzlement
Exploration	Exchanging information, brainstorming
Integration	Connecting ideas, creating solutions
Resolution	Applying new ideas

Coding scheme of select indicators modified from Table 7.1 Community of Inquiry Categories and Indicators (Garrison, 2017, p. 28) with additional indicators from Garrison (2017).

enabled me to organize my course very thoughtfully, intentionally, and cohesively." The online courses showcased a variety of technologies. Participants described these tools and resources as a "pandora box of amazing tools to explore" and "a trove of additional resources to enhance my online experiences with teaching and learning." One participant added, "Every unit provided a take-home message that I could use/incorporate/or avoid in creating my own online course."

In the Plan & Design course, participants completed a detailed module plan to align learning objectives with assessments, activities, and content. In the Facilitation & Management course, participants completed an online journal to reflect on the strategies they would use to address common online teaching challenges. Both documents prompted participants to ask questions of facilitators. Participants indicated that the module plan and the journal acted as a "blueprint for my course." As one participant shared, these documents helped "wrap everything up from that course module, to write down any concerns, share some thoughts about those concerns, describe how I was going to handle whatever it was we were working on, and then get facilitator feedback."

Direct Instruction

Direct instruction methods include diagnosing misconceptions, sharing knowledge from diverse sources, confirming understanding through assessments and feedback, presenting content and questions, and focusing discussion on specific issues (Garrison, 2017). Both courses in the blended learning community provided a variety of perspectives from experienced online instructors, many who were past participants, through live presentations and video testimonials. Participants said a strength of the learning community was exposure to a variety of perspectives: "There was really a team approach" in the program. Multiple program facilitators and guest speakers offered reflections on their own personal experiences of online course design and instruction. "The knowledgeable instructional team for this course and the associated instructional designers are a valuable source of advice, support, and inspiration," noted one participant.

Program facilitators provided feedback on participants' module plans, journals, and assignments. As one participant summarized, the "meaningful and authentic feedback, ideas, and questions helped push my thinking on the activities." Many also said the feedback was influential to both their continued participation and to what they implemented in their own courses. "The thoughtful feedback on the assignments was extremely helpful, not just from a relevance point of view, but also from an accountability point of view." Other participants added that the facilitators encouraged them to "come up with more ideas" and offered different perspectives, suggestions, and approaches to consider: "They were willing to push us on our assumptions."

Facilitating Discourse

Educators need to draw in participants to share ideas, prompt discussion, set the climate for learning, and build understanding (Garrison, 2017). The learning community facilitators encouraged participants to share challenges and ideas during online discussions and synchronous sessions: "You couldn't really just sit in the corner and do nothing." This participant added that he realized the program encouraged idea sharing across colleagues: "We're all there to learn and to help each other. So, I think that was obvious from the way you guys presented it." He added that the program facilitators "were really good about helping answer questions in the small groups and just think about how you can make this work." During large-group discussions held in person or via synchronous video conference, "We would kind of sum up some of our ideas and concerns or thoughts, it was then nice to get, you know, again, a little bit more feedback then from the whole class."

Social Presence

Social presence represents participants' ability to develop relationships, engage in open communication, and identify with the community (Garrison, 2017). Social presence strategies build a respectful and purposeful environment in which it is safe to take risks, share ideas, and express concerns. The opportunity to build social presence was one of the primary reasons that the lead facilitator selected the learning community approach for this professional development program.

The following analysis comprises the key social presence strategies used in the faculty learning community that were cited most often by the participants as having impacted their perceptions of and practices for teaching online. The results are categorized by the three indicators of social presence included in the CoI coding scheme: Personal/Affective Communication, Open Communication, and Group Cohesion.

Personal/Affective Communication

Affective communication represents interpersonal expression that develops a safe, welcoming, trusting, and respectful environment. Affective communication can be established through humor, self-disclosure, graphic symbols, and other forms of emotive language (Garrison, 2017).

Participants most frequently cited the affective communication practices of the facilitators as having shaped their experience in the learning community. Social presence has been defined as using communication to project one's personality in a way that allows an individual to be perceived by others as a "real person" (Kreijns et al., 2014). Participants indicated that the "energy and enthusiasm" and "encouraging, supportive, and tolerant" approach of the "extremely friendly" facilitators led to a sense of real human presence in the course. One participant indicated that feeling there was a "real person there" made the course "more enjoyable and engaging."

As Garrison (2017) notes, the purpose of affective communication is to establish an inclusive and respectful learning environment that allows for critical inquiry and purposeful discourse. That is, establishing a welcoming environment that permits participants to be seen as real people serves a broader educational goal. The program director sent personalized messages to encourage participation and to remind participants of course deadlines. Participants said the encouraging, personalized reminders impacted their motivation and "created a sense of urgency" to complete the course work. After experiencing the facilitators' flexibility and understanding of issues that caused them to miss deadlines, participants considered how they could, as one instructor noted, find more "humane ways of dealing with deadlines." Another participant explained, "It's definitely made me want to be more present in my courses."

Open Communication

A learning community supports open communication when participants are able to freely express agreement and dissent in a respectful, trusting environment (Garrison, 2017). The learning community offered opportunities for congregation and free talk among participants in order to support the development of collegial relationships, in particular through in-person sessions and the "Online Café" and "Share Resources" discussion forums. Every face-to-face meeting began with a shared meal and 15 minutes for informal conversation. The webinars also provided opportunities for informal conversations before and after each session.

Asynchronous and synchronous discussions made frequent use of small-group breakouts. Participants regularly cited these small groups as configurations that, for many, allowed for more comfortable open communication than did the whole-group discussions: "It was nice to be able to . . . in the small groups feel a little bit more comfortable sharing ideas, getting some feedback." Participants also spoke to their colleagues' respectful, supportive, and critical engagement with the group conversations: "There wasn't really any judgement, and there was a lot of support there."

Group Cohesion

Defined as learners' sense of identification with the community of inquiry, group cohesion supports purposeful discourse. Garrison (2017) cites the use of *we* and *our* as verbal markers of participants' sense of group cohesion. Participants regularly used the words *community*, *collegial[ity]*, and *camaraderie* in speaking about their experience in the group.

During the synchronous face-to-face and webinar sessions, participants were intentionally placed with departmental or disciplinary colleagues in an effort to build on existing local connections. Lunch sessions in particular supported the development of community and group affiliation. Participants cited these opportunities for informal dialogue as "normal people having a normal conversation." They spoke also to the "social value of breaking bread together" and that the communal meal "provides a warm and inviting atmosphere for sharing and discussion."

Participants found value in working with others who faced similar challenges and opportunities in their teaching practices. Indeed, many participants spoke about the importance of talking with others "on similar journeys," a common experience that led one respondent to "sense that I am not alone on campus." Participants shared that "teaching is a solitary activity" that can "at times feel like a lonely enterprise." Participants viewed their colleagues in the program as a "wider support system" that was newly available to them.

Cognitive Presence

Cognitive presence is "the extent to which learners are able to construct and confirm meaning through sustained reflection and discourse" (Garrison et al., 2001, p. 11). The primary focus of cognitive presence is to develop a higher-order thinking process (i.e., critical thinking or practical inquiry) that integrates existing learning with new learning through reflection, discussion, and feedback. The

124 Karen Skibba and Maria Widmer

following analysis of the learning community is organized by the four processes of cognitive presence: Triggering Event, Exploration, Integration, and Resolution.

Triggering Event

The first phase of Cognitive Presence is the triggering event, or the recognition of a problem or issue (Garrison, 2017). Participants came to the learning community with a number of concerns about teaching online that they were hoping to resolve. Most were new to teaching online ("I had no earthly idea on how to teach online"), though others had prior online teaching experience. Those who had some online teaching experience said they were "thrown into it" without any training. One participant who had previously taught online said, "I was a little sheepish that I had been teaching for so long without really getting any training or resources about how to do it well." These concerns led participants to register for the learning community:

> If I was going to develop this course online, I wanted to get the best information about how to do that. And certainly the [blended faculty learning community] is without a doubt the best resource at [the university], as to how to develop an online course.

Both courses solicited participants' challenges and concerns about teaching online in introductory and topical discussion forums, during meetings, and through collaborative activities. Many openly shared that they came to the community with skepticism, apprehension, reluctance, and a negative perception of online teaching and learning. One participant shared:

> I had no idea how an online class worked or how I could structure it successfully to be a good learning experience for the students. Frankly, I'm not sure why I agreed to develop a class online in the first place.

Many others had heard "horror" stories of online courses that were "hated by students" and others that were "watered down" and "not as rigorous." Participants also shared concerns about their ability as online instructors to address academic misconduct, engage students, provide feedback, personalize instruction, build rapport, and manage their time—especially in courses with 100 to 1,000 students. The conversations were open, honest, and sometimes emotional. This was possible because, as noted in Social Presence, the facilitators established a "safe environment" to share questions and concerns.

Exploration

The exploration phase includes information exchange, suggestions for consideration, and brainstorming in search of relevant resources and ideas (Garrison, 2017).

The learning community activities engaged participants in individual reflection and collaboration. As one participant explained, the facilitators "continuously challenged participants to reevaluate what students want and need." Participants also collaborated on group discussions to collectively identify solutions to shared challenges such as assessment, academic honesty, managing course workload, and building online learning communities. One participant said that they found the collaboration "so helpful to hear how other people were implementing the content and troubleshooting issues."

The reflective activities and discussions were instrumental to transforming participants' ideas of and practices for teaching online. One participant summarized, "Taking the course has given me time to pause and reflect on my current teaching practices and to be inspired to make use of some new ideas." In-person and online synchronous meetings provided additional opportunities to reflect on these resources and further explore solutions by "bounc[ing] different ideas" off each other and guest speakers. Through these exchanges, one participant said: "Now I have five or six different solutions versus just maybe the one or two I was thinking about."

Integration

The integration phase involves connecting ideas and creating solutions as a "process of constructing a meaningful solution or explanation" (Garrison, 2017, p. 66). This process took place throughout many of the activities detailed earlier. In particular, participants worked toward integration through a series of "application activities." These activities allowed participants to create important documents and activities for use directly in their own courses. They also gave an opportunity to experiment with a variety of collaboration technologies from the perspective of an online student. Building their course through participation in the program proved impactful: "There is something to be said about immediacy here. I can go from reading about a new idea or activity to try to implement it right away."

Resolution

The final phase, resolution, takes place when learners "critically assesses the viability of the proposed solution through direct or vicarious application" (Garrison, 2017, p. 66). Participants at the end of the learning community had a choice of a final project designed to support continued progress on their course. Most completed a course map that provided a "big picture" of the course design and prompted instructors to "think critically about transforming" their courses. Others created video content that "forced" instructors to use technology, with the videos ultimately used directly in their courses. A final option was to create a template that "plotted out" the full content for one course module. Many participants modified and improved their final projects before using them directly in their own courses. One participant reflected on the impact of the final project: "I've completely reconceived my course, how I'm going to structure, what my objectives will be. All improvements for the better, which wouldn't have occurred to me without [the learning community]."

At the end of both courses, a final "Lessons Learned" discussion allowed participants to share the ways in which their opinions about online teaching had changed and the strategies they planned to apply in their own courses. This concluding discussion proved an important way for participants to reflect on what they had learned and experienced. At the end of the learning community, participants shared more positive perspectives about online teaching, noting how they felt "prepared," "confident," "better equipped," "enthusiastic," "totally ready to move the course forward," "excited by the endless opportunities," and with "a renewed enthusiasm and enjoyment for teaching."

Others shared how their perception of teaching online had evolved significantly, "drastically changed," and "dispelled a lot of the myths." Many said their "bias against online learning is gone." One participant noted that prior to enrolling, "I really didn't feel that an online course could offer a learning experience comparable to a face-to-face class. I now feel like the resources provided and the ideas discussed through the two courses this year have changed my mind."

Discussion of Research Questions

This approach to the faculty learning community format was inspired by Skibba's (2012) research, which found it was important for instructors to take responsibility for their own learning, immediately apply what they learn, and use self-assessments and reflection. The blended learning community incorporated these adult learning principles in purposeful alignment with the CoI presences.

Interviews and surveys conducted after participants had completed the learning community and taught their own online courses revealed the program's lasting impact on participants' perceptions of and practices for online education. Survey results include the following: 97% (N = 290) reported gaining practical knowledge to apply to their own courses, and 98% (N = 211) of those who taught online said participating in the program improved the quality of their online course.

Many of the strategies shared in the CoI analysis were incorporated directly into the participants' online courses. Participants proudly shared their positive student ratings and credited the learning community because they "knew what to do and knew how to do it." As one participant shared, "I was prepared and ready to transition my face-to-face course online, all while maintaining high quality learning and collaboration."

Participants also spoke more broadly to the program's impact on their perceptions of online education, primarily noting a new understanding that online education can be as successful as a face-to-face course, given the use of effective strategies: "Online learning works and is as effective. . . . [Y]ou can feel comfortable as an instructor that nets the same kind of benefit to your students that you could give them through a face-to-face class."

This study adds to the faculty development and CoI literature through a rich qualitative analysis using the powerful words of instructors reflecting on the impact of a large, blended faculty learning community. The following summary of key findings answers the two research questions: Which methods utilized in a blended faculty learning community, categorized by the presences of the community of inquiry framework, had the most impact on participants' perceptions and practices of online course design and teaching? Why were these methods impactful?

Student Experience: Modeling of Community of Inquiry Presences

This case study analysis supports the finding that all three CoI presences—social presence, teaching presence, and cognitive presence—contributed to a meaningful learning experience through which instructors reconsidered their perceptions and practices of online education. Vaughan and Garrison's (2016) analysis of the face-to-face and online sessions of a comparable faculty learning community also concluded that "the key to creating a cohesive, purposeful and worthwhile community of inquiry is the integration of social, teaching and cognitive presence" (p. 150).

The interaction of all three presences contributed to the holistic student learning experience. It was this meta-experience of being a student that most impacted participants' perceptions of and practices for online education. Most participants indicated that this was the first time they had experienced being an online student and it was "humbling and eye-opening." One participant summarized, "Being an online student was essential to our collective learning and our absorption of the relevance of this new material." The student experience encouraged instructors, as one said, "to want to make it a more positive and engaging experience with different ways to learn (webinars, video lectures, group work etc.)." In post-course surveys, 97% of respondents (N = 293) said that the experience of being an online student was important to what they learned about online teaching and student learning.

Being situated as online students allowed participants to learn the challenges of and strategies for designing, teaching, and improving student learning in an online course. This direct experience included the "trauma" and "frustrations" of keeping up with activities and missing deadlines. As one participant noted, "I kept finding myself getting behind—I guess I was being a 'true' student:-)." Participants also experienced what it was like not to get responses in discussion forums. One noted, "When I fell to the depths of despair" when no one was

128 Karen Skibba and Maria Widmer

contributing to the group discussion forum, "[the main facilitator] sent me emails of encouragement."

Turning in assignments late and contacting the instructor for needed extensions, participants found their own behaviors aligned with those of their students. This led participants to gain more "empathy" and "compassion" through a better understanding of online students' personal situations, concerns, and fears—particularly salient during the COVID-19 pandemic. They learned firsthand what it meant to design and teach a humane and learner-centered online course.

Blended Experience: Multimodal Interaction and Reflection

The blended or meta-experience, in which participants engaged first in online modules followed by face-to-face or webinar sessions, also proved impactful. Synchronous meetings brought together program facilitators and participants for deeper discussions and collaboration on the topics addressed in the online materials. The learning community created an open, trusting environment in which instructors could share questions, challenges, ideas, and aspirations. One participant summarized that the facilitators in both the online courses and synchronous meetings "did a lot of work to ensure that we felt like members of a community."

The findings in this case study align with Vaughan and Garrison's (2016) conclusion that a blended faculty learning community approach creates "a flexible and accessible environment for faculty to engage in sustained critical reflection and discourse" (p. 150). Research participants said that offering a choice of in-person or webinar meetings provided needed flexibility for their schedules. Live sessions allowed participants to experience webinars from the student perspective and created variety in engaging with course information. The face-to-face and webinar sessions were often described as being "more fun." The webinars helped instructors "with a real sense of how I can utilize webinars in my own online and blended courses."

Direct experience in online courses allowed instructors to be "immersed and spend some time ruminating on the content." At the live meetings, with guidance from facilitators, participants would reflect "more deeply" about the student experience, the online instructional content, and their plans to apply strategies in their own courses. The meetings also created a structure of accountability that motivated participants to review the online content in order to be prepared to discuss it with their peers: "With everybody else coming prepared, I felt that level of responsibility to do the same. Even if I was busy, I would review the material before I came to face to face, or before the webinar."

This blend of immersion in an online course and meta-reflection during webinars and face-to-face meetings impacted participants' ideas of and practices for teaching online. One participant summarized: "Without this constant multimodal interaction with colleagues, I'm not sure that I would have learned as much or paid as close attention to the lessons/strategies of [the program]."

Conclusion

The holistic learning experience that emerges from the interaction of teaching, social, and cognitive presence supports instructors in transforming their perceptions and practices—not only for online and blended courses, but for all their courses. This was evidenced by the positive student evaluations that participants shared.

This impact was most immediately salient in March 2020, when instruction was quickly moved to a remote format due to the COVID-19 pandemic. Participants reported that their experience in the blended learning community allowed for a more rapid and effective transition to remote teaching. Now campus experts in online education, participants were called on to support their colleagues with online teaching during the pandemic and continue to lead ongoing online initiatives.

A significant investment of time and support is necessary for instructors to engage in meaningful collaboration, reflection, and applied practice through a faculty learning community. These experiences result in an enduring transformation of teaching that is critical to student success in online education. Further research into applications of the CoI framework in professional development would provide faculty developers with additional evidence-based strategies to successfully guide instructors through this transformation.

Contributors

Thanks to Karin Spader for organizing the data and to Norm Vaughan for reviewing the interview guide.

References

Anderson, T., Rourke, L., Garrison, D. R., & Archer, W. (2001). Journal of asynchronous learning networks. *Journal of Asynchronous Learning Networks, 5*(2), 1–17.

Cox, M. D. (2004). Introduction to faculty learning communities. In M. D. Cox & L. Richlin (Eds.), *New directions for teaching and learning* (Vol. 97, pp. 5–23). Wiley.

Garrett, R., Legon, R., & Fredericksen, E. E. (2020). CHLOE 4: Navigating the mainstream, the changing landscape of online education. *Quality Matters*. http://qualitymatters.org/qa-resources/resource-center/articles-resources/CHLOE-project

Garrison, D. R. (2017). *E-learning in the 21st century: A community of inquiry framework for research and practice* (3rd ed.). Routledge, Taylor and Francis.

Garrison, D. R., Anderson, T., & Archer, W. (2001). Critical thinking, cognitive presence, and computer conferencing in distance education. *American Journal of Distance Education, 15*(1), 7–23.

Kreijns, K., Van Acker, F., & Vermeulen, M. (2014). Community of inquiry: Social presence revisited. *E-Learning and Digital Media, 11*(01). Available at: https://doi.org/10.2304/elea.2014.11.1.5

Laster, S., Otte, G., Picciano, A. G., & Sorg, S. (2005, April 18). *Redefining blended learning* [Conference session]. 2005 Sloan-C Workshop on Blended Learning.

Lincoln, Y. S., & Guba, E. G. (1985). *Naturalistic inquiry.* Sage.

Merriam, S. B. (1998). *Qualitative research and case study applications in education.* Jossey-Bass.

Skibba, K. (2012). Adult learning influence on faculty learning cycle: Individual and shared reflections while learning to teach online lead to pedagogical transformations. In J. Keengwe & L. Kyei-Blankson (Eds.), *Virtual mentoring for teachers: Online professional development practices* (pp. 263–291). IGI Global.

Vaughan, N., & Garrison, R. (2016). A blended faculty community of inquiry: Linking leadership, course redesign, and evaluation. *Canadian Journal of University Continuing Education, 32*(2), 67–92.

Wicks, D. A., Craft, B. B., Mason, G. N., Gritter, K., & Bolding, K. (2015). An investigation into the community of inquiry in blended classrooms by a faculty learning community. *Internet and Higher Education, 25*(1), 53–62.

8
IMPACT ANALYSIS OF TEN YEARS OF BLENDED LEARNING

Concepcion B. Godev and Jaesoon An

Due to the coronavirus pandemic, institutions of higher education were forced to move swiftly from face-to-face instruction to some form of technology-mediated instruction in order to complete the second half, or the last third, of the Spring 2020 semester (Toquero, 2020; Crawford et al., 2020). As in many parts of the world, administrators, faculty, and students throughout the United States had little time to do an orderly transition to remote instruction. Colleges and universities have met this challenge with various degrees of success, depending on the level of existing instructional technology they may have had integrated in their teaching and learning management of face-to-face courses.

This research[1] examined how ten years of blended learning initiatives shaped the transformation of teaching and learning at UNC Charlotte,[2] specifically in terms of impact on instructional modes and the interaction of academic units with those supporting blended learning. We will also reflect on how the implementation of blended instruction over the last ten years may have provided the needed level of readiness for the quick transitioning to online teaching motivated by pandemic social distancing policies enacted in the spring of 2020.

In this chapter, the terms *blended teaching* and *blended learning*, as adopted at UNC Charlotte, refer to the delivery mode of instruction that combines face-to-face instructional time with 25% to 75% of online instructional time,[3] with online content presented through a learning management system (LMS). The source of the content within the LMS may include a wide range of instructional tools such as an e-textbook, digitized documents from the campus library, open-access content, surveys, quizzes, discussion forums, and other materials authored by instructors.

In what follows, we will discuss how our first institutionally led experimentation with blended teaching began, ushering in a sustained campus-wide dialogue

DOI: 10.4324/9781003037736-11

132 Concepcion B. Godev and Jaesoon An

about teaching that continues to date. This dialogue has further promoted scholarship of teaching and learning as faculty examined teaching critically in order to be effective in the blended learning environment.

Gradual Implementation of Blended Teaching

The institutional plans of the last 15 years (UNC Charlotte, 2015, 2017) have given prominence to the goal of continuing to serve the growing demand for higher education. The university's ability to realize this goal has depended on developing the infrastructure and teaching culture that can sustain both blended and online teaching. When the leadership took the first step to examine why blended teaching should be implemented and saw its potential for the teaching enterprise, events were set in motion to support the migration to blended teaching.

The systematic implementation of blended teaching began with the question of how blended instruction could extend the capacity of the university to serve more students in the near future. The quickly evolving instructional technology (Siemens et al., 2015) offered tangible possibilities in 2008 for the implementation of some form of virtual instruction. This was considered a promising venue that could aid in accommodating the anticipated enrollment growth of the university. The Center for Teaching and Learning (CTL) led the effort of exploring how that question could be answered by different departments and what department could best take the first step by participating in a pilot program that would support multi-section course redesign. This effort led to the establishment of a program called Large Course Redesign (An, 2014). Indeed, implementing blended teaching required overhauling how students learned and how they were taught. The term *large course redesign* was adopted in keeping with the National Center for Academic Transformation (NCAT) nomenclature to designate large-enrollment courses (Graves & Twigg, 2006; Rosenthal & Weitz, 2012). The cautious approach that the administration took in 2008 in order to implement blended teaching and bring it to the level at which it is today mirrors the careful type of planning that Picciano (2015) would recommend a few years later, thus averting the obstacles that usually emerge when transformational initiatives are implemented too quickly.

Piloting the Redesign of a Large Course

The first phase of the implementation of blended learning on campus was focused on large-enrollment, primarily freshman courses. These courses were of interest to the redesign program because they presented opportunities for different ways to manage the classroom space more efficiently. For the first redesigned pilot course on campus, CTL selected the two-semester course sequence of first-year Spanish.[4] The pilot project, whose main goal was to replace 50% of the in-class time with online assignments, was structured according to the guidelines of the National Center for Academic Transformation (NCAT)[5] (1999–2018c). NCAT provided opportunities to review the pilot project at different stages by sponsoring attendance to NCAT's institutes and annual conference as part of the university's participation in the NCAT's Colleagues Committed to Redesign program (National Center for Academic Transformation, 1999–2018b). NCAT large-course redesign guidelines kept the pilot process anchored in the scholarship of teaching and learning (SoTL). Elements that later were integrated into the blended teaching implementation in first-year Spanish were grounded in pilot project results, comparing redesigned first-year Spanish courses to those previously taught face to face. The focus on evidence-based decisions, influencing the final implementation of the blended delivery of first-year Spanish, established a model to foster the scholarship of teaching and learning across disciplines typically not engaged in this type of research.

At the time of the pilot, UNC Charlotte was similar to many other institutions of higher education, where SoTL was seldom a component of the research agenda of faculty outside the college of education. Some years later, Moskal (2016) remarked that SoTL continued to have a peripheral role in disciplines other than education and cautioned colleagues in those disciplines to ascertain if this type of research was valued for purposes of professional advancement. One factor that contributed to the success of the first large-course redesign pilot was that faculty were interested in the research process associated with it. One of the outcomes of this interest was the analysis of data that provided useful insight into how blended teaching affected the way instructors were managing their time (Godev, 2014). The data derived from this analysis proved useful for the administration to understand matters of workload and compensation in the context of first-year language courses and for other academic units that gradually would start experimenting with blended learning in their own course redesign projects.

Beyond the First Large-Course Redesign Pilot

As departments explored the potential advantages of redesigning large courses, they were able to recognize promising pedagogical benefits that had been eclipsed by the initial thrust of maximizing classroom space efficiencies. One of the major drivers for some departments to participate in large-course redesign was to explore how students could interact with the subject matter in ways that were not possible in a traditional lecture-hall setting (McAlpin & An, 2012). The anticipated outcome of making improvements in the pedagogy of the course was that students would engage more deeply with the subject matter, which could also have a positive effect on retaining students. The search for ways to improve learning led the way to incorporating instructional technology at a time of rapid developments in the publishing industry. These developments included online interactive instructional materials that could help instructors keep students on task and provide instructors with time-saving, interactive, machine-graded activities with automated feedback. In 2009, the e-textbook industry had just reached the point of being able to offer interactive e-textbooks and e-workbooks in a large variety of subjects (Butler, 2009). The possibilities for directed independent learning offered by the new generation of interactive materials were further enhanced by learning management systems (LMS) that seamlessly integrated communication tools, assignment and quizzing tools, and learning objects chosen by instructors, which were essential elements to the implementation of blended learning. The ease of use of Moodle, which was adopted in 2008 and used until it was replaced by Canvas in 2016, encouraged faculty to integrate it into their teaching. Today more than 87% of the faculty use Canvas,[6] either to enhance face-to-face courses or to teach blended or online courses.

In the years that followed the first large-course redesign pilot, blended learning continued to foster experimenting with digital instructional materials and with redefining the roles of instructors and students in the teaching and learning enterprise (UNC Charlotte, n.d.c). That experimentation has led to a steady increase in the number of blended (see Tables 8.1 and 8.2, and Figures 8.1 and 8.2) and online courses.

An interesting trend that can be observed is the increase in online courses, which is outpacing the number of blended courses both in the summer and in regular semesters. This outcome is somewhat unexpected as one would have imagined that the move to teaching online would have first gone through a more extensive blended learning phase. A tentative explanation is, on the one hand, that the university's Office of Distance Education had been providing generous

TABLE 8.1 Courses Offered in Fall and Spring Semesters by Instructional Type

Year	Blended		Online		Face to Face	
	%	N	%	N	%	N*
2009–10	0.00%	0	2.90%	243	97.10%	8,140
2010–11	0.50%	43	3.12%	267	96.38%	8,258
2011–12	1.27%	113	3.44%	306	95.29%	8,486
2012–13	2.50%	229	4.29%	393	93.21%	8,539
2013–14	2.79%	263	5.51%	520	91.70%	8,651
2014–15	3.17%	311	5.18%	509	91.65%	9,000
2015–16	3.24%	322	5.70%	566	91.06%	9,046
2016–17	4.33%	444	6.39%	655	89.27%	9,147
2017–18	5.05%	533	7.25%	765	87.69%	9,247
2018–19	5.13%	545	7.62%	810	87.26%	9,278
2019–20	5.37%	553	9.53%	981	85.09%	8,756

* The number of face-to-face courses includes a small number of interactive television (iTV) courses. Teaching in iTV courses and face-to-face courses is very similar. On average, five iTV courses per academic year were offered in 2009 through 2020.

Ten Years of Blended Learning 135

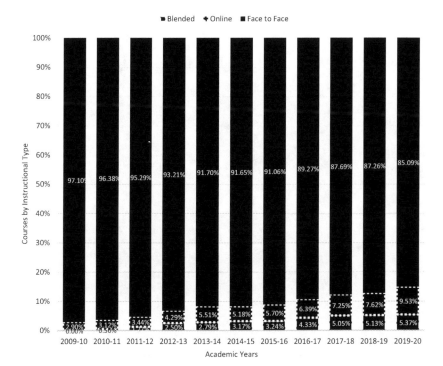

FIGURE 8.1 Courses Offered in Fall and Spring Semesters by Instructional Type

TABLE 8.2 Courses Offered in Summer Semesters by Instructional Type

Year	Blended %	N	Online %	N	Face to Face %	N
2010	0.00%	0	11.57%	141	88.43%	1,078
2011	0.73%	9	12.84%	158	86.43%	1,064
2012	3.32%	42	16.44%	208	80.24%	1,015
2013	4.49%	53	18.39%	217	77.12%	910
2014	4.62%	56	23.86%	289	71.51%	866
2015	5.17%	66	26.88%	343	67.95%	867
2016	8.50%	109	30.63%	393	60.87%	781
2017	6.95%	95	34.33%	469	58.71%	802
2018	7.06%	105	37.26%	554	55.68%	828
2019	6.44%	101	40.41%	634	53.15%	834*

* The number of face-to-face courses in Summer 2019 includes four interactive television (iTV) courses. Teaching in iTV courses and face-to-face courses is very similar.

136 Concepcion B. Godev and Jaesoon An

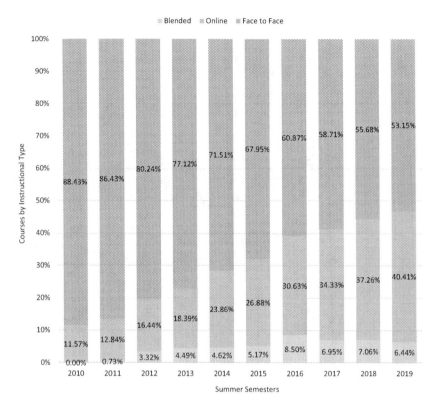

FIGURE 8.2 Courses Offered in Summer Semesters by Instructional Type

support—namely, grants and training—to faculty and departments that were interested in developing online courses and degrees, even before the first institutionally led experimentation with blended teaching began in 2009; on the other hand, the second author of this chapter has observed a recurrent pattern of faculty moving directly, if through a slow course development process, from face-to-face to online teaching because of the flexibility afforded by being connected to the students in virtual space. LMS self-efficacy, defined by Zheng et al. (2018) as the level of confidence users have to integrate LMS functionalities into their teaching, may be another factor that explains online teaching outpacing blended teaching. Even in face-to-face courses, instructional technology is used extensively as a course enhancer; as we indicated earlier, more than 87% of the faculty use Canvas to handle some element or elements of their teaching (UNC Charlotte, 2016). Instructors who may have enhanced their courses over time using LMS tools may have found it unnecessary to undergo a blended teaching phase before moving to online teaching.

Impact of Ten Years of Blended Learning

According to Halverson et al. (2012), Garrison and Kanuka (2004) was the most cited blended learning research article from 2000 to 2011. This work was highly consulted because it addressed issues related to the infrastructure needed to support blended learning at a time when many universities were exploring that topic (Halverson et al., 2014). In reviewing this highly cited work, we were able to recognize the authors' prophetic vision about where blended learning was headed, at a transformative moment when many institutions of higher education, UNC Charlotte among them, were far from adopting blended teaching as a mainstream form of instruction. Their prescient vision articulated a number of transformations that universities would necessarily be bound to undergo in order to harness the potential of blended learning for the benefit of higher education's mission of educating lifelong learners in the era of information technology. Students would have to conceive anew their role as students in a more self-directed type of learning in a more virtual space. Similarly, instructors would have to be more intentional about how to incorporate more student-centered techniques as well as new ways of assessing learning outcomes. The authors also pointed out that, in the process of implementing blended learning, both students and faculty would need institutional support to learn and teach, respectively, in new ways.

As predicted by Garrison and Kanuka (2004), the efforts to implement blended learning in large courses at UNC Charlotte led to gradually increasing discussions about teaching in general, as well as teaching in virtual environments in particular. In trying to understand how instructional technology could enhance and modify prior teaching methods, faculty had to examine every element in the courses that they wanted to redesign, from learning objectives to assessment and time on task. In this regard, we saw the changing role of teachers unfold in the way that Badley and Habeshaw (1991) had explained when the internet as an instructional resource had just begun to make its entrance into higher education. Instructors had to expand the scope of what they considered their prime responsibility: namely, being experts in their field of research. In part organically and in part intentionally, instructors had to incorporate teaching development into their professional plans and goals in order to be more effective teachers in emerging new environments. Teachers who were developing and teaching blended courses realized that being knowledgeable about pedagogy was central to succeeding in the task of redesigning a course and teaching in blended environments. Additionally, instructors had to adapt to the fast-paced change of technologies underpinning instructional virtual environments, the swift adaptation being the result of the frequent upgrading of learning management systems (LMS) and periodical migrations to new LMS altogether. Since 2002, when UNC Charlotte adopted its first enterprise-wide LMS, instructors have had to learn their way around five different LMS. The latest change to a new LMS occurred in 2016 (UNC

138 Concepcion B. Godev and Jaesoon An

Charlotte, 2016). Furthermore, faculty need to learn new functionalities when LMS upgrades occur, typically once a year.

The Center for Teaching and Learning as Catalyzer of Teaching Innovation

The gradual transformation of the teaching landscape has occurred under the leadership of the Center for Teaching Learning (CTL). Through the Large-Course Redesign program and subsequent faculty development initiatives relevant to blended learning, this unit has architected cross-unit collaboration that enables the administration's vision of increased access to higher education for diverse prospective students. Faculty interest in experimenting with virtual instruction has evolved from reluctance a decade ago to substantial engagement in blended and online teaching today. Next, we describe the CTL initiatives and how faculty mentoring their peers is interwoven into these initiatives in order to stimulate reflective dialogue on teaching and learning in general and on blended and online environments in particular.

The Role of Scholarship of Teaching and Learning (SoTL) Grants

The framework underpinning the Large-Course Redesign (LCR) program was informed by the principles that define the scholarship of teaching and learning. While redesigning the course format, participating faculty members collected data on student grades and perceptions to assess changes from their prior instructional methods. The faculty participating in the initial round of projects served as LCR redesign scholars to help the next round of participants with the course redesign and SoTL. The research feedback loop was set in motion as LCR projects provided impetus for the SoTL program, which started in 2009 and, in turn, informed research-based course design revisions or adjustments. As shown in the list of SoTL projects funded (UNC Charlotte, n.d.d), Spanish and chemistry LCR projects were showcased in the inaugural year. Some of these SoTL-funded projects have led to publications by faculty who carried them out (Heafner & Plaisance, 2013; Godev, 2014; Cao & Grabchak, 2019).

In addition to the LCR and SoTL programs, the Center for Teaching and Learning has led other faculty development initiatives to foster and guide the design of blended courses, such as Active Learning Academy and Quality Matters. These initiatives, which are described next, have helped sustain blended and online teaching at UNC Charlotte.

Active Learning Academy and Active Classrooms

As faculty began to recognize the pedagogical benefits of blended learning, interest in integrating active learning strategies emerged. Several instructors recognized the pedagogical potential of flipped classrooms (O'Flaherty & Phillips, 2015), in which students work through online course content individually first and then participate in the on-campus classroom activities for deeper and active learning. To enable effective exploration and adoption of flipped and active learning pedagogies, CTL launched the Active Learning Academy (UNC Charlotte, n.d.a), a program that facilitated regular meetings of groups of faculty to discuss and exchange ideas on diverse active learning strategies such as collaborative learning, service learning, and project-based learning. Active learning leaders were recruited to lead the academy activities. At the same time, academic affairs funded the construction of two state-of-the-art, technology-enhanced, active-learning classrooms in the building where the CTL office was located. CTL supported the effective utilization of active-learning classrooms as well as class scheduling in conjunction with the Active Learning Academy in this pilot phase. Meanwhile, several more active-learning classrooms were built throughout the campus, and finally, their scheduling was integrated into the regular classroom scheduling system. Keith-Le and Morgan (2020) provide a detailed account of the significant contribution made by the Active Learning Academy program, which remains active to date, to the development of faculty as blended, online, and face-to-face instructors.

Distance Education and Quality Matters Course Development (QMCD)

While initiatives like LCR, SoTL, and Active Learning Academy provided faculty development opportunities for the university's general faculty community, the Office of Distance Education (DE) had a strategic plan for blended and online courses to increase the offering of DE programs. The DE office had funding available for the "faculty developers" of online or blended courses but did not house any instructional designers. At the beginning of the CTL and DE collaboration, the second author of this chapter was the only instructional designer at CTL. Led by the instructional designer, CTL staff members started offering two consultations per course being redesigned. A wave of academic program requests for faculty development support made it apparent that the university needed course design quality standards. Quality Matters (QM)[7] training and course design review programs were then made available to faculty, and two instructional designers and a QM specialist were hired to meet the increasing demand for course development support. With the new CTL team in place plus the QM support for faculty developers, CTL was able to launch the Quality Matters Course Development (QMCD) program. Cohorts of online or blended course faculty were supported through a semester-long timeline and the QMCD phases. Throughout the cohort timeframe, faculty developers had regular individual consultations with their assigned instructional designer, who would guide them on how to use different templates and rubrics to build the entire course on

140 Concepcion B. Godev and Jaesoon An

Canvas (UNC Charlotte, n.d.e). Once the faculty cohorts completed the QMCD program, they moved on to the QM internal review process, where they were assigned to QM faculty fellows, who had the QM peer reviewer certification, to review their courses and determine if they met the QM standards. Faculty developers received another round of feedback on the course design before submitting the course to an external course review administered by the QM organization.

Beyond the Faculty Development Initiatives

Both LCR and QMCD programs were project-based course design initiatives in which faculty cohorts produced and taught blended or online courses, incorporating these skills into their professional experience. Support teams consisted of instructional designers and technologists, video producers, DE program managers, and librarians. This interdepartmental project approach resulted in strengthened collaboration among different support units. This collaboration resulted in the formation of the Teaching and Learning Connection, which comprises the Center for Teaching and Learning (CTL), the Office of Distance Education (DE), Audiovisual Integration and Support for Learning Environments (AISLE), and continuing education (CE).

Conclusion

Looking at the evolution of the use of instructional technology at UNC Charlotte, the findings described by Sorcinelli et al. (2006) in "Faculty Development in the Age of the Network" have been confirmed. Faculty and students adapted their way of teaching and learning as instructional technology tools were made available and were perceived as teaching assets. In this change, the Center for Teaching and Learning became a hub for dialogue about implementation of instructional technologies that serve the field-specific teaching and learning needs of the myriad academic units on campus. The teaching initiatives that CTL has launched have laid the foundation for sustained inquiry about blended learning and teaching in general. At the same time, while CTL has been the hub for dialogue and provided support, both instructional and technical, it has also been intentional in having faculty drive that dialogue and support peers. CTL's contribution to the transformation of teaching has catalyzed a change in how faculty conceptualize their role; this is tangible evidence that administrators have made it a priority to support faculty development in the area of teaching.

How students fare in any teaching environment depends substantially on how faculty are faring in their approach to teaching, regardless of the modality. It also depends on the subject matter, individual preferences, and prior experience (Park, 2018). The very nature of the growth pace of blended and online learning, conservative but yet steady, is what has made blended and online learning sustainable at UNC Charlotte and, in our estimation, what will continue to guarantee its future direction.

The campus was increasing the implementation of both blended and online teaching before the coronavirus pandemic forced university employees and students to work remotely beginning mid-March 2020. At that point, most courses had completed two-thirds of the semester. Courses, regardless of their initial modality, were then taught in a fully online environment, with professors and students having just one week to make it happen. Had this happened in 2009, when the first blended course was being piloted, the university would likely not have been able to continue business operations due to lack of instructional technology and faculty, student, and institutional readiness. Ekmekci and Bergstrand (2010) described such a situation in their study on the business continuity readiness of 20 universities if faced with a disruptive event.

The disruption caused by the coronavirus pandemic has tested campus readiness to continue business operations both at the administrative and teaching level. UNC Charlotte's commitment to building a robust infrastructure has paid off.

The newly minted Teaching and Learning Connections unit, with the assistance of faculty mentors (UNC Charlotte, n.d.b), was able to coordinate the training and support for the Spring 2020 online migration and Summer 2020 exclusive online delivery and prepare faculty for blended or online instruction in Fall 2020, with the contingency of completing the semester entirely online if the pandemic worsens. We anticipate that blended and online learning will continue to be supported as the university returns to post-COVID-19 instruction.

Notes

1. The authors would like to thank Susan Miller, from the office of institutional research at UNC Charlotte, for her assistance with the data supplied in this chapter, and the Center for Teaching and Learning at UNC Charlotte for making public documents that have assisted our research.
2. The University of North Carolina at Charlotte is a state university that enrolls some 24,000 undergraduate students and some 5,500 graduate students (UNC Charlotte, n.d.f). It employs some 1,555 faculty; 69% of the faculty are full-time employees (College Factual, n.d.).
3. The percentage of online instructional time in blended courses may usually be determined by the faculty teaching a course, if the course is a single-section course, or by the department if the course is a multi-section course.
4. Pyke (2010) includes a description of the piloted redesign for first-year Spanish.
5. NCAT (1999–2018c) describes six models for large-course redesign; the replacement model is among the most frequently used models. For a brief history of NCAT, the reader may consult NCAT (1999–2018a).
6. The estimate of LMS use by 87% of the faculty is conservative. This is the estimated use documented in UNC Charlotte (2016).
7. Quality Matters is a set of rubrics and standards whose purpose is to guide online course developers through the course design process according to best practices that have been empirically proven to work (Quality Matters, n.d.).

References

An, J. (2014). Large course redesign at UNC Charlotte. *KAERA Research Forum*, *1*(2), 17–23. www.k-aera.org/wp-content/uploads/2014/09/KAERA-Research-Forum_Vol_1_No_2.pdf

Badley, G., & Habeshaw, T. (1991). The changing role of the teacher in higher education. *Journal of In-Service Education*, *17*(3), 212–218.

Butler, D. (2009). Technology: The textbook of the future. *Nature*, *458*(7238), 568–570. https://doi.org/10.1038/458568a

Cao, L., & Grabchak, M. (2019, May). Interactive preparatory work in a flipped programming course. In *Proceedings of the ACM Conference on Global Computing Education* (pp. 229–235). ACM.

College Factual (n.d.). *The University of North Carolina at Charlotte student to faculty ratio & faculty composition*. Retrieved June 23, 2020, from www.collegefactual.com/colleges/university-of-north-carolina-at-charlotte/academic-life/faculty-composition/

Crawford, J., Butler-Henderson, K., Rudolph, J., & Glowatz, M. (2020). COVID-19: 20 countries' higher education intra-period digital pedagogy responses. *Journal of Applied Teaching and Learning (JALT)*, *3*(1).

Ekmekci, O., & Bergstrand, J. (2010). Agility in higher education: Planning for business continuity in the face of an H1N1 pandemic. *S.A.M. Advanced Management Journal*, *75*(4), 20–30.

Garrison, D., & Kanuka, H. (2004). Blended learning: Uncovering its transformative potential in higher education. *The Internet and Higher Education*, *7*(2), 95–105. https://doi.org/10.1016/j.iheduc.2004.02.001

Godev, C. (2014). First-year hybrid Spanish courses: How instructors manage their time. *Hispania*, *97*(1), 21–31. https://doi.org/10.1353/hpn.2014.0020

Graves, W., & Twigg, C. (2006). The future of course redesign and the National Center for Academic Transformation: An interview with Carol A. Twigg. *Innovate: Journal of Online Education*, *2*(3), 1–5.

Halverson, L., Graham, C., Spring, K., & Drysdale, J. (2012). An analysis of high impact scholarship and publication trends in blended learning. *Distance Education*, *33*(3), 381–413. https://doi.org/10.1080/01587919.2012.723166

Halverson, L. R., Graham, C. R., Spring, K. J., Drysdale, J. S., & Henrie, C. R. (2014). A thematic analysis of the most highly cited scholarship in the first decade of blended learning research. *The Internet and Higher Education*, *20*, 20–34. https://doi.org/10.1016/j.iheduc.2013.09.004

Heafner, T. L., & Plaisance, M. (2013). Windows into teaching and learning: Uncovering the potential for meaningful remote field experiences in distance teacher education. In R. Hartshorne, T. L. Heafner, & T. Petty (Eds.), *Teacher education programs and online learning tools: Innovations in teacher preparation* (pp. 454–475). IGI Global.

Keith-Le, J. A., & Morgan, M. P. (Eds.). (2020). *Faculty experiences in active learning. A collection of strategies for implementing active learning across disciplines*. J. Murrey Atkins Library at UNC Charlotte. https://doi.org/10.5149/9781469660042_Keith-Le

McAlpin, V., & An, J. (2012). Student success at UNC Charlotte. *A Series of Working Papers*, *1*, 1–9. https://provost.uncc.edu/sites/provost.uncc.edu/files/media/Student-Success-Vol-1-Large-Course-Redesign.pdf

Moskal, P. D. (2016). Incorporating the scholarship of teaching and learning (SoTL) into instruction. In C. D. Dziuban, A. G. Picciano, C. R. Graham, & P. D. Moskal (Eds.), *Conducting research in online and blended learning environments* (pp. 114–126). Routledge.

National Center for Academic Transformation (NCAT) (1999–2018a). *Colleagues committed to redesign (C2R): Project descriptions sorted by discipline*. Retrieved June 5, 2020, from www.thencat.org/RedesignAlliance/C2R/C2R_ProjDiscipline.html

National Center for Academic Transformation (NCAT) (1999–2018b). *How to organize a campus-wide course redesign program using NCAT's methodology*. Retrieved June 5, 2020, from www.thencat.org/Guides/Campus/CW_TOC.html

National Center for Academic Transformation (NCAT) (1999–2018c). *How to redesign a college course using NCAT's methodology*. Retrieved June 5, 2020, from www.thencat.org/Guides/AllDisciplines/TOC.html

O'Flaherty, J., & Phillips, C. (2015). The use of flipped classrooms in higher education: A scoping review. *The Internet and Higher Education*, *25*, 85–95. https://doi.org/10.1016/j.iheduc.2015.02.002

Park, E. E. (2018). *Student success in a large-size hybrid learning course—a study of student backgrounds, online video quizzes, and persistence* [Doctoral dissertation]. The University of North Carolina. ProQuest Dissertations Publishing.

Picciano, A. (2015). Planning for online education: A systems model. *Journal of Asynchronous Learning Networks*, *19*(5), 142–158. https://doi.org/10.24059/olj.v19i5.548

Pyke, G. (2010). *Colleagues committed to redesign (C2R): The University of North Carolina at Charlotte, Elementary Spanish I*. www.thencat.org/RedesignAlliance/C2R/R3/UNCC_Abstract.htm

Quality Matters (n.d.). *QM rubrics & standards*. Retrieved July 10, 2020, from www.qualitymatters.org/qa-resources/rubric-standards

Rosenthal, D., & Weitz, R. (2012). Large-course redesign via blended learning: A post-implementation assessment across institutions. *International Journal on E-Learning*, *11*(2), 189–207.

Siemens, G., Gašević, D., & Dawson, S. (2015). *Preparing for the digital university: A review of the history and current state of distance, blended and online learning*. Athabasca University. https://research.monash.edu/en/publications/preparing-for-the-digital-university-a-review-of-the-history-and

Sorcinelli, M. D., Austin, A. E., Eddy, P. L., & Beach, A. L. (2006). *Creating the future of faculty development*. Anker Publishing.

Toquero, C. M. (2020). Challenges and opportunities for higher education amid the COVID-19 pandemic: The Philippine context. *Pedagogical Research*, *5*(4).

UNC Charlotte (2015). *Institutional plan 2011–2016*. Retrieved May 29, 2020, from https://chancellor.uncc.edu/sites/chancellor.uncc.edu/files/media/Institutional-Plan-2011-16.pdf

UNC Charlotte (2016). *Recommendation to adopt the Canvas learning management system for UNC Charlotte*. Retrieved May 17, 2020, from https://teaching.uncc.edu/sites/teaching.uncc.edu/files/media/files/LMSEval/FinalReportoftheLearningManagementSystemEvaluationCommitteeMarch2016.pdf

UNC Charlotte (2017). *Institutional plan 2016–2021*. Retrieved May 29, 2020, from https://chancellor.uncc.edu/sites/chancellor.uncc.edu/files/media/Institutional-Plan-2016.pdf

UNC Charlotte (n.d.a). *Active Learning Academy*. Retrieved June 30, 2020, from https://teaching.uncc.edu/ActiveLearning

UNC Charlotte (n.d.b). *Faculty training and technology upgrades*. Retrieved June 30, 2020, from https://provost.uncc.edu/faculty-resources-government/planning-fall-2020-reopening/faculty-training-and-technology-upgrades

UNC Charlotte (n.d.c). *Large course redesign projects at UNC Charlotte.* Retrieved June 30, 2020, from https://teaching.uncc.edu/services-we-provide/large-course-redesign/projects

UNC Charlotte (n.d.d). *Projects funded.* Retrieved June 30, 2020, from https://teaching.uncc.edu/learning-resources/sotl/grants/projects-funded

UNC Charlotte (n.d.e). *QM course development.* Retrieved June 30, 2020, from https://teaching.uncc.edu/services-programs/onlinedistance-ed-course-design/qm-course-development

UNC Charlotte (n.d.f). *University profile: About UNC Charlotte.* Retrieved May 29, 2020, from https://admissions.uncc.edu/about-unc-charlotte/university-profile

Zheng, Y., Wang, J., Doll, W., Deng, X., & Williams, M. (2018). The impact of organisational support, technical support, and self-efficacy on faculty perceived benefits of using learning management system. *Behaviour & Information Technology, 37*(4), 311–319. https://doi.org/10.1080/0144929X.2018.1436590

SECTION IV
Adaptive Learning Research

9
EFFICACY OF ADAPTIVE LEARNING IN BLENDED COURSES

Jeremy Anderson, Heather Bushey, Maura Devlin, and Amanda Gould

Since its inception in 1999, the continuing education division of Bay Path University (BPU), serving adult women undergraduates, has endeavored to address the iron triangle of higher education—cost, quality, and access (Immerwahr et al., 2008; Daniel et al., 2010)—via innovative pedagogical and administrative strategies. Though still tied to seat time, accelerated six-week sessions delivered on Saturdays provided access to a more affordable educational experience, as the cost was lower than a residential, coming-of-age experience. However, quality remained variable, with most courses being taught by adjunct instructors who developed their own curriculum. More recent innovations, facilitated by technology, have fused quality and access to low-cost virtual learning experiences through a centralized course management model. Technology-enabled curricular innovations that address the iron triangle are the subject of this chapter, which aims to assess the impact of adaptive blended course delivery on student achievement and satisfaction.

Purpose of the Study

Technological innovations have allowed BPU to expand upon access and affordability aspects of the iron triangle by profoundly shaping high-quality teaching and learning experiences with funding from a federal grant. In 2013, BPU launched Social Online Universal Learning (SOUL), a model built on evidenced-based practices, at the American Women's College (TAWC) division. SOUL capitalizes on technology and data to ensure that micro-level interactions and macro-level workflows and processes lead toward student success and graduation. Micro-level interactions between student and course instructors ensure students receive prompt and frequent feedback on strengths and ways to improve academically

DOI: 10.4324/9781003037736-13

and among advisors and students to ensure students understand policies and pathways to graduation. At the macro-level, data and technology bolster students' safety nets through aligned instructor, advisor, peer, and mentor supports. To ensure instructional quality and the consistency required for micro- and macro-level interactions to support students effectively, TAWC uses a centralized course development model and master course shells in its learning management system. Consistent business rules govern the functioning of courses, including expectations for feedback on assignments, professional advisor and student engagement, and faculty and student interaction.

SOUL consists of six components informed by research on best practices for distance learners. Included in the model are an accelerated six-week course schedule; mandatory student orientation; faculty training; wraparound supports, specific interventions and proactive outreach by staff informed by predictive analytic data on student activity; and digital spaces for peer-to-peer social and academic engagement. The last aspect of SOUL is adaptive learning courseware, embedded in 25% of TAWC courses, which facilitates personalized learning, promotes Universal Design for Learning practices, and delivers micro- and macro-level teaching and learning processes. Data on granular lessons allow instructors to provide just-in-time remediation as necessary, as well as a shared visual for students and faculty of course learning maps that show the concept hierarchy and student performance by concept. All aspects of SOUL combine to promote "high-tech high-touch" practices to personalize students' learning, promoting persistence and degree completion. By the conclusion of the federal grant in 2018, TAWC had developed 60 adaptive courses and began converting five-hour on-ground classes on Saturdays into blended experiences to make use of these adaptive modules in a blended format.

The rationale for developing blended learning experiences is presented in the literature review that is next and is guided by the balancing of access, cost, and quality. Measurement of student learning from these adaptive, blended experiences informs the research questions in this study. This study contributes to the literature in the data-driven way that administrators at TAWC gauge student success as they change delivery models to address the iron triangle and expands limited student learning evidence on use of adaptive learning systems in blended courses.

Literature Review

In investing in an adaptive learning system (ALS), academic program directors and instructional designers explored its promise of enhancing learning gains by harnessing big data, customizing learning at scale (Anderson & Bushey, 2017), and leveraging technology to keep costs low. The two primary pedagogical frameworks that undergird adaptive course development are personalized and universally accessible learning (Anderson et al., 2019). Capitalizing on a technological solution in fully online courses addressed Bloom's dilemma (1984), the two-standard-deviation gap in student learning outcomes between those learning via traditional classroom settings and those learning via one-on-one instruction, by incorporating machine learning to adapt to students' individualized learning needs at scale, allowing the course instructor to intervene in students' learning with the exact support needed at just the right time.

Adaptive Learning Systems

The ALS emerged from the development of computer-assisted instruction (CAI), which frequently was aimed at rendering teaching and learning more accessible and scalable. A core element of an ALS, borrowed from CAI systems developed in the 1970s, is a linkage between faculty-defined skills and knowledge schemas (alternately, maps) and data gleaned from assessment questions to tailor learning experiences to student needs (Carbonell, 1970; Barr et al., 1976). The ALS presents questions to students and uses a machine-learning algorithm to react to data generated by students' answers and to detect patterns in learners' interactions (Pugliese, 2016). Where ALS depart from earlier CAI is in the capacity to use big data to better gauge the nonlinearity of learning complexity and the engagement patterns of digital learning, facilitating interventions in complex learning processes (van den Bogaard et al., 2018; Dziuban et al., 2019).

ALS also present more and varied teaching and learning opportunities (Hinckle & Moskal, 2018; Dziuban, 2017; Picciano, 2019), which foster student engagement and promote academic self-efficacy and through which course instructors can make timely adjustments. Depending on the ALS, the system may use data to provide supplemental content, suggest an alternative form of the learning content, or free students to control their own learning paths through the curriculum (Brusilovsky & Peylo, 2003, Dziuban, 2017; van den Bogaard et al., 2018). Learning analytics embedded in ALS also empower the instructor to remediate course-wide challenges; engage with students in targeted, personalized interactions; and address students' individual needs (Anderson & Bushey, 2017). In these ways, the ALS hold promise for providing improved learning outcomes.

Efficacy of Adaptive on Student Learning

Adaptive learning, while not yet fully solving Bloom's dilemma (1984), has led to student learning results that are comparable to other educational delivery formats. TAWC's research conducted through a randomized control trial indicates that the ALS yielded mixed results in overall course grades when comparing fully online courses to fully online courses with embedded adaptive learning (Anderson et al., 2019). The greatest student learning gains were found in math courses, possibly because discrete concepts in math needed for mastery of each activity work well in the ALS. However, in tracking entering students exposed to its entire SOUL

150 Anderson, Bushey, Devlin, and Gould

model, of which adaptive learning is one key element, for re-enrollment in the fall semester of its second year, TAWC saw a first-to-second-year retention rate approximately 10% higher than the comparable national average (Anderson & Bushey, 2017), which its administrators the attribute to the holistic way that faculty and student advisors engage to support student success via adaptive learning analytics.

Since the ALS is designed to personalize learning in a way that scales human one-to-one tutoring, an important meta-analysis (vanLehn, 2011) found that certain forms of technology-mediated tutoring attained outcomes equivalent to human tutoring. Other early institutional research has shown that student learning in ALS is similar to student learning without ALS in other formats (Dziuban et al., 2016, Dziuban, Graham et al., 2018). These findings suggest that adaptive learning systems promise to add quality to learning experiences while promoting greater access. While an ALS undoubtedly has costs, developing adaptive courses in a centralized course management model can effectively reduce cost, concurrently addressing all three aspects of the iron triangle.

Blended Course Delivery

The definition of blended learning continues to be ambiguous, though it generally is defined as a combination of online learning and face-to-face instruction (Oliver & Trigwell, 2005; Sharpe et al., 2006; Allen et al., 2007; Mayadas & Picciano, 2007; Parsad et al., 2008; Picciano, 2009; Dziuban, Graham et al., 2018). There has been some definitional consensus that reducing seat time is part of what makes a learning experience blended, though the quantification of the seat-time reduction varies, with the National Center for Education Statistics defining blended courses vaguely "as a combination of online and in-class instruction with reduced in-class seat time for students" (Parsad et al., 2008, p. 1), while a prominent early study defined blended courses more specifically as courses in which 30% to 79% of seat time was replaced by online activity (Allen et al., 2007, p. 5). For the purposes of this study, TAWC adopts the definition from Allen et al. (2007) since the college reduced seat time by 50% on Saturdays in its quest for increased access.

Much of the literature on blended learning is devoted to understanding the modality, student and instructor preferences, and institutional requirements to make blended adoptions successful. Indeed, early research on blended learning sought to understand the scope of blending learning among higher educational institutions (Allen et al., 2007). More recent scholarship on blended learning has identified other research domains, most notably how blended learning affects teaching and learning as they relate to learners' behaviors, motivations, and use of time (Dziuban, Graham et al., 2018).

Efficacy of Blended Delivery on Student Learning

Findings related to student success with blended learning have been promising. In a study involving 1,431 students taking an accounting course in a blended learning modality, López-Pérez et al. (2011) found that exam scores increased and withdrawal rates decreased compared to fully online learning. They further found that improved exam scores in blended learning were correlated with students' perceptions of motivation that the inter-related distance learning and face-to-face learning components fostered, suggesting that the impact of blended learning may work via affective variables.

Supporting the theme of academic achievement in blended learning, Dziuban, Graham et al. (2018), using a sample of over 100,00 students studying in three modalities—face to face, fully online, and blended—found that students' overall course grades in face-to-face courses generally were lower than grades in fully online courses, which, in turn, generally were lower than grades in blended courses. These findings held true when controlling for students' minority or non-minority status. Moreover, withdrawal rates among students learning in a blended environment were lower than in fully online and face-to-face courses.

A meta-analysis described in a report from the Online Learning Consortium identified empirical studies comparing fully online learning and blended learning, with results indicating that blended learning yielded more improved student outcomes than fully online learning environments (Buban, 2018). While the report did not find a clear reason for students' gains in the blended learning format, it suggested six factors—a focus on intentional instructional design, students' increased focus on task, students' increased interaction and engagement, enhanced guidance in digital platforms, online access to learning materials, and students' greater ability to self-direct and personalize learning—that may act individually or in combination to yield positive results. Early research on blended learning found similarly that blended learning supports an enhanced sense of community in students (Rovai & Jordan, 2004). All factors are consistent with TAWC's pedagogical approach to its online and blended learning environments (Anderson et al., 2019).

Pedagogical Similarities—Adaptive and Blended Learning

Pedagogical similarities between adaptive learning and blended learning suggest that the most revolutionary practices have promise to transform teaching and learning, while the more daunting among them remind us of the intentional planning needed to veer from traditional delivery models and the importance of using data to evaluate student impact. Blended and adaptive course designs require intensive advance planning and active, just-in-time responsiveness among faculty (Moskal et al., 2013; Shea et al., 2015; Dziuban, Graham et al., 2018).

Changes to the instructional roles required by both adaptive learning and blended learning run counter to methods that faculty have used and the ways they were socialized to academia (Anderson & Bushey, 2017; Lorenzetti, 2011; Mennella, 2016; Dziuban, 2017; Dziuban, Graham et al., 2018; Picciano, 2019). Teaching ALS-enhanced or blended courses therefore requires new technical and instructional skills, collaboration with instructional designers, and change management processes.

If institutions take advantage of technology to enhance time-honored teaching methods to align greater access with quality, there could be tremendous changes to academia. With both blended and adaptive learning, time is no longer constant, which would force reevaluation of the common currency of higher education, seat time (Lorenzetti, 2011; Mennella, 2016; Dziuban, 2017). In both modalities, students progress to their own satisfaction and control their learning (Lorenzetti, 2011; Dziuban, 2017; Dziuban, Graham et al., 2018), shifting more control of the "ownership" of teaching and learning from the faculty member to the student. The benefits in terms of flexibility could be enormous, facilitating greater adaptability on the part of faculty and meeting students where and how they learn (Lorenzetti, 2011; Dziuban, 2017; Buban, 2018). Based on the literature and guided by the imperative to address the iron triangle, TAWC sought to redesign courses with this adaptability to address student needs.

Methodology

This convergent parallel mixed-methods study sought to relate quantitative and qualitative analysis (Creswell, 2009) to answer the research question of whether or not transitioning from traditional on-ground delivery to adaptive blended delivery led to positive academic outcomes and perceptions for students. A positive finding would inform continued development of adaptive blended courses at the institution and could be applied as a best practice at other institutions that are considering implementing adaptive learning.

Quantitative Methods

The following hypotheses were tested using four years of course outcomes data stored in the student information system (SIS) at the college:

Hypothesis #1: The average final grade, by course, will increase when comparing on-ground sections in the 2016–2017 and 2017–2018 academic years to adaptive blended sections in the 2018–2019 and 2019–2020 academic years.

Hypothesis #2: The proportion of students earning a D, an F, or a W, by course, will decrease when comparing on-ground sections in the 2016–2017 and 2017–2018 academic years to adaptive blended sections in the 2018–2019 and 2019–2020 academic years.

Adaptive Learning in Blended Courses **153**

Preparing the Data

The dependent variables in the study were average grades and the proportion of D, F, or withdrawal (i.e., W) grades. Faculty members entered grades for each student who was enrolled in a section after the drop deadline in the SIS using categorical letters—A, B, etc. An Excel extract from the SIS included columns for the students' identification numbers, course codes, section codes, academic year, academic session, and letter grade. Each row represented a student's enrollment and grade in a course section. In total, the data file contained 1,515 grades earned and 29 withdrawals across 221 sections of 26 courses.

Additional preparation was necessary to carry out testing. For Hypothesis 1, letter grades needed to be converted to numbers to calculate averages. The four-point grade point value in the institution's published undergraduate grading matrix provided a translation for letters to numbers. All grade point values, except for grades of W, which did not have a grade point equivalent, were entered into a new column called Grade Point Earned. In the case of Hypothesis 2, the researchers added an additional column—DFW Flag—that was populated with binary values of 0 for grades of A, B, and C and 1 for grades of D, F, and W to facilitate the calculation of DFW rates.

The independent variable in the study was the course delivery mode, either on ground or adaptive blended. Data extracted from the SIS did not readily identify these categories, so translation was necessary. The university registrar applied a series of characters to each section of the SIS, which were readily converted to the delivery modes. A new column in the data set—Course Delivery Flag—contained binary values of 0 for on-ground sections and 1 for adaptive blended sections.

Analysis Plan

Hypothesis 1 implied a comparison of means test. The researchers chose to employ the Student's t-test since Lumley et al. (2002) demonstrated that this method is robust even when the assumption of normality is not upheld. In cases in which the group variances were unequal, the researchers instead followed Field's (2013) recommendation to use Welch's t-test. Upon importing the Excel data file into SPSS, the split-file function made it possible to group all analyses by course codes. Next, the independent samples t-test, grouped on the values in Course Delivery Flag, yielded at the course level descriptive statistics for each delivery mode and students' and Welch's t-test results.

Data analysis for Hypothesis 2 was possible in Excel. The researchers first filtered the data set to view grades for a single course across the four academic years of the study. The Course Delivery Flag column values then served as the basis to group grades into categories for delivery mode. DFW rates for each course delivery mode were based on the sum of the values in the DFW Flag column divided by the total number of grades in the column. This process was necessary for each of the courses in the study.

Qualitative Methods

Concurrently, the researchers used the qualitative method of content analysis to determine if students had positive perceptions of their learning experiences in the adaptive blended sections in the 2018–2019 and 2019–2020 academic years. The data source for analysis was open-ended items on course evaluations completed by students in the penultimate week of the course. In each course evaluation, a series of 19 questions adapted from Dziuban et al. (2017) were asked to gauge each student's perception of their course experience and the adaptive system's contribution to their learning experience. Responses were captured through a combination of Likert-type and open-ended responses. The researchers completed open and axial coding by hand to identify themes in open-ended responses. Using grounded theory research (Creswell, 2009), the researchers were able to draw conclusions about the community of learners who participated in the adaptive blended courses in the 2018–2019 and 2019–2020 academic years and their perceptions of their learning experiences.

Preparing the Data

Course evaluations from adaptive blended courses in the 2018–2019 and 2019–2020 academic years were downloaded from the LMS into an Excel spreadsheet. The collated data represented 23 adaptive blended courses and 55 unique course sections. Of the nineteen questions on the survey, eight Likert-type questions and two open-response questions were pertinent to the research question; all other questions were eliminated from the data set. The researchers calculated the proportion of students selecting each choice on the Likert-type questions for all such questions.

Results

Hypothesis 1

Descriptive statistics included in the independent samples t-test in SPSS and presented in Table 9.1 showed that average course grades increased in 15 courses and decreased in 11 courses when shifting from on-ground delivery to adaptive blended delivery. Standard deviations also decreased in 20 courses, indicating that grades generally clustered closer to the mean in adaptive blended courses than in on-ground courses. While these results lent mixed support for Hypothesis 1,

Adaptive Learning in Blended Courses **155**

TABLE 9.1 Descriptive Statistics and t-Test Results for On-Ground and Adaptive Blended Sections

Course	Ground N	Ground M	Ground SD	Blend N	Blend M	Blend SD	t value	df	p
ACC100	47	3.01	0.83	4	2.42	0.32	1.41	49.00	.165
ACC101	49	2.98	1.08	4	3.17	0.58	-0.34	51.00	.733
BSC109	98	3.06	0.91	26	3.08	0.83	-0.10	122.00	.924
BUS215	24	3.29	1.23	4	3.17	0.84	0.20	26.00	.845
BUS226	31	2.86	1.24	12	2.19	1.45	1.51	41.00	.140
BUS235	36	2.88	1.26	4	3.17	0.34	-0.45	38.00	.655
BUS300	20	3.67	0.89	10	3.47	0.65	0.63	28.00	.533
BUS327	38	3.23	0.89	17	3.71	0.35	-2.85[a]	52.55	.006[b]
BUS491	28	3.41	0.91	14	3.62	0.73	-0.76	40.00	.450
ECO240	12	3.28	1.02	27	3.11	1.00	0.48	37.00	.636
ENG114	79	3.09	1.3	8	3.21	0.56	-0.25	85.00	.805
ENG124	250	3.14	1.31	58	3.30	1.16	-0.88	306.00	.380
ENG134	47	3.00	1.19	16	2.40	1.24	1.74	61.00	.087
HIS114	59	3.15	1.21	13	3.18	1.08	-0.07	70.00	.940
HIS115	22	3.53	0.94	22	2.38	1.64	2.86[a]	33.46	.007[b]
HIS315	14	3.76	0.63	7	3.24	0.81	1.63	19.00	.120
HUM11	4	2.58	1.34	10	2.67	1.22	-0.12	12.00	.910
MAT104	19	3.04	1.36	18	3.21	0.71	-0.48[a]	27.54	.638
MAT112	36	2.4	1.21	22	2.94	1.02	-1.74	56.00	.087
MAT120	75	3.15	0.94	47	3.21	0.87	-0.37	120.00	.716
PSY101	30	2.66	1.66	11	3.15	1.46	-0.87	39.00	.388
PSY206	16	3.15	1.08	6	2.78	1.54	0.64	20.00	.532
PSY323	33	3.15	1.12	11	2.85	1.54	0.70	42.00	.485
PSY340	27	2.84	1.32	3	2.89	1.17	-0.06	28.00	.951
PSY370	19	3.76	0.43	9	3.74	0.40	0.09	26.00	.929
SOC200	9	3.26	0.91	10	3.70	0.33	-1.37[a]	9.92	.201

Columns labeled "Ground" correspond to on-ground sections and "Blend" to adaptive blended sections.

N: total observations, excluding non-numeric values (i.e., grades of withdrawal)

M: average grade using a four-point grade-point scale

[a] results of a Welch's t-test; equal variances not assumed

[b] significant at p < .05

differences in average course grades were significant and above the critical level in only 2 of 26 courses, HIS115 and BUS327. Students in on-ground sections of HIS115 ($M = 3.53$) performed better than students in adaptive blended sections ($M = 2.38$), $t(33.46) = 2.86$, $p = .007$. For BUS327, students performed better in adaptive blended sections ($M = 3.71$) than in on-ground sections ($M = 3.23$), $t(52.55) = -2.85$, $p = .006$. Small sample sizes for the adaptive blended delivery model, including 12 courses where n was ten or fewer, limited the power of many of the remaining tests (Field, 2013).

Hypothesis 2

To test Hypothesis 2, the researchers compared the DFW rates between on-ground and adaptive blended sections of each course and then aggregated DFW rates of all courses for each condition (Table 9.2). DFW rates decreased in 14 of 26 courses, stayed the same in 2 courses, and increased in 10 courses. These analyses provided some support for Hypothesis 2. Given the small sample size for the adaptive blended condition in many courses, the course-level comparison could have been misleading on its own. Aggregating DFW rates provided a worthwhile alternative view. There was an aggregate drop in the rate of 6.6% ($n = 961$) in the 14 courses that showed decreases in DFW rates when adaptive blended delivery was introduced. For the 10 courses that saw an increase in DFW rates under the adaptive blended condition, the aggregate increase was 17.4% ($n = 536$). A final

TABLE 9.2 DFW Rates for On-Ground and Adaptive Blended Sections

Course	On-ground N	On-ground DFW rate (%)	Adaptive Blended N	Adaptive Blended DFW rate (%)	Change in DFW rate (%)
ACC100	48	8.3	5	20.0	11.7
ACC101	49	12.2	4	0.0	-12.2
BSC109	99	6.1	26	3.8	-2.3
BUS215	24	12.5	4	0.0	-12.5
BUS226	31	12.9	12	25.0	12.1
BUS235	39	20.5	4	0.0	-20.5
BUS300	20	5.0	10	0.0	-5.0
BUS327	38	5.3	17	0.0	-5.3
BUS491	28	3.6	14	0.0	-3.6
ECO240	13	7.7	28	10.7	3.0
ENG114	80	13.8	8	0.0	-13.8
ENG124	254	14.6	59	10.2	-4.4
ENG134	48	14.6	17	23.5	8.9
HIS114	60	11.7	14	21.4	9.7
HIS115	22	4.5	22	31.8	27.3
HIS315	14	0.0	8	12.5	12.5
HUM101	4	25.0	10	10.0	-15.0
MAT104	20	20.0	19	5.3	-14.7
MAT112	36	22.2	22	9.1	-13.1
MAT120	78	7.7	49	10.2	2.5
PSY101	31	32.3	12	25.0	-7.3
PSY206	16	6.3	6	16.7	10.4
PSY323	34	8.8	11	18.2	9.4
PSY340	27	14.8	3	0.0	-14.8
PSY370	19	0.0	9	0.0	0.0
SOC200	9	0.0	10	0.0	0.0
Total	1,141	11.9	403	10.9	-1.0

N: total observations, including grades of withdrawal

Adaptive Learning in Blended Courses **157**

aggregation of DFWs by delivery method across all courses showed an overall drop in DFW rates of 1% from the on-ground condition (11.92%, $n = 1,141$) to the adaptive blended condition (10.92%, $n = 403$). This result lent additional support for an affirmative finding for Hypothesis 2.

Qualitative Analysis

An analysis of the qualitative data allowed the researchers to articulate the student experience in adaptive blended courses and draw conclusions from students' perceptions of how the adaptive technology impacted their learning. The following themes were present in open responses:

- accessibility of academic content
- engagement of learners
- pace of learning
- volume of content covered

A majority of students were pleased with their experiences in adaptive blended courses and were able to articulate the benefits through their responses on the course evaluation. When asked if the ALS helped them better learn the course material, 53% of students either agreed or strongly agreed that it was helpful. In addition to the adaptive blended courses assisting a majority of the students in learning the course material better, students also indicated that they learned better with access to adaptive technology, more so than in other courses in which they did not have access to the adaptive technology. When asked to make the comparison between ease of learning with the adaptive technology and courses without, 64% of students either agreed or strongly agreed that the adaptive blended course experience helped them learn better than a traditional course. For many students, the adaptive component to the course proved to be a good complement to the face-to-face instruction provided by the faculty member. One student commented that she liked "that [the ALS] introduced terms that I had never heard before. It prepared me for what the professor would be talking about. I liked that it let you keep going back to work on the areas you were struggling with."

Besides aiding in their learning and academic progress, 61% of students also believed that the personalized feedback received through the ALS assisted them in staying on track in the course and focused on the course objectives. A personalized learning experience is critical to the success of a student. Having the ability to meet their unique needs and keep them engaged in their course can lead to a positive academic experience with positive academic outcomes.

Students who completed the course evaluations were asked to elaborate on what they enjoyed about their course experience. When asked specifically to identify their favorite part about adaptive technology, 52% of students reported that learning in the adaptive blended format was engaging for all types of learners.

One student stated that she "liked that it gave you an assortment of questions and the ability to use a different learning option if needed."

Another benefit to the personalized nature of an adaptive blended course is the level of engagement it provides to each student. Engagement with course materials in a unique and varied way based on the needs of each student is a pillar of the adaptive course experience. Of students enrolled in these courses, 57% of those surveyed either agreed or strongly agreed that the adaptive technology increased their engagement with the course content.

While the varied content offered in the adaptive platform provided more opportunities for students to engage with the course material, students admitted that it did feel like too much content was presented at times (39% of respondents), and, ultimately, 50% of students stated that they spent more or much more time working in their adaptive blended course than they did in a course without the ALS.

With a majority of the responses favoring the adaptive blended course model and 62% of students stating that if given the chance, they would take another course that included adaptive technology, the researchers are optimistic about the future trajectory of adaptive learning and the continued positive impact it can have on learners. The students surveyed recognize the value-add of the blended learning model of an adaptive blended course, "however, the strong possibility exists that blended learning, like quality, is observer dependent and may not exist outside of our perceptions of the concept" (Dziuban, Howlin et al., 2018, p. 12).

Implications

Implications for Practice

The goal of this study was to validate positive impacts on student outcomes given the utilization of adaptive frameworks and reduced face time in blended courses. There were mixed results on the academic outcomes, though they generally were more positive than negative. These findings suggest that adaptive blended delivery provided greater access in many cases to quality learning experiences, while containing instructional costs and ensuring quality through the data-rich learning platform. Practitioners considering the use of an ALS may wish to review the trends in findings across subject domains to determine where to begin an adoption. The courses in this study in which DFW rates declined and course grades improved most—core offerings such as English and math—are foundational requirements on which most academic work builds and may be good targets at other institutions. A depth of content knowledge in these courses likely has longer term effects that spill into later coursework, especially when adaptive content can be mapped across course sequences. Additionally, qualitative analysis confirmed that students perceived heightened motivation and a feeling of control over learning in the adaptive blended mode. Even in courses with lower performance, the positive affective outcomes and the opportunity to use big data from the ALS to facilitate ongoing improvements to course design justify continued adoption of the ALS at BPU and consideration of adoption at other institutions.

Implications for Research

Part of the value of integrating adaptive learning platforms into a blended learning experience was the accumulation of learning analytics that otherwise would have been uncollectable in traditional face-to-face learning. These analytics provided more detail on behaviors of students interacting with content, practicing, revising, and responding to pre- and post-tests. Analytics beyond standard grading mechanisms applied by instructors or the circumstantial needs for students to potentially withdraw could shed more light on learning gains. The ability to capture these data could be used to drive further studies on the specific behaviors and forms of engagement of faculty and students that lead to the quantitative and qualitative results of this study. For example, ways in which faculty use the ALS to improve local instruction in their sections, such as personalizing interventions through data insights, was out of the scope of this study and is ripe for future qualitative exploration. Therefore, revisiting the study after faculty further develop skill in the use of the ALS, which also would yield larger sample sizes to improve the power of the statistical tests, may be telling.

Also, the finding that standard deviations in course grades decreased in the adaptive blended condition for 20 of 26 courses lent credence to Bloom's (1984) finding that personalized tutoring and mastery learning, both hallmarks of adaptive learning, resulted in less dispersion in grades. Additional studies would be helpful to verify this finding and to investigate the effect sizes predicted by Bloom (1984) and vanLehn (2011). Conversely, the mixed results on learning gains did not coincide with Bloom's (1984) and vanLehn's (2011) predictions for improved learning across the board when fusing personalization and mastery learning. It will be important to ascertain if the patterns in outcomes by subject domain hold true as sample sizes increase at BPU and as other institutions adopt ALSs in adaptive blended courses.

Conclusion

As methods for teaching and learning continue to evolve in response to the changing needs of learners, and through advancing engagement with technology and data in our learning environments, a commitment to the iron triangle—cost, quality, and access—needs to remain at the forefront. We believe that adaptive learning incorporated into blended courses allows for student-instructor contact but also increases access to learner data for both students and faculty to help enhance student and faculty engagement.

160 Anderson, Bushey, Devlin, and Gould

References

Allen, I. E., Seaman, J., & Garrett, R. (2007). *Blending in: The extent and promise of blended education in the United States.* Sloan Consortium. Retrieved from www.onlinelearning survey.com/reports/blending-in.pdf

Anderson, J., & Bushey, H. (2017, June 19). The journey to adaptive learning at the American women's college. *EDUCAUSE Review.* https://er.educause.edu/articles/2017/6/journey-to-adaptive-learning-at-the-american-womens-college

Anderson, J., Bushey, H., Devlin, M., & Gould, A. (2019). Cultivating student engagement in a personalized online learning environment. In E. Alqurashi (Ed.), *Handbook of research on fostering student engagement with instructional technology in higher education* (pp. 267–287). IGI Global.

Barr, A., Beard, M., & Atkinson, R. C. (1976). The computer as a tutorial laboratory: The Stanford BIP project. *International Journal of Man-Machine Studies, 8*(5), 567–596. https://doi.org/10.1016/s0020-7373(76)80021-1

Bloom, B. (1984). The 2 sigma problem: The search for methods of group instruction as effective as one-to-one tutoring. *Educational Researcher, 13*(6), 4–16. https://doi.org/1 0.3102/0013189x013006004

Brusilovsky, P., & Peylo, C. (2003). Adaptive and intelligent web-based educational systems. *International Journal of Artificial Intelligence in Education, 13*(2–4), 159–172.

Buban, J. (2018). Online and blended learning: Selections from the field. In *Online learning consortium.* Routledge. www.routledge.com/rsc/downloads/OLC_Free Book_Online__Blended_Learning.pdf?utm_source=crcpress.com&utm_medium= referral

Carbonell, J. (1970). AI in CAI: An artificial-intelligence approach to computer-assisted Instruction. *IEEE Transactions on Man Machine Systems, 11*(4), 190–202. https://doi.org/10.1109/tmms.1970.299942

Creswell, J. W. (2009). *Research design: Qualitative, quantitative, and mixed methods approaches* (3rd ed.). Sage.

Daniel, J., Kanwar, A., & Uvalić-Trumbić, S. (2010). Breaking higher education's iron triangle: Access, cost, and quality. *Change Magazine, 41*(2), 30–35. https://doi.org/10.3200/chng.41.2.30-35

Dziuban, C. (2017). The technology of adaptive learning. *Education Technology Insights.* https://digital-solution.educationtechnologyinsights.com/cxoinsights/the-technol ogy-of-adaptive-learning-nid-280.html

Dziuban, C., Graham, C. R., Moskal, P., Norberg, A, & Sicilia, N. (2018). Blended learning: The new normal and emerging technologies. *International Journal of Educational Technology in Higher Education, 15*(3), 1–16. https://doi.org/10.1186/s41239-017-0087-5

Dziuban, C., Howlin, C., Moskal, P., Johnson, C., Eid, M., & Kmetz, B. (2019). Adaptive learning: Context and complexity. *E-Mentor, 5*(77), 7–39. https://doi.org/10.15219/em77.1384

Dziuban, C., Howlin, C., Moskal, P., Johnson, C., Parker, L., & Campbell, M. (2018). Adaptive learning: A stabilizing influence across disciplines and universities. *Online Learning, 22*(3), 7–39. https://doi.org/10.24059/olj.v22i3.1465

Dziuban, C., Moskal, P., & Hartman, J. (2016). *Adapting to learn, learning to adapt.* EDU-CAUSE Center for Analysis and Research. https://library.educause.edu/-/media/files/library/2016/9/erb1610.pdf

Dziuban, C., Moskal, P., Johnson, C., & Evans, D. (2017). Adaptive learning: A tale of two contexts. *Current Issues in Emerging eLearning, 4*(1), 26–62.

Field, A. (2013). *Discovering statistics using IBM SPSS statistics* (4th ed.). Sage.

Hinckle, J., & Moskal, P. (2018). A preliminary examination of adaptive case studies in nursing pathophysiology. *Current Issues in Emerging eLearning, 5*(1), 20–28. https://scholarworks.umb.edu/ciee/vol5/iss1/3/

Immerwahr, J., Johnson, J., & Gasbarra, P. (2008). *The iron triangle: College presidents talk about costs, access, and quality.* The National Center for Public Policy and Higher Education. https://vtechworks.lib.vt.edu/bitstream/handle/10919/83320/IronTriangleCollege.pdf?sequence=1&isAllowed=y

López-Pérez, M. V., Pérez-López, M. C., & Rodríguez-Ariza, L. (2011). Blended learning in higher education: Students' perceptions and their relation to outcomes. *Computers & Education, 56*(3), 818–826. https://doi.org/10.1016/j.compedu.2010.10.023

Lorenzetti, J. P. (2011). The benefits of blended learning explained. *Faculty Focus.* www.facultyfocus.com/articles/blended-flipped-learning/the-benefits-of-blended-learning-explained/

Lumley, T., Diehr, P., Emerson, S., & Chen L. (2002). The importance of the normality assumption in large public health data sets. *Annual Review of Public Health, 23*, 151–169.

Mayadas, A. G., & Picciano, F. (2007). Blended learning and localness: The means and the end. *Journal of Asynchronous Learning Networks, 11*(1), 3–7. https://doi.org/10.24059/olj.v11i1.1730

Mennella, T. (2016). Comparing the efficacy of flipped vs. alternative active learning in a college genetics course. *The American Biology Teacher, 78*, 471–479.

Moskal, P., Dziuban, C., & Hartman, J. (2013). Blended learning: A dangerous idea? *The Internet and Higher Education, 18*, 15–23. https://doi.org/10.1016/j.iheduc.2012.12.001

Oliver, M., & Trigwell, K. (2005). Can "blended learning" be redeemed? *E-Learning, 2*(1), 17–26. https://doi.org/10.2304/elea.2005.2.1.2

Parsad, B., Lewis, L., & Tice, P. (2008). *Distance education at degree-granting postsecondary institutions: 2006–07.* National Center for Education Statistics. https://nces.ed.gov/pubs2009/2009044.pdf

Picciano, A. G. (2009). Blending with purpose: The multimodal model. *Journal of Asynchronous Learning Network, 13*(1). https://doi.org/10.24059/olj.v13i1.1673

Picciano, A. G. (2019). Artificial intelligence and the academy's loss of purpose. *Online Learning, 23*(3), 270–284. https://doi.org/10.24059/olj.v23i3.2023

Pugliese, L. (2016, October 17). Adaptive learning systems: Surviving the storm. *EDUCAUSE Review.* Retrieved from https://er.educause.edu/articles/2016/10/adaptive-learning-systems-surviving-the-storm

Rovai, A. P., & Jordan, H. M. (2004). Blended learning and sense of community: A comparative analysis with traditional and fully online graduate courses. *International Review of Research in Open and Distance Learning, 5*(2), 1–13.

Sharpe, R., Benfield, G., Roberts, G., & Francis, R. (2006). *The undergraduate experience of blended learning: A review of UK literature and research.* The Higher Education Academy. http://citeseerx.ist.psu.edu/viewdoc/download?doi=10.1.1.624.5359&rep=rep1&type=pdf

Shea, J., Joaquin, M. E., & Gorzycki, M. (2015). Hybrid course design: Promoting student engagement and success. *Journal of Public Affairs Education, 21*(4), 539–556. https://doi.org/10.1080/15236803.2015.12002219

van den Bogaard, M. E. D., Howlin, C., Lindsay, E., & Morgan, J. (2018). *Patterns of students' curriculum engagement in an on-demand online curriculum: An exploratory study at Charles Sturt University*. Proceedings of the 46th SEFI Annual Conference. www.sefi.be/wp-content/uploads/2018/10/SEFI-Proceedings-2-October-2018.pdf

vanLehn, K. (2011). The relative effectiveness of human tutoring, intelligent tutoring systems, and other tutoring systems. *Educational Psychologist, 46*(4), 197–221. http://doi.org/10.1080/00461520.2011.611369

10

ADAPTIVE AND ACTIVE

The Integration of Adaptive Courseware Through the Lens of Blended Learning

Janelle D. Voegele and Raiza Dottin

Authors Note

The authors would like to express our appreciation to the Bill and Melinda Gates Foundation and the Association of Public and Land Grant Universities for their support of this project.

Adaptive learning systems are emerging as promising digital learning environments with the potential to personalize academic content in response to students' diverse learning needs. Adaptive learning platforms "employ algorithms, assessments, student feedback, instructor adjustments/interventions, and various media to deliver new learning material to students who have achieved mastery and remediation to those who have not" (Educause Learning Initiative, 2017). Adaptive learning can address issues of equity in student achievement, preparation, and persistence (Thompson et al., 2019) and can scale real-time student learning assessment that "not only allows students to have their own learning path with individual learning nodes or steps, but also provides various formative and summative assessments of the students' learning performance" (Cai, 2018).

Adaptive learning seems well suited to blended course formats (Cai, 2018; Thompson et al., 2019). In blended learning, generally defined as the practice of strategically integrating digital and classroom learning experiences, adaptive systems offer personalized instruction coupled with the opportunity to extend adaptive learning synchronously with peers and instructors. Some findings suggest that adaptive learning is more effective when utilized in a blended environment (Johanes & Lagerstrom, 2017; Means et al., 2014). Yet more research is

DOI: 10.4324/9781003037736-14

needed on the effective integration of adaptive systems into blended learning contexts. Scholarship has focused on specific student outcomes or students' perspectives on digital technology and less on student perspectives related to learning organization and design (Roberts et al., 2016; West et al., 2020). An important consideration becomes understanding students' perspectives on the blend of adaptive learning and their experiences in the rest of a course. Through this, we may gain greater insight into the variability of student outcomes found in research on adaptive learning.

This chapter reports results from a two-year study that examined student experiences in 108 undergraduate courses representing 11 disciplines, all of which incorporated adaptive learning platforms into blended course curricula. Although persistence rates were variable across course offerings, three programs with the highest decrease in "not passing" rates were also rated highest overall by students on measures of learning effectiveness, including those connected to effective blended design.

Adaptive Learning and Student Persistence

Research on the impact of adaptive learning on college persistence has focused primarily on course completion, followed by module or assignment completion (Farmer et al., 2019; Gebhardt, 2018). Some results have been quite promising; for example, Arizona State reported a 18% increase in college algebra pass rates over two years, and Colorado Technical University saw improved pass rates in introductory online courses of 5% to 10% (Johanes & Lagerstrom, 2017).

However, as adaptive learning initiatives have begun to scale up, persistence outcomes have been mixed. For example, 10,000 students across multiple campuses participated in an Adaptive Learning Market Acceleration Program (ALMAP) initiative. Adaptive courseware had "no measurable effect" on course completion rates when compared to non-adaptive course counterparts (Johanes & Lagerstrom, 2017). Describing an adaptive learning study across nine higher education institutions, Briggs et al. (2019) reported small but statistically significant gains in course academic outcomes, passing rates and satisfaction for four-year campuses, while two-year colleges showed no significant academic outcomes and lower course satisfaction scores. Salami and Omiteru (2015) observe that prevailing orientations to teaching may or may not resonate with approaches to adaptive learning in all programs or institutions.

Student Perceptions of Adaptive Learning

Much of the research on students' perceptions has emphasized their experiences with adaptive platforms, effectiveness of adaptive tools, and use of technology (West et al., 2020). Recent scholarship has examined perceived adaptive learning effectiveness, some of which has reported positive learning experiences overall

(Dziuban et al., 2017; Farmer et al., 2019; Serhan, 2017), increased learning (Alshammari et al., 2015), increased interactivity with content (Farmer et al., 2019), increased perceived competence (Sun et al., 2018), and improved learning due to immediate feedback (Dziuban et al., 2017; van Seters et al., 2012). Interestingly, a few studies report that although some students rate certain aspects of adaptive systems as more difficult, this does not appear to impact an overall positive view of the adaptive learning environment (Dziuban et al., 2017; Sun et al., 2018).

Research on perceived adaptive learning barriers has revealed some commonly reported challenges, such as increased time needed to navigate adaptive platforms and confusing module design structures (Farmer et al., 2019; Richards-Babb et al., 2018; Sun et al., 2018), problems with technology (Farmer et al., 2019), insufficient targeted feedback when unable to progress (Liu et al., 2017), overwhelming content (Briggs et al., 2019), and student anxiety connected to content knowledge and/or poor module performance (Roberts et al., 2016).

While research on students' perceptions is emerging and mixed, findings raise many questions about the impact of course design and pedagogical approach. As White (2020) points out, part of the challenge may be that in many studies, teaching styles and approaches to course organization and design are not accounted for. The nature of the blend may vary considerably, even between courses in the same study. There is a need to know more about which blended design practices leverage the potential of adaptive learning for student persistence and deeper learning.

The Context: Adaptive Learning at Portland State University

Portland State University (PSU), located in downtown Portland, Oregon, is a public, urban university serving approximately 25,000 students. This current study was administered through PSU's Office of Academic Innovation (OAI). OAI combines expertise areas in postsecondary education, curriculum development, digital learning, instructional design, digital learning, high impact practices, and assessment. OAI titled the project Active and Adaptive, to reinforce the goal of active learning strategies combined with students having mastered foundational concepts prior to attending class. Utilizing backward design and elements that support a blended learning approach (Caufield, 2011; Linder, 2017; Wiggins & McTighe, 2005), teams partnered with participating programs on course design.

Method

To examine persistence and student perspectives on learning, three sources of data were obtained during the two-and-a-half-year study period: persistence data measured by a comparison of "not passing" (NP) rates for courses before and during the study, quantitative survey items, and qualitative survey questions. The reasoning for collecting and examining three data sources was an attempt by the researchers to incorporate multiple approaches to explore the integration of adaptive courseware (Johnson & Onwuegbuzie, 2004).

Student persistence and experience data were collected in 108 undergraduate courses representing 11 disciplines during the two-and-a-half-year study period (see Table 10.1).

Surveys were distributed to students in all participating adaptive course sections from Fall 2018 to Winter 2020; 2,816 students, or 34.3% of enrolled students, completed surveys. The following section provides study findings from the three sources of data collected during the study period.

"Not Passing" Grade Report

Student persistence was measured through an analysis of "not passing" (NP) grade marks recorded for redesigned adaptive courses compared to previous non-adaptive course sections. For this study, NP grade reports reflected the percentage of no-pass grades out of the total grade reports for a course. Per the university Office of the Registrars' grading scale system, NP grade letters are identified as D, D-, F, and no-pass or NP for undergraduate courses. NP grade reports were analyzed by the researchers for all adaptive courses deployed during the study and compared to non-adaptive course offerings of the same discipline and subject matter for the two years before the study start date in fall of 2017.

Student Survey

Student experience of adaptive learning was measured through a mid-quarter survey. The student survey consisted of 14 Likert scale questions and 2 open-ended questions. The survey was designed to collect (a) perceptions of the adaptive

TABLE 10.1 Participating Disciplines and College Course Level During Study (Fall 2017–Winter 2020)

Discipline	Course Level	Total Course Sections
Biology	100	6
Business Administration	100, 200	6
Chemistry	100, 200, 300	12
Computer Science	100	2
Mathematics	100, 200	21
Philosophy	200, 300	2
Physics	200	7
Spanish	200	1
Statistics	200	25
University Studies	100	3
Writing	300	3

Note: Total number of students enrolled across sections: 9,659

Adaptive and Active **167**

platform, (b) perceptions of adaptive learning, and (c) perceptions of connection between digital and classroom learning.

This chapter focuses on five Likert scale questions and two open-ended questions that measured perceived elements of adaptive learning, perceived adaptive/course integration, and facilitators and barriers to learning. Integrating content and activities across course formats, utilizing digital learning information to inform course organization, timely feedback, and strategic preparation for classroom activity contribute to effective blended design (Caufield, 2011; Linder, 2017):

1. The adaptive courseware helped me prepare for class.
2. The adaptive courseware helped me prepare for quizzes and exams.
3. Feedback in the adaptive platform helped me stay on track.
4. Instructor uses students' work in the adaptive platform to inform teaching and/or class activities.
5. The work I do in the adaptive platform and class activities are connected.

Open-ended questions:

6. What aspects of the course, if any, increased your learning?
7. What aspects of the course, if any, were barriers to your learning?

Surveys were deployed to students digitally during week six of the ten-week course quarter. Course instructors were provided with a summary report of survey data, as well as recommendations made by students for the use of adaptive courseware in future course sections.

Findings

Summary of Student Survey Data

This chapter focuses on the portion of the study survey that explored the perceived impact of adaptive courseware on student learning, perceived connections between adaptive and other course elements, and open-ended questions regarding facilitators of and barriers to learning. Table 10.2 provides the overall mean of student ratings related to "strongly agree" (SA) and "agree" (A) statements recorded for each of the selected study questions.

Survey Responses: All Study Participants

As seen from Table 10.2, students' responses to learning items were generally positive. Students selected statement 1, "The adaptive platform helped me prepare for class," as the highest-rated (strongly agree and agree) at 74.78%, followed by

168 Janelle D. Voegele and Raiza Dottin

TABLE 10.2 Student Responses on Active and Adaptive Implementation Survey (1–5) for Adaptive Disciplines from Fall 2019–Winter 2020

Statement	Strongly Agree (SA)	Agree (A)	Total
	M	M	
1. The adaptive platform helped me prepare for class.	33.92	40.86	74.78
2. The adaptive platform helped me prepare for quizzes and exams.	33.53	38.11	71.64
3. The adaptive platform helped me stay on track.	20.83	28.06	48.88
4. Instructor(s) use(s) students' work in adaptive platform to inform teaching and/or class activities.	22.70	28.89	51.59
5. The work I do in the adaptive platform and class activities were connected.	33.30	37.81	71.10

Note: 1 = Strongly Agree (SA), 2 = Agree (A); total n = 2,816

statement 2, "The adaptive platform helped me prepare for quizzes and exams," the second highest-rated at 71.64%. Statement 3, "The adaptive platform helped me stay on track" was the lowest rated (strongly agree and agree) at 48.88%. When examining student sentiment on the integration or blending of the adaptive courseware with course curriculum and activities, students rated (strongly agree and agree) statement 4, "Instructor(s) use(s) students' work in adaptive platform to inform teaching and/or class activities" at 51.59%. However, students rated (strongly agree and agree) statement 5, "The work I do in the adaptive platform and class activities were connected" at 71.10%.

When analyzing survey responses across participating programs, the researchers noted that students in 3 of the 11 disciplines—biology (BI), physics (PHYS), and statistics (STATS)—selected "strongly agree" or "agree" on all five statements by 50% or greater. Additionally, data isolated from these programs also revealed a different preference pattern for certain survey items. Table 10.3 provides a comparison of the overall "strongly agree" and "agree" mean for the 3 disciplines to the overall mean for all 11 adaptive disciplines.

Survey Responses: Biology, Physics and Statistics

In contrast to survey data from all disciplines, responses from students in BI, PHYS, and STATS revealed a different pattern (Table 10.3). Students in these programs selected statement 5, "The work I do in the adaptive platform and class activities

Adaptive and Active **169**

TABLE 10.3 Student Responses on Active and Adaptive Implementation Survey for Biology (BI), Physics (PHYS), and Statistics (STAT) to All Adaptive Disciplines from Fall 2019–Winter 2020

Statement	SA/A [BI, PHYS, STAT]	SA/A [All 11 Disciplines]
	M	M
1. The adaptive platform helped me prepare for class.	79.46	74.78
2. The adaptive platform helped me prepare for quizzes and exams.	78.07	71.64
3. Feedback in the adaptive platform helped me stay on track.	57.49	48.88
4. Instructor(s) use(s) students' work in adaptive platform to inform teaching and/or class activities.	59.49	51.59
5. The work I do in the adaptive platform and class activities were connected.	86.97	71.10

Note: 1 = Strongly Agree (SA), 2 = Agree (A)

were connected" as the highest-rated (strongly agree and agree) at 86.97%, followed by statement 1, "The adaptive platform helped me prepare for class," at 79.46%. However, as was consistent across the study, statement 3, "Feedback in the adaptive platform helped me stay on track" was the lowest-rated (strongly agree and agree) at 57.49%, followed by statement 4, "Instructor(s) use(s) students' work in adaptive platform to inform teaching and/or class activities" at 59.49%, although the three programs' combined mean for each of these two questions was higher than mean scores for all disciplines (+8.61 and +7.90, respectively).

Having noted these earlier patterns of higher scores on the learning environment items, the researchers wondered how the NP data for BI, PHYS, and STATS would compare to data for all adaptive courses. The following section summarizes the NP grade report data across disciplines and the comparative analysis with the aforementioned three courses.

Summary of "Not Passing" Data

To examine student persistence, a comparative analysis was conducted of "not passing" (NP) grade marks for all adaptive course offerings during the study period and previous non-adaptive course offerings over the two-year period prior to the start of the study. The researchers determined that only eight of the disciplines represented in the study had enough sample groups to conduct an independent-samples t-test successfully. In analyzing NP grade reports for these disciplines, two years before the start of the study in fall 2017 (M = 10.59, SD = 4.46) and during the two-and-a-half-year

170 Janelle D. Voegele and Raiza Dottin

TABLE 10.4 Summary of "Not Passing" Grade Reports Pre-study (Fall 2015–2017) and During Study Period (Fall 2017–Winter 2020) for All Disciplines Compared to BI/PHYS/STAT Independent Samples t-Test

Disciplines	Pre-study M (n=2,078)	Pre-study SD	During Study M (n=343)	During Study SD	p-value (2-tailed)
All Disciplines	10.59	4.46	10.99	6.99	.869
Biology (BI)	9.32	6.52	6.56	2.19	.469
Physics (PHYS)	14.54	7.56	10.55	7.51	.427
Statistics (STAT)	8.57	0.81	7.47	2.94	.567
Total	10.81	4.96	8.19	4.21	.488

study period (M = 10.99, SD = 6.99), an independent t-test revealed no overall statistical significance, $t(14) = .168$, $p = .869$. Next, the researchers isolated the NP grade mark data for BI, PHYS, and STATS, as shown in Table 10.4.

A comparative analysis of NP rates with all adaptive courses in the study revealed modestly lower NP rates for BI, PHYS, AND STAT compared to the mean NP rates for all combined disciplines. Although NP scores for physics were only .44 lower than the mean for combined disciplines, this program's pre-study NP rates were among the highest for all programs (M = 14.54), resulting in a net reduction in NP rates of -3.99.

In summary, the researchers noted a consistency in select disciplines that showed an overall positive trend in student persistence and learning experiences for adaptive blended courses. Specifically, biology, physics, and statistics were the three disciplines that (a) received higher than average "strongly agree" and "agree" rates on the survey learning environment items, particularly on items reflecting a blend of digital and classroom activities; (b) were among the disciplines with the lowest NP rates; and (c) showed a modest decrease in "no passing" rates by 1.1 or greater compared to the same courses before the adoption of adaptive learning. To further understand students' perceptions for all adaptive disciplines, student responses to the survey open-ended questions were assessed through a qualitative analysis.

Qualitative Survey Themes

In addition to the scaled survey questions, the survey contained the following open-ended questions:

1. What aspects of the course, if any, increased your learning?
2. What aspects of the course, if any, were barriers to your learning?

Analysis of repeating ideas across all course sections resulted in the following themes.

Perceptions of Integration Between Adaptive and Classroom Learning

The most common theme across adaptive courses was the integration (or lack of integration) between the adaptive learning environment and the rest of the course experience. This repeated theme was found in response to both what was helping and what was a barrier to learning:

> Instructor could help us so much more effectively, because the class was partly based off [adaptive system]. . . . [W]ay better than just, "any questions from your homework?"
>
> I liked how [platform] and the class went together, and linked for a stronger support system for learning. . . . [O]ur professor also showed us where most of us were having challenges and then focused on those things.
>
> [Platform] did not really go with what was being taught in class . . . so rather than preparing you for tests, [platform] just gave additional information for the subjects.
>
> The adaptive homework didn't have anything to do with class, so after a while, I just gave up doing the homework.

Self-Paced Learning

Students reported that the ability to go through material at their own pace increased their learning. Three subthemes related to self-paced learning were flexibility, real-time feedback, and practice for mastery.

> Using [adaptive platform] made it easier for me to move at my own pace and I didn't feel crushed or suffocated by the material. I continued to learn when I was ready to learn and I didn't feel like I was letting myself down.
>
> I enjoyed covering the material online and receiving instant feedback before coming to class. It made it easier for concepts to click, while the professor went over the material.
>
> [Adaptive platform] helped me break down each subject and master it by repetition which really worked for me.

Challenges with Adaptive Platforms

Students also reported navigation and technology challenges with the adaptive platforms, barriers attributed to platform and/or module design, and time commitment due to module load:

> [Adaptive platform] wasted my time by providing unnecessary information . . . failed to provide more examples when I needed additional instruction, and failed to take into account lucky guesses on my part which caused it to skip over lesson materials that I needed.

When we reach the end . . . a button pops up that asks if we want more examples. If the "yes" is clicked, [platform] repeats the same examples it just provided. I have learned that when [platform] states a particular module will take about 10 minutes, it takes me about an hour. A "20 minute" module takes about two hours to complete.

It is interesting to note that despite some challenges, 74% of students agreed or strongly agreed that adaptive activities helped them to prepare for class. This seeming incongruity was reflected in the following student observation:

The [platform] glitches and the time it takes to get to the end are totally worth it when I can actually understand what's going on in class . . . or on the other hand, when I can get the extra help on my own time and schedule.

In summary, students' perceptions in the present study mirror several recent findings connected to adaptive learning effectiveness, including the value of immediate and targeted feedback, flexibility, and increased interactivity with content (Dziuban et al., 2017; Farmer et al., 2019). Barriers described by students in adaptive literature and the current study include increased time needed to navigate adaptive platforms, technology challenges, and module design (Briggs et al., 2019; Liu et al., 2017). In addition, findings from the current study offer some insight into students' experiences with adaptive platforms in relation to their adaptive blended learning environments, to be discussed in the final section.

What Adaptive Learning Can Learn from Blended Learning

Among the proposed models for personalizing learning in higher education today, Thompson et al. (2019) observe that "one of the most challenging to implement . . . is the skillful integration of adaptive learning within a blended learning context" (p. 36). An encouraging result from this study was that most students agreed that adaptive systems were helpful on many items connected to learning, including items reflecting effective blended learning design. Although the change in NP grades was not significant overall, a pattern emerged among three disciplines, all of which had higher-than-average scores for survey items reflecting the learning process and blended design and also showed among the highest improvement in "not passing" grades. This improvement was emerging and modest at the time of this study, yet the findings did suggest some areas for further investigation into adaptive learning in blended contexts.

For example, this study raised questions about students' experiences with real-time adaptive feedback and the impact on subsequent class organization and activities. Lower scores on the survey item "Feedback in the adaptive platform helped me stay on track" could connect to a range of experiences reported by students, including technical problems, increased time to complete assignments, and perceptions of integration between the adaptive platform and classroom activities. As evidenced in the qualitative analysis, adaptive activities were perceived as more effective for learning in those courses that were also rated higher for the perceived connections between learning environments. Two blended learning practices that emerged as key for students in adaptive environments were integration and the use of digital data.

Blended Adaptive Learning: Integration

By far the most commonly expressed observation about the adapted blended environment was the perceived integration (or lack of integration) between the adaptive experience and the rest of the course environment, design, and structure. Students for whom the connection between adaptive and classroom experience was weak or nonexistent expressed confusion and lack of motivation to complete modules. Students who agreed that classroom and adaptive learning were connected specifically commented on that connection—in other words, did not take it for granted—in terms of how they built on their prior understanding and deepened their learning. More investigation is needed on how deliberate connections between students' adaptive learning experiences and course organization and activities are facilitated.

Blended Adaptive Learning: Data Practices

Related to perceptions of integration was the perceived use of digital data to assess student activity, as well as the use of that information to guide instruction and student growth. When students perceived that their digital activity was utilized in connection to course organization, they commented on how that connection impacted their learning and engagement. The courses in this study varied widely as to how digital activity was monitored and utilized. Several faculty found this particular teaching activity very challenging, including decisions on how to communicate and implement their observations on the digital environment and where to prioritize time on students' challenges, particularly in large-enrollment courses. This may provide insight into the seemingly contradictory findings in which many students perceived adaptive learning to be connected with the rest of their course learning experiences, and yet fewer agreed that instructors used adaptive learning data to inform their classes. It is likely that class time was informed by adaptive learning data in many courses, but in some cases, it may have reflected in the choice of lecture materials or in other ways not immediately apparent to students.

What Blended Learning Can Learn from Adaptive Learning

Graham and Robinson (2007) wondered whether blended courses undertaken primarily for purposes of access and convenience could become stepping stones to more transformational course practices. Similarly, Thompson et al. (2019) address the centrality of faculty in advancing innovative adaptive blended learning models and the importance of a strategic approach to institutional and professional development, one that focuses on the underlying beliefs and values of blended learning. On the other hand, it is reasonable to suggest that adaptive platforms as a springboard for deeper and more meaningful engagement will reflect deeply held instructional beliefs that such a springboard is central to the process of learning. What did our students' adaptive experiences teach us about future professional development in transformative, adaptive blended course design?

Invest in Faculty as Partners in Research Over the Long Term

The adoption of significantly new directions in curriculum and instruction is iterative and often takes a great deal of time. Long-term scholarly partnerships that emphasized what faculty were trying to achieve saw more satisfactory results in the long term, generating questions about which blended practices would best support instructors' adaptive goals and how we would know.

Start Small

Planning for a thoughtfully integrated blended course design is complex; adding adaptive learning increases the complexity. Starting small can create early successes and feedback to strengthen the adaptive/classroom blend. During this study, particularly in courses rated higher for the adaptive/classroom connection by students, a steady but gradual increase in applying adaptive learning lessons to blended design was noted by the researchers.

For example, one might begin with an adaptive approach to one module or particularly challenging concept, incorporate adaptive learning as a low-stakes (minimally graded) activity, or pilot one new teaching strategy to connect students' adaptive work to the classroom.

Formative Assessment Interpretation and Strategies Are Key

The potential of adaptive platforms to provide faculty with large amounts of real-time, in-depth information on students' learning pathways has been widely discussed in terms of a more pedagogically active, responsive classroom environment. Less commonly acknowledged are the complexities in formative assessment interpretation and real-time instructional responses, as well as the effort involved in learning and applying these skills for many instructors (Lopez-Pastor & Sicilia-Camacho, 2016). The Latin root of assessment, *assidere*, or "to sit beside," connotes an "observing/learning from students' learning" orientation that has not traditionally been emphasized in postsecondary instruction. Discipline-specific strategies for efficiently interpreting emergent, real-time student learning data should be included in preparation for adaptive blended learning. In addition, skills for quickly incorporating that data into ongoing instructional planning can increase the likelihood of a flexible, iterative approach to adaptive blended design, as well as integrated adaptive and classroom experiences.

Conclusion

As educators explore the elements of blended course design that leverage the potential of adaptive learning, there are many early insights that can inform efforts to improve student persistence and learning outcomes. Conversely, adaptive learning insights applied toward evolving blended course models hold promise for a dynamic interplay between detailed, real-time formative data on student learning and a flexible, iterative, and engaged learning environment. The results of this study indicate that despite some challenges, most students agreed that their learning was supported, reinforced, and enhanced by the incorporation of adaptive learning, particularly in environments that reflected perceptions of integrated, blended design. As we assess—or "sit beside"—our students on their journeys with adaptive blended learning, their insights can inform a new future for blended models in higher education.

References

Alshammari, M., Anane, R., & Hendley, R. J. (2015). Design and usability evaluation of adaptive e-learning systems based on learner knowledge and learning style. In J. Abascal, S. Barbosa, M. Fetter, T. Gross, P. Palanque, & M. Winkler (Eds), *Human-computer interaction—INTERACT* (Vol. 1, pp. 584–591). Springer. https://doi.org/10.1007/978-3-319-22668-2

Briggs, A., Anderson, T., Gebrekristos, A. S., Simon, A., & Mei, A. (2019). *Evaluation of adaptive learning in statistics (ALiS): Testing an online adaptive platform at nine postsecondary institutions in Maryland.* Urban Institute.

Cai, R. (2018). Adaptive learning practice for online learning and assessment. *Proceedings of the 2018 International Conference on Distance Education and Learning*, 103–108. https://doi.org/10.1145/3231848.3231868

Caufield, J. (2011). *How to design and teach a blended course: Achieving student-centered learning through blended classroom, online and experiential activities.* Stylus.

Dziuban, C., Moskal, P., Johnston, C., & Evans, D. (2017). Adaptive learning: A tale of two contexts. *Current Issues in Emerging eLearning, 4*(1), 26–62.

Educause Learning Initiative (2017). *7 things you should know about adaptive learning.* https://library.educause.edu/~/media/files/library/2017/1/eli7140.pdf

Farmer, E. C., Catalano, A. J., & Halpern, A. J. (2019). Exploring student preference between textbook chapters and adaptive learning lessons in an introductory environmental geology course. *TechTrends*, *64*, 150–157. https://doi.org/10.1007/s11528-019-00435-w

Gebhardt, K. (2018). Adaptive learning courseware as a tool to build foundational content mastery: Evidence from principles of microeconomics. *Current Issues in Emerging eLearning*, *5*(1). https://scholarworks.umb.edu/ciee/vol5/iss1/2

Graham, C., & Robinson, R. (2007). Realizing the transformational potential of blended learning: Comparing cases of transforming blends and enhancing blends in higher education. In A. G. Picciano & C. Dzuiban (Eds.), *Blended learning: Research perspectives.* Needham, MA: The Sloan Consortium.

Johanes, P., & Lagerstrom, L. (2017). *Adaptive learning: The premise, promise, and pitfalls.* Proceedings of the 124th ASEE Annual Conference and Exposition. Presented at the American Society for Engineering Education (ASEE) Annual Conference and Exposition.

Johnson, R. B., & Onwuegbuzie, A. J. (2004). Mixed methods research: A research paradigm whose time has come. *Educational Researcher*, *33*(7), 14–26. https://doi.org/10.3102%2F0013189X033007014

Linder, K. E. (2017). *The blended course design workbook: A practical guide.* Stylus.

Liu, M., McKelroy, E., Corliss, S. B., & Carrigan, J. (2017). Investigating the effect of an adaptive learning intervention on students' learning. *Educational Technology Research and Development*, *65*(6), 1605–1625. http://doi.org/10.1007/s11423-017-9542-1

Lopez-Pastor, V., & Sicilia-Camacho, A. (2016). Formative and shared assessment in higher education: Lessons learned and challenges for the future. *Assessment and Evaluation in Higher Education*, *42*(1), 77–97. https://doi.org/10.1080/02602938.2015.1083535

Means, B., Peters, V., & Zheng, Y. (2014). *Lessons from five years of funding digital courseware by the Gates Foundation and SRI Research: SRI.* www.sri.com/sites/default/files/publications/psexecsummary_1.pdf

Richards-Babb, M. R., Curtis, R., Ratcliff, B., Roy, A., & Mikalik, T. (2018). General chemistry student attitudes and success with use of online homework: Traditional-responsive versus adaptive-responsive. *Journal of Chemical Education*, *95*(5), 691–699. https://doi.org/10.1021/acs.jchemed.7b00829

Roberts, L. D., Howell, J. A., Seaman, K., & Gibson, D. C. (2016). Student attitudes toward learning analytics in higher education: "The Fitbit version of the learning world." *Frontiers in Psychology*, *9*, 1–11. https://doi.org/10.3389/fpsyg.2016.01959

Salami, T. O., & Omiteru, E. O. (2015). E-textbooks and the digital natives: A study of first-year chemistry students attitudes toward e-textbooks. In K. Daus & R. Rigsby (Eds.), *The promise of chemical education: Assessing our students' needs* (pp. 45–59). American Chemical Society.

Serhan, D. (2017). Students' attitudes toward the use of adaptive learning systems in learning college algebra. In P. Resta & S. Smith (Eds.), *Proceedings of society for information technology & teacher education international conference, 2005–2010.* Association for the Advancement of Computing in Education (AACE). www.learntechlib.org/primary/p/177492/

Sun, Q., Norman, T. J., & Abdourazakou, Y. (2018). Perceived value of interactive digital textbook and adaptive learning: Implications on student learning effectiveness. *Journal of Education for Business*, *93*(7), 323–331. https://doi.org/10.1080/08832323.2018.1493422

Thompson, K., Jowallah, R., & Cavanagh, T. B. (2019). "Solve the big problems": Leading through strategic innovation in blended teaching and learning. In Y. Qian & G. Huang, (Eds.), *Technology leadership for innovation in higher education* (pp. 26–48). IGI Global.

van Seters, J. R., Wellink, J., Tramper, J., Goedhart, M. J., & Ossevoort, M. A. (2012). A web-based adaptive tutor to teach PCR primer design. *Biochemistry and Molecular Biology Education, 40*(1), 8–13. https://doi.org/10.1002/bmb.20563

West, D., Luzeckyj, A., Toohey, D., Vanderlelie, J., & Searle, B. (2020). Do academics and university administrators really know better? The ethics of positioning student perspectives in learning analytics. *Australasian Journal of Educational Technology, 36*(2), 60–70. https://doi.org/10.14742/ajet.4653

White, G. (2020). Adaptive learning technology relationship with student learning outcomes. *Journal of Information Technology Education: Research, 19*, 113–130. https://doi.org/10.28945/4526

Wiggins, G. P., & McTighe, J. (2005). *Understanding by design*. ASCD.

11

A BLENDED LEARNING CASE STUDY

Geo Exploration, Adaptive Learning, and Visual Knowledge Acquisition

Mark Jack Smith

Adaptive and blended learning have specific training applications aboard ships in remote locations where operations require onboard personnel to acquire knowledge and competence quickly (Bonk & Graham, 2005; Chiva et al., 2010; Dziuban et. al., 2018; Picciano et al., 2013). Petroleum Geo-Services (PGS), a marine seismic company, created a blended modality by deploying an adaptive learning (AL) solution to a multinational group of mechanics amassing data on seismic survey vessels. One of a limited number of companies worldwide, PGS produces seismic images of the earth's subsurface beneath the ocean floor. Given the constraints of the offshore environment and employee (crew) configuration, a commercial need for cost-effective and efficient learning modalities motivated interest in AL. Theoretical learning, coupled with new, practical, on-the-job learning assessment added to the AL modality, will transform how PGS trains its offshore employees.

Combining knowledge data with operational scenarios will provide a unique feedback loop; practical knowledge assessment will augment blended learning solutions. These enhancements will increase operational effectiveness, improve the sustainability of the equipment, avoid costly delays created by technical downtime, and require less crew and onshore personnel to operate and manage the equipment. AL also appears to be the logical next step in the development of learning modalities for employees in PGS who work half the year, live in over 30 countries, and are crewed to vessels working offshore in multiple, changing remote locations. Because of rapid retraining requirements, PGS chose hydraulics as the area in which to pilot AL, even though current market forces have delayed large-scale introduction for commercial energy enterprises.

Although AL is at its introduction stage at PGS and the possibilities for cost-effective, verifiable, and continual knowledge creation and renewal are

DOI: 10.4324/9781003037736-15

A Blended Learning Case Study **179**

not completely understood, the company understands AL's potential. AL offers e-learning, new modalities like gamification, and the integration of these platforms with performance management that will create a new learning and development paradigm that improves the quality of learning and development for existing crew and provides more effective training for new and existing crew to gain more verifiable competency levels.

Marine Seismic Data Acquisition

Marine seismic data acquisition is a relatively new and cyclical industry in the oil and gas sector. Cyclical industries present challenges for competency development and management programs to onboard new personnel, train them quickly in the up cycle, and protect competency investments in the down cycle. As in most oil services businesses, cost efficiency mandates through the cycle.

Founded in 1991, PGS produces data primarily used by national and international oil companies to determine their exploration risks and strategies for both undeveloped and developed areas. Data is acquired using proprietary streamers that contain hydrophones to record continuous sound waves generated from the vessel. These recorded sounds are returned to the vessel for quality control and initial processing. The final processing of the data happens over several months in onshore processing centers.

PGS regularly innovates configurations and survey design to match client needs, and seismic data manipulation develops at a rapid pace, requiring new or updated training and confirmation for offshore crew competency. Technology development is continuous in PGS as they overcome operational and geological challenges and apply new technologies.

Streamers and their configuration determine data quality, illumination, and acquisition efficiency and are selected based on geophysical and geological objectives. PGS successfully combines data quality objectives with requirements for safe and efficient operations. Up to 16 streamers as long as 10 kilometers in length spaced between 100 to 200 meters apart are towed behind the vessel at up to 25 meters' depths. Streamer spreads can cover the size of the island of Manhattan. Configurations and survey design are constantly innovated to match client needs and seismic data manipulation advances. These innovations develop at a rapid pace, requiring new or updated training and confirmation for offshore crew competency. Technology development is continuous in PGS as operational and geological challenges need to be overcome, and new technologies are applied.

While maintaining an excellent safety record, the multiple disciplines onboard use proprietary equipment and manage dynamic geophysical constructs and systems. This is truer in PGS than in our competitors because the majority of our seismic equipment, including streamers and software, is proprietary, requiring in-house expertise to maintain equipment sustainability.

180 Mark Jack Smith

Offshore Seismic Crew Training Profile

The competency of the offshore crew is essential to the safe and efficient acquisition of high-quality data. Vessels work across the world, and poor-quality seismic data, including geographical location data, can be costly, especially if the vessel must revisit the survey area.

The 24- to 28-member seismic crew working on a PGS vessel typically work a five- or six-week schedule offshore, followed by an equal number of days on leave. Multiple weeks in remote locations require a high level of onboard competency because decisions often cannot wait for consultations with experts onshore.

The crew competencies are generally grouped into five categories. Each department is governed by a seismic crew manager or chief with up to six subordinates. Each area requires a unique technical skill and an educational focus and shares a common safety and performance management process linked to competency profiles, supported by specific training programs.

The departments are as follows:

- Geophysicists analyze, investigate, and perform quality control on the seismic data acquired. This position has the primary responsibility for ensuring that the data acquired meets client specifications.
- Mechanics operate and maintain the mechanical seismic equipment onboard. They perform quality control on and maintain the seismic source systems, in-sea equipment positioning, towing and handling hardware, and a variety of other mechanical and seismic equipment.
- Navigators plan the acquisition path, schedule, and are responsible for positioning the vessel and all in-sea navigational equipment to ensure accurate positional information of the seismic data acquired.
- Observers operate the seismic recording instruments and seismic streamers, while constantly monitoring the signal-versus-noise characteristics to ensure acceptable data quality. Deployment, recovery, and maintenance of seismic streamers and in-sea equipment are other important aspects of the observers' responsibility.

These highly specific competency profiles need customized educational requirements. To update competency, PGS prefers a pedagogical approach to its on-the-job training. Annual performance assessments that appraise specific competency requirements link training leveraging directly into individual annual training plans. Profiles, processes, and training programs are continuously monitored, and management analyzes the data collected in the aggregate to improve competency profiles, impact of training modalities, etc. Unlike the regulated maritime industry, seismic crew are not required to qualify their knowledge of what are often proprietary equipment, software and routines objectively.

Four to five hundred seismic crews living in over 30 different countries create a uniquely daunting training and development challenge as their routines are repeatedly changing. Traditional classroom training for seismic crew is costly because they must travel during their earned leave period to sites usually in Norway or the United Kingdom. Besides the training cost, and room and board, PGS compensates the crew for working during their earned leave period. The additional cost of wages with travel costs is on average USD 6,000 per crew member. Even though training is expensive, traditionally only attendance and attendees' opinion of the training are regularly assessed. PGS holds a common assumption that professionals need only be exposed to knowledge to gain knowledge. As AL was evaluated and its potential better understood, the weakness of this traditional approach became increasingly clear: it did not support improved operational efficiency.

The AL Journey

Early in the company's history, the dominant learning modality for theoretical knowledge was self-study. This modality consisted of multiple pages of explanations of theory, practices, or technical specifications that crewmembers were required to read. Once read, the trainees would present the document to their superior or chief, who then confirmed that the crewmember had read and understood the document.

PGS's long-standing policy is to employ multiple nationalities to create a balanced culture onboard and to mitigate changes in taxation and employment issues that can occur in the countries in which the crewmembers reside. A good working knowledge of English is required to work offshore on a PGS vessel.

Although the policy is beneficial over time, it does create language and cultural complications for training seismic crew. Specifically, theoretical training can be difficult if the instructor and the crew do not have English as their first language.

Learning modalities and formats have evolved significantly during the last 15 to 20 years at PGS, though management rarely addressed the level of achieved learning. The crew preferred the classroom modality, although it was expensive. PGS also assumed that those trained would impart their newly acquired knowledge to their subordinates. This was and is a flawed model since there is no assessment of the knowledge gained by the superior, nor did it account for the pedagogical competencies of the superior.

Many educational institutions recognized the development of the internet as an effective modality to deliver blended courses to compensate for limited classroom space. For faculty, blended courses were opportunities to infuse new engagement into established courses or, for some, to provide a transitional opportunity between fully face-to-face and fully online instruction. For students, blended courses offered the conveniences of online learning combined with the social

182 Mark Jack Smith

and instructional interactions that may not lend themselves to distance delivery (Dziuban et al., 2011). These strategies are all relevant for commercial enterprises, too, but access to the internet was, until recently, limited and prohibitively expensive in the offshore environment. The increasing satellite communications efficiency (bandwidth) and falling telecommunications costs motivated PGS training management to develop and introduce new technology learning modalities that would better manage costs and decrease the ever-increasing pace at which crew receives new training.

In 2008, generic off-the-shelf e-learning courses were related to specific software operating systems used onboard (e.g., Linux). They were much more cost effective than sending crew to a week-long training session during their leave and seen as more effective than reading a book. No competency achievement was recorded or documented, only progress toward a minimum completion or pass-level requirement configured in the e-learning platform. Completion was primarily driven by cost. Most e-learning costs were based on how many crewmembers started the e-learning module, so the crew was pushed to complete the courses to justify the expenditure.

In 2009, PGS partnered with a Norwegian-based e-learning development firm to create a custom-made blended learning solution for seismic crew trainees in the mechanical, navigation and observer departments. The program was called eMAST (electronic marine acquisition seismic training) and was developed with an educator from the e-learning development firm, who worked with technical specialists to structure the curriculum (Hallingstad, 2012).

While development was more costly to PGS, the reuse of the modality was more cost effective. Crew took their training at home during their leave periods, on the internet, or onboard with their superior. The data collection, however, was rarely leveraged to improve the quality of the material, determine learner preferences, or determine weak performers. Neither was the observed completion of tasks onboard incorporated into the evaluation.

Around 2012, PGS offered specific e-learning modules from the eMAST program to promote cross-department understanding and to document senior crew competency. Many senior crew members complained that, among other things, the training was a waste of time, given their years of experience. Based on this feedback, PGS gave the senior crew the option of just taking the test at the end of the e-learning module to document their understanding; the software accommodated the action.

Initial test reports from the system soon indicated that a high level of senior crew did not achieve the 80% correct response rates required to document completion of the e-learning module. The implication was clear—the theoretical competency of some experienced crew could not be documented to the desired level, even though most had completed their required self-study eMAST modules, attended expensive onshore training, etc.

From 2009, e-learning proliferated in compliance and safety training modules that were developed with educators. Our experience with e-learning is that it is most effective for seismic crew with academic backgrounds who have an aptitude that lends itself to self-study and have a keen interest in the subject, which increases their motivation to persevere. It is less effective and even disliked by crew when completing e-learning became required for subjects they found less relevant to their work.

The introduction of e-learning and blended learning solutions created large amounts of data, as did the collection of electronic crew assessments of their own learning. Though collected and analyzed, it was rarely leveraged from more than completion metrics and anecdotal reviews of modality effectiveness. PGS continued to offer traditional classroom training despite the expense, but it was not popular enough with crew when they had to travel to take the course during their free period.

The employment relationship added another factor when assessing competency in training. Employees and crew, given their lack of interpersonal contact with onshore management, feared being demoted or terminated if they did not pass a test or meet a standard, which created a natural skepticism about competency assessment. Onboard management evaluated knowledge levels in annual performance appraisals, but the data clearly showed their reluctance to point out development needs unless they were visible or critical (e.g., lack of understanding of safety procedures, specific operational, or technical knowledge below the level relative to the crewmember's seniority and held position).

Another reflection that, in hindsight, makes AL attractive: 200 trainees completed the eMAST program from 2012 to 2014, but PGS did not meaningfully use the data gathered from e-learning completion and blended learning mentor signoff on hundreds of tasks to improve the quality of the curriculum.

PGS also employs a large group of field engineers with varying abilities and interests to provide onboard classroom training. Because the training they provide is not uniform, documentation of knowledge taught is difficult. They also have no efficient system to document the instruction that they provide, and crews who work 12-hour shifts often do not have time to participate in their training.

Other training modalities offered onboard include cross-department table-top sessions and newly introduced simulator training. Feedback on the table-top sessions is positive but provides no assessment of improved competency—only confirmation of training attendance and attendees' opinions of personal training relevance. The simulator training is expensive and popular primarily for onboard management on specially built classroom-based simulators in Norway that aim to improve management of incidents and hazards in offshore operations. The simulator training does not contain any pre- or post-assessment competency and only measures individual satisfaction and the training's relevance to the participant.

184   Mark Jack Smith

Looking retrospectively at the historical success of learning programs in PGS, the increasing amount of under-utilized data generated and the potential for more efficient delivery of learning became obvious.

AL Learning and Cost Effectiveness

AL's attractiveness is its learning verification and cost-effective recognition of who needs to learn general and specific competences or subsets of them. Explaining the difference between AL learning and learning management would be the main challenge.

In late 2014, oil companies wanted a more substantive verification of competence than what the traditional training paradigm provided. Oil company shareholders mandated better cost management and viewed the oil companies' costs as unsustainable after a precipitous drop in oil prices. The circumstances severely impacted PGS. From 2015 to early 2018, PGS laid off almost 50% of offshore crews as they removed vessels from the market. PGS had to cut its own costs while maintaining a high level of crew competency.

Oil companies ensure effective operations through a variety of methods, chiefly by auditing their providers' processes and systems. In 2015, a major multinational oil company in a routine audit asked a simple question: How do you know that the crews working on our marine seismic surveys are competent? I answered that we ensure seismic crew complete required training. The auditor repeated his question. This simple question revealed that PGS customers were no longer satisfied with the traditional model of crew attendance in required training.

By pure chance, Charles D. Dziuban, PhD, from the University of Central Florida was in Oslo and offered to speak to PGS training management about the introduction of adaptive learning in major universities in the United States and other countries. The ability to verify competency in a cost-effective manner that was time effective for crew was a natural progression from blended learning and, in some cases, a more attractive option than traditional classroom courses (Dziuban et al., 2011, 2017).

The Realizeit (Realizeit, 2020) platform used by the University of Central Florida offered the most sophisticated knowledge management approach, compared to other platforms. Realizeit's platform integrates with learning management systems to provide course content navigation. The system can be content agnostic; instructors create and build courses within the system, and the system allows users to ingest content from existing materials. After initial contact with Realizeit, who were positive to the challenge, and a better understanding of the functionality of their AL platform, PGS decided to develop and pilot one course as a proof of concept.

Selecting which of the four onboard departments to pilot the course was easy—the navigation department, which had the most expensive training experience. The software provider in Scotland hosted the navigation classroom courses:

A Blended Learning Case Study **185**

three-to-four-day courses that taught navigators how to use the software through offshore scenario simulations. The verification of knowledge provided by the Realizeit platform seemed ideal as it tested knowledge of theories and procedure needed to determine the geographical positioning of acquired marine data—critical data for their customers.

After several meetings, including a full demonstration of Realizeit, the software provider was no longer interested. The company viewed the platform as another learning management system. Some evidence exists that offering fully online training might be seen as a threat to a company's existing business model, or, as in many institutions, a strong bias exists toward the classroom learning modality.

Hydraulics

PGS offshore training management explored other options. The education groups found that the theoretical understanding of hydraulics among mechanics was increasingly critical for the operation of vessels, particularly since the newest vessels in PGS's fleet have a fully integrated hydraulics system. If these hydraulic systems do not function, they will have a dramatic negative commercial impact on operations.

Operations have become increasingly more complicated as PGS deploys larger vessels with the need for faster recovery of multimillion-dollar streamers. PGS has invested over $20 million per vessel in the back-deck systems that use hydraulics. These hydraulic systems require continual maintenance to avoid environmental risk from hydraulic oil leaks. In seismic marine operations, hydraulic equipment is also left idle for significant periods and, when used, is only used for short periods. This means special attention must be paid to the preservation of the systems and their functions.

A week-long course offered by the hydraulics vendor did not provide the certainty of knowledge acquisition but was popular with the mechanics, while at the same time, hydraulic-related incidents, failures, and repairs on the vessels supported the need for more urgent action. The solution was to hire specialized field engineers to train and advise offshore operations.

The mechanical department at the fleet level of approximately 100 crew had little time for onboard training, and the company would still not be able to verify competency. AL provided the solution that could reduce costs and likely reduce capital expenditure if crew became more competent in maintaining equipment.

Creating the Hydraulics AL Modules

Once the company determined hydraulics to be the best subject to pilot AL, the complications and challenges to the mechanics became clear: mechanics' computer literacy, aptitude, and comfort varied widely. The 2018 technical training

186 Mark Jack Smith

survey showed a strong preference and interest for classroom and on-the-job training; 74% agreed that training was important to their job. Onboard field engineers reported that mechanics had a clear preference for visual and cognitive learning formats. Positive feedback loops inherent in AL-motivated learning eased the concern about a formal designation of achievement based on assessment; monetary rewards for learning achievement have proven to be motivating.

After securing management buy-in to piloting AL in PGS with hydraulics, the company recruited the field engineer responsible for onboard hydraulic training. His large collection of material, however, was not pedagogically structured and required assessment protocols. The field engineer, who lives in Thailand, partnered with an educator from Realizeit based in Chicago. Management's skepticism about the geographical distance proved unfounded since the Realizeit platform provides effective collaboration, while video conferencing provided sufficient additional interaction.

Initial development time—two months for four modules—proved too ambitious due to the field engineer's availability, the sourcing of visual content, and the investigation of copyright compliancy, both essential for PGS as a commercial enterprise.

PGS initially approached academic institutes in Europe specializing in hydraulic education to incorporate their material into PGS's AL modules. They were not interested in the new AL modality or in converting their material to a more interactive format; their response was basically "Use the book that we published." Like the navigation software providers, these institutes held traditional classroom courses.

Positively, the most visual material gathered to date were YouTube videos. YouTube, a Google-owned website, allows users to upload videos, share and comment on other videos, subscribe to other users' channels, and make money by monetizing their videos (Kravčík et al., 2016). These independently produced videos were available to anyone and provided the visual content that PGS would otherwise need to develop. PGS approached the independent authors of the YouTube material to determine usage and copyright fees and discovered that the videos are free to watch through the YouTube platform. YouTube compensates authors through the CPM (cost per thousand) model that represents revenue per thousand views. With copyright issues solved, two of the planned four modules were ready for rollout.

PGS compensated crew for their achievement in each module, not their time, defining achievement-level compensation for competent, expert, and mastery. Crew had the option to improve their learning, affording the opportunity for training management to check on crew perseverance in the subject. PGS contacted crew who completed each module to lower than the highest defined level (mastery), and they provided anecdotal feedback that some crew were interested in (intellectual curiosity), while others were not—these crew members felt they knew enough to function in their job.

Measuring the Success of the Hydraulics AL Modules

Mechanics have responded positively to adaptive learning as a modality with the embedded videos, as evidenced by their willingness to complete the modules in their free time. Over 50% of mechanics have completed one of the two available modules as of June 2020. AL allows students and, in this case, crew to complete learning at their own pace where there is internet access. Additionally, AL demonstrates a competent, expert, or mastery level of competency before and after completing each module.

The range of knowledge from pre– to post–module completion revealed just how inefficient the previous training modalities were, given the wide variety of knowledge documented on the AL platform. The assessed starting knowledge of hydraulics in the first two modules ranged from 33% to 97%. Further, there was no correlation between crew who had previously attended the aforementioned vendor-provided training or company sponsored field course. Knowledge gains assessed on the platform for the first 40 participants who engaged with three or more topics also varied widely. The highest knowledge gain was 41% from an assessed starting knowledge of 33% and as low as 5% from an assessed starting knowledge of 74%.

A secondary effect of the AL modality among mechanics is the positive feedback loop created by the inherent progress reporting AL provides with the economic incentive. Specifically, crew are compensated for the expertise they quickly exhibited while others are paid to increase their knowledge at their own personal pace. The additional two hydraulic modules are planned for the fall of 2020, although the worldwide COVID-19 pandemic has delayed most training development across the industry and, in most cases, forced management and employees to focus on downsizing. When the market stabilizes, the expectation is that the value of the hydraulics modules will increase as the feedback data is mined to improve assessments and module content.

Potential Long-Term Value

Blended learning combined with adaptive learning supports the critical digitization and automation processes that most commercial enterprises experience. In an industry like marine seismic data acquisition and interpretation, training data from every step in the processes provides operational efficiency improvement; capital expenditure reduction; and, most importantly, offshore safety.

Long-term value can be realized by adding a component to the blended adaptive learning mix. Predictive learning analytics can tailor instruction to the needs of individuals or cohorts of crew members (Ruiz-Calleja et al., 2017). Realizeit provides a suite of outcome data in real time for baseline status, knowledge acquisition, growth, and learning engagement. The intersection of the adaptive modality and analytics yields learning information in real time that builds an autocatalytic instructional loop. Adaptive learning intersecting with blending learning produces a just-in-time supply chain learning model because the elements of adaptive and supply chain management coincide (Johnson et al., 2020). Blending and analytics produce a uniquely structured method for combining visual learning into a diagnostic framework. This results in what was experienced in this case study—an emergent learning environment that transcends the individual elements where their interaction is more important than individual considerations.

Additional long-term value comes from what we have learned in this pilot case study. Crew members in the mechanical department feel that additional technical training is important for proper job performance, and the personalized learning protocol is a value-added component for them. Crew have a strong desire for additional training, and many feel that it should be available while onboard the vessels. They wish to learn by doing but are somewhat ambivalent about the effectiveness of e-learning. Their most convincing response recognizes that the content of training should dictate the presentation method.

AL platforms such as Realizeit have the potential to become sources of knowledge development, inventories, and the rapid deployment of new knowledge and can become important business and operational data sources in multiple industries. AL platforms allow managers to instantly train employees on the specific competency improvement needs and assess them pre- and post-training. The application of these and other new developments has long-term potential for PGS, especially as pressure to lower costs and increase efficiency drive digitization, and are essential to improve business management and ensure safe operations. The real long value will come from the next phase of this case study, in which PGS examines the relationships among technical knowledge acquisition, problem solving, and job performance. Blending multiple learning modalities has the potential to address these issues on seismic data acquisition vessels and in industries where job training is a continuous process. If there is a new normal, its index case is here.

References

Bonk, C. J., & Graham, C. R. (2005). *The handbook of blended learning: Global perspectives, local designs*. Pfeiffer Publishing.

Chiva, R., Grandío, A., & Alegre, J. (2010). Adaptive and generative learning: Implications from complexity theories. *International Journal of Management Reviews, 12*(2), 114–129.

Dziuban, C., Graham, C. R., Moskal, P. D., Norberg, A., & Sicilia, N. (2018). Blended learning: The new normal and emerging technologies. *International Journal of Technology in Higher Education, 15*(3), 1–16.

Dziuban, C., Hartman, J., Cavanagh, T., & Moskal, P. (2011). Blended courses as drivers of institutional transformation. In A. Kitchenham (Ed.), *Blended learning across disciplines: Models for implementation* (pp. 17–37). IGI Global.

Dziuban, C., Howlin, C., Johnson, C., & Moskal, P. (2017). An adaptive learning partnership. *EDUCAUSE Review*, 1–19.

Hallingstad, T. (2012). *PGS eMAST trainee level handbook & eLearning*. Petroleum Geo-Services A/S.

Johnson, A., Dziuban, C., Eid, M., & Howlin, C. (2020, January). *Supply chain management and adaptive learning*. Realizeit Labs.

Kravčík, M., Nicolaescu, P., Siddiqui, A., & Klamma, R. (2016, October). Adaptive video techniques for informal learning support in workplace environments. In *International symposium on emerging technologies for education* (pp. 533–543). Springer.

Picciano, A. G., Dziuban, C. D., & Graham, C. R. (2013). *Blended learning: Research perspectives* (Vol. 2). Routledge.

Realizeit (2020, July 15). *An intelligent learning and analytics platform*. http://realizeitlearning.com/

Ruiz-Calleja, A., Prieto, L. P., Ley, T., Rodríguez-Triana, M. J., & Dennerlein, S. (2017, September). Learning analytics for professional and workplace learning: A literature review. In *European conference on technology enhanced learning* (pp. 164–178). Springer.

SECTION V

K–12 Perspectives

12

COMPETENCIES AND PRACTICES FOR GUIDING K–12 BLENDED TEACHER READINESS

Cecil R. Short, Courtney Hanny, Michelle Jensen, Karen Arnesen, and Charles R. Graham

The increase in blended teaching (BT) across K–12 contexts is difficult to measure because "blended teaching" is defined and implemented in a variety of ways (Graham, 2013; Hrastinski, 2019). Some define BT as using a combination of both in-person and online modalities (Allen & Seaman, 2010; Garrison & Kanuka, 2004; Graham, 2006), while others include certain pedagogical implications within their definition (Alammary et al., 2014; Bower et al., 2015; Diep et al., 2017; Garrison & Vaughan, 2008; Picciano, 2009; Staker & Horn, 2012; Zacharis, 2015). The most common definition in K–12 contexts is part of this latter category, describing BT as "at least in part through online delivery, with some element of student control over time, place, path and/or pace" (Horn & Staker, 2011, p. 3). Watson and Murin (2014) also require some student control over "time/pace/path/place," adding that blended learning (BL) "changes the instructional model away from one-to-many (teacher-to-students) instruction and toward a personalized, data-driven approach" (p. 13). These definitions describe personalization as essential to BT. While some effective blends have aspects of personalization, such pedagogy is not essential to creating a blend (Arnesen et al., 2019). Measuring K–12 implementation of BL is difficult due to definitional murkiness and because implementation can happen at the school level, be led by individual teachers, or remain within individual classrooms (Graham, 2019).

We define BT competencies as the knowledge, skills, and abilities that teachers need to teach in BL contexts, building from competencies presented in *K–12 Blended Learning: A Guide to Personalized Learning and Online Integration* (Graham, Borup, Short et al., 2019). These competencies approach BL in the broadest sense, as an umbrella term for any combination of both online and in-person instruction (Graham, 2013, 2019), and are therefore pedagogically agnostic. Regardless of chosen pedagogies, BT requires a significant paradigm shift for teachers as it

DOI: 10.4324/9781003037736-17

differs from the traditional teaching methods many experienced as students and have been trained to use as pre-service and in-service teachers (Greene & Hale, 2017). Various sources have identified or suggested competencies necessary for BT but have not evaluated them in terms of prevalence in practice. Pulham and Graham (2018) reviewed 17 documents with K–12 BT competencies and synthesized six competency areas for BT. Subsequently, Pulham et al. (2018) found that many of the individual competencies identified were not specific to BT contexts.

There are pedagogical implications for understanding and identifying the most influential BT competencies. Greene and Hale (2017) called for pre-service and in-service training for blended and online teaching, explaining that twenty-first-century teachers may be expected to "facilitate learning that lives up to the potential of both modes of education" (p. 147). As BL becomes more prevalent, teacher preparation programs need to prepare novice teachers for BT. Pre-service curriculum will need to include competencies specific to blended pedagogy because generic teaching competencies do not capture all the skills necessary for BT (Pulham et al., 2018). Identifying competency areas that are relevant to BT in K–12 contexts will help teacher educators know what to emphasize in their pre-service training and how to assist in-service teachers, administrators, and professional development leaders as they transition traditional, in-person classes to blended classes.

Literature Review

As demand for BL increases (Barbour, 2017), understanding the relative prevalence of BT competencies becomes more urgent (Dziuban et al., 2018; Eisenbach, 2016). Researchers have demonstrated that skills and practices associated with BT are not the same as those needed for in-person or online teaching (Pulham et al., 2018; Graham, Borup, Short et al., 2019). Based on frameworks presented in literature, BT is not simply the addition of technology to the classroom (Archambault et al., 2014; Bjekic et al., 2010; Oliver & Stallings, 2014). Yet most PD programs targeting BL focus on technology tools instead of blended competencies (Graham, Borup, Pulham et al., 2019). Since the competencies associated with BT vary so dramatically from those of other forms of teaching, blended education requires a more deliberate and specific emphasis on professional development (Eisenbach, 2016; Ojaleye & Awofala, 2018; Pulham et al., 2018).

Many researchers have identified specific competencies to improve educators' successful implementation of BL (Akarawang et al., 2015; Anthony, 2019; Bjekic et al., 2010; Oliver & Stallings, 2014; Pulham & Graham, 2018). Pulham and Graham (2018) identified eight pre-service teacher competency areas for online and blended learning. Graham, Borup, Pulham et al. (2019) built on this research, creating a rigorously validated framework with 13 competency areas, through

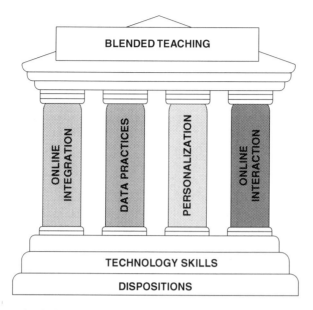

FIGURE 12.1 Blended Teaching Competency Framework
Source: (Graham, Borup, Short et al., 2019)

which teachers could assess their readiness to start blending. Graham, Borup, Short et al. (2019) refined this work in their guide to BT with a framework consisting of foundational dispositions and technology skills, with four competency areas: online integration, data practices, personalization, and online interaction (Figure 12.1). These competency areas were used to direct the research presented in this chapter.

Research Questions

This research sought to connect the competency areas from Graham, Borup, Short et al. (2019) to current K–12 BT practices by answering the following questions:

1. How do proposed BT competency areas relate to actual K–12 BT pedagogical practices?
2. What examples can be found of quality BT practices within the competency areas of online integration, data practices, personalization, and online interaction?
3. What areas for potential growth for experienced K–12 blended teachers are revealed by investigation of BT competency areas?

Methods

We answered these questions by implementing two separate though related methodologies. First, we analyzed BT artifacts to establish the prevalence of proposed competency areas in BT practices. Second, we analyzed interviews of teachers with BT experience to uncover examples of effective established practices as well as practices needing further development within each competency area.

Artifact Analysis

The artifacts included 959 observations, interviews, and videos created by the Learning Accelerator, a non-profit group dedicated to connecting K–12 blended practitioners to the knowledge, tools, and networks needed to effectively blend and personalize instruction. The artifacts were collected from over a dozen K–12 districts and span all grade levels. BT competencies from Graham, Borup, Short et al. (2019) were used as a priori codes to analyze the artifacts. We completed independent coding of 372 randomly sampled artifacts, allowing for generalizability to all artifacts with a confidence level of 95% (+/-4%).

Interview Analysis

We identified prospective participants for the interviews through working relationships, recommendations from district-level leaders, recruitment at various conferences, and professional partnerships such as the Learning Accelerator, the Clayton Christensen Institute, and the Digital Learning Collaborative. We requested interviews from strong candidates through email and asked other candidates to fill out a survey designed to vet participants not selected for the first round of interviews. Survey respondents indicating BT experience received additional interview invitations. Participants were located domestically and from various content areas: English language arts, social studies, math, science, computer science, visual and performing arts, and others (see Table 12.1). Their teaching

TABLE 12.1 Interview Sampling Strategy Across Grade Levels and Subject Areas

Number of interviews	Grade levels	Subjects
2	K–3	General
3	4–6	General
3	7–12	Humanities (language arts, foreign languages)
3	7–12	Social sciences (social studies, history)
3	7–12	STEM (science, engineering, math)
3	7–12	Arts (visual arts, performing arts, music)
3	7–12	Other (physical education, health, FACS, special education)

experience ranged from 2 to 20 or more years, and each teacher had at least 1 year of BT experience.

When candidates agreed to participate, they signed an informed consent form and scheduled an interview. We conducted semi-structured interviews, lasting approximately 90 minutes, using a video conferencing platform that automatically generates transcriptions. We designed the interview protocol to explore participants' implementation of the four competency areas identified by Graham, Borup, Short et al. (2019). Research assistants prepared and anonymized the video transcriptions, which we uploaded to NVivo for coding using a thematic analysis based on the four competency areas presented by Graham, Borup, Short, and Archambault.

After thematic coding, we coded interviews again identifying specific BT practices in each interview, then ranked the practices according to the codes in Table 12.2. Example details varied from interviewees concisely explaining what they used to record online feedback to a multiple paragraph description of how a teacher managed a station rotation within the BT classroom. Researchers coded three interviews together to make sure the rating codes captured the practices in the interviews. Following norming sessions with three more interviews, two researchers independently coded five interviews and compared coding to reveal an interrater reliability of 80.3% on over 25% of the sample. Upon reaching this interrater reliability, the two researchers independently coded the remaining nine interviews.

Limitations

Our findings have been limited by the scope of the artifacts we analyzed and the experiences of the teachers we interviewed. The artifacts may have

TABLE 12.2 Rating Codes for Blended Teaching Practices

Code	Description
Not present	The practice was not found. The interviewee may have talked about the competency with no intention of implementing it and/or had not arrived at the point of ideation.
Emerging	A practice was evident but still in the beginning phases of development. The interviewee was trying it out or had reflected on the possibility of doing it. The practice was in the idea stages or had barely emerged as an applied practice.
Developing	This practice was being developed but showed room for improvement. This example could help someone starting out, but was not a prime example of the competency.
Mastery	This practice was well developed and exemplary of what the competency looks like in practice.

underrepresented online interaction examples due to the focus of the Learning Accelerator on the other three competency areas. Despite this limitation, the artifacts illustrated that practices for online integration, data practices, and personalization go beyond the teachers we interviewed. A limitation of the interview data was that many of the teachers came from school districts similar in student demographic data, and all of them had successfully implemented BT strategies into their classes. A more diversified sample of teachers, who had various levels of BT experiences and were teaching in more varied contexts, could yield different insights into the patterns of implementation across competency areas.

Findings

The skills for online integration, data practices, and personalization were ubiquitous throughout the BT artifacts, with data practices and personalization skills often co-occurring. Online interaction skills appeared in fewer artifacts than the other three, though this might be due to the Learning Accelerator's exclusion of online interaction as one of their core areas of BT or because this area may be difficult to capture through classroom observations. Figure 12.2 displays the number of artifacts that had at least one competency from each of Graham, Borup, Short et al.'s (2019) competency areas. The prevalence of BT examples in online integration, data practices, and personalization may suggest that these areas are more developed than online interaction, and the abundance of personalization practices may suggest that it is the most developed. Alternatively, the greater representation of personalization practices may suggest a greater emphasis on observing

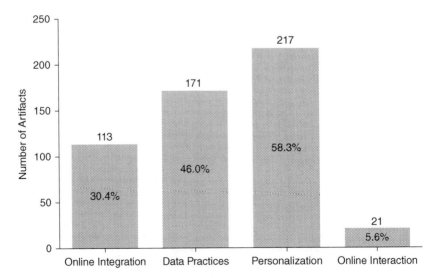

FIGURE 12.2 Competency Area Representation Across 372 Blended Teaching Artifacts

Guiding K–12 Blended Teacher Readiness **199**

personalization practices, due to the popularity and increasing focus of this area within the field of K–12 education. To better understand specific practices within competency areas, we used data collected from our interviews.

The interviews revealed that many effective practices are being used across competency areas and that online interactions may be more developed than the artifact analysis suggests (see Figure 12.3). Perhaps because the teachers interviewed were all experienced with K–12 BT, most of the practices they discussed were coded as masterful. Online integration practices outnumbered the other areas, likely because this area included (a) using the online space with the in-person space and (b) managing the use of the online space, as well as the co-occurrence of online integration with the other three competency areas. The breakdown of practices across categories can be seen in Table 12.3.

To better understand what these practices may look like across contexts and how areas of established practices may differ from areas with room for development, we looked at each competency area and compared practices across the content areas. The following sections highlight examples of best practices as well as practices that seem to need more development.

Online Integration

Online integration had the highest number of mastery and non-mastery practices among the four competency areas. Thus, practices specifically related to online integration were widely used and extensively developed among interviewees, which was anticipated as online integration is the core competency needed to blend. We coded online integration practices into two sub-categories identified in

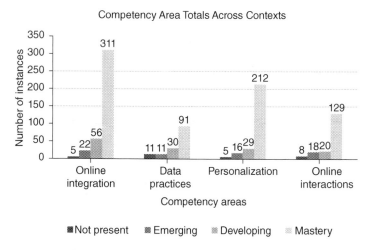

FIGURE 12.3 Prevalence of Practices Within Competency Areas in 20 Blended Teacher Interviews

TABLE 12.3 Ratings of Blended Teaching Practices Coded in Teacher Interviews

	Online integration	Data practices	Personal-ization	Online interaction
Coded blended practices	400	145	262	184
Percent at mastery	77.8%	62%	80.9%	75.5%
Percent below mastery	22.3%	37.2%	19.1%	24.5%
Percent at developing	14.5%	22.1%	11.1%	10.9%
Percent at emerging	6.3%	7.6%	6.1%	9.2%
Percent at not present	1.5%	7.6%	1.9%	4.4%
Ratio of non-mastery practices to mastery practices	89:311	54:91	25:106	45:139

Note: Percentages do not always add up to 100% because numbers are rounded.

TABLE 12.4 Distribution of Ratings for Coded Practices Within Online Integration

Rating	Integration		Management	
	#	%	#	%
Not present	5	1.7%	1	0.9%
Emerging	21	7.2%	4	3.7%
Developing	36	12.4%	22	17.9%
Mastery	229	78.7%	82	75.2%

Table 12.4 as integration (purposefully combining online and in-person instruction) and management (effectively managing the online environment, blended rotations, hardware and software, student online help, etc.). Integration, with 291 practices, had 72.8% of the coded practices, while management, with 109 practices, had 27.3%. Table 12.4 shows the percentage of the total practices in both integration and management for each competency level.

Examples of Quality Practices

Quality management practices commonly centered on teaching and practicing/reviewing. Teachers with mastery practices took time to teach students how to move with, use, and otherwise manage devices; how to log in and save documents; how to use the classroom LMS, including submitting assignments and communicating with the teacher and other students; how to give and receive appropriate feedback; how to avoid cyber bullying; and how to use educational and online programs. Teachers practiced and reviewed this training until students felt comfortable using technology and knew how to be safe and civil. Teachers with mastery-level management practices also developed methods for monitoring students as they used devices, to ensure they were using devices for educational purposes.

Three of the most commonly used online/in-person integration practices were providing video instruction, video feedback, and video-based assessments. Instruction included math and coding teachers using short videos to explain problems that students struggled with, targeting the videos to students who needed the instruction. Similarly, after using in-class time to discuss objectives, goals, and procedures for a project, a sewing teacher provided videos to show instructions for the students' specific projects. Feedback was impactful as language arts teachers used both video and written feedback on students' Google docs. Broad topics that occurred frequently in students' work developed into in-person discussions. Assessment was accomplished as a choir and a health teacher used class time to teach and practice sight singing and CPR, respectively, then conducted video assessments to make sure the students could perform what they had learned.

Other mastery practices were unique to a specific content area. For example, a social science teacher arranged for students to meet online with students in Tunisia. Students discussed their daily lives and cultures, as well as issues that concerned them. After meeting with the Tunisian students, the class met together to discuss what they had learned, particularly the concerns the Tunisian students had expressed. Then they formed groups; each group chose one aspect of the concerns they had discussed and created a presentation, which they shared with the rest of the school. Closer to home, students in a health class went on a video ride-along experience with a police detective, after which the school officer talked to them in class about gangs. Based on what they learned, student groups researched different types of substance abuse and created infographics, posters, and videos.

Areas for Potential Growth

Most teachers who struggled with management practices either lacked experience in teaching how to use specific technologies or were frustrated with not knowing how to work with students who (a) misused the online space by playing games or watching YouTube videos or (b) were unkind to other students in online discussions, feedback, or collaboration. Teachers felt especially vulnerable when they were helping other students or working with small groups and could not adequately monitor those students who were working on devices.

Teachers using integration practices worked toward growth in several areas. Common areas included finding good programs (e.g., writing assessment tools), finding ways to use devices not available for every student, learning to use new technology (e.g., video or sound editing in a music class), feeling overwhelmed with the number of programs and amount of information available and having insufficient time to evaluate their adequacy for a specific learning objective or environment, and ensuring that "exciting" technology use can actually contribute to learning.

Data Practices

The category of data practices was found to have the fewest mastery level practices and the most developing practices relative to the number of mastery practices (see Table 12.3). The underrepresentation of data practices may be due to lack of confidence across all mastery levels. Interviewees began their answers with expressions like "I'm new" and "I am not the best"; a mastery-level practice for setting and tracking goals was prefaced with "I'm still working on that." Many teachers found themselves forced to delve deeper into data practices for the first time during the pandemic teaching period, and most expressed eagerness to learn how to use data practices to their advantage after schools reopen.

Among the data practices, clear distinctions were found between teachers using data (a) to evaluate student performance and student activity and (b) to evaluate individual students or an entire class, as evidenced by Table 12.5. Some practices do not appear in Table 12.5 because they collected data not associated with activity or performance, such as student preferences, while other practices are counted twice because they compiled both kinds of data: for example, time spent and scores earned within a learning program.

Examples of Quality Practices

Most teachers with mastery-level data practices found that these practices made the work of meeting student needs easier, faster, and more organized. They used individual student data to give constructive individualized feedback to students and to identify struggling students to offer them additional support. For example, one teacher created a remediation course in Canvas and used data to decide who to enroll in that course. Some teachers also used these data to form heterogeneous groups, placing struggling students with those already at mastery. Many teachers used dashboards and charts provided by educational programs, explaining that the students liked the visual feedback and became more intrinsically motivated when they could set their own goals. Mastery practices using student activity data helped teachers track and offer support to students who struggled to manage their own time on the computer. Additionally, teachers used performance data more

TABLE 12.5 Types and Prevalence of Data Used in Blended Practices Coded in Teacher Interviews

	Individual student instances	Class-wide instances
Performance data (assessments, exams, assignment scores, etc.)	60	23
Activity data (participation, engagement, effort, etc.)	25	5

frequently in communication with parents, either to solicit their support or to explain why a student was not performing well.

Notably, most of the class-wide data practices were coded at mastery and were used by teachers who had other mastery-level data practices as well. Teachers used class-wide performance data to understand how to best change their assessments, assignments, or overall pedagogy, as these data allowed them to "get a finger on the pulse" of classrooms in their entirety. One teacher frequently gave short surveys to her students, and within ten minutes, she had the information she needed to adjust her instruction for the next class. Class-wide activity data were used to track class engagement in specific programs or with various assignments. For example, a teacher used software to monitor student time because he had noticed class productivity was much lower when students were not engaged. Other teachers used class-wide surveys to understand if students were enjoying the activities and structure of the course and to determine whether instructional changes were needed. The positive responses teachers received from these surveys motivated them in their attempts to blend and improve their practices.

Areas for Potential Growth

Teachers struggling to implement data practices experienced two major difficulties: inexperience generating data and inefficiency using data. Some teachers were unsure of how to use the technological resources and software available. For example, a few teachers collected and tracked all student information on paper, resulting in a much more limited and rigid use of data. Other teachers were uncomfortable with specific dashboards or with their LMS and therefore did not use the technology's data capabilities. One teacher explained that she usually forgot to check the students' data, but when she tried, she became overwhelmed by the quantity of data, with each program presenting student progress in a different way. Another teacher commented on the pressure of having "so many options [of data-tracking software] out there." Other teachers deliberately chose to avoid collecting data, believing that data practices restricted assignments to multiple-choice questions, thus creating equity concerns or allowing students to more easily manipulate their scores.

Personalization

Our analysis sought personalization practices that focused on giving students choice over their own time, place, pace, path, and learning goals. These dimensions of personalization are most commonly associated with the Christensen Institute's definition of BL (Staker & Horn, 2012) but add the dimension of "goals" from Graham, Borup, Short et al. (2019). Our analysis revealed practices that allowed students to personalize their learning and practices related to managing personalized learning, the two being distributed fairly evenly across contexts.

The only area that seemed to have fewer personalized learning practices was the area of "other." The distribution of practices within each content area can be seen in Figure 12.4.

Table 12.6 illustrates the five personalization dimensions (time, place, pace, path, goals) mentioned by interviewees when discussing their practices, as well as the level of development and implementation of their practice—not present, but emerging; developing; or mastery. Of the 262 coded practices, 20 (7.6%) referred to time, 34 (13.0%) to place, 71 (27.1%) to pace, 80 (30.5%) to path, and 57 (21.8%) to goals. As mentioned, some of the practices did not focus on a specific dimension because they focused on implementation or management. In some cases, teachers personalized learning for their students instead of allowing students to have control over their choice, referred to by Graham, Borup, Short et al. (2019) as "differentiation." Additionally, some of the practices could fit into multiple dimensions, such as a mastery-level

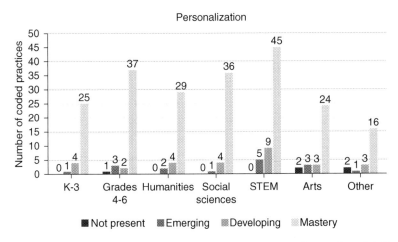

FIGURE 12.4 Ratings for Personalization Practices Across Grade Levels and Subject Contexts

TABLE 12.6 Distribution of Ratings for Coded Practices Within Personalization

Rating	Dimensions of personalization									
	Time		Place		Pace		Path		Goals	
	#	%	#	%	#	%	#	%	#	%
Not present	0	0.0%	0	0.0%	3	4.2%	0	0.0%	3	5.3%
Emerging	2	10.0%	4	11.8%	2	2.8%	3	3.8%	3	5.3%
Developing	1	5.0%	1	2.9%	4	5.6%	9	11.3%	0	17.5%
Mastery	7	85.0%	9	85.3%	62	87.3%	68	85.0%	41	71.9%

practice from a computer coding teacher who personalized across all five dimensions by allowing students to choose their own goals, choose from a variety of resources to meet those goals, and work at their own pace either in or outside class.

Examples of Quality Practices

Mastery-level practices were found both for managing personalized learning and for allowing students to have some control over their own learning. Examples of mastery-level management practices included motivating students with recognition, praise, or micro-credentials; organizing the classroom to allow for student choice; using data to guide student learning; and working with students who might resist or abuse increased control over their learning. Most of the mastery-level practices within the dimensions of personalization consisted of pace (62 practices) and path (68 practices), with personalized goals also being a fairly common mastery-level dimension (41 practices). Personalization of goals was found more frequently in the upper grades, while personalizing pace and path were more common practices per interviewee in the lower grades (K–6). Some mastery practices allowed for personalizing across multiple dimensions, including management strategies. A K–3 teacher used adaptive software to allow students to work at their own time, place, pace, and path in the classroom and recruited parents to assist learning from home. The teacher encouraged working ahead or getting caught up from home by celebrating student progression in class. Using adaptive software was also an important part of personalizing across all dimensions in grades 4 through 6.

Areas for Potential Growth

Time and place appeared fewer times during the interviews than the other dimensions and mostly focused on allowing students to learn at home, though there were a few practices within personalizing place that focused on flexible seating, allowing students to work in groups instead of on their own and allowing students to work anywhere in the building. The practices marked as "not present" reflected a lack of desirable adaptive software that would allow students to work at their own pace and on an appropriate level based on their skill or development. Emerging and developing practices, while not very common across the interviews, primarily represented teachers' desires to do more blending within their classroom, such as flipping more instruction or allowing students to have greater flexibility within certain lessons or standards. The dimensions of path and goals had the most developing practices, despite path having more mastery-level practices. This may suggest that personalization of goals represents the dimension with the most room for further growth.

Online Interaction

Our analysis focused on two categories of online interactions. Teacher-to-student interactions occurred as teachers used the online space to communicate with students or provide feedback to them. Student-to-student interactions occurred when students participated in discussions (written or video based), collaboration, or peer review. The category of online interaction included fewer mastery-level practices than online integration and personalization but more than data practices (see Figure 12.3). Thus, online interaction seemed to be practiced less often among interviewees and might not be as well developed. Student-to-student online interactions were frequent in upper elementary and secondary grades, but less common in K–3. Figure 12.5 illustrates the prevalence of online integration practices across contexts.

Table 12.7 shows the distribution of practices among the various types of teacher-to-student and student-to-student interactions. With a total of 158

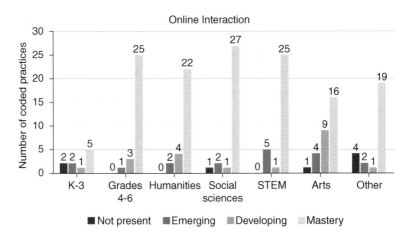

FIGURE 12.5 Practice Ratings for Online Interaction Across Contexts

TABLE 12.7 Distribution of Ratings for Coded Practices Within Online Interaction

Rating	Dimensions of Online Interaction									
	S-S Collaboration		S-S Discussion		S-S Peer review		T-S Feedback		T-S Communication	
	#	%	#	%	#	%	#	%	#	%
Not present	3	10.3%	1	4.0%	1	8.3%	3	8.3%	25	44.6%
Emerging	1	3.4%	5	20.0%	1	8.3%	5	13.9%	6	10.7%
Developing	4	13.8%	3	12.0%	3	25.0%	3	8.3%	4	7.1%
Mastery	21	72.4%	16	64.0%	7	58.3%	25	69.4%	21	37.5%
Total	9	18.4%	25	15.8%	12	7.6%	36	22.8%	56	35.4%

practices, 29 (18.4%) referenced student-to-student collaboration; 25 (15.8%) student-to-student discussion; 12 (7.6%) student-to-student peer review; 36 (22.8%) teacher-to-student feedback; and 56 (35.4%) teacher-to-student communication. Although teacher-to-student communication garnered the highest number of coded practices, student-to-student collaboration had the highest percentage of coded mastery practices.

Examples of Quality Practices

Although online interaction practices seemed to be less developed, many mastery-level practices were used across contexts. Online discussion through an LMS was a common practice that required students to post an initial response to a prompt and then reply in a directed way to several peers. Teachers interviewed found this practice beneficial because it "gives everyone a megaphone . . . in a context that's comfortable," "gives them [a] mechanism for thoughtful reflection," and allows the teacher to coach students regarding "the kinds of words that you can use when you're disagreeing with someone to get your point across but still be appropriate." Another mastery-level practice was requiring online peer reviews, which often improved students' work by giving them insight into their own strengths and weaknesses. Students also collaborated online, usually through tools that allowed them to work simultaneously in the online space, such as Google docs and slides, editing and commenting on the same file. One teacher described the benefits of student collaboration as "connecting with other learners during the process of learning" and suggested that this encouraged his students to "think differently about production of the work, but also to take feedback that [they] can critically incorporate into [their] work."

Teachers with mastery-level practices also found that online interactions enriched their relationships with their students by providing an additional means of communication. These interactions were seen as less threatening and more private than other forms of communication, allowing students to share personal and educational concerns that they would not have otherwise felt comfortable expressing. Teachers offered support for these students' needs in person or by contacting parents or administrators in especially concerning situations. One teacher doubted that he could have obtained the help some of his students needed without the online interactions. Teachers also expressed that they learned more about students' unique personalities and interests through digital interactions. Teacher-to-student online interaction also enabled teachers to stay connected with students who were chronically absent.

Teachers also interacted online with students through feedback on assignments. They found this method of providing feedback faster, easier, more effective, and more personal: "I think those asynchronous little nuggets are the pieces where I feel more connected to the kids than just when I high-five them walking in the door." Several teachers mentioned leaving video or audio feedback and expressed a belief that students responded better to it than to written feedback. Teachers benefited from a shortened feedback cycle, allowing students to revise and resubmit assignments and receive feedback several times before submitting a final product.

Areas for Potential Growth

Teachers who did not have mastery practices for online interaction believed that student-to-student communication would be more effective in person or were concerned with their students' ability to interact online and struggled to help their students develop the necessary abilities. Among K–3 teachers, online interaction was very rare, with only five practices per interview (Figure 12.7). These teachers expressed concern that their students were too young and lacked the independent technical and social skills necessary to interact online. Teachers who lacked mastery practices also claimed that interacting with their students online was ineffective and lacked meaning and that this adversely affected their relationships with students, claiming that the students lacked the skills to utilize online feedback and manage digital content.

Conclusions

The rapid increase in BL use across K–12 education necessitates understanding the core competencies for K–12 BT. Training pre-service teachers or providing professional development to in-service teachers requires deep understanding of the skills that they need to use effectively. This chapter focuses on BT competencies as implemented in practice by experienced educators. We analyzed hundreds of BT artifacts and interviewed 20 experienced blended teachers in the primary grades as well as across all major subject domains in the secondary grades. Some important insights from the research are summarized in Table 12.8, followed by discussion of their potential implications.

To be particularly noted in this research is that we should feel hopeful about the ability of teachers to develop BT competency. While there was some variation according to grade level and subject taught, overall, the teachers demonstrated a broad range of practices within the four core competencies. Richer case examples are needed specific to the subject domains, especially for elective subjects, as examples of practice are easier to find for required subject areas like math, English language arts, science, and social studies. Teachers of the arts; physical education; family, home, and consumer sciences; and world languages need more specific instances.

Online integration is the only BT competency essential to all blends; the definition of *blend* requires this competency. Although the data presented show online integration less emphasized in the BT artifacts (see Figure 12.2), it had the highest representation among teacher practices mentioned in the interviews

Guiding K–12 Blended Teacher Readiness **209**

TABLE 12.8 Important Observations Summarized from the Research

Competency area	Observations
General	• All four competency areas used for analysis were represented in teachers' practices across grades and subjects (see Figure 12.3). • Interviewees discussed mostly practices that were seen as masterful (see Figure 12.3).
Online integration	• Competencies were divided into two categories: integration of online learning and management of the online space. • More practices were found for integration than for management, though the percentage of mastery-level practices was approximately the same (see Table 12.4).
Data practices	• This competency area showed the fewest mastery-level practices of all the areas (see Figure 12.3). • Practices focused mostly on individual student performance data (see Table 12.5).
Personalization	• Personalization was well represented in both the artifacts and mastery-level practices in the interviews. • Pace and path were the most commonly personalized dimensions in the mastery-level practices (see Table 12.6).
Online interaction	• This was the least represented competency in the professional development artifacts (see Figure 12.1). • This was also the least developed competency area in K–3 according to teacher interviews (see Figure 12.7).

(see Figure 12.3). Many teachers accomplished online integration with various kinds of adaptive or educational software, such as literacy programs or virtual labs. Other teachers lamented the lack of educational software specific to their content areas, explaining that they created their own online materials. As many new blended teachers may feel the need for abundant online resources to begin integrating the online space by creating new content, professional development materials might be targeted to helping them understand the scope and sequencing of beginning to blend.

Based on our findings, data practices is a competency that needs more emphasis in BT professional development, as teachers seem to be weakest in this area. Some of the less disruptive models of BT (e.g., rotation models) do not require data use. However, effective data practices can enhance the use of rotation models and become essential to using more disruptive models that emphasize personalized and mastery-based approaches to learning. Such BT models hold a lot of promise but may not be practically implemented without the digitally organized data that (a) help teachers see student learning patterns and (b) inform adjustments to student learning paths.

Practices related to personalization were well represented in the artifact analysis and in mastery-level practices within the interviews. However, space for growth was apparent with personalizing time, place, and goals, which were represented at lower levels than personalizing pace and path. Teachers may feel more confined within time, place, and goals than with other dimensions of personalization, as they must provide instruction within the school day and in the classroom, with the requirement to meet specific learning objectives. More research is needed to fully understand if the dimensions of personalization are equal in importance, both to student learning and to pedagogy, or if dimensions such as pace and path are more important, as suggested by our data. An additional factor in determining the importance of these dimensions may be to consider the traits students must develop to become effective adult learners who have the choice and ability to pursue their own learning goals.

Online interactions is the competency area that may have the most room for development. As likely expected, online interactions were less frequent in the elementary grades, as many of the practices in this area are more developmentally appropriate for older students. However, the occurrence of mastery-level practices within these lower grades suggests that elementary students may be capable of meaningful interactions online if given the appropriate tools and training to do so. Perhaps a more prevalent barrier to implementing online interactions was teachers' beliefs about their utility. Many teachers seemed to feel that their students could not benefit from online interactions or handle them responsibly and that the opportunity to have effective in-person interactions outweighed the need for online interactions. If teachers were more aware of the potential benefits of student-student and teacher-student online interactions, some of which were highlighted in our findings, they might decide that the costs of implementing such interactions are justified. Future research could highlight such benefits in order to make them clearer for teachers wanting to use various BT models.

The overall findings in this chapter provide a valuable foundation for future research focusing on K–12 BT knowledge, skills, and abilities. The prevalence of certain competency areas in the artifacts and interviews analyzed may reflect the order in which teachers begin developing BT competencies or the importance they attribute to some competency areas over others. For example, teachers may concentrate first on online integration, with a desire to obtain the benefits of other competency areas that frequently overlap with it. Our findings may also suggest that experienced blended teachers value certain competency areas over others due to their ease of implementation or their perceived benefit and value to students. Regardless of implication, it seems clear that many experienced blended teachers have implemented practices that have transformed the way they teach and provided various advantages to students.

Future research should use the findings in this chapter as a starting point to uncover more detailed and specific information about BT pedagogies, including what is needed to prepare K–12 teachers to blend effectively. Future observations, interviews, and analyses could uncover the prevalence of specific practices within the competency areas we have explored, possibly expanding those findings to other areas such as essential BT dispositions and technology skills. More in-depth analyses could uncover specific practices for each competency area within K–12 contexts and also explain teachers' rationale for implementing such practices. Our analysis clarified that teachers choose to blend for varied reasons and that they have found multiple benefits as a result of their blending. Discussing such benefits was outside the scope of this chapter, but future research regarding such benefits could provide valuable motivation for teachers, districts, and states moving toward BT. Understanding specific BT motivations, skills, practices, and knowledge across K–12 contexts can help teacher educators, teachers, administrators, and districts identify teachers' BT strengths and weaknesses to provide professional development that will help teachers better serve students while easing teachers' transition to BT.

References

Akarawang, C., Kidrakran, P., & Nuangchalerm, P. (2015). Enhancing ICT competency for teachers in the Thailand basic education system. *International Education Studies*, *8*(6), 1–8. https://doi.org/10.5539/ies.v8n6p1

Alammary, A., Sheard, J., & Carbone, A. (2014). Blended learning in higher education: Three different design approaches. *Australasian Journal of Educational Technology*, *30*(4), 440–454.

Allen, I. E., & Seaman, J. (2010). *Class differences: Online education in the United States, 2010*. Sloan Consortium (NJ1).

Anthony, E. (2019). (Blended) learning: How traditional best teaching practices impact blended elementary classrooms. *Journal of Online Learning Research*, *5*(1), 25–48. Retrieved June 10, 2020, from https://eric.ed.gov/?id=EJ1208838

Archambault, L., DeBruler, K., & Freidhoff, J. (2014). K–12 online and blended teacher licensure: Striking a balance between policy and preparedness. *Journal of Technology and Teacher Education*, *22*(1), 83–106.

Arnesen, K. T., Graham, C., R., Short, C. R., & Archibald, D. (2019). Experiences with personalized learning in a blended teaching course for preservice teachers. *Journal of Online Learning Research*, *5*(3), 251–274. www.learntechlib.org/primary/p/210637/

Barbour, M. K. (2017). K–12 online learning and school choice. In R. A. Fox & N. K. Buchanan (Eds.), *The Wiley handbook of school choice* (pp. 421–440). John Wiley and Sons. https://doi.org/10.1002/9781119082361.ch29

Bjekic, D., Krneta, R., & Milosevic, D. (2010). Teacher education from e-learner to e-teacher: Master curriculum. *Turkish Online Journal of Educational Technology*, *9*(1), 202–212. https://files.eric.ed.gov/fulltext/EJ875783.pdf

Bower, M., Dalgarno, B., Kennedy, G. E., Lee, M. J., & Kenney, J. (2015). Design and implementation factors in blended synchronous learning environments: Outcomes from a cross-case analysis. *Computers & Education*, *86*, 1–17.

Diep, A. N., Zhu, C., Struyven, K., & Blieck, Y. (2017). Who or what contributes to student satisfaction in different blended learning modalities? *British Journal of Educational Technology*, *48*(2), 473–489.

Dziuban, C., Graham, C., Moskal, P., Norberg, A., & Sicilia, N. (2018). Blended learning: The new normal and emerging technologies. *International Journal of Educational Technology in Higher Education*, *15*(3). https://doi.org/10.1186/s41239-017-0087-5

Eisenbach, B. B. (2016). Considering the virtual classroom: A call to middle level education programs. *Middle Grades Review*, *2*(1), 1–6. https://eric.ed.gov/?id=EJ1154849

Garrison, D. R., & Kanuka, H. (2004). Blended learning: Uncovering its transformative potential in higher education. *The Internet and Higher Education*, *7*(2), 95–105.

Garrison, D. R., & Vaughan, N. D. (2008). *Blended learning in higher education: Framework, principles, and guidelines*. John Wiley & Sons.

Graham, C. R. (2006). Blended learning systems. In C. J. Bonk & C. R. Graham (Eds.), *The handbook of blended learning: Global perspectives, local designs* (pp. 3–21). Pfeiffer Publishing.

Graham, C. R. (2013). Emerging practice and research in blended learning. In M. G. Moore (Ed.), *Handbook of distance education* (3rd ed., pp. 333–350). Routledge.

Graham, C. R. (2019). Current research in blended learning. In M. G. Moore & W. C. Diehl (Eds.), *Handbook of distance education* (4th ed., pp. 173–188). Routledge.

Graham, C. R., Borup, J., Pulham, E., & Larsen, R. (2019). K–12 blended teaching readiness: Model and instrument development. *Journal of Research on Technology in Education*, *51*(3), 239–258. https://doi.org/10.1080/15391523.2019.1586601

Graham, C., Borup, J., Short, C., & Archambault, L. (2019). *K–12 blended teaching: A guide to personalized learning and online integration*. Independently Published. https://edtech books.org/k12blended

Greene, K., & Hale, W. (2017). The state of 21st century learning in the K–12 world of the United States: Online and blended learning opportunities for American elementary and secondary students. *Journal of Educational Multimedia and Hypermedia*, *26*(2), 131–159. www.learntechlib.org/p/174164/

Horn, M., & Staker, H. (2011). *The rise of K–12 blended learning*. Seattle: The Innosight Institute. https://www.christenseninstitute.org/wp-content/uploads/2013/04/The-rise-of-K-12-blended-learning.pdf

Hrastinski, S. (2019). What do we mean by blended learning? *TechTrends*, *63*(5), 564–569.

Ojaleye, O., & Awofala, A. O. A. (2018). Blended learning and problem-based learning instructional strategies as determinants of senior secondary school students' achievement in algebra. *International Journal of Research in Education and Science*, *4*(2), 486–501. https://doi.org/10.21890/ijres.428286

Oliver, K. M., & Stallings, D. T. (2014). Preparing teachers for emerging blended learning environments. *Journal of Technology & Teacher Education*, *22*(1), 57–81. www.learntech lib.org/p/112374/

Picciano, A. G. (2009). Blending with purpose: The multimodal model. *Journal of Asynchronous Learning Networks*, *13*(1), 7–18.

Pulham, E. B., & Graham, C. R. (2018). Comparing K–12 online and blended teaching competencies: A literature review. *Distance Education*, *39*(3), 411–432. https://doi.org/10.1080/01587919.2018.1476840

Pulham, E. B., Graham, C. R., & Short, C. R. (2018). Generic vs. modality-specific competencies for K—12 online and blended teaching. *Journal of Online Learning Research*, *4*(1), 33–52. https://files.eric.ed.gov/fulltext/EJ1174455.pdf

Staker, H., & Horn, M. B. (2012). *Classifying K–12 blended learning*. Innosight Institute.

Watson, J., & Murin, A. (2014). A history of K-12 online and blended instruction in the United States. In *Handbook of research on K-12 online and blended learning*. Pittsburgh: ETC Press. https://dl.acm.org/doi/10.5555/2811036.2811038

Zacharis, N. Z. (2015). A multivariate approach to predicting student outcomes in web-enabled blended learning courses. *The Internet and Higher Education, 27*, 44–53.

13

EXAMINING PEER-TO-PEER SUPPORTS IN K–12 BLENDED ACADEMIC COMMUNITIES OF ENGAGEMENT

Jered Borup, Shea Walters, and Rebecca Stimson

K–12 students in the United States are increasingly enrolling in online courses, especially at the high school level (Schwirzke et al., 2018). While full-time online programs have quickly expanded as a popular option in many states, the majority of K–12 students enroll in one or two online courses to supplement their in-person coursework (Digital Learning Collaborative, 2019). In fact, some states such as Michigan have required students to have an online learning experience prior to graduation (Watson et al., 2014). Online students are also motivated to seek opportunities to learn online for many other reasons, including to access courses not available locally (especially in rural settings), to gain added flexibility in their learning schedule so they can pursue other academic or personal interests, and to retake courses that were previously failed.

While students and schools move online in an attempt to overcome some of the challenges they encounter in an in-person setting, online courses themselves come with unique challenges. For instance, K–12 students are less likely to successfully complete online courses than in-person courses (Freidhoff, 2020). Even when students pass their online courses, some have questioned the quality of their learning experiences (Molnar et al., 2019). For instance, there is some indication that online courses fail to provide students with meaningful opportunities to communicate and collaborate with their peers (Gill et al., 2015). This is especially concerning because communication and collaboration skills have been identified as highly important in the modern workforce (National Education Association, n.d.).

A national survey of 100 full-time online charter schools found that 60% relied on an independent study model with little or no learner-learner interaction (Gill et al., 2015). While this study examined full-time charter schools, it can be even more difficult to provide learner-learner communication and

DOI: 10.4324/9781003037736-18

Peer-to-Peer Supports in K–12 Communities **215**

collaboration in supplemental online courses that lack uniform start and end dates. Requiring common start and due dates would help facilitate learner-learner interactions. However, programs have resisted hard deadlines because they remove the flexibility in pacing that many students require and that has made online learning popular (Garrison, 2009). This is especially true in supplemental programs in which a single online course section the teacher has students enrolled in various school districts, each with its own academic calendar.

Blended learning may help maintain a high level of flexibility in students' pace of learning while still increasing the amount of learner-learner interaction. For instance, some students who take an online course actually complete the course in a physical lab with other students who may or not be enrolled in the same online course. Students' work is then facilitated by an in-person adult (see Figure 13.1). This on-site facilitator is not a content expert but is instead tasked with encouraging interactions and ensuring that students make adequate progress in their online course (Borup, 2018).

In these blended environments students have two sets of peer groups—online peers and in-person peers (Borup, Graham et al., 2020). However, research has been largely focused on the learner-learner interactions that occur in the online course, and little is known regarding how learners support each other in person.

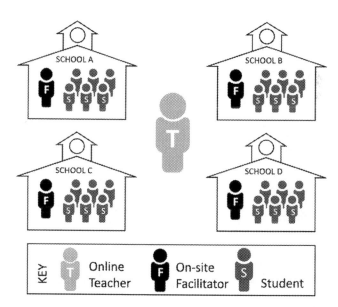

FIGURE 13.1 Blended Learning Model in Which a Single Course Section Has an Online Teacher and Students Across Multiple Brick-and-Mortar Schools.

Note: At each school, there is an on-site facilitator.

The purpose of this research is to examine student perceptions of their interactions with their in-person and online peers as they worked to complete an online course in a physical classroom.

Theoretical Framework

Online and blended student interactions and support frameworks tend to focus on interactions between the student and others who are officially within the same course. While helpful, these frameworks ignore some of the most important types of support that blended and online students receive. These additional supports are especially important for K–12 learners, who commonly lack the self-regulation abilities to be successful independently—especially in online environments. For instance, Oviatt et al. (2018) analyzed 1,055 surveys from students who had completed an online independent study program and found that the large majority of the support students received came from local teachers, parents, and peers who were not part of their course.

To better understand student support in online and blended environments, Borup, Graham et al. (2020) developed the Academic Communities of Engagement (ACE) framework that provided a more expansive lens for examining support structures than previous frameworks. The ACE framework focuses on how others support students' academic engagement or "the energy exerted toward productive involvement with course learning activities" (p. 810; see Figure 13.2).

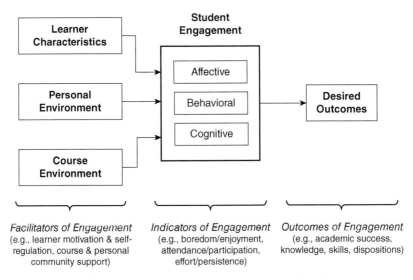

FIGURE 13.2 Model of Student Engagement Highlighting the Facilitators, Indicators, and Outcomes of Student Engagement

Source: (Borup, Walters et al., 2020, p. 811)

Specifically, the ACE framework identified the following indicators of academic engagement:

- Affective engagement: "The emotional energy associated with involvement in course learning activities" (p. 813).
- Behavioral engagement: "The physical behaviors (energy) associated with completing course learning activity requirements" (p. 813).
- Cognitive engagement: "The mental energy exerted towards productive involvement with course learning activities" (p. 813).

The framework contends that all three indicators of engagement are necessary for academic success (see Figure 13.3). Often, academic success is used as a euphemism for grades or learning, whereas the ACE framework takes a broader perspective. Too often grades do not reflect actual learning, and it is possible for students who learn a great deal to actually fail a course due to poor behavioral engagement such as absences or not turning in work on time. Of the three types of indicators of academic engagement, affective engagement is the most overlooked, although it can be extremely important

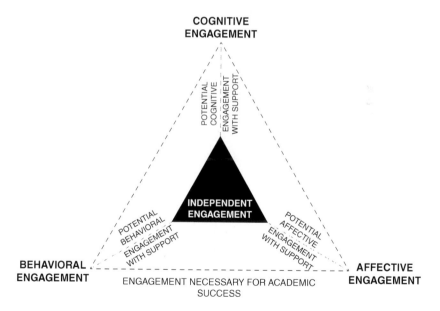

FIGURE 13.3 Indicators of Engagement Necessary for Academic Success

Source: (Borup, Walters et al., 2020, p. 815)

Note: The area of the inner triangle represents students' ability to be independently engaged with the potential of being scaffolded by others who assist them in reaching a higher level of affective, behavioral, or cognitive engagement represented by the outer triangle.

218 J. Borup, S. Walters, and R. Stimson

to achieving academic success. While learning objectives focus on "what students know and can do" (Kuh et al., 2014, p. 5), student-teacher relationships can be the "starting point for promoting school success" (Roorda et al., 2011, p. 520). Meta-analyses have identified an important relationship between student emotions and academic outcomes (Roorda et al., 2011; Tze et al., 2016). Affective engagement is especially important in online learning environments because students are prone to feeling isolated and unmotivated to learn (Symeonides & Childs, 2015).

Students vary in their ability to independently engage in online and blended courses, and each student likely has different ability levels to engage affectively, behaviorally, and cognitively. Those abilities likely change based on the learning environment, the course subject, or even a specific topic within a course. While it is possible for some students to independently engage in a course and reach full academic success without much, if any, support from others, most students do require a degree of support from others to be successful. This is especially true of younger students who tend to be less developed than adults, but there are cases in which the opposite can be true, and a middle school student may be better able to independently engage in a course than a university student.

The goal of ACE is to provide students with the support necessary to bridge the gap between what is required academically and what the student can do independently (see Figure 13.4). Specifically, the ACE framework identifies two support communities:

- The course community is made up of actors (e.g., teachers, support staff, course mates) who are official members of a course and whose relationship with the student is a result of the student's enrollment in the course.
- The personal community is made up of actors (e.g., family and friends) who have long-lasting relationships with the student but likely do not formally contribute to the course.

Building on Vygotsky's (1978) zone of proximal development, the ACE framework contends that a student's ability to engage in learning activities increases when supported by actors within the student's course and personal communities. The authors of the ACE framework identified support elements aligned with each of the engagement indicators (see Figure 13.5).

As the ACE framework is new, little research has been applied to it. As a result, we used the ACE framework to guide the analysis of eight K–12 student focus groups in three schools with a total of 51 student participants. The majority of the focus group questions addressed students' perceptions of the supports provided by online teachers and on-site facilitators, the analysis of which was published in an earlier article (Borup et al., 2019). This chapter reports on findings from the analysis of students' comments regarding their interactions with peers.

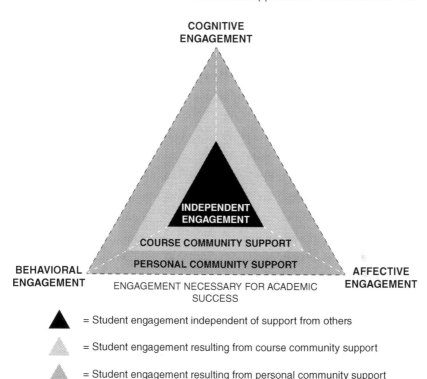

FIGURE 13.4 Engagement Necessary for Academic Success

Source: (Borup, Graham et al., 2020, p. 815)

Note: The inner black triangle represents a student's engagement independent of support from others. The engagement resulting from course community support is represented in yellow, and the engagement resulting from personal community support is represented in red. The order of the support the student receives is itnerchangeable in the figure and does not reflect a necessary sequence. The goal of support communities is to help the student increase engagement to the level necessary for academic success, as represented by the dotted line.

Methods

Three brick-and-mortar schools provided the context for this research. Section 21f of Michigan Public Act No. 60 (2013) required that online students' local brick-and-mortar schools provide students with an on-site facilitator. As a result, when students enrolled in an online course, they were supported by both an online teacher and an on-site facilitator. Our previous research identified schools with high online student pass rates (85% or higher) and then interviewed on-site facilitators at those schools to better understand how students were being supported (Borup et al., 2019). Of the 12 interviewed facilitators, 11 worked with

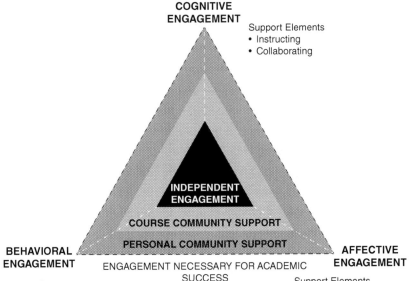

FIGURE 13.5 The ACE Model with Support Elements Aligned to the Three Types of Engagement

Source: (Borup, Graham et al., 2020, p. 818)

students who attended a daily lab. We then followed up by selecting three high schools from the original twelve that were willing to invite students to participate in student focus groups, following parental consent. The three schools had student populations ranging from 650 to 820 and were in cities with populations ranging from 4,500 to 8,000.

Data Collection

Data collection began with facilitators sending home parental consent and student assent forms. All students who returned both were invited to participate in a focus group. In total, 51 students participated in eight focus groups that ranged in size from four to nine students. Four focus groups were conducted at one high school, and two were conducted in each of the other two high schools. The focus group questions focused on the different support elements, but the focus groups were semi-structured, allowing those conducting the focus groups to ask follow-up questions regarding types of support not included in the focus group protocol.

It is important to note that the focus groups were conducted prior to the creation of the ACE framework. The creation of the focus group questions was guided by a predecessor to the ACE framework, the Adolescent Communities of Engagement framework. Comparing and contrasting the two frameworks is beyond the scope of this chapter, but those who are interested in learning more can read the ACE framework paper (Borup, Graham et al., 2020). For the purposes of this chapter, we will note that the support elements are similar across both frameworks, so the focus group questions would have been similar even if we had used the ACE framework.

Data Analysis

The focus group discussions were audio recorded and transcribed. The person who conducted the focus group then listened to the audio recording while reading the transcript. While listening, he or she checked for accuracy while also attempting to match the comments with the participants. Following, the transcripts were provided to students who were asked to check for accuracy. However, none of the students returned any corrections, concerns, or elaborations.

Each of the final transcripts was analyzed by coding comments into as many different categories as possible, while also comparing them to all previously coded comments, a process Glaser (1965) called the "basic, defining rule for the constant comparative method" (p. 439). Similar categories were also grouped under larger themes. These grouping decisions were guided by, but not limited to, the ACE framework. The entire research team met three times during the analysis to review the coding, share insights, and discuss how the categories could be grouped into larger themes. When disagreements arose, they were discussed until consensus was achieved.

Findings

Analysis of the eight student focus groups revealed that students received high levels of support from their online teachers, on-site facilitators, and peers. The majority of students' comments focused on the support received from on-site facilitators and online teachers (or lack of online teacher support). Those findings are shared in a previously published article (Borup et al., 2019), and this section will share findings related to the support students provided and received from other students.

Students reported receiving support elements aligned with cognitive and affective engagement but not behavioral engagement. Additionally, most of the support they received was aimed at improving cognitive presence. While students interacted frequently with their online peers in discussion boards, the participants expressed the perception that the most significant support came from in-person peers—especially those who attended the same lab time.

Supporting Cognitive Engagement

Most of the focus group comments related to how peer-provided support helped improve students' cognitive engagement. Students reported that their cognitive engagement was mostly impacted by peers at their brick-and-mortar schools. Greta explained, and those in her focus group agreed, that she turned to people in her own school for help because it was "easier to email students in your school instead of random people." This also included students who did not attend the in-person lab time. At times, students turned to those with whom they had previously developed a relationship. This was highlighted by Kara when she shared her experience with a course her boyfriend had previously taken. She stated, "If I'm ever stuck, it's pretty much the exact same thing, so if I'm stuck, he'll help me with that." Brianna shared a similar experience, relating how she turned to her sister who was taking the same online course. While Brianna and her sister had different instructors, the course assignments appeared to be the same, and the siblings frequently supported each other throughout the course.

While there was some indication that students were being supported by peers who did not attend their in-person lab, the large majority of instructional support seemed to be provided by students who attended the same lab time. In fact, some students like Sheila would actually turn to a peer in their lab "before asking [their online] teacher because it's easier." Janet found that some of her peers provided unsolicited support to let her know when she was doing something incorrectly and guided her through the correct way to complete a problem or assignment. Most often students reported actively requesting instructional support from their peers. Peers who were concurrently taking or who had previously taken the course were especially helpful, but even peers who were not in those categories could also prove helpful. For assistance with his game design course, Ryan explained that he would circle his lab and ask his peers to take a moment to play his games. This would enable him to use their perspectives and interactions with the game to figure out what might be wrong with the game and receive feedback to help him fix the issues. He found that type of support "actually helps a lot for doing better in the class." Warren also used students in his lab to assist him when he was having difficulty with his baseball course. According to Warren, there was one peer in particular who was very knowledgeable about baseball and therefore proved especially helpful.

Students also interacted with their online peers primarily in discussion boards—a regular activity in most of their courses. Typically, the discussion board required students to post a response to the discussion prompt and then reply to two of their peers' posts. Most students found that most discussion board activities were repetitious and did not help them better understand content. Amanda best expressed this sentiment:

> For every discussion I've had to do so far, there's been a rubric, and you have to have multiple paragraphs, specific things you have to include. . . .

Everyone is literally saying the same thing and . . . when it's all the same stuff and it isn't personal in any way, it takes all the meaning away from it, and it's not even like you're talking to other students. It's pretty much like you're just reading the same thing over and over again, and you're just making this answer up as you go. You're doing it to meet the requirements, not to actually have a collaboration.

Christy shared that she had to use the discussion board a lot for her personal finance class, but she and others "don't ever go back to" the discussion once they have replied to two of their peers' posts. Even the responses students received to their discussion board posts were viewed as unhelpful and forced. Common peer replies were "Oh, great job," "I totally agree with that," and "I like this about your post." As a result, students found the comments were not "personal." Layla shared why the replies she posted were impersonal: "When we do discussions, I don't really like it because I have to post on other people's posts, and I don't know what to say." Avery actually compared the online discussion boards to her in-person focus group, where students were "bouncing off each other's ideas" but found that "you can't really do that with online posts." Sheila summarized, "My least favorite thing on [the online courses] is the discussion boards."

While the majority of student comments regarding online discussion board activities were negative, some indicated they could prove helpful. A few students stated they would sometimes use their peers' discussion board comments to help guide them if they were having a difficult time understanding the assignment. Sarah shared the following experience: "I was looking at one prompt, and I keep looking at it, and I'm like, 'I don't even know what this says. What is this asking me?' So I looked at a couple, and then I got a better idea." Her experience was mirrored by a few other students within her focus group. Ryan explained a similar experience and added, "I'm kind of just looking at your work and making my work based on yours."

Warren saw the potential of discussion board activities and believed they would be beneficial if students treated "the discussion board like a discussion." Avery agreed that discussions could be effective in some subject areas:

> It depends on the class, because the film studies, it'd be a lot easier to do . . . because it's talking about a movie, but whereas in like oceanography . . . it's like a lot of facts and stuff, so everybody would be getting the same thing.

Students in her focus group agreed that discussions were beneficial when students were able to share "different opinions."

While students reported that they frequently communicated with peers and provided each other with instructional support, there was less evidence they actually collaborated with each other to complete assignments. Most of the collaboration students described occurred with other students in their lab. Heath said,

"One major advantage of the lab setting is that if you're with people that are in the same course, it's easier to get through it if you can collaborate on it." Christy also described collaborating with other students for American Sign Language (ASL). She and her peers would all do their signing "videos together because usually they're group assignments . . . and so it was easier because we didn't have to do it all on our own."

In most courses, collaboration was optional, but collaboration with online peers could also be required in some cases. Heather mentioned a collaborative research project with four of her online peers that extended through Thanksgiving break, making it especially difficult to collaborate. Students in her focus group agreed that mandatory collaboration with online peers was "awful" because "how are you all going to have the same exact time frame to do things?"

Some students shared that, in theory, collaboration could be beneficial because it could make them "more determined to get it done." However, in practice, they found that collaboration was "not really functional." Heather argued that because so much work was done independently throughout class, when it came time for collaboration, one of two things would happen: "either everybody's already collaborated, or nobody's there yet." Amanda believed that if online courses could figure out the logistics necessary for collaboration, "it would be helpful, and it would just be nice to have [opportunities to collaborate]."

Supporting Affective Engagement

While students commented less frequently regarding support elements aligned to affective engagement than to those aligned with cognitive engagement, peers did appear to impact students' affective engagement by creating a sense of excitement and urgency for their learning and developing relationships.

Rather than providing each other with words of engagement, students found they were driven to complete assignments when they knew where their peers were in the course. This added a sense of excitement and competition as students wanted to exceed or match the progress of their peers. This type of motivation primarily came from other students at their local school. Cara said she talked to friends at her school to see where they were in the class and would use that to gauge where she should be. To that, Sarah replied, "It's like a competition." Larry agreed with the competitive influence: "My friend that's taking the same course, I ask her, 'So, where are you in the course right now?' and she answers a few units before me, and I'm like, 'I'm winning.'" Similarly, Brynn explained that in her online course, she was able to determine where her online peers were in the course, which inspired her to do more.

Being in a lab with peers who were engaged in their learning also appeared to encourage others to "naturally follow along." Rory said that "Sociologically speaking, seeing other people doing their work, it makes you want to [do the same]. . . . It's just that peer-to-peer thing." Craig agreed and said that when he is around people, he will "actually get more work done." However, not all students agreed, and some found that working in the presence of other students proved distracting. Sarah explained, "See, I'm personally the opposite. If I'm around more students that I know, I'm like, 'Oh, I can do this later tonight.' I will talk to those people."

Students did not believe that their online peers had an impact on their affective engagement, in part because they did not feel a sense of closeness or familiarity with them. While their courses commonly had ice-breakers or "bonding projects," students found them ineffective. Cory stated that he felt "probably less connected to my [online] students than my [online] teacher, and personally that's not saying that much." Delilah believed she would have felt closer to her online peers if the discussion board activities were actual discussions with more back and forth because as they were currently constructed "you never got a response back so you're kind of talking to yourself."

Conversation within one of the focus groups actually showed students not wanting to interact with their online peers because they took online classes to actively avoid interaction with others. Sammy shared that, if given the choice, she "wouldn't have talked to anyone in the [online] class." Norm mentioned that he took an online course so he could work by himself and "just focus on that instead of interacting with other people." Tyler felt the same: "I'm doing this because I enjoy the material, not because I want to make friends." Tyler was not the only one who felt this way. Sidrah added that she did not even want to interact with others in the lab. Rather, she decided to take the online course so she could "put her headphones in during the class" and focus on completing the assignments.

Only Kayleigh shared a positive experience of feeling a sense of closeness with her online peers. In her ASL class, they had to film themselves, and she felt that seeing other peoples' videos started a connection with some students, and she "actually became friends with two or three of the kids" through email exchanges, social media pages, and the sharing of phone numbers.

Discussion

Distance education has a long history, but high levels of learner-learner interactions have only become commonplace since the advent of the internet. Over 30 years ago, Moore (1989) predicted that learner-learner interactions would "be a challenge to our thinking and practice" (p. 4). While over the last three decades, our field has clearly come to better understand the potential of learner-learner interactions, it is just as clear that it continues to be a challenge to our practice.

Graham et al. (2014) explained that "by their very nature [frameworks] tend to establish a common language and focus for the activities that take place in a scholarly community" (p. 71). Mishra and Koehler (2006) added that frameworks are helpful because they draw researchers' attention to the most important questions to answer and provide guidance on what data to collect to answer those questions, how to analyze those data, and the interpretations that can be made based on those findings. In order to be effective, frameworks cannot include all possible factors and should focus on what is most important (Ferdig et al., 2009). Whetten (1989) similarly explained that frameworks all have boundaries that can create some tension when deciding if a factor should be included or excluded.

Building on previous theoretical frameworks, the ACE framework provides a more inclusive lens for examining student interactions and support from actors within both the course community and the student's personal community. This research highlights the importance of examining both communities. If we had only examined peer-to-peer interactions and support in the course community, we would have had a narrow perception and concluded that students received little to no support from their peers. However, because our research was guided by the ACE framework, we recognized the peer-provided support in their personal communities and saw that students were indeed receiving valuable support from in-person peers. What is less well understood is how a student's course community and personal community can work in concert to support students, an area where additional research would be helpful.

Course Community Peers

In-person K–12 education has moved toward more collaboration- and discussion-rich forms of learning, such as guided inquiry, problem-based learning, and project-based learning. This shift is intended to provide students with authentic learning opportunities while helping them develop communication and collaboration skills. At the same time, K–-12 online courses have remained focused on learner-content and learner-teacher interactions with only supplemental opportunities to share their thoughts. For instance, in this research, students commonly participated in discussion board activities but largely found them unhelpful. Students were asked to post a response to a discussion board prompt and then reply to two peers' posts. This repetition proved monotonous for many of the focus group participants. One student summarized this sentiment: "It's all the same stuff, and it isn't personal in any way; it takes all the meaning away from it, and it's not even like you're talking to other students." Students also recommended that discussion board activities be changed so that they are "like a discussion" where students can share "different opinions." This supports Murphy and Rodriquez-Manzanares (2009) recommendation that discussions be centered "on controversial issues so that students have to provide their opinion" (p. 18). However, if teachers ask students to discuss controversial topics, it is especially important that they have established clear netiquette guidelines so that controversy does not slip into inappropriate conflict or even bullying. Students shared that this is easier within some subjects such as "film studies" than other subjects that focus more on factual information. We recommend that researchers examine the similarities and differences in discussions across content areas in online and blended courses.

While controversy may be less common in some content areas, Dubuclet et al. (2015) analyzed discussion board comments in math and computer science courses and found that students were able to still express differing opinions. In fact, student responses were more in-depth when students disagreed than when students quickly reached consensus on a topic. The authors also recognized that some students may fear expressing their honest opinions that may be seen negatively by others. Their analysis also highlighted that while setting clear expectations for student participation is important, the quantity of the participation was less of an indicator of student learning than was the quality of the prompt and subsequent responses because "students typically displayed the cognitive skill prompted by the questions" (p. 292). Pesek (2017) added that students should be allowed to respond in multiple ways such as text, video, and images. While the design of a discussion activity is important, online teacher facilitation practices will also play a critical role in students' experiences, and online teachers would benefit from professional development focused on facilitating meaningful online discussions.

One reason students compared posting to a discussion board to "talking to yourself" is they were unable to develop a sense of closeness with other students. This is in part due to their expectations and perceptions of online learning. For instance, some students shared that they enrolled in an online course so they would not have to interact with others. Courses commonly had ice-breaker discussion activities at the start of the semester, but students found them ineffective. The only individual who reported successfully forming relationships with online peers was a student in an ASL course that required students to communicate using video recordings. Research in higher education has found that asynchronous video communication can help efficiently establish a sense of community (Borup et al., 2014), but research examining the practice is lacking in K–12. The growing popularity of video-enabled tools such as Flipgrid, Padlet, and VoiceThread may have been changing practice and can provide opportunities for research. However, before adopting these tools, programs should carefully consider student privacy and data security. Garrett Dikkers (2018) highlighted that online programs commonly have discussions, but programs lack the research to know how to use them to increase student engagement in a way that improves student outcomes. We join Garrett Dikkers (2018) in his call for more research on online discussion boards in an attempt to identify best practices.

Personal Community Peers

Compared to their course community peers, students received more support from peers in their personal communities, especially—but not exclusively—from those who attended the same lab times. Even when students were not in the same online course, their proximity allowed them to share feedback, knowledge, and interests with each other. It seemed to be especially helpful when a student had previously taken the same course. One of the responsibilities of on-site facilitators can be to facilitate learner-learner interactions (Borup, 2018). Research has found that on-site facilitator professional development can help improve student performance, and this research supports the need for professional development to include strategies for facilitating learner-learner interactions.

This research examined perceptions of students who learned in a lab, an opportunity not available to all students. Additional research is needed to examine strategies that facilitate learner-learner support when students are not learning in a lab setting. For instance, members of the honor society at a cyber charter school served as peer mentors and tutors in courses they had previously taken (Borup, Walters et al., 2020), and similar approaches could be taken at brick-and-mortar schools.

Conclusion

The educational community has increasingly emphasized the importance of learner-learner interactions and collaboration, and yet these opportunities seem elusive in online learning environments. In this research, we found that K–12 students who enrolled in online courses to supplement their in-person coursework frequently participated in discussion board activities with other students but largely found those interactions to be unhelpful. Considering its importance, much more research is needed that examines effective strategies for facilitating meaningful learner-learner communication and collaboration. Additionally, this research found that the majority of learner-learner support was actually occurring locally and outside the official online learning environment. More research is needed to understand the impacts of that support and how the course community can encourage and strengthen those types of opportunities. The ACE framework provides a lens for understanding the types of support that students receive from both their course community and their personal community. As a new framework, additional qualitative research can prove helpful in refining or expanding the elements included in the framework. Validated instruments would also be helpful and allow for new types of research. This type of research is challenging but can potentially have important impacts on learning outcomes.

References

Borup, J. (2018). On-site and online facilitators: Current and future direction for research. In K. Kennedy & R. Ferdig (Eds.), *Handbook of research on K–12 online and blended learning* (2nd ed., pp. 423–442). ETC Press. http://repository.cmu.edu/etcpress/82/

Borup, J., Chambers, C., & Stimson, R. (2019). K–12 student perceptions of online teacher and on-site facilitator support in supplemental online courses. *Online Learning*, 23(4), 253–280. Retrieved from https://olj.onlinelearningconsortium.org/index.php/olj/article/view/1565/874

Borup, J., Graham, C. R., West, R. E., Archambault, L., & Spring, K. J. (2020). Academic communities of engagement: An expansive lens for examining support structures in blended and online learning. *Educational Technology Research and Development, 68*, 807–832. https://doi.org/10.1007/s11423-020-09744-x

Borup, J., Walters, S., & Call-Cummings, M. (2020). Student perceptions of their interactions with peers at a cyber charter high school. *Online Learning, 24*(2), 207–224. https://doi.org/10.24059/olj.v24i2.2015

Borup, J., West, R. E., Thomas, R. A., & Graham, C. R. (2014). Examining the impact of video feedback on instructor social presence in blended courses. *The International Review of Research in Open and Distributed Learning, 15*, 232–256.

Digital Learning Collaborative (2019). *Snapshot 2019: A review of K–12 online, blended, and digital learning.* www.evergreenedgroup.com/s/DLC-KP-Snapshot2019.pdf

Dubuclet, K. S., Lou, Y., & MacGregor, K. (2015). Design and cognitive level of student dialogue in secondary school online courses. *American Journal of Distance Education, 29*(4), 283–296. https://doi.org/10.1080/08923647.2015.1085722

Ferdig, R. E., Cavanaugh, C., DiPietro, M., Black, E., & Dawson, K. (2009). Virtual schooling standards and best practices for teacher education. *Journal of Technology and Teacher Education, 17*(4), 479–503.

Freidhoff, J. R. (2020). *Michigan's K–12 virtual learning effectiveness report 2018–19.* Michigan Virtual University. https://michiganvirtual.org/research/publications/michigans-k-12-virtual-learning-effectiveness-report-2018-19/

Garrett Dikkers, A. (2018). Social interaction in K–12 online learning. In K. Kennedy & R. Ferdig (Eds.), *Handbook of research on K–12 online and blended learning* (2nd ed., pp. 509–522). ETC Press. http://repository.cmu.edu/etcpress/82/

Garrison, R. (2009). Implications of online learning for the conceptual development and practice of distance education. *Journal of Distance Education, 23*(2), 93–104.

Gill, B., Walsh, L., Wulsin, C. S., Matulewicz, H., Severn, V., Grau, E., Lee, A., & Kerwin, T. (2015). *Inside online charter schools.* Walton Family Foundation and Mathematica Policy Research. www.mathematica-mpr.com/~/media/publications/pdfs/education/inside_online_charter_schools.pdf

Glaser, B. G. (1965). The constant comparative method of qualitative analysis. *Social Problems, 12*(4), 436–445. www.jstor.org/stable/798843

Graham, C. R., Henrie, C. R., & Gibbons, A. S. (2014). Developing models and theory for blended learning research. In A. G. Picciano, C. D. Dziuban, & C. R. Graham (Eds.), *Blended learning: Research perspectives* (Vol. 2, Issue 801, pp. 13–33). Taylor & Francis.

Kuh, G. D., Jankowski, N., Ikenberry, S. O., & Kinzie, J. (2014). *Knowing what students know and can do: The current state of student learning outcomes assessment in US colleges and universities.* National Institute for Learning Outcomes Assessment. www.learningoutcomeassessment.org/documents/2013AbridgedSurveyReportFinal.pdf

Michigan Public Act § No. 60 (2013). www.legislature.mi.gov/docu-ments/2013-2014/publicact/htm/2013-PA-0060.htm

Mishra, P., & Koehler, M. J. (2006). Technological pedagogical content knowledge: A framework for teacher knowledge. *Teachers College Record, 108*(6), 1017–1054.

Molnar, A., Miron, G., Elgeberi, N., Barbour, M. K., Huerta, L., Shafer, S. R., & Rice, J. K. (2019). *Virtual schools in the U.S. 2019.* National Education Policy Center. Retrieved from http://nepc.colorado.edu/publication/virtual-schools-annual-2019

Moore, M. G. (1989). Editorial: Three types of interaction. *The American Journal of Distance Education, 3*(2), 1–6.

Murphy, E., & Rodríguez-Manzanares, M. A. (2009). Teachers' perspectives on motivation in high school distance education. *Journal of Distance Education, 23*(3), 1–24.

National Education Association (n.d.). *Preparing 21st century students for a global society: An educator's guide to the "four Cs."* www.nea.org/assets/docs/A-Guide-to-Four-Cs.pdf

Oviatt, D. R., Graham, C. R., Davies, R. S., & Borup, J. (2018). Online student use of a proximate community of engagement in an independent study program. *Online Learning Journal, 22*(1). https://doi.org/10.24059/olj.v22i1.1153

Pesek, J. (2017). Discussion of controversial issues in an online teacher preparation course. In P. Resta & S. Smith (Eds.), *Proceedings of society for information technology & teacher education international conference* (pp. 280–282). Association for the Advancement of Computing in Education (AACE). www.learntechlib.org/primary/p/177298/

Roorda, D. L., Koomen, H. M. Y., Split, J. L., & Oort, F. J. (2011). The influence of affective teacher-student relationships on students' school engagement and achievement: A meta-analytic approach. *Review of Educational Research, 81*(4), 493–529. https://doi.org/10.3102/0034654311421793

Schwirzke, K., Vashaw, L., & Watson, J. (2018). A history of K–12 online and blended instruction in the United States. In K. Kennedy & R. Ferdig (Eds.), *Handbook of research on K–12 online and blended learning* (2nd ed., pp. 423–442). ETC Press. http://repository.cmu.edu/etcpress/82/

Symeonides, R., & Childs, C. (2015). The personal experience of online learning: An interpretative phenomenological analysis. *Computers in Human Behavior, 51*, 539–545. https://doi.org/10.1016/j.chb.2015.05.015

Tze, V. M. C., Daniels, L. M., & Klassen, R. M. (2016). Evaluating the relationship between boredom and academic outcomes: A meta-analysis. *Educational Psychology Review, 28*, 119–144. https://doi.org/10.1007/s10648-015-9301-y

Vygotsky, L. S. (1978). *Mind in society: The development of higher psychological processes* (M. Cole, Ed.). Harvard University Press.

Watson, J., Pape, L., Murin, A., Gemin, B., & Vashaw, L. (2014). *Keeping pace with K–12 online learning.* www.kpk12.com/wp-content/uploads/EEG_KP2014-fnl-lr.pdf

Whetten, D. A. (1989). What constitutes a theoretical contribution? *The Academy of Management Review, 14*(4), 490–495. https://doi.org/10.2307/258554

14

INTELLECTUAL AGENCY OF LINGUISTICALLY DIVERSE STUDENTS WITH DISABILITIES IN A BLENDED LEARNING ENVIRONMENT

Mary Frances Rice and Mark Stevens

Early definitions of blended learning included any ratio of advanced internet technologies alongside in-person instruction (Staker & Horn, 2012). While advocates of blended learning under this open definition believed that various models and configurations would lead to greater opportunities for all students, these promises are still emerging. Some approaches to blended learning take mastery orientations, where data obtained through online adaptive software is used to identify cognitive gaps and fill them through additional scaffolded tasks (Hoxie et al., 2014; Mohammed, 2017; Staker, 2011). Other approaches embrace learner preferences in accordance with constructivist principles (Smith & Suzuki, 2015). Learner preference may be highly supported or loosely supported in such environments.

Using blended learning to support targeted content mastery and affective learner control does not have to be an either-or proposition (Dewey, 1938). For example, Graham (2006) outlined three blended learning levels on a continuum of technology integration in blended classrooms, starting with enabling blends, moving to enhancing blends, and then continuing to transforming blends. Each type increases the sophistication of the technology use and affords additional autonomy to the learners. Rhythms of activity that alternate between approaches to blended learning may influence decisions about how resources such as technological devices are allocated, as well as how teachers and students spend the time they have together for in-person instruction.

The age and developmental needs of learners also warrant consideration in designing classroom routines and learning orientations for blended learning. For learners in the middle grades, learner control is important because early adolescence should be a time when young people explore their talents and skills (Noddings, 2013). Identifying personal and academic strengths is important to

DOI: 10.4324/9781003037736-19

envisioning a productive and stable adult life. From a psychosocial development perspective, exploration is also important for the positive resolution of identity during adolescence through learning to trust others and oneself, recognizing one's autonomy and the autonomy of others, taking initiative to do tasks that will meet one's goals, and learning the benefits of being industrious (Erikson, 1968). To meaningfully explore, learners need freedom to engage with subject matter that meets their immediate needs while also building knowledge, skills, and dispositions that will be valuable in the future (Dewey, 1938). Aspirations for high-quality, identity-supportive middle-level learning could be met in blended learning environments when learners engage in tasks that are sufficiently structured to provide organized opportunities to learn intended subject matter but sufficiently supportive of personal preferences that extend the inquiry beyond the subject matter.

Purpose of the Study

Blended learning has been advocated for students with disabilities as a way to increase access to technology use as well as to meet inclusion goals (Basham et al., 2015). However, previous research on this topic is slim, especially at the middle level (Rice & Dykman, 2018). Blended learning has also been advocated for supporting English learners in the middle-level setting (Stevens, 2016). However, English learners in middle-level blended settings are also under-researched. Studies of middle-level learners with present or previous English-learner status *and* who have disability identifications are even rarer. With such a fledgling research base, there are many things that would be useful to know about middle-level learners who are linguistically diverse and who have disabilities in a blended environment. Nevertheless, considering the importance of understanding the self at this age, we asked, How do individual learners of English with disabilities use their agency in a blended learning environment?

Conceptual Framework

The conceptual framework for this study favored blended learning routines emphasizing learner control as fundamentally grounded in self-determination (Deci & Ryan, 2012). Although regulation of learning was initially understood through stimulus-response that operated apart from individual thought, more modern conceptions acknowledge the role of social context in decision-making during learning (Noddings, 2013). In fact, recent research in K–12 online learning suggests that communities of engagement are more important than individual efforts, but individual needs should still be considered in instructional design (Borup et al., 2020).

We began this research operating under the premise that instructional design generally, but especially in online learning environments, should strive to balance cognitive support through structured activities with affective considerations that promote investment in the subject matter (Carter et al., 2020). Structure should be present, but not so strict that learners lose affective interest. Structured learning opportunities are also important because self-regulation models were developed for late adolescent and emerging adult university students, rather than early adolescents in middle school (Erikson, 1968; Pintrich, 1999).

Balancing structure and learner control was also a goal in Dewey's (1938) educational philosophy. Specifically, Dewey argued for a balance between the highly structured traditional curriculum of his day and the newly emerging progressive schools that offered, in his opinion, too much freedom. Even so, Dewey felt that teachers should be cautious about exercising authority, and they should leave most control to students. He wrote:

> The educator is responsible for a knowledge of individuals and for a knowledge of subject matter that will enable activities to be selected which lend themselves to social organization, an organization in which all individuals have an opportunity to contribute something, and in which all participants are the chief carrier of control.
>
> *(Dewey, 1938, p. 56)*

Dewey favored learner control because he believed children would be kinder, more thoughtful citizens if they were guided to intellectual freedom. He also thought that society was changing, particularly in regards to technology, and learners would need intellectual flexibility to deal with the onslaught of new problems posed to democratic communities as they experienced rapid innovation. Dewey's prescience should afford him a special kind of relevance in blended learning environments.

Learner Control

Some advocates of blended learning have also recommended high degrees of learner control (O'Byrne & Pytash, 2015). Specifically, advocates of blended learning have insisted on the importance of learner control over time, place, path, and/or pace (Staker & Horn, 2012). Also, Graham et al. (2019) argued that instead of including goals in the personalization of the learning path, learning goals should be conceptualized as a separate idea because choosing *what* one will learn is different than choosing *how* one will learn.

When learners are in control of time, place, path, and/or pace, they share the responsibility of organizing their learning with their teacher (Deweyan, 1938). One model for such organization is the self-regulation of learning model (Zimmerman & Risemberg, 1997). This model is cyclical and has three phases: forethought, performance, and reflection. Each phase requires learners to understand their resources in their environments and to think metacognitively about how those resources will contribute to their learning. To support self-regulation, teachers are encouraged to use regulatory *apparati*, including tools, strategies, and routines, to structure the task to ensure learners move through the phases and achieve learning goals (Pape et al., 2003; Roscoe et al., 2013). However, when the environment is too tightly managed, learners only have the illusion of control. Such might be the case when learners answer scripted questions or fill in short answers.

Learner Agency

Alongside theories suggesting learners need environmental *apparati* to support individual motivation, theories of intellectual agency suggest that learners are constantly making choices within a context, and learning is not organized by tools and strategies alone (Anyon, 2009; Archer, 2013). These choices go beyond cognitive efforts to be stimulated intellectually or avoid difficult mental labor. Instead, these choices guide self-making within a space. Giddens and Archer both argued that individuals are agents at the point when they consciously choose one course of action over another (Archer, 2003; Giddens, 1979). Further, these choices are not personal, but relational (Burkitt, 2016). In relational agency, decisions are made based on the need to preserve and validate relationships with people as well as objects. Unfortunately, students with disabilities and English learners often find themselves in educational contexts that highlight what they cannot do rather than what they can. More troubling, these challenges are often made public in the classroom and jeopardize constructive teacher-student relationships (Menken & Kleyn, 2010; Pham & Martin, 2016; Trent et al., 1998).

When students fail to act in ways that align with planned regulatory *apparati*, teachers might assume that learners were acting to avoid punishment or increase emotional pleasure. The response under these assumptions might be to provide more *apparati*. When decisions are regarded as willful, then students run the risk of having what they do (or do not do) taken as resistance or as non-cooperation (Anyon, 1981). In this study, we took the perspective of intellectual agency for interpreting student actions. We assumed that students wanted to do the tasks and that they sought out the best ways they could learn using the resources—personal and environmental—to which they had access. In short, we wanted to understand students as intellectual agents alongside the *apparati* available to them.

Literature Review

Previous research has been scant regarding both English learners and students with disabilities at the middle level. Stevens (2018) found that multimodal blended learning had a significant positive impact on social studies content and vocabulary learning and a positive, though not large, impact on reading comprehension. The seventh graders in Stevens's study expressed positive opinions regarding the use of the multimodal bended approach. In another study, Stevens and Rice (2016) considered blended learning in a highly diverse middle-level classroom and found diligent dialogue and social presence were used collaboratively between learners in an effort to cross the boundaries between virtual and actual worlds. In this boundary crossing, problems were resolved, and off-task behavior was redirected as students and the teacher engaged relationally during the learning.

For students with disabilities, there is also little research about blended learning. One such study was from Bottge et al. (2014), who found that middle-level students with disabilities who participated in a blended mathematics curriculum outperformed students with disabilities who did not use the technologically enhanced materials in the blended learning environment. However, Pace and Mellard (2016) found that middle school students with disabilities performed below students without disabilities in a blended learning intervention where the online reading program was prioritized as a data source over the in-person instruction. While content materials that are on- or offline are part of blended learning, this environment also enables new types of interpersonal interactions in various spaces (Graham et al., 2019). Part of the reason that conclusions might be difficult to draw from previous research, besides the fact that there have been so few studies where blended learning theories are explicitly and intentionally applied, is that some studies have focused on the technology and instructional materials (Bottge et al., 2014; Pace & Mellard, 2016), and others seem to have focused more on the relationships between learners and their teacher (Stevens & Rice, 2016) when actually, both are important.

Clearly, more research about how English learners and students with disabilities engage in blended learning would be useful. For students with disabilities, there is a particular need to understand engagement and learning strategies since participating in schooling alongside peers is a key component of the Individuals with Disabilities in Education Act (2004). When students without disabilities are doing blended learning, students with disabilities should also have access per federal law. For English learning, understanding agency as a relational concept has implications for taking on identities as English speakers in addition to maintaining identities related to the first language (Norton & Pavlenko, 2019). In the current study, a small group of students with disabilities who were also English learners navigated the blended learning environment for their learning.

Methods

Merriam (1998) defined qualitative case study as "an intensive, holistic description and analysis of a bounded phenomenon such as a program, an institution, a person, a process, or a social unit" (p. xiii). Our case study approach to this phenomenon emphasized meaning over essence (Heidegger, 2009). A case study had three attributes: (a) a focus on particular situation, event, program, or phenomenon; (b) a rich, thick description of the phenomenon under study); and (c) information to draw readers' understanding of the phenomenon under study).

Participants

Four seventh-grade students were selected as focal students from a larger inquiry into engagement in a blended learning classroom. Each of the students had been identified with at least one learning disability and had a current Individualized Educational Program per IDEA (2004). Two of the students were dual-identified as English learners in addition to having a disability, while the other two had been classified as English learners but had been exited after achieving WIDA proficiency levels of 6, which is standard practice (Willner & Monroe, 2016). These students attended a highly diverse urban middle school in the Southeastern United States. Table 14.1 offers additional information about the students.

Data Collection

Major types of data were collected for analysis during this study included lesson materials, observations, student work, informal interviews with students, and researcher communications.

TABLE 14.1 Participant Information

Name	English Proficiency Level	Gender	Additional Information Related to Special Education Needs
Josue	6-Exited	M	Specific challenges consisted of (a) reading/decoding multisyllabic words and (b) writing/multi-paragraph essays and compositions.
Isabella	6-Exited	F	Specific learning challenges included (a) reading/identifying the main idea, making predictions, and interpreting text; (b) math/multiplication and division; (c) writing/drafting, editing, spelling, capitalization, and punctuation.
Lucia	3-Developing	F	Specific learning challenges included (a) study skills; (b) reading/identifying the main idea, making predictions, interpreting text; and (c) writing/cohesive paragraphs.
Emilia	3-Developing	F	Specific learning challenges included (a) study skills; (b) reading/identifying the main idea, making predictions, interpreting text, and identifying the theme; and (c) writing/generating a paragraph on a topic.

Lesson Materials and Assignments

Lesson materials consisted of both final materials and interim drafts. The students were learning about World War II. Their project was to evaluate two types of influences—leaders and media—and develop theories to share about how these influences contributed to the ill feelings and confusion before and during the war. Students had access to a series of teacher-built modules that were thematic, rather than chronological, in accordance with recommendations for history teaching that leads to stronger language and literacy skills (Metro, 2017). Themes from these modules included Recruiting Youth Participation, Earning the Trust of the Masses, Maintaining Loyalty, Making Hate Popular in the Media, and Resistance to Harmful Ideas. These modules were built within an LMS platform with directions, links, and spaces for student responses. These modules had been revised according to feedback from previous middle school students in this class, university graduate students, and other practicing teachers.

Observations

Students were observed every day during the unit about World War II. During these observations, we interacted with the students to hold instructional conversations, monitor their work, and answer questions. This was true of all students, whether they were study participants or not. For study participants, we kept field notes and anecdotal logs of conversations and other classroom activity related to the research questions.

Student Work

In accordance with goals for sponsoring agency among the learners, students chose from a menu of short activities in the modules designed to take 30 to 45 minutes each (Ward, 2012). These assignments were focused on single topics relating to the theme of the module and involved either answering directed questions or using graphic organizers (VanFossen, 2000; Ward). Students were allowed to enter the open internet to search for additional materials for their responses. Responses from these activities were gathered as data. Other data related to student work included search histories available through student accounts, drafts of work saved in LMS spaces, and formal and informal student reflections about their progress.

Informal Interviews

Small-group discussions and whole-class discussions were held daily, and students conferenced with one another if they chose. Students also shared their work with peers online, offline, and during whole-class events. During these small-group discussions, students shared their impressions of the assignment, talked about things that worked well, and discussed their lives outside school. Although students who were not in the study participated in these informal small group and one-on-one interviews, data was only collected and analyzed for participating students.

Researcher Communications

The researchers wrote daily emails to one another in the process of conducting the study. These became data for analysis.

Data Analysis

"Making sense out of data involves consolidating, reducing, and interpreting what people have said and what the researcher has seen and read—it is the process of making meaning" (Merriam, 1998, p. 178). Using recursive and dynamic data collection and analysis, "is not to say that the analysis is finished when all the data have been collected. Quite the opposite. Analysis becomes more intensive as the study progresses, and once all the data are in" (Merriam, 1998, p. 155). After the data had been collected, the researchers performed a cross analysis to discover how the students engaged to make meaning of the texts they were presented. During this process, the researchers made comparisons between the various data forms to identify places of overlap as well as inconsistency. Data were read by researchers searching for instances of agency by students and then choices were mapped for each student. Then, the maps were laid against student explanations and teacher interpretations of behavior. Finally, the researchers performed a secondary analysis to identify themes across cases. These themes constituted the findings.

Findings

Students demonstrated intellectual agency in three ways: (a) agency over with whom to collaborate, (b) agency over materials and modes of learning (online versus in person), and (c) agency over how to manage their learning time inside and outside school.

Agency Over Collaborative Interactions

All students in the class chose where they sat as a way to personalize the location of their learning. Students were also encouraged to decide when and how they wanted to collaborate with peers. Some students worked with different classmates on different tasks, and others had consistent partners.

Isabella exercised agency in this regard by working with a friend on a shared cloud document. The collaboration involved having a conversation about the topic of the Nazi harassment of Jewish individuals. Isabella and her friend debated whether and to what extent Nazis were intentionally malicious or if they were merely reacting to poor information proffered by a few individuals. At the end of the conversation, Isabella and her friend shared a position that the boycott was about revenge, and then she used additional evidence to argue that the Nazi party not only was sharing lies, but also knew they were.

Lucia became interested in Isabella's conversation and later went to work with Isabella's partner as well. Lucia asked if they could focus on the Nazi boycott of 1933. Lucia wrote:

> The Nazis said the boycott was revenge against the Jews because Jews in Germany, as well as Jews in other countries, assisted by foreign newspaper people, were publishing stories around the work to damage Nazi Germany's reputation. Meanwhile, Nazis said the stories about bad things happening against the Jews were not true. It was a lie and they said it anyway. Those bad things really were happening.

In what Lucia wrote, she attributed understandings gleaned from the conversations that emerged as Isabella and Lucia worked with the same partner. She communicated a position about her interpretation of the events. Her interpretation was not just a conclusion born of cognition and individual reasoning—it was a conclusion born out of social convergence. These three students were listening to each other, sharing ideas, practicing ways to write them, and then completing responses. Lucia did not have access to the shared document that Isabella and the other student were working on, but she did share in the constructed meaning that emerged during the event.

Agency Over Materials and Modes of Learning

Students demonstrated intellectual agency by deciding what materials and modes they would use. They often exercised this agency in determining whether and how to extend or alter assignments.

Josue used his time in class to identify specific parts of Nazi's Final Solution. He realized early in his reading and through a clip he watched that this solution was genocide—to take people's lives. As an expansion of the assignment, Josue organized these pieces of the plan according to what he felt was their level of severity and justified his choices with explanations in his own words. Josue also made specific choices about what types of texts he wanted to use during this project and in which modalities. He alternated between modes (text, audio, images, and video) as he identified parts of the Final Solution, which included work camps, death camps, and liberation. While designing such a task might seem a little dark, the task served as a way for Josue to think about the nature of hatred when it becomes ensconced in policy. It also allowed him to practice with terms

240 Mary Frances Rice and Mark Stevens

related to the topic and use them for cognitive tasks like summarization, paraphrasing, and even argument through his justifications.

Another example of this came from Isabella. She made a personal connection to Winston Churchill's "We Shall Fight on the Beaches" speech. She wrote:

> I had to defend my friend in a situation. I talked to somebody who was talking bad about her. When I did that, they were nicer to my friend.

Although the initial assigned task was merely to interpret meaning in an abstract way, through rephrasing of the historical content, Isabella took the idea of interpretation and enhanced it through a personal connection. When the teacher saw what Isabella had done, he shared her response with the class and encouraged them to make personal connections if they wished. Some students did make these connections in later assignments.

Lucia demonstrated agency through her work with Winston Churchill's speech. Although she had engaged with Isabella and another classmate earlier, for this portion of the unit, she worked by herself. She began by identifying keywords in the text and then identifying their meanings. Although the teacher had recommended some content words in the module, such as *empire* and *republic*, Lucia chose her own words, such as *odious*, *apparatus*, and *subjugate*. Then Lucia made herself an interactive, multimodal glossary of the words and shared this with other students during small group.

Emilia decided to study political cartoons instead of reading about the boycott. She located a cartoon related to Hitler crawling out of the large rolled-up copy of the Versailles Treaty to respond to a teacher-generated question: What were the terms of the Treaty of Versailles? She wrote "shrink the military and admit the war was their fault" but did not mention the rise of Hitler being a by-product in her written response. Instead, she added the cartoon to her document and submitted it. It took extra time and work to locate the image, more time than it would have to write something like "and it also brought Hitler to power."

Agency Over Work Routines Inside and Outside School

Although the examples shared so far feature students choosing projects and guiding their own work, students did not always want to work. For example, Josue started work on a Defeat of Germany timeline that required exploration of five events through production of slides that shared (a) event name, (b) picture. (c) explanation of picture, (d) countries involved, and (e) the outcome. Although Josue often completed all the parts of many activities, he chose to make only one slide. Further, on this particular slide, he only included three of the elements, even though the three friends he worked with finished.

Besides not doing work, sometimes students would do work and then not submit it. Lucia failed to complete several activities, even with urging from her teacher or offers from peers to work together. One day in particular, she inexplicably deleted several slides from a presentation she was working on and instead claimed that she had done nothing for the day.

Sometimes students produced work that was oddly inaccurate. For example, Emilia attempted an analysis of a political cartoon related to the beginning of World War II with Hitler balancing a gun on his nose with the world on top of that. Her analysis stated it showed "a gun shooting the world." While it did show both a gun and the world, there was no shooting. When her interpretation was questioned, Emilia shrugged. When asked if she wanted to work with a peer or see what other students were writing, she said no.

While some members of the class chose to do work on these projects at home, none of these four students did. However, the students in the study did not have internet access at home, and they did not live in communities where libraries were close or travel by walking or bike riding was reasonable. Such circumstances highlight the importance of agency happening in a relationship with other people as well as resources. Even if these students wished to work outside school, they simply did not have the equipment and the internet access to do so. Thus, their choices about how to spend their time in school were all the more important— this was their only chance to work on the assignments.

Discussion

These findings have important implications for organizing blended environments that support intellectual agency and are not just technologically flush for English learners who also have disabilities. The students in this study are from socioeconomic circumstances where they could have ended up in learning spaces with much surveillance, where they could be completely ignored by the teacher and their peers, or where they were only assigned rote, low-skilled work (Anyon, 1981). Instead, these students were active choice makers who were sufficiently industrious, often over and above what would typically be expected of them as English learners with disabilities (Trent et al., 1998). For these students, doing blended learning was more than just being able to do an assignment on the computer and have small- and whole-group instruction. It was an opportunity to imagine themselves in positive spaces, to use technologies, to express their thoughts, and to build and maintain social relationships.

Agency as Support for Intellectual Challenge

Looking at the official documents outlining student challenges in Table 14.1, readers might not have expected they would be successful with their work most of the time. Researchers have found that English learners, students with disabilities, and particularly dual-identified learners are often positioned in deficit (Hoover & Patton, 2005; Kim & García, 2014). In this particular blended learning environment, these students were generally able to do work they wanted to do and interact with their peers. As for critics who might say, "But what about the standards?" we would respond that students' modifications of their work actually yielded stronger learning than what was originally posed in the task. For example, when Emilia picked general high-frequency words over content vocabulary, her selections were more aligned to recommendations from vocabulary research (Beck et al., 2013). Moreover, not restricting student language to tidy fill-in-the-blank assignments resulted in higher word production and complex discourse. This is important because the assignment was not merely about learning facts about a bygone war. From a Deweyan (1938) perspective, this unit was an opportunity to learn what occupation and oppression look like, which is important for social participation because of its ongoing, immediate relevance.

Agency to Engage or Not to

While it might be worth considering what else or what more students might learn in an environment geared toward mastery of discrete skills, the findings of the study demonstrate the reverse is also true. What do students not learn, who do they not interact with, and what do they not produce when they are in highly structured blended learning environments? Remember the position of Dewey (1938)—that the goal is for a balance that enables learners to use modern resources, such as digital technologies, to cope with contemporary problems *and* participate in social democracy. Particularly when it comes to students with disabilities and English learners, these goals of inclusion need more careful consideration. For proof that these needs have not yet been carefully considered, all one must do is consult the relatively tiny research base supported by only a few individuals and groups (Rice & Dykman, 2018). The evidence is in the lack of studies.

These findings also provide insight into the perceived dichotomy between engagement and non-engagement. Instead of an either-or proposition, engagement was best seen as an ongoing relational negotiation, more compatible with a continuum metaphor than a switch. Further, students made strategic choices to maximize (or survive) a learning experience. Their choices were more complex than did they plan, perform, and evaluate (Zimmerman & Risemberg, 1997). Part of the exchange in allowing intellectual agency over with whom to work, what tasks to do, and how to do them was that sometimes, students would choose to do nothing or choose to share nothing. Some of this nothing might be tied to not knowing what to do or not being intellectually stimulated to do it. Some might also come from psychosocial tensions endemic to adolescent development (Erikson, 1968). Nevertheless, it is in these moments, when students who usually do something do nothing, that teachers may see how well their classes support student agency. Often after these episodes of nothing (part of the class period, maybe a whole one), students would return and do something . . . lots of things, even. Moreover, adulthood affords the choice to do nothing, often with impunity. Even so, during these times of nothing in blended learning, what are appropriate responses from teachers who believe in agency and understand relational adolescent development? This is a question for future research.

Agency as Relational

These findings highlight agency in its relational features (Burkitt, 2016). When the students in this study asked for help, they preferred to ask for it from a peer. Sometimes this help solicitation was in the form of a quick question, and sometimes it was an invitation for collaboration through in-person conversation or with documents. Students made different choices on different days with different content. Again, while some of these choices might be about not understanding language or having certain skills, some of it is also social. Maybe a student feels like being alone. Maybe something happened in another class. Maybe friendships and alliances shifted in accordance with development (Erikson, 1968). The point is that learner control is not tethered exclusively to the stimulation of working with technology or very narrow choices, such as choosing the order of the tasks. Learner control, when fully embraced, encompasses a wide range of decisions learners might make. Supporting these choices requires relational interest from the teacher and other adults on- and offline that goes beyond merely keeping students on task. This is especially important for students who are English learners and/or who have disabilities because these are two groups of students who have trouble acquiring and maintaining social relationships in school and with teachers (Menken & Kleyn, 2010; Pham & Murray, 2016; Trent et al., 1998). Can blended learning structures contribute to a greater sense of inclusion in schools? Hopefully, but more research is needed on how structures support and constrain agency while supporting and constraining achievement.

Conclusion

This study focused on students with disabilities who were also English learners as they made choices in a blended learning classroom. The students leveraged their agency to make choices about with whom to work and how to engage with the materials. Students also made decisions about their rhythms of work that included not working at times. The findings support the advocacy position that English learners and students with disabilities should be included in blended learning classrooms. These students are agents, doing their best to navigate their adolescence as well as their language and functional challenges. They are active thinkers and learners. Studying students in blended learning environments should honor agency and include diverse students. We close with a paraphrase from Anyon (2009): Let us not let theories about these populations do our thinking for us. Let us engage and observe and include.

References

Anyon, J. (1981). Social class and school knowledge. *Curriculum Inquiry, 11*(1), 3–42.

Anyon, J. (2009). *Theory and educational research: Toward a critical social explanation.* Routledge.

Archer, M. S. (2003). *Structure, agency and the internal conversation.* Cambridge University Press.

Archer, M. S. (2013). The ontological status of subjectivity: The missing link between structure and agency. In *Contributions to social ontology* (pp. 31–45). Routledge.

Basham, J. D., Stahl, W., Ortiz, K. R., Rice, M. F., & Smith, S. J. (2015). *Equity matters: Digital and online learning for students with disabilities.* Center on Online Learning and Students with Disabilities.

Beck, I. L., McKeown, M. G., & Kucan, L. (2013). *Bringing words to life: Robust vocabulary instruction.* Guilford Press.

Borup, J., Graham, C. R., West, R. E., Archambault, L., & Spring, K. J. (2020). Academic communities of engagement: An expansive lens for examining support structures in blended and online learning. *Educational Technology Research and Development, 68*(2), 807–832.

Bottge, B. A., Ma, X., Gassaway, L., Toland, M. D., Butler, M., & Cho, S. J. (2014). Effects of blended instructional models on math performance. *Exceptional Children, 80*(4), 423–437.

Burkitt, I. (2016). Relational agency: Relational sociology, agency and interaction. *European Journal of Social Theory, 19*(3), 322–339.

Carter, R. A., Rice, M., Yang, S., & Jackson, H. (2020). Self-regulated learning in online learning environments: Strategies for remote learning. *Information and Learning Sciences. 121*(5/6), 321–329.

Deci, E. L., & Ryan, R. M. (2012). Self-determination theory. In P. A. M. Van Lange, A. W. Kruglanski, & E. T. Higgins (Eds.), *Handbook of theories of social psychology* (pp. 416–436). Sage. https://doi.org/10.4135/9781446249215.n21

Dewey, J. (1938). *Experience and education.* Collier Books.

Erikson, E. H. (1968). *Identity: Youth and crisis* (Vol. 7). W. W. Norton & Company.

Giddens, A. (1979). *Central problems in social theory: Action, structure, and contradiction in social analysis* (Vol. 241). University of California Press.

Graham, C. R. (2006). Blended learning systems: Definitions, current trends, and future directions. In C. J. Bonk & C. R. Graham (Eds.) *The handbook of blended learning: Global perspectives, local designs* (pp. 3–21). Pfeiffer Publishing.

Graham, C. R., Borup, J., Short, C. R., & Archambault, L. (2019). *K–12 blended teaching: A guide to personalized learning and online integration.* EdTechBooks.org. http://edtech books.org/k12blended

Heidegger, M. (2009). *Basic concepts of Aristotelian philosophy.* Indiana University Press.

Hoover, J. J., & Patton, J. R. (2005). Differentiating curriculum and instruction for English-language learners with special needs. *Intervention in School and Clinic, 40*(4), 231–235. https://doi.org/10.1177/10534512050400040401

Hoxie, A. M., Stillman, J., & Chesal, K. (2014). Blended learning in New York City. In A. G. Picciano, C. D. Dziuban, & C. R. Graham (Eds.), *Blended learning research perspectives* (pp. 304–324). Routledge.

Individuals with Disabilities Education Act [IDEA], P.L. 108–446, 20 U.S.C. § 1400 (2004).

Kim, W. G., & García, S. B. (2014). Long-term English language learners' perceptions of their language and academic learning experiences. *Remedial and Special Education, 35*(5), 300–312. https://doi.org/10.1177/0741932514525047

Menken, K., & Kleyn, T. (2010). The long-term impact of subtractive schooling in the educational experiences of secondary English language learners. *International Journal of Bilingual Education and Bilingualism, 13*(4), 399–417.

Merriam, S. B. (1998). *Qualitative research and case study applications in education: Revised and expanded from case study research in education.* Jossey-Bass.

Metro, R. (2017). *Teaching US history thematically: Document-based lessons for the secondary classroom.* Teachers College Press.

Mohammed, S. (2017). Connecting research and practice to understand efficacy in K–12 blended learning. *Journal of Online Learning Research, 3*(1), 1–4.

Noddings, N. (2013). *Education and democracy in the 21st century.* Teachers College Press.

Norton, B., & Pavlenko, A. (2019). Imagined communities, identity, and English language learning in a multilingual world. In X. Gao (Ed.), *Second handbook of English language teaching.* Springer.

O'Byrne, W. I., & Pytash, K. E. (2015). Hybrid and blended learning: Modifying pedagogy across path, pace, time, and place. *Journal of Adolescent & Adult Literacy, 59*(2), 137–140.

Pace, J. R., & Mellard, D. F. (2016). Reading achievement and reading efficacy changes for middle school students with disabilities through blended learning instruction. *Journal of Special Education Technology, 31*(3), 156–169.

Pape, S. J., Bell, C. V., & Yetkin, I. E. (2003). Developing mathematical thinking and self-regulated learning: A teaching experiment in a seventh-grade mathematics classroom. *Educational Studies in Mathematics, 53*(3), 179–202.

Pham, Y. K., & Murray, C. (2016). Social relationships among adolescents with disabilities: Unique and cumulative associations with adjustment. *Exceptional Children, 82*(2), 234–250.

Pintrich, P. R. (1999). The role of motivation in promoting and sustaining self-regulated learning. *International Journal of Educational Research, 31*(6), 459–470.

Rice, M., & Dykman, B. (2018). The emerging research base for online learning and students with disabilities. In R. Ferdig & K. Kennedy (Eds.), *Handbook of research on K–12 online and blended learning* (pp. 189–206). ETC Press.

Roscoe, R. D., Segedy, J. R., Sulcer, B., Jeong, H., & Biswas, G. (2013). Shallow strategy development in a teachable agent environment designed to support self-regulated learning. *Computers & Education, 62*, 286–297.

Smith, J. G., & Suzuki, S. (2015). Embedded blended learning within an algebra classroom: A multimedia capture experiment. *Journal of Computer Assisted Learning, 31*(2), 133–147.

Staker, H. (2011). *The rise of K-12 blended learning: Profiles of emerging models.* Innosight Institute. Retrieved from https://files.eric.ed.gov/fulltext/ED535181.pdf

Staker, H., & Horn, M. B. (2012). *Classifying K–12 blended learning.* Innosight Institute. https://eric.ed.gov/?id=ED535180

Stevens, M. (2016). Space for all: Middle level students in blended learning environments. *Voices from the Middle, 24*(2), 50–55.

Stevens, M. (2018). *Technology enhanced learning for English language learners* [Unpublished doctoral dissertation]. George Mason University.

Stevens, M., & Rice, M. (2016). Inquiring into presence in a middle level blended learning classroom. *Journal of Online Learning Research*, 2(4), 447–473.

Trent, S. C., Artiles, A. J., & Englert, C. S. (1998). From deficit thinking to social constructivism: A review of theory, research, and practice in special education. *Review of Research in Education*, 23(1), 277–307.

VanFossen, P. J. (2000). Using the Internet to create primary source teaching packets (cover story). *Social Studies*, 91(6), 244.

Ward, A. E. (2012). Teaching civil war mobilization with online primary sources. *OAH Magazine of History*, 26(2), 37.

Willner, L. S., & Monroe, M. (2016). *The WIDA accessibility and accommodations framework: Considerations influencing the framework development.* https://wida.wisc.edu/sites/default/files/resource/WIDA-Accessibility-Accommodations-Framework.pdf

Zimmerman, B. J., & Risemberg, R. (1997). Self-regulatory dimensions of academic learning and motivation. In G. Phye (Ed.), *Handbook of academic learning: Construction of knowledge* (pp. 105–125). Elsevier. https://doi.org/10.1016/B978-0-12-554255-5.X5000-5

15
MULTIMODAL BLENDED LEARNING AND ENGLISH LANGUAGE LEARNERS

Mark Stevens

Examination of the Problem

The problem of this study, English language learner (ELL) achievement in blended technology-enhanced contexts, rests in the consideration of several issues. These include (a) who are ELLs? (b) the growing populations of ELLs, (c) the strategies implemented, (d) persisting achievement gaps, and (e) the negative impacts of gaps.

Who Are ELLs?

In the context of this study, ELLs were students who had limitations speaking, reading, writing, or understanding English (Ahmed Badawi, 2019). One particular detail that increases understanding of them is that 80% of ELLs in the US speak Spanish at home (NCES, 2019b).

Growing Population of ELLs

Growing populations of English language learners (ELLs) in US schools and concerns about academic achievement present challenges (Snyder et al., 2017). This growth is reflected in data at the national, state, school district, and local school level. In the 16 years from 2000 to 2016, the number of ELLs in US public schools increased by 52%, from 307,295 to 466,405 (NCES, 2019a). In Virginia, where this study took place, the number of ELLs has grown from 36,802 in 2000 to 162,377 in 2019, an increase of 441% (NCES, 2018). From 2003–2004 to 2018–2019, the following ELL growth occurred in the study context: (a) study

DOI: 10.4324/9781003037736-20

Strategies Implemented

The responses of school districts to the challenges posed by this growth have varied. Some have positively impacted ELLs with strategies such as the use of bilingual learning (Nordstrom, 2015), individual differentiation (Baecher et al., 2012), and a focus on vocabulary development (Chung, 2012). However other school district actions have been less than equitable, including (a) segregating ELLs by language ability (Carreira, 2007), (b) fast-paced learning (Abedi & Herman, 2010), and (c) failure to involve the home culture of ELLs (Carreira, 2007).

Persisting Achievement Gaps

Although school districts have implemented practices to address the needs of ELLs, achievement gaps persist (Colgren & Sappington, 2015). On a national basis, from 1992 to 2019, the reading comprehension gap between all eighth-grade students and ELLs averaged 42% (NCES, 2019b, 2020). Between 2001 and 2014, gaps between all students and ELLs on social studies averaged 39% (NCES, 2020).

These gaps appear on a state, district, and school level as well. Reading comprehension gaps from the 2013–2014 through 2017–2018 school years averaged 19% at the state (Virginia), 20% at the participant school district, and 23% at the participant school level (VDOE, 2016, 2019). Social studies achievement gaps for the same period were 16% at the state (Virginia), 18% at the participant school district, and 24% at the participant school level (VDOE, 2016, 2019).

Negative Impacts of Gaps

Achievement gaps like these can have negative impacts on ELLs. One is the development of feelings of disenfranchisement from the educational process among Latinos, who represent 80% of ELLs (Gonzales & Shields, 2015; NCCTQ, 2009). Additionally, Fry (2003) found low levels of English language proficiency increased the probability ELLs would drop out of school. In fact, from the 2015–2016 to the 2018–2019 school years, ELLs at the high school that will be attended by most students at the study school averaged 49% of the school population but 91% of the dropouts (VDOE, 2017a, 2017b, 2019, 2020).

The personal treatment of ELLs, based on their understanding gaps, paints a particularly troubling picture (Hung et al., 2019). Rodriguez (1993), described his schooling experience as an ELL: "The Spanish had been beaten out of me in the early years of school—and I didn't learn English very well either" (p. 219). This behavior continues, as a middle school ELL shared with a school superintendent that "too often I heard, maestro, they don't want me there. They told me to come back when I learn English" (Lavadenz et al., 2019, p. 184). These behaviors result in learners struggling with self-worth, which can impact achievement (Ghaith, 2019). The continuing challenges experienced by ELLs calls for increased focus on developing English literacy.

Concepts Relevant to Study

In order to increase understanding of the approach designed to address ELL literacy problems, several areas will be examined, including (a) blended learning, (b) multimodal learning, (c) reading comprehension, and (d) social studies learning.

Blended Learning

Blended learning can be understood as the purposeful combination of online and face-to-face instructional strategies (Graham, 2013; Menon, 2019). Furthermore, it includes the combination of hardware (computers, tablets, phones), software (web sites, productivity applications), and online networks to promote learning (Giannakos & Darra, 2019). The relevance of blended learning as an instructional practice derives from multiple aspects, including that it supports students worldwide in the effort to self-direct the construction of knowledge (Kundu et al., 2020). This work is guided by active teacher engagement during the design, delivery, and redesign of learning (Anderson et al., 2001; Borup et al., 2014).

In order to better understand blended learning, two examples can be examined. Trainin et al. (2016) studied a social studies/science intervention using expressive reading websites, highlighted textual passages, and scaffolded vocabulary and found learners experienced significant gains in fluency and comprehension. Dalton (2015) examined a program that used images and live-action video to support learner investigation of US westward expansion and determined learners not only understood content better, but also developed multimodal (text, images, audio, video) composing skills.

Other benefits are related to blended learning. Researchers have found it can have a positive impact on ELL learning in general, and reading ability particularly (Altiner, 2019; Yeop, 2019). One reason for this is blended learning supports differentiated instruction through teacher-student collaboration, which encourages learner independence (Haelermans et al., 2015; Oliver et al., 2019).

Constraints also exist when using blended learning. Some schools deploy an insufficient amount of technology to make it work efficiently (Kundu et al., 2020). Also, technology quality can be so poor that effective learning does not happen, thereby blocking access to blended learning (Mor & Winters, 2008).

Multimodal Learning

Multimodal learning involves the interrelationship of imagery, music, voice audio, written digital text, video, and animation learners use to actively create and share meaning in a self-directed way (Doerr-Stevens & Buckley-Marudas, 2019; Serafini, 2012). Even though these modes extend beyond traditional print sources, they are understood through the traditional literacy practices of "decoding, comprehension, and production" (Gomez et al., 2010, p. 21).

Benefits have been realized with multimodal learning. Learning using at least two of the modes creates a situation in which the logics of time and space combine to allow learners to personally differentiate use of resources to meet their own needs (Kress & Selander, 2012). Specifically beneficial to ELLs, research has found language knowledge growth results from the multimodal interaction of words and symbols, thus allowing struggling learners to accurately create meaning for themselves (Bakhtin, 1981; Dalton & Jocius, 2013). In particular, videos have been found helpful in supporting ELLs in correctly using English vowels, consonants, suffixes, and prefixes, thereby improving learning (Ahmed Badawi, 2019).

Reading Comprehension

Examining reading comprehension, an element of ELL achievement gaps, opened a window into the design of an approach that proved helpful. Reading comprehension is a multimodal process in which a reader interacts with text, and what occurs while reading is ongoing: to decode and comprehend content that is being read (Ahmed et al., 2016). Skill with vocabulary is essential in this process (Davis, 1944; Khataee, 2019), and lack of it is a major factor in low levels of reading comprehension for Latino/a ELLs and other learners (Garcia, 1991; Karademir & Gorgoz, 2019). Comprehension of what is being read also involves fluency, which describes learner actions reading text passages easily, thereby demonstrating word part awareness and understanding (Ahmed Badawi, 2019; Elkonin, 1963).

ELLs' problems in this area are various. One involves comprehension being adversely impacted when ELLs lack content background knowledge (Brown, 2007; Khataee, 2019). Closely related is the trouble ELLs face mastering content and vocabulary while also learning English (Clemens et al., 2018). These challenges to reading comprehension contribute to the achievement gaps mentioned and magnify the necessity of identifying an approach that serves ELL needs.

Social Studies Learning

Social studies learning is a multifaceted concept based in five different content areas: economics, geography, history, law, and religion. The traditional teacher-centric approach used in these areas involves presentation of essential content by

Multimodal Blended Learning and ELLs 251

lecture, with heavy dependence on text alone (Capin & Vaughn, 2017). Teacher-directed social studies lessons also start with review and depend on the use of textbooks and worksheets (Scruggs et al., 2012).

A more progressive approach to social studies learning includes a focus on reading comprehension, concentration on guiding learners with organizational and thinking strategies, and involves collaborative learning. One example of this is known as collaborative strategic reading (CSR), which is designed to activate prior knowledge, read new social studies texts, develop vocabulary learning strategies, help learners monitor their own understanding, correct comprehension problems, and summarize with collaborative questioning (Boardman et al., 2016). Another example is the United States History for Engaged Reading (USHER) curriculum, which develops similar strategies, as well as supporting motivation to read and understand US history (Taboada Barber et al., 2015). Many of these ideas impacted the development of the approach studied.

Methodology

This study examined how a multimodal blended learning (MMBL) approach (see Figure 15.1) supported learners, particularly ELLs, in reading, vocabulary, and content knowledge development in a middle-level social studies class. The MMBL is a system in which learners use multimodal blended instruction in a learner-centered way, supported by teacher and parent interaction.

In order to examine the influence of the MMBL, system research questions were constructed that examined the effect of the intervention on ELL learners'

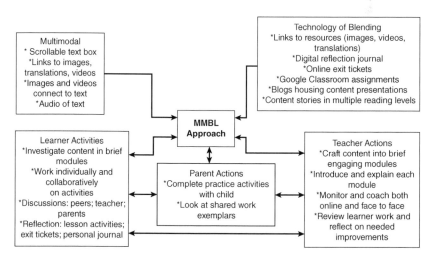

FIGURE 15.1 Diagram of Multimodal Blended Learning System (MMBL)

academic achievement and how learners viewed the intervention. They included the following:

1. Is there a difference in social studies content knowledge achievement between ELLs who use the MMBL and those who primarily learn through teacher-directed instruction?
2. Is there a difference in social studies vocabulary knowledge achievement between ELLs who use the MMBL and those who learn primarily through teacher-directed instruction?
3. Is there a difference in the ability to read social studies text between ELLs who use the MMBL and those who primarily learn through teacher-directed instruction?
4. What do ELLs report about their experiences using the MMBL?

Study Design

A quasi-experimental comparative design examined the MMBL's influence on learning. This approach used "two natural intact groups, one experimental, the other control," that, while not identical, were similar (Campbell & Stanley, 1963, p. 15). This design supported causal inferences regarding the effectiveness of the educational intervention because randomized assignment to experimental and control groups could not be conducted (Kim & Steiner, 2016; Tilley, 2006). These groups were in different schools, where the students had no contact with each other, due to the ethics of withholding the possibly effective MMBL strategies from learners who would see the benefits gained by others (Tilley, 2006).

Methods

The study followed a mixed-methods approach, using both quantitative and qualitative methods, to support triangulation and reach for greater insight on the MMBL's influence on ELL learning versus if only one method were used (Maxwell & Loomis, 2003).

Quantitative Methods in the Study

This study used quantitative methods to explore research questions one through four. The quantitative variables used included learner scores on content/vocabulary post-tests for each of the two units taught, as well as learner scores on pre- and post-study social studies reading comprehension tests (Johnson & Christensen, 2014).

Qualitative Methods in the Study

Qualitative data were collected using interviews to examine the MMBL within the context of its use—a strategy useful when studying intervention development

(Baxter & Jack, 2008). This approach supported the credibility and confirmability of the study by informing interpretation of quantitative data by giving learners voice (Anfara et al., 2002; Yin, 2011).

Participants

Participants consisted of seventh- grade learners enrolled in social studies classes in two schools in a large public school district in the Mid-Atlantic. This district serves 188,000 learners, 29% classified as ELLs (School Division, Student Membership Demographics). For purposes of comparison, General Education (Gen. Ed.) seventh-grade general education history classes were used for participation in the study by both the MMBL and the teacher-directed (TD) schools. Thirty-nine students at the TD school and 54 at the MMBL site completed the assent/consent process. The TD school had 34% of their population of 910 identified as ELLs, with learning gaps of 30% and 19% in reading comprehension and social studies, respectively (VDOE, 2019). The MMBL school had 30% of their population of 1,891 identified as ELLs, with learning gaps of 38% and 31% in reading comprehension and social studies, respectively (VDOE, 2019).

Once classrooms were identified, purposeful sampling was used to select ELL participants within the classes of cooperating teachers at each school most likely to provide the information and understanding sought, many being Latino/a. Their ELL levels were identified by the World-Class Instructional Design and Assessment (WIDA) standards (WIDA, 2007). The numbers in each setting can be seen in Table 15.1.

Interview Participants

Learners were selected for interviewing by purposive sampling of the already-identified ELLs. This was based on both teacher recommendation of learners viewed as most able to express opinions and the desire to select a group of learners that would be as representative as possible of all ELLs involved in the study settings. The 11 interviewees by ELL level were (a) Levels 3–4 = 4, (b) Level 6 = 6, and (c) Level 10 = 1.

TABLE 15.1 ELL Levels of Study Participants

ELL WIDA Levels	TD Group Totals	MMBLS2 Group Totals
Level 1–2 (Enter/Begin)	3 = 8%	5 = 9%
Level 3–4 (Develop/Expand)	7 = 18%	14 = 26%
Level 6 (Reaching)	24 = 61%	34 = 63%
Level 10 (Refused services)	5 = 13%	1 = 3 %
Totals	39	54

Description of Study Treatments

Learners in both the TD and MMBL groups completed two consecutive US history units covering the 1920s and the Great Depression and New Deal time periods. These units were designed to support learning that meets state learning objectives. These approaches are explained and contrasted in Table 15.2.

Quantitative Data Sources

Several quantitative instruments were used, including (a) separate post-unit 1920s and Great Depression/New Deal content and vocabulary tests and (b) social studies pre- and post-reading comprehension tests. Selection of questions for these was guided by participating teacher input, state and national standardized test questions from both fourth- and eighth-grade reading and social studies, and critical friend review. Once given, the scores from each unit's assessment (1920s and Great Depression/New Deal) were combined to produce one dependent variable of social studies content knowledge and one of social studies vocabulary knowledge necessary for comparative purposes.

Qualitative Data Sources

The qualitative instrument used was an interview protocol that guided semi-structured interviews. The process of developing the protocol involved multiple steps, including (a) review of data from a student survey given during a pilot of the MMBL; (b) feedback from two scholars familiar with the MMBL; (c)

TABLE 15.2 Study Treatment Descriptions

Multimodal Blended Learning	*Teacher Directed*
Teacher supports students working in a self-directed way.	Teacher explains details the day of lesson and controls pacing.
List of modules provided in Google Classroom so learners know in advance all topics.	Objectives listed the day of the lesson on whiteboard.
A separate Google Classroom assignment for each module, containing (a) module work plan providing learning objectives, steps to be taken, and links to content presentations and translation tools; (b) activity document for each module; and (c) links to exit ticket surveys.	Paper learning documents passed out and collected the day of the lesson.
Online personal reflection journal, supported by whole and small group discussion.	Whole-class reflection at end of lesson.
Engaged teacher presence, both on- and offline, during and after school.	Teacher monitors and supports students in classroom.

construction of a proto-interview protocol, piloted with learners who had used a version of the MMBL the previous school year; and (d) construction of the final 16-question protocol.

Data Collection

The first step in data gathering was administration of the reading comprehension pre-test in both settings. Then work was done on the 1920s unit, followed by the 1920s post-unit content-vocabulary test. After work was done on the Great Depression/New Deal unit, that post-unit content-vocabulary test was given. Following that, learners took the social studies reading comprehension post-test. The last step involved interviews with the 11 learners chosen from among all MMBL participating classes.

Data Analysis

The analysis of data depended on the objective of the question. The first three questions examined the effect of the two learning approaches (MMBL and TD) on learner knowledge and used independent t-tests for two samples to process relevant data. The independent test was chosen because, while the MMBL and TD groups were similar demographically, they were unconnected samples including no common subjects (Lowry, 2017). Analysis of the fourth question used learner interviews and followed a hybrid approach, employing deductive and inductive coding to identify thematic understandings (Fereday & Muir-Cochrane, 2006).

Results/Findings

Findings from the study have been organized into the following sections to support understanding: (a) social studies content knowledge, (b) social studies vocabulary knowledge, (c) social studies reading comprehension, and (d) ELLs reporting of experiences using the MMBL.

Social Studies Content Knowledge

The first question of the study assessed social studies content knowledge between ELLs using the MMBL and those in the TD group. The assessment scores for the 1920s and Great Depression/New Deal units were added together, resulting in a total of 35 questions. Results showed a statistically significant difference on the content test performance between MMBL learner (M = 28.15) and teacher-directed learner scores (M = 24.72). The effect size was also calculated and found to be d = 0.74, which translates to a 69.8% chance any randomly chosen MMBL learner would score higher in social studies content assessments than any randomly chosen TD learner.

Social Studies Vocabulary Knowledge

The second question of the study assessed social studies vocabulary knowledge achievement between ELLs using the MMBL and those in the TD group. The assessment scores for both units were added together, resulting in 22 total questions. Calculations demonstrated a statistically significant difference in the vocabulary test performance between MMBL learner (M = 20.22) and TD learner scores (M = 18.13). The effect size was also calculated and found to be d = 0.795, which translates to a 70.9% chance any randomly chosen MMBL learner would score higher in social studies content assessments than any randomly chosen TD learner.

Social Studies Reading Comprehension

The third question of the study assessed the difference in the ability to read social studies text between ELLs using the MMBL and those in TD instruction. A 14-question assessment was used after both study units finished. Results indicated no statistically significant difference between MMBL learner (M = 11.04) and TD learner scores (M = 10.03). The effect size was also calculated and found to be d = 0.35, which translates to a 59.5% chance any randomly chosen MMBL learner would score higher in social studies content assessments than any randomly chosen TD learner.

ELLs Report Experiences Using MMBL

The fifth research question asked, "What do ELLs report about their experiences using MMBL?" The 11 interviews analyzed demonstrated ELLs had a range of reactions connected to using the MMBL, including (a) the multimodal approach, (b) technology tools in blended learning, (c) peer interaction, (d) teacher support, and (e) parent input.

General learner views of the MMBL are useful to consider. In fact, they were overwhelmingly positive, such as Benjamin saying, "I liked being in charge of my own learning." Sophia stated she liked the MMBL because it helped her understand what she was reading: "I listened to the text. . . . [I]f I didn't understand what it meant I was able to watch the videos and understand." Robert, in effect, summarized a major point made by other participants when he shared, "It was my teacher; she gave me the confidence to make all of this work."

However, a few concerns were expressed. Amelia shared, "I wanted to do the at-home activities, but Mom does not understand English well enough to help me." Liam indicated his opinion of collaboration when he advised, "I really wanted more opportunity to work in small groups, but not with people trying to not do the work." Isabella advised, "The videos really help me understand things, but there should be more." Effort was expended to locate more negative views to challenge the markedly positive nature of participant opinions, but I was not able to locate any, thereby confirming the positive nature of learner experiences.

Opinions of Multimodal Approach

Multimodal learning, which combines text, audio, images, and video to relay a message, was described by participants through their experiences using the MMBL. Amelia said videos helped her understand the text about music and dance in the 1920s. Olivia described how the multimodal approach made it easier because the pictures showed what it looked like, the text and image captions asked questions that made her think, and she could find answers later when she read text. Both of them explained that while their teacher did not specifically explain multimodal learning, they helped them figure out how to use it.

Learners mentioned other specific ways the multimodal approach helped. Charlotte said the colorization and bolding of text improved content understanding by organizing information and focusing reading effort. Sophia described how the audio helped her by saying, "All you have to do is click the play button, and it just starts reading. All you have to do is follow." Leonard stated the videos helped him understand the written text and explained they could be "funny and educational at the same time." Learners also appreciated how the images included gave a stronger understanding of what they were reading and helped them avoid the boring practice of just using worksheets.

Technology Tools Opinions

One component of the MMBL that learners found beneficial was the use and combination of technology tools. Google Classroom was seen by learners as supporting ease of access to learning, self-regulation, flexibility, and organization. Thomas described the self-regulation and flexibility Google Classroom enabled by saying it helped him get to everything he needed on his own, in his own way, without having to wait for the teacher.

The work plan document available on Google Classroom provided learners detailed directions and necessary resource links to complete each lesson. Sophia and Charlotte felt the step-by-step directions it contained made it easy to know what to do and get to those necessary links. James stated this organization kept him from making mistakes.

Module content was contained in a series of Google Blogger posts, which learners found useful. Amelia stated the scrolling feature of the box in each blog post containing the text, images, and videos was easy to use to make the content move up and down as she needed. James found the videos embedded inside the scrollable box easy to use. Most learners actually stated the multimodal resources the blog made available in one place supported reading and vocabulary comprehension.

258 Mark Stevens

A podcasting tool (www.spreaker.com/) provided an embeddable play bar that controlled audio of module text within Google Blogger module posts. Learners saw the ability to pause and rewind audio with this tool as particularly useful.

Google Surveys proved useful as module reflection tools. Thomas advised he was able to use the surveys to "tell my teachers if it [MMBL lesson] is good, or if it's bad, or if I didn't like it." Cooperating teachers confirmed they used these responses to modify lessons as needed. Robert said the surveys helped him because they "made you think back to what you'd done."

Participants pointed out that while these tools usually worked easily, problems could occur, but were quickly addressed by their teacher.

Opinions of Peer Interaction

One component of the MMBL was the ability to collaborate with peers on learning activities. Amelia described it by saying, "It wasn't really that hard to work with them (peers) doing all the lessons." Others decided to limit their peer interaction to a minimum, which Thomas described by saying, "I'm a quiet person, but sometimes my classmates ask me for my help. Most of the time I was silent and worked on my own." Olivia enjoyed the flexible interaction possible, stating, "It was actually interesting because you would either work in a group or with a partner or on your own." Sophia's description of this was typical of many learners: "During class the teacher helped us share documents, and work on it together on our own. We would share parts and we would double check each other's work, like we switched." Another powerful example of peer interaction came from James, who said, "My friend was absent one day, and the next day was a little behind, so she asked me what she was supposed to do and I told her."

Opinions of Teacher Support

Learners felt teacher interaction helped them successfully use the MMBL. Isabella stated this started from the beginning of a lesson when her teacher would give "explanations of it [how to do the lesson] that [were] really helpful." Leonard said his teacher always noticed who needed help: "Whenever I had a question, even when I didn't, she would come over and look at what I'm doing and then advise me to do something or fix something that I did." Benjamin reported his teacher noticed when this coaching confused learners and took steps to clarify what was needed. When compared to the understanding of the TD approach provided by teachers in that setting, MMBL teacher support was easier to access both individually and in small groups, actively encouraged learner self-direction, and was often offered without being asked for.

Opinions of Parent Input

Parent input occurred in various ways, spurring a variety of learner opinions. Olivia said that while she did not do the at-home activities provided with each lesson with her parents, she did complete regular unit assignments with them around in case she needed help. Leonard described how his dad helped him with one of the at-home activities and eventually said about the MMBL: "This is actually a fun way to learn." Although learners did realize benefits of at-home activities, they were not widely used. It is possible English fluency prevented this as Thomas reported, "My Mom and Dad don't speak English."

Discussion

The findings of this study painted a picture of positive outcomes. In order to fully contemplate this, several ideas were considered, including (a) overall endorsement of MMBL, (b) why the MMBL achieved positive results, (c) why ELLs benefited from the MMBL approach, and (d) reading comprehension performance and possibilities. Each is discussed next. In addition, ideas related to limitations and recommendations will be shared.

Overall Endorsement of MMBL

The MMBL proved to positively impact social studies reading, vocabulary, and content learning and was viewed favorably by learners. In order to achieve this effect, the MMBL used all source modes (audio, video, images, and text) in a combined fashion, along with digital text. Researchers have found similar effects related to the use of:

- images (Dalton & Grisham, 2013)
- audio (Bogard & Mcmackin, 2012)
- video (Hafner, 2015)

Why the MMBL Achieved Positive Results

The MMBL achieved positive results due to the actions of teachers and the engagement of learners. One way the positive influence of MMBL teachers became clear was that testing data showed MMBL learners performed better than learners in a TD approach, and active teacher presence, mentioned by learners, was necessary to make that happen (Anderson et al., 2001; Borup et al., 2014). Learner engagement was described in different ways, one being their appreciation of working in a self-directed manner (Luo, 2018). Additionally, collaborative work was mentioned as causing a more focused effort (Capin & Vaughn, 2017).

Why ELLs Benefited from the MMBL Approach

Various strategies found to help ELLs with challenges in an English-centric environment were used in the MMBL system, including:

- individualized instruction (Baecher et al., 2012)
- bilingual learning (Cisco & Padrón, 2012)
- development of vocabulary knowledge (Chung, 2012)
- intentional efforts to motivate and engage (Taboada Barber et al., 2015)
- employment of multimodal learning (Dalton & Jocius, 2013)
- using various technology tools (Ortlieb et al., 2014)

Reading Comprehension Performance and Possibilities

Reading comprehension is a stable construct that can take as long as ten years to achieve significant improvement (Wanzek et al., 2017). Even though this is the case, and the MMBL was used only for six weeks, it had a positive impact on the reading comprehension of those employing it. There is a possibility that longer implementation of the MMBL would have produced even greater growth.

Limitations

It is worthwhile to consider the limitations of this study as that can increase the validity of what has been found (Shipman, 2014). In order to focus attention, the limitations discussed will deal with design of the MMBL system and implementation of the study.

Design of MMBL

It took considerable time to design, construct, and redesign, as necessary, all MMBL components for each lesson. Concern also emerged related to the accessibility of the MMBL assignments to all learners, including support in different languages. In addition, some did not have access to safe locations outside school where they could use computers to work on lessons. This was addressed in part by offering after-school sessions in the classrooms.

Study Implementation

Implementation limitations exist that impacted this study. One was there was no way to account for the influence on ELLs of using the MMBL in classes with non-ELLs. In some ways, that may not be a serious limitation because the social presence of learners positively influences others' cognitive actions (Garrison et al., 2001). Additionally, the effectiveness of the study was limited by lack of access to

WIDA Level One or Two students. If this has been possible, deeper examination could have been made of the impact language ability has on MMBL benefits.

References

Abedi, J., & Herman, J. (2010). Assessing English language learners' opportunity to learn mathematics: Issues and limitations. *Teachers College Record, 112*(3), 723–746.

Ahmed, Y., Francis, D. J., York, M., Fletcher, J. M., Barnes, M., & Kulesz, P. (2016). Validation of the direct and inferential mediation (DIME) model of reading comprehension in grades 7 through 12. *Contemporary Educational Psychology, 44*, 68–82. https://doi.org/10.1016/j.cedpsych.2016.02.002

Ahmed Badawi, M. F. (2019). The effect of explicit English morphology instruction on EFL secondary school students' morphological awareness and reading comprehension. *English Language Teaching, 12*(4), 166–178. https://doi.org/10.5539/elt.v12n4p166

Altiner, C. (2019). Integrating a computer-based flashcard program into academic vocabulary learning. *The Turkish Online Journal of Educational Technology, 18*(1), 44–62. https://doi.org/10.31274/etd-180810-375

Anderson, T., Rourke, L., Garrison, D. R., & Archer, W. (2001). Assessing teaching presence in a computer conferencing context. *Journal of Asynchronous Learning Networks, 5*(2), 1–17.

Anfara, V. A., Brown, K. M., & Mangione, T. L. (2002). Qualitative analysis on stage: Making the research process more public. *Educational Researcher, 31*(7), 28–38. https://doi.org/10.3102/0013189X031007028

Baecher, L., Artigliere, M., Patterson, D. K., & Spatzer, A. (2012). Differentiated instruction for English language learners as "variations on a theme." *Middle School Journal, 43*(3), 14–21. https://doi.org/10.1080/00940771.2012.11461807

Bakhtin, M. M. (1981). *The dialogic imagination: Four essays. Bakhtinian perspectives on language, literacy and learning*. Cambridge University Press.

Baxter, P., & Jack, S. (2008). Qualitative case study methodology: Study design and implementation for novice researchers. *The Qualitative Report Volume, 13*(4), 544–559. https://doi.org/10.2174/1874434600802010058

Boardman, A. G., Buckley, P., Vaughn, S., Roberts, G., Scornavacco, K., & Klingner, J. K. (2016). Relationship between implementation of collaborative strategic reading and student outcomes for adolescents with disabilities. *Journal of Learning Disabilities, 49*(6), 644–657. http://doi.org/10.1177/0022219416640784

Bogard, J. M., & Mcmackin, M. C. (2012). Combining traditional and new literacies in a 21st-century writing workshop. *Reading Teacher, 65*(5), 313–323. https://doi.org/10.1002/TRTR.01048

Borup, J., West, R. E., Graham, C. R., & Davies, R. S. (2014). The adolescent community of engagement: A framework for research on adolescent online learning. *Journal of Technology and Teacher Education, 22*(1), 107–129.

Brown, C. L. (2007). Strategies for making social studies texts more comprehensible for English-language learners. *The Social Studies, 98*(5), 185–188.

Campbell, D., & Stanley, J. (1963). *Experimental and quasi-experimental designs for research*. Houghton Mifflin.

Capin, P., & Vaughn, S. (2017). Improving reading and social studies learning for secondary students with reading disabilities. *Teaching Exceptional Children, 49*(4), 249–261. https://doi.org/10.1177/0040059917691043

Carreira, M. (2007). Spanish-for-native-speaker matters: Narrowing the Latino achievement gap through Spanish language instruction. *Heritage Language Journal, 5*(1), 147–171.

Chung, S. F. (2012). Research-based vocabulary instruction for English language learners. *The Reading Matrix, 12*(2), 105–120.

Cisco, B. K., & Padrón, Y. (2012). Investigating vocabulary and reading strategies with middle grades English language learners: A research synthesis. *Research in Middle Level Education Online, 36*(4), 1–23.

Clemens, N. H., Oslund, E., Kwok, O. M., Fogarty, M., Simmons, D., & Davis, J. L. (2018). Skill moderators of the effects of a reading comprehension intervention. *Exceptional Children, 85*(2), 197–211. https://doi.org/10.1177/0014402918787339

Colgren, C., & Sappington, N. (2015). Closing the achievement gap means transformation. *NCPEA Education Leadership Review of Doctoral Research, 2*(1), 24–33. http://jeb.sagepub.com/cgi/doi/10.3102/1076998611411918

Dalton, B. (2015). Level up with multimodal composition in social studies. *Reading Teacher, 68*(4), 296–302. https://doi.org/10.1002/trtr.1319

Dalton, B., & Grisham, D. L. (2013). Love that book: Multimodal response to literature. *Reading Teacher, 67*(3), 220–225. https://doi.org/10.1002/TRTR.1206

Dalton, B., & Jocius, R. (2013). From struggling reader to digital reader and multimodal composer. In E. T. Ortlieb & E. H. Cheek, Jr. (Eds.), *School-based interventions for struggling readers, K–8 literacy research, practice, and evaluation* (pp. 79–97). Emerald.

Davis, F. B. (1944). Fundamental factors of comprehension in reading. *Psychometrika, 9*(3), 185–197.

Doerr-Stevens, C., & Buckley-Marudas, M. (2019). Hearing knowledge into action: Mobilizing sound for multicultural imaginaries. *International Journal of Multicultural Education, 21*(1), 105–124. https://doi.org/10.18251/ijme.v21i1.1735

Elkonin, D. B. (1963). The psychology of mastering the elements of reading. In B. Simon & J. Simon (Eds.), *Educational psychology in the U.S.S.R.* (pp. 165–179). Routledge.

Fereday, J., & Muir-Cochrane, E. (2006). Demonstrating rigor using thematic analysis: A hybrid approach of inductive and deductive coding and theme development. *International Journal of Qualitative Methods, 5*(1), 80–92.

Fry, R. (2003). *Hispanic youth dropping out of US schools: Measuring the challenge.* Pew Hispanic Center.

Garcia, G. E. (1991). Factors influencing the English reading test performance of Spanish-speaking Hispanic students. *Reading Research Quarterly, 26,* 371–392.

Garrison, D. R., Anderson, T., & Archer, W. (2001). Critical thinking, cognitive presence, and computer conferencing in distance education. *American Journal of Distance Education, 15*(1), 7–23. https://doi.org/10.1080/08923640109527071

Ghaith, G. (2019). The interplay of selected demotivation determinants and achievement in EFL critical reading and writing. *The Electronic Journal for English as a Second Language, 22*(4), 1–16. http://tesl-ej.org/pdf/ej88/a11.pdf

Giannakos, V., & Darra, M. (2019). The contribution of computer-supported collaborative learning to the development of collaboration between students: Results of pilot implementation in Greek secondary education. *International Education Studies, 12*(3), 158–169. https://doi.org/10.5539/ies.v12n3p158

Gomez, M. L., Schieble, M. B., Curwood, J. S., & Hassett, D. D. (2010). Technology, learning, and instruction: Distributed cognition in the secondary English classroom. *Literacy, 44*(1), 20–27.

Gonzales, S. M., & Shields, C. M. (2015). Education "reform" in Latino Detroit: Achievement gap or colonial legacy? *Race Ethnicity and Education*, *18*(3), 321–340.

Graham, C. (2013). Emerging practice and research in blended learning. In M. G. Moore (Ed.), *Handbook of distance education* (3rd ed., pp. 333–350). Routledge.

Haelermans, C., Ghysels, J., & Prince, F. (2015). Increasing performance by differentiated teaching? Experimental evidence of the student benefits of digital differentiation. *British Journal of Educational Technology*, *46*(6), 1161–1174. http://doi.org/10.1111/bjet.12209

Hafner, C. A. (2015). Remix culture and English language teaching: The expression of learner voice in digital multimodal compositions. *TESOL Quarterly*, *49*(3), 486–509. http://doi.org/10.1016/j.tate.2009.04.009

Hung, M., Smith, W. A., Voss, M. W., Franklin, J. D., Gu, Y., & Bounsanga, J. (2019). Exploring student achievement gaps in school districts across the United States. *Education and Urban Society*, 1–19. https://doi.org/10.1177/0013124519833442

Johnson, R. B., & Christensen, L. (2014). *Educational research: Quantitative, qualitative and mixed methods approaches*. Sage.

Karademir, C. A., & Gorgoz, S. (2019). English teachers' problems encountered in teaching four basic language skills. *International Education Studies*, *12*(4), 118–127. https://doi.org/10.5539/ies.v12n4p118

Khataee, E. (2019). The effect of THIEVES strategy on EFL learners' reading comprehension. *International Journal of Instruction*, *12*(2), 667–682.

Kim, Y., & Steiner, P. (2016). Quasi-experimental designs for causal inference. *Educational Psychologist*, *51*(3–4), 394–405.

Kress, G., & Selander, S. (2012). Multimodal design, learning and cultures of recognition. *Internet and Higher Education*, *15*(4), 265–268. http://doi.org/10.1016/j.iheduc.2011.12.003

Kundu, A., Rice, M., & Bej, T. (2020). *Time to engage: Implementing math and literacy blended learning routines in an Indian elementary classroom* [Manuscript in preparation].

Lavadenz, M., Armas, E. G., Murillo, M. A., & Jáuregui Hodge, S. (2019). Equity for English learners: Evidence from four years of California's local control funding formula. *Peabody Journal of Education*, *94*(2), 176–192. https://doi.org/10.1080/01619 56X.2019.1598113

Lowry, R. (2017). *Concepts & applications of inferential statistics*. Retrieved September 30, 2017, from http://vassarstats.net/textbook/

Luo, T. (2018). Connected education: Teachers' attitudes towards student learning in a 1:1 technology middle school environment. *Journal of Online Learning Research*, *4*(1), 87–116. www.learntechlib.org/p/180512/

Maxwell, J. A., & Loomis, D. (2003). Mixed method design: An alternative approach. In A. Tashakkori & C. Teddlie (Eds.), *Handbook of mixed methods in the social and behavioral sciences* (pp. 241–271). Sage.

Menon, S. (2019). Designing online materials for blended learning: Optimising on bookwidgets. *International Journal of Linguistics, Literature and Translation*, *2*(3), 166–174. https://doi.org/10.32996/ijllt.2019.2.2.10

Mor, Y., & Winters, N. (2008). Participatory design in open education: A workshop model for developing a pattern language. *Journal of Interactive Media in Education*, *1*, 1–16. http://doi.org/10.5334/2008-13

National Center for Education Statistics (NCES) (2018). *English language learner (ELL) students enrolled in public elementary and secondary schools, by state: Selected years, fall 2000 through fall 2016* (NCES 204.20). Institute of Education Sciences, US Department of Education. https://nces.ed.gov/programs/digest/d18/tables/dt18_204.20.asp

National Center for Education Statistics (NCES) (2019a). *English language learners in public schools* (NCES 204.20). Institute of Education Sciences, US Department of Education. https://nces.ed.gov/programs/digest/d18/tables/dt18_204.20.asp

National Center for Educational Statistics (NCES) (2019b). *Digest of education statistics 2017* (NCES 2018–070). Institute of Education Sciences, US Department of Education. https://nces.ed.gov/pubs2018/2018070.pdf

National Center for Educational Statistics (NCES) (2020). *The nation's report card.* www.nationsreportcard.gov/ndecore/xplore/NDE

National Comprehensive Center for Teacher Quality (NCCTQ) (2009). *Teaching English language learners: A complex system.* http://files.eric.ed.gov/fulltext/ED521323.pdf

Nordstrom, J. (2015). Flexible bilingualism through multimodal practices: Studying K–12 community languages online. *International Journal of Bilingual Education and Bilingualism, 18*(4), 395–408. https://doi.org/10.1080/13670050.2014.909773

Oliver, K. M., Cook, M. P., & Wiseman, A. (2019). Teachers' first experiences with global projects: Emerging collaboration and cultural awareness. *Journal of Online Learning Research, 5*(1), 65–96.

Ortlieb, E., Sargent, S., & Moreland, M. (2014). Evaluating the efficacy of using a digital reading environment to improve reading comprehension within a reading clinic. *Reading Psychology, 35*(5), 397–421. https://doi.org/10.1080/02702711.2012.683236

Rodriguez, L. J. (1993). *Always running—La Vida loca: Gang days in L.A.* Touchstone.

Scruggs, T. E., Mastropieri, M. A., & Marshak, L. (2012). Peer-mediated instruction in inclusive secondary social studies learning: Direct and indirect learning effects. *Learning Disabilities Research and Practice, 27*(1), 12–20. https://doi.org/10.1111/j.1540-5826.2011.00346.x

Serafini, F. (2012). Reading multimodal texts in the 21st century. *Research in the Schools, 19*(1), 26–32.

Shipman, M. D. (2014). *The limits of social research* (4th ed.). Routledge.

Snyder, E., Witmer, S. E., & Schmitt, H. (2017). English language learners and reading instruction: A review of the literature. *Preventing School Failure, 61*(2), 136–145. https://doi.org/10.1080/1045988X.2016.1219301

Taboada Barber, A., Buehl, M. M., Kidd, J. K., Sturtevant, E. G., Richey Nuland, L., & Beck, J. (2015). Reading engagement in social studies: Exploring the role of a social studies literacy intervention on reading comprehension, reading self-efficacy, and engagement in middle school students with different language backgrounds. *Reading Psychology, 36*(1), 31–85.

Tilley, N. (2006). Quasi-experiment. In V. Jupp (Ed.), *The Sage dictionary of social research methods* (pp. 615–619). Sage.

Trainin, G., Hayden, H. E., Wilson, K., & Erickson, J. (2016). Examining the impact of QuickReads' technology and print formats on fluency, comprehension, and vocabulary development for elementary students. *Journal of Research on Educational Effectiveness, 9*(1), 93–116. http://doi.org/10.1080/19345747.2016.1164778

Virginia Department of Education (VDOE) (2016). Graphs presenting standards of learning testing results for all tested content from 2013–2016. *School Quality Profiles.* http://schoolquality.virginia.gov/

Virginia Department of Education (VDOE) (2017a). *Fall membership for the commonwealth of Virginia.* http://schoolquality.virginia.gov/schools/glasgow-middle#fndtn-desktopTabs-enrollment

Virginia Department of Education (VDOE) (2017b, June). *Fall membership for the commonwealth of Virginia.* www.doe.virginia.gov/statistics_reports/enrollment/fall_member ship/report_data.shtml

Virginia Department of Education (VDOE) (2019). *Virginia state quality profile.* http://schoolquality.virginia.gov/virginia-state-quality-profile#desktopTabs-2

Virginia Department of Education (VDOE) (2020). *Fall membership build-a-table.* https://p1pe.doe.virginia.gov/apex/f?p=180:1:13584886102023:SHOW_REPORT:NO:::

Wanzek, J., Petscher, Y., Otaiba, S. A., Rivas, B. K., Jones, F. G., Kent, S. C., & Schatschneider, C. (2017). Effects of a year-long supplemental reading intervention for students with reading difficulties in fourth grade. *Journal of Educational Psychology, 109*(8), 1103–1119.

World-Class Instructional Design and Assessment Consortium (WIDA) (2007). *Understanding the WIDA English language proficiency standards.* WIDA.

Yeop, M. A. (2019). Implementation of ICT policy (blended learning approach): Investigating factors of behavioural intention and use behaviour. *International Journal of Instruction, 12*(1), 767–782.

Yin, P. K. (2011). *Qualitative research from start to finish.* The Guilford Press.

SECTION VI

International Perspectives

16
NEGOTIATING THE BLEND

George R. Bradford and Anders Norberg

Blended learning (BL) has influenced education for the past 20 years, becoming quite normal for higher education (Dziuban et al., 2018) and a remarkable occurrence for such a loosely defined concept as the word *blend*, especially when applied to the central concept of learning.

Although understanding what BL is or can be seems specific to professionals in the education field and their students, asking the general public its definition may raise questions rather than answers:

- What do you mean by *learning* can be *blended*?
- What things are actually blended?
- Is there such a thing as unblended learning?
- Has learning always been blended, or is this a recent development?
- Can teaching be blended as well?
- There seem to be many components in a BL mix: technologies, environments, learning materials, and even pedagogies. Should it always be something old and something new?
- Is it a blend when lectures combine with book readings?
- What can be gained or lost with blended learning? For teachers? For students? For institutions?
- Will teachers and/or students still be blending 30 years from now?

The BL concept may not be as intuitively understood as we had hoped because, primarily, it is developed against the backdrop of terms such as *distance learning*, *online learning*, and *e-learning*. The approach does suggest a middle road—not disruption, but an incorporation of two systems: an existing one and a new and sometimes complex one. This chapter addresses the combination of the

DOI: 10.4324/9781003037736-22

A Dissection of the Term Blended Learning

Learning

Today, learning and blended learning seem to be inextricably bound as a unified concept—a phenomenon not approached through educational psychology, but at the semantic level.

A systematic search on Google shows that *learning* is a more popular term than *teaching* (Norberg, 2017, p. 16ff), especially when combined with modern terms such as *digital, virtual, mobile, online, e-learning, cloud, internet,* etc. Oliver and Trigwell (2005, pp. 21–22) found that the BL concept in the literature dealt primarily with the organization of teaching and course design, and not learning as such. They argued that the word *learning* should "rightfully be returned to the learners" (2005, p. 24). The authors tend to agree. Learning is reasonably the students' purview because they may use combinations of new and old, digital and analogue instructional technologies, in ways other than advised by the teaching design. Sharpe, Benfield, Roberts, and Francis call this student blended perspective "under reported and under researched" (2006, p. 3). These students' strategies for blending are difficult to discuss, since the term *blended learning* (BL) mostly relates to course design and teaching. The use of *learning* to mean *teaching* today is more student centered than previously, though all teaching cannot be reasonably equated with learning; such a concept obscures the pedagogical problem. Much is taught but not learned, and much is learned without teaching. Biesta finds that we live in a world of *learnification* of education, "the redefinition of all things educational in terms of learning" (2019, p. 549), which he views as a commercial marketing phenomenon. Universities do not market their teaching; they instead try to sell student learning. Biesta finds this problematic because it should be possible to talk about teaching and learning separately, and he suggests a "rediscovery of teaching." A possible conflict-remediating concept is Vygotsky's *obuchenie* (обучение)—in English, *training*—a Russian word for his development of a teaching-learning social process in which students and teachers interact with one another, with technology, and with the world, and all are involved in both learning and teaching (Vygotsky, 1978). Cole (2009) finds the word difficult to translate but notes that it serves as a good concept. Teaching can be characterized by a combination of media, environments, and methods, old and new, while learning cannot be so easily rendered—a conception of a *blended obuchenie*, the social teaching-learning process.

Blended

Blend is a strange choice to introduce new technology into education and does not always inspire a positive connotation. *Hybrid* is not much better. Something blended is generally not as expansive or exclusive as something in a pure form, and the term *blended* does not come with any instructional protocols embedded in the concept. Which kind of blends are we talking about? If we assume the chemical association, do we want an *emulsion*, like oil and water that will always have to be stirred to keep it blended? Perhaps, we want a *light flavoring* like salt and pepper to a conventional dish; or *a solution*, in which the magic is in the mix that becomes something new once blended, but in a controlled way; or possibly a *reaction* as in handling explosive material?

In most languages, BL is called *blended learning*, borrowing the English term, but it often has a national translation that may emphasize different aspects of the blend by including more content: In German, we have *Integriertes Lernen*, in Finnish *Solatuva oppinem*; both describe a blend as an ongoing *integration* of new technology into something already existing. That appears to be a sustainable, inclusive, and practical way to think of *blend*—an *integration*. New technology, in any field, is complex and usually not as rewarding as decision makers may initially hope. Integration demands experimentation, tinkering, evaluation, critical thinking, and repeated attempts. Integration respects the existing and traditional and does not promise that the new will completely replace the old. The goal is enhancement, not disruption. With technology integration, people usually replicate the existing and traditional with new tools, hoping to achieve some increased effectiveness. New technology, however, often has more unexpected transformation to offer (Christensen et al., 2015; Li et al., 2018; Taleb, 2007). An ongoing technology integration process may thereby not bring any immediate disruption but can, with time, transform what we consider as normal or mainstream.

Blended + Learning

The synthesis of *learning* and *blend*, BL, may be a linguistic category mistake (see Ryle, 2009, p. 8f): as, for example, "the number two is blue" or "the theory of relativity is eating breakfast." Learning is not one of those concepts that easily blend. Learning is learning—a brain mechanism still not fully understood and explained.

The literature offers many well-known definitions of blended learning (BL). Authors have precise interpretations of what BL could or should be, what the components are, what BL should be used for, and how. Serious conflicts to the construction of their blend or research regarding BL are few; teachers and researchers construct their blends, or research regarding it, in relative harmony. Seldom does one hear a teacher or scientist criticizing someone else's blend. ("You

272 George R. Bradford and Anders Norberg

are not really blending!") Sharpe, Benfield, Roberts, and Francis recommend use of the term *blended learning* because of its lack of definition or clarity, serving practitioners as a negotiable term, an umbrella under which to conduct teaching and learning experiments, including new technology (2005, p. 4). Is it possible that the term BL gains its general acceptance at the cost of its low content ratio? Laumakis et al. (2009) use the concept of a boundary object (Star, 1989) to imagine the reference width of BL as a unity in vision. Oliver and Trigwell (2005) seriously questioned the use of the metaphor *blend*, while still not questioning information communications technologies' (ICT) integration in teaching and learning. Driscoll states that "the point is that blended learning means different things to different people . . . which illustrates its widely untapped potential" (2002, p. 1).

A Time and Process Perspective

The authors do not have any new ingenious definition of blended learning (BL) to propose but find that a time- and process-based approach is useful for working with and understanding the integration of new ICT into a contemporary normality of the teaching-learning process. Hopefully, this perspective can encompass most BL definitions and learning theories at the meta-level. This focus concentrates on how social synchronous interactions in a teaching/learning process shift with more flexible asynchronous individual work and interactions and how new ICT can shift the teaching-learning pattern. As synchronous modalities, we think of not only classroom lectures, but also video conferences, chats, telepresence robotics, synchronous audio conferences, and even Twitter exchanges. Asynchronous modalities can include working assignments, readings, participating in forum discussions, trailblazing desktop research, watching recorded lectures, and so on. Please note that in this time model, both synchronous and asynchronous activities can be internet based or not, digital or not. A lecturing teacher in a classroom assigning readings and homework is also blending. Writings, prints, books, paper notes, and even classrooms are also ICT, although not digital. Norberg et al. (2011) categorize how, in this classic pattern, new digital ICT can help us design better teaching-learning processes in this time perspective by support, migration, synchronous location, flow, and empowerment.

The question becomes that if we study blended learning (BL) using time as the perspective, where technology integration can bring innovation to teaching and learning, how do we frame this? BL seems too fluid and not sticky. What path can we take to let it find its organic-level *obuchenie* approach? Coincidently, we found another approach with Russian origins that can be helpful: activity theory.

Activity Mediation and the Blend

There is varying potential for what faculty can do using BL strategies. The advantage blended learning presents is its flexibility because there are many possible

Negotiating the Blend **273**

ways to blend teaching. The price, however, is the inability to conduct comparative analyses. BL designs among institutions are founded on their unique academic ecologies, which differ considerably, though conducting a self-study repeatedly has the advantage of informing practice and offering opportunities to explore possibilities for sustaining innovation (Moskal et al., 2013). Using a case-study approach can resonate with readers if they see themselves in another's work, while the structured approach that is replicable offers the opportunity to assess the sustainability of BL practices.

A Self-Study Example

The case-study method is a good fit for organizational self-studies, leading an investigator to answer the how and why within the ecology of their own organization. Inductive reasoning that frames research questions can facilitate theory building (Myers, 2013) and further position the case study as optimal when studying something with clear start-end boundaries (Yin, 2014, 2016), such as examining blended learning (BL) practices grounded in course term schedules.

Studies of effectiveness will be unbalanced if they leave out context. Holistic studies (e.g., ethnography, phenomenology), offering the potential to be informative, can be unwieldy, especially in short time frames that should be repeated in two-year cycles. The solution to the conundrum of choice between less data from studies omitting context and those fully embracing expanded information is activity theory: a descriptive framework, a meta-theory (Engeström, 2000; Engeström et al., 2007) that can provide perspective on human enterprise (Arnseth, 2008). Activity theory originates from work by Soviet psychologists Alexei Leont'ev, Sergei Rubinstein, and Lev Vygotsky but is modified and used as a tool to study work in social psychology, education, professional training, and ergonomics (Cole & Engeström, 1993) or, most recently, complex contractual relationships and their influence on faculty teaching practice (Ramani, 2020). Activity theory is useful when paired with the case-study method because it provides structure for inquiry by locating patterns between relationships and interactions.

The mediational triangle of activity theory (Figure 16.1) frames inquiry planning. The subject of this inquiry is a teaching faculty member, an innovator or early adopter, or perhaps the opposite. The action we study is the faculty member's teaching practice using blended learning strategies. Rules and policies influencing blended learning might be found in institutional directives or strategic plans, employment contracts directing how the faculty will divide time, federal laws and directives such as copyright or the Americans with Disabilities Act. Roles reflect the types of positions held by individuals in or outside the organization with whom the instructor interacts. Roles might include help desk teams; software, or media support; instructional designers; and also supervisors, teaching assistants, and students. The community embodies colleagues at the institution, or beyond, and other individuals or groups the faculty may depend upon in the

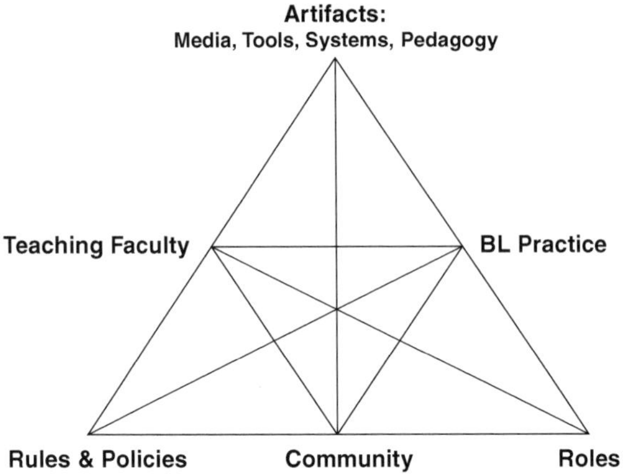

274 George R. Bradford and Anders Norberg

FIGURE 16.1 A Modified Activity Theory Mediation Triangle

practice of teaching and applying blended learning principles. Artifacts are the collection of tools used to teach or innovate. Besides the obvious collection of books (paper or digital), articles, recordings, images, lab equipment, hard and software tools, and networks, artifacts include pedagogy used to deliver instruction. Where research provides evidence-based methods for instruction, pedagogy involves a choice among tools and practices that can be used for teaching. Taken broadly, the list gives us potential sources for inquiry.

Sources are factors that influence the practice of teaching or innovating teaching through the use of blended learning plans. In Engeström's expanded model modified by our short list of factors, the lines represent relationships in a state of tension; when everything works, we note the lack of tension, or harmony. Relationships can be expressed as single- or bi-directional conflicts, in which one side or the other is the source of increasing tension—both when the two sides contribute to its bi-directional nature. If a faculty member lacks a system password for an LMS (an artifact), there is a single source of tension from the tool to the faculty. If a faculty member works with an instructional designer (a role) and both find fault with each other (e.g., the faculty believes the ID is unqualified, a poor communicator, or unorganized, and the ID considers the faculty close-minded and unfamiliar with educational research), there is bi-directional tension. Following a path of inquiry that explores these relationships yields rich data on what might be preventing effective teaching or innovative practices.

Simplifying the self-study, we suggest one or two focused questions to be answered: for instance, am I innovating my teaching practice by integrating modalities used in a blend, and how is my use of blended learning effective? This involves a case-study method structured to identify key factors influencing teaching practices, a semi-structured inquiry plan to collect information, and a review method to identify and explore themes of observed tension in any observed relationships between influential sources. For planning an inquiry strategy, Table 16.1 presents a sample of relationship sources between a teaching faculty and their blended learning practices. The sources you identify specific to your organization may differ from this sample.

Characterize Blended Learning and Innovation in Your Organization

As we have argued, blended learning (BL) is a boundary object, so flexible in how it is described, used, and studied that it seems impossible to describe as a specific practice (Moskal et al., 2013) or in a universal definition. We have also argued that a virtue of BL is its flexibility, in which innovation maximizes teaching effectiveness to the current student generation. For a self-study, a focusing

TABLE 16.1 Sample Sources for Inquiry for Modified Activity Theory

Rules & Policies	Community	Roles	Artifacts/Tools
Institutional and departmental policies	Senior leadership	Faculty teaching	Learning management systems
Employment contract requirements (apportionment of time & responsibility)	Institutional services & staff	Faculty research	Email and messaging systems
Term teaching deadlines	Administrative support	Faculty service	Social networking tools
Deadlines for research and service	Department colleagues	Co-teaching faculty or adjuncts	Application-specific tools
Copyright & fair use laws	Institutional colleagues	Instructional designers	Library systems
Americans with Disabilities Act (ADA) requirements	Colleagues in your field	Technologists	Data systems and platforms
	Teaching and learning centers	Help desks	Lab equipment
	Board of trustees or advisory boards	Software application support	Computer set-up
		Librarian	Pedagogies used
			Resources: books, recordings, images, digital files

276 George R. Bradford and Anders Norberg

question begins with asking what is blended in our teaching and what we mean when we ask if we are innovating. What is it we should evaluate? Can we sustain inquiry to continue seeking innovative opportunities? Similar to blended learning's flexibility is innovation because it can be found in many odd corners of an institution. Some perspectives on innovative practice by experienced educational professionals reflect the range where innovation might be found (all quotes collected through interviews in 2011):

- "Balance the projected costs against future value."
  (Dr. Joel Hartman, Vice Provost for Information Technologies and Resources, University of Central Florida)
- "Open up instructional design practices . . . Try the unconventional."
  (Dr. Larry Ragan, Director-Instructional Design & Development Continuing and Distance Education/World Campus, Penn State University)
- "Look to internal resources who experiment."
  (Dr. William Patterson, eLearning Innovations and Entrepreneurial Partnerships, University of South Florida)
- "Develop collaborative environments, let students own and innovate while you facilitate."
  (Dr. Howard Rheingold, Berkley and Stanford Universities, author of *Tools for Thought* (www.rheingold.com/texts/tft/), *The Virtual Community* (www.rheingold.com/vc/book/), and *Smart Mobs* (www.smartmobs.com))

While the variety of perspectives is confusing, it is possible to simplify the targets for a self-study to characterize blended learning practices and examine your organization for opportunities to sustain innovation.

Innovation might be new technology or old technology used differently, new pedagogy or established pedagogy blended with another new approach or established way. Innovation might be an adjustment to policy (e.g., change a course's traditional session schedule), implementing a new target for your organization's strategic plan (e.g., plans will make extensive use of active learning), or deploying a new session delivery platform. Innovation can be one, some, or even none of such changes to practice. One strategy previously argued is the use of time as a principle factor for considering learning (Norberg et al., 2011). Using a time-based model distinguishes between when a student is active synchronously with peers and teachers and when they are interacting asynchronously. Thus, when planning activities and the blends of interactions, we suggest using a course schedule's arrow of time as rows in an Excel file and columns to hold details of synchronous and asynchronous plans. While this table appears like our familiar schedule in a syllabus, we suggest an approach that includes depicting dependencies among activities by including details in a column linked to follow-on row items: if there is an asynchronous activity preceding or following a synchronous one, what is the dependency, and how will it be made relevant? Will it be assessed? This simple innovation allows exploration of the student experience by seeing the flow of activities and how they are mutually reinforcing learning and illuminating time on task. Characterizing innovation in your institution should guide inquiry while also supporting its emergence as a finding in the study. Following Norberg et al.'s suggestion for innovation opportunities, Table 16.2 presents an updated approach to guide inquiry and planning for blending modality and course activities that includes pedagogy, technology, and policy.

Exploratory sources provide awareness of your institution, but they can also be derived through a modified activity theory study. Data may need to include student course evaluations, graduation rates, and employment placement percentages. While these numbers constitute a surrogate life insurance policy for most educational institutions, they do not express their quintessence. Following the sources identified in the modified active learning table, combined with potential sources of innovation in an enhanced time-based model, research inquiry can focus on finding sources of tension between faculty members and their teaching practices.

Data collection in this approach follows a review of records (student performance, completion/graduation rates, job placement, etc.) and focus groups or interviews. The notable exception for the approach is that focus groups and inquiries should be semi-structured to allow the researcher flexibility to follow the relationship structure between faculty and the various sources. Inquiry focuses on identifying relationships that are harmonious (i.e., working without tension) or that exhibit tension as being single or bidirectional. This work of thematic extraction corresponds to grounded theory allowing a coding scheme that confirms strategies, such as data validation and triangulation. The unique contribution of using modified activity theory derives from representing themes visually with the mediating triangle.

To illustrate single or bidirectional tension, a colleague to one of the authors completed a study of a complex business relationship with an academic institution using a modified activity theory design. In Figure 16.2, Ramani (2020) depicts a theme derived from a research study on whether online program management companies influence faculty approaches to teaching design. In this sample theme, Figure 16.2 displays the contract's permitted use of teaching assistants (TAs), who had a positive effect on both students and faculty.

In one instance, Ramani's analysis yielded multiple negative influences on faculty, as illustrated with bi-directional arrows. Figure 16.3 shows tensions created by partial contract failure that aggravated faculty frustrations leading to motivation loss toward teaching.

Modified activity theory used in this way opened a door to reveal sources that influence activities, sometimes in positive ways, other times not. Poor attitudes toward teaching design for online learning would not usually be linked to failures to meet contract obligations. In instances like this, an expression of tension presents an opportunity to innovate. Adjustments that reduce or remove tension

278 George R. Bradford and Anders Norberg

TABLE 16.2 Innovation Opportunities Using an Enhanced Time-based Model

Opportunity type	Guiding questions	Innovation ideas or starters
Support	How can I extend and innovate support for learning?	Offer blended virtual office hours; integrate instant messaging technology students use; innovate discussion board designs; prompt students to share what works
Migration	What and where in my course can I change modality?	Traditional modality switches are synchronous presentations to/from asynchronous (e.g., flipped classroom); consider modality switching for assessments, such as diagnostic, low-stakes formative polling, or minute papers from/to either; consider giving students a choice
Location	Are there specific activities requiring co-location? Are there some that do not? Can I vary co-location?	Activities may require co-location (e.g., science labs, physical and occupational therapy sessions, some counselling); separate activities to permit remote participation; co-location requirements can also be moved within or beyond course time boundaries
Flow	Do my activity plans flow in the course schedule? Do the parts connect? Is everything mutually reinforcing?	Flow becomes visible when you map key details (e.g., presentations, in-session activities, homework, assessments); a timeline depicting dependencies and strategies is useful to differentiate blends of modality, support, or empowerment
Learner empowerment	Where can I give control and choice to students? When and why should I control access to resources?	Students prefer having access to all resources immediately: publish everything from course start; integrate choice into activities; include modeling success; give students simple directions and to have them take initiatives
Pedagogy choices	Does my choice of pedagogy permit innovating? Can I infuse pedagogies?	Standard lectures can be reworked into activity blocks to improve focus and engagement while retaining concept presentations; activities emphasize hands-on practice; peer teaching can be infused with block-design active learning—students innovate, demonstrate, and model practice
Technology enhancements	Do my students think the technology is "old"? Are students using technologies that are equally effective?	Technology advances are opportunities to innovate and blend: trends to consider include social networking that bundles media sharing, remixing, and collaboration; augmented reality; and adaptive learning advances that simplify learner modeling, course design, and effectiveness measuring

Negotiating the Blend 279

Opportunity type	Guiding questions	Innovation ideas or starters
Policy-related or other administrative changes	Are there adjustments to policy that can improve teaching and learning? Are there strategic directives I can leverage to innovate?	Policy changes can yield sustainable innovation: advocate new course structures beyond the conventional; advocate long term through incremental implementation or deployment; model active learning strategically coupled to effectiveness evaluations, new hire orientations, and performance reviews

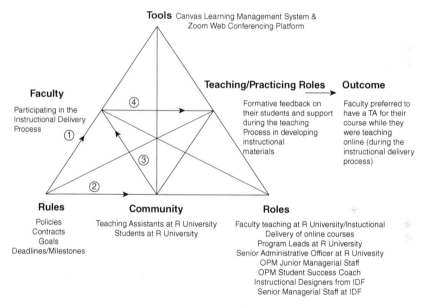

FIGURE 16.2 A Unidirectional Tension in Study Employing Modified Activity Theory

Source: (Ramani, 2020, used with permission)

may lead to improved teaching and student experience. Following opportunities to innovate suggested in Table 16.2 may alleviate an existing tension, create new positive tension, or elevate student experience. The modified activity theory approach is sufficiently flexible to explore an ecology that may be impacting teaching. Periodic replication of this kind of study creates a model for sustaining innovation. The holistic approach is very useful in identifying opportunities to innovate practice.

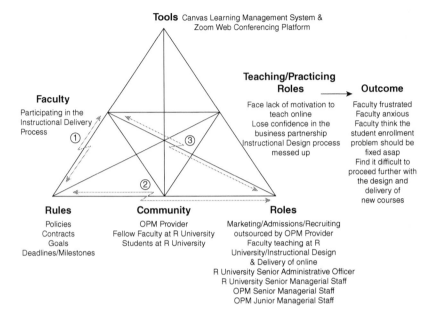

FIGURE 16.3 Bidirectional Tension in Study Employing Modified Activity Theory

Source: (Ramani, 2020, used with permission)

A Final Word . . .

Will we still be blending 30 years from now, in 2050? The answer seems to be most assuredly yes. New technology has integrated into existing teaching and learning processes throughout history. What we have called an innovation, however, becomes part of normality because technology integration is vital to the process. Further, the digital ICT we are working with now in education predominantly lower the friction of information. It is easier to communicate over distances with good quality and to access, exchange, edit and create information with diminished transport damages. This function, closely aligned with internet-based technology, cannot be said to be the revolutionary new characteristic with digital technology. Information processing outside the human brain, by algorithms, robots, computer programs, and artificial intelligence, repositions the role of humans in the world in learning analytics and adaptive learning to gain ideas about future blends, when teachers and students cooperate with ICT to improve the teaching-learning activity.

References

Arnseth, H. C. (2008). Activity theory and situated learning theory: Contrasting views of educational practice. *Pedagogy, Culture & Society*, *16*(3), 289–302. https://doi.org/10.1080/14681360802346663

Biesta, G. (2019). Should teaching be re(dis)covered? Introduction to a symposium. *Studies in Philosophy and Education, 38*(5), 549–553.

Christensen, C. M., Raynor, M. E., & McDonald, R. (2015). What is disruptive innovation? *Harvard Business Review, 93*(12), 44–53.

Cole, M. (2009). The perils of translation: A first step in reconsidering Vygotsky's theory of development in relation to formal education. *Mind, Culture, and Activity, 16*, 291–295.

Cole, M., & Engeström, Y. (1993). A cultural-historical approach to distributed cognition. In G. Salomon (Ed.), *Distributed cognitions: Psychological and educational considerations* (1st ed., pp. 1–46). Cambridge University Press.

Driscoll, M. (2002). Blended learning: Let's get beyond the hype. *E-Learning, 1*(4), 1–4.

Dziuban, C., Graham, C. R., Moskal, P. D., Norberg, A., & Sicilia, N. (2018). Blended learning: The new normal and emerging technologies. *International Journal of Educational Technology in Higher Education, 15*(1), 3.

Engeström, Y. (2000). Activity theory as a framework for analyzing and redesigning work. *Ergonomics, 43*(7), 960–974. https://doi.org/10.1080/001401300409143

Engeström, Y., Miettinen, R., & Punamaki, R. (2007). *Perspectives on activity theory*. Cambridge University Press.

Laumakis, M., Graham, C., & Dziuban, C. (2009). The Sloan-C pillars and boundary objects as a framework for evaluating blended learning. *Journal of Asynchronous Learning Networks, 13*(1), 75–87.

Li, M., Porter, A. L., & Suominen, A. (2018). Insights into relationships between disruptive technology/innovation and emerging technology: A bibliometric perspective. *Technological Forecasting and Social Change, 129*, 285–296.

Moskal, P., Dziuban, C., & Hartman, J. (2013). Blended learning: A dangerous idea? *The Internet and Higher Education, 18*, 15–23.

Myers, M. D. (2013). *Qualitative research in business & management*. Sage.

Norberg, A. (2017). *From blended learning to learning onlife: ICTs, time and access in higher education* [Doctoral dissertation]. Umeå University.

Norberg, A., Dziuban, C. D., & Moskal, P. D. (2011). A time-based blended learning model. *On the Horizon, 19*(3).

Oliver, M., & Trigwell, K. (2005). Can "blended learning" be redeemed? *E-Learning and Digital Media, 2*(1), 17–26.

Ramani, S. (2020). *The impact of a university/online program management provider partnership on faculty approaches to teaching design: A case study using activity theory* [Dissertations and Theses (2441597559)]. Claremont University Consortium.

Ryle, G. (2009). *The concept of mind*. Routledge.

Sharpe, R., Benfield, G., Roberts, G., & Francis, R. (2006). The undergraduate experience of blended e-learning: A review of UK literature and practice. *The Higher Education Academy*, 1–103.

Star, S. L. (1989). The structure of ill-structured solutions: Boundary objects and heterogeneous distributed problem solving. In *Distributed artificial intelligence* (pp. 37–54). Morgan Kaufmann.

Taleb, N. N. (2007). *The black swan: The impact of the highly improbable* (Vol. 2). Random House.

Vygotsky, L. S. (1978). *Mind in society*. Harvard University Press.

Yin, R. K. (2014). *Case study research* (5th ed.). Sage.

Yin, R. K. (2016). *Qualitative research from start to finish* (2nd ed.). The Guilford Press.

17

BLENDED LEARNING AND SHARED METACOGNITION

What Is the Connection?

Norman D. Vaughan

Introduction

This chapter explores the connection between blended learning and shared metacognition through the lens of the community of inquiry framework (Garrison, 2017). The educational research literature has indicated that a blended approach to teaching and learning might provide an optimal environment for enhancing student engagement and success (Dziuban et al., 2018). The idea of blending different learning experiences has been in existence since humans started thinking about teaching (Williams, 2003). The ongoing infusion of web-based technologies into the learning and teaching process has highlighted the potential of blended learning (Dziuban et al., 2016). Collaborative web-based applications have created new opportunities for students to interact with their peers, teachers, and content.

Blended learning is often defined as the combination of face-to-face and online learning (Sharpe et al., 2006; Williams, 2002). Ron Bleed, the former vice chancellor of information technologies at Maricopa College, argues that this is not a sufficient definition for blended learning as it simply implies "bolting" technology onto a traditional course, using digital technologies as an add-on to teach a difficult concept, or adding supplemental information. He suggests that blended learning should be viewed as an opportunity to redesign how courses are developed, scheduled, and delivered through a combination of physical and virtual instruction: "bricks and clicks" (Bleed, 2001). Joining the best features of in-class teaching with the best features of online learning that promote active, self-directed learning opportunities with added flexibility should be the goal of this redesigned approach (Garnham & Kaleta, 2002; Littlejohn & Pegler, 2007; Norberg et al., 2011). Garrison and Vaughan (2008) echo this sentiment when they

DOI: 10.4324/9781003037736-23

Blended Learning and Shared Metacognition 283

state that "blended learning is the organic integration of thoughtfully selected and complementary face-to-face and online approaches and technologies" (p. 148).

Most of the recent definitions for blended courses indicate that this approach to learning offers potential for improving how we deal with content, social interaction, reflection, higher-order thinking, problem solving, collaborative learning, and more authentic assessment in higher education, which could potentially lead to a greater sense of student engagement (Graham, 2006; Mayadas & Picciano, 2007; Norberg et al., 2011). Moskal et al. (2013) further suggest that "blended learning has become an evolving, responsive, and dynamic process that in many respects is organic, defying all attempts at universal definition" (p. 15).

Campus-based environments have their roots in educational systems in which classes have been delivered by teachers in synchronous class lecture settings. Initially, blended learning was used to complement these synchronous lectures through the use of asynchronous discussion forums and learning management systems such as Canvas, Blackboard, and Moodle. With the advent of synchronous tools, such as Zoom and Adobe Connect, opportunities have been created to provide students with both synchronous and asynchronous communication possibilities (Figure 17.1).

Power (2008) has coined the term *online blended learning* to describe the simultaneous and complimentary integration and implementation of an asynchronous-mode learning environment (i.e., a learning management system, or LMS) and a synchronous desktop conferencing environment (i.e., virtual classroom). This conception of blended learning has been further expanded by the Sunchild E-Learning Community framework (Vaughan et al., 2013), which fully integrates face-to-face and online synchronous and asynchronous learning opportunities for their students, who physically work with mentors at local learning centers and communicate with highly qualified online teachers who are located off-site (Figure 17.2).

There has been an increased focus on the topic of student engagement in higher education in light of rising tuition costs and concerns about student success and

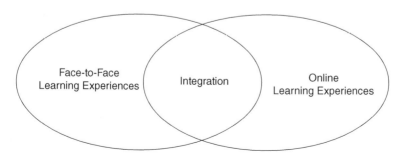

FIGURE 17.1 Campus-based Learning Approach

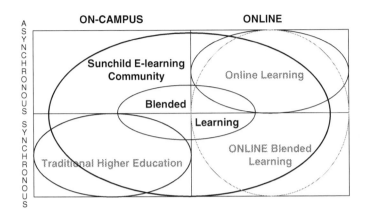

FIGURE 17.2 Sunchild e-Learning Community Program Framework

retention rates (Regier, 2014). In order to address these issues, Littky and Grabelle (2004) advocate for a curriculum redesign that stresses relevance, relationships, and rigor (3Rs of engagement). It has been suggested that such a redesign would enable students to meaningfully engage in sustained learning experiences that may lead to a state of optimal flow, which Csíkszentmihályi (1990) defines as "the mental state of operation in which the person is fully immersed in what he or she is doing by a feeling of energized focus, full involvement, and success in the process of the activity" (p. 9).

At the core of meaningful student engagement is the concept of metacognition, which is simply "thinking about one's thinking" (Chick, 2013, n.p.). Metacognition is key to learning how to learn. Metacognitive approaches to learning start with designing and planning the learning experience. Metacognition means increasing awareness of the learning process and taking responsibility for controlling the learning process (Garrison, 2017).

Recently, the focus in higher education has shifted from an individualistic to a more collaborative approach to learning (Kromydas, 2017). This has led Garrison and Akyol (2015a) to develop a shared metacognition construct, which is based on the community of inquiry framework (Garrison et al., 2000).

This research study investigates how a blended course can be designed, facilitated, and directed to help students develop their capacity for shared metacognition.

Theoretical Framework

Garrison (2017) states that the community of inquiry (CoI) theoretical framework can provide the "context to conceptually and operationally define and operationalize metacognition in a socially shared environment" (p. 62). The three key elements or dimensions of the CoI framework are social, cognitive, and teaching presence (Figure 17.3). It is at the convergence of these three mutually

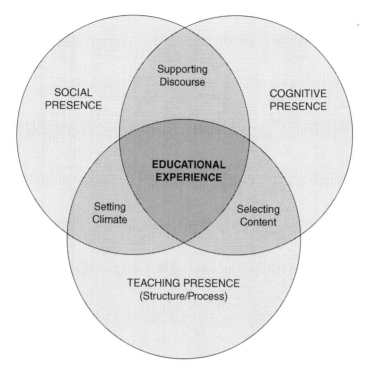

FIGURE 17.3 Community of Inquiry Framework

Source: (Garrison, 2017)

reinforcing elements that a collaborative constructivist educational experience is realized. Social presence creates the environment for trust, open communication, and group cohesion. Cognitive presence has been defined "as the extent to which learners are able to construct and confirm meaning through sustained reflection and discourse in a critical community of inquiry" (Garrison et al., 2001, p. 11). It has been operationalized through the developmental phases of inquiry—triggering events, exploration, integration, and resolution. The third and cohesive element, teaching presence, is associated with the design, facilitation, and direction of a community of inquiry. It is the unifying force that brings together the social and cognitive processes directed to personally meaningful and educationally worthwhile outcomes.

Shared metacognition (MC) exists at the intersection of the cognitive and teaching presence constructs and goes to the heart of a deep and meaningful educational learning experience (Figure 17.4). Consequently, we must understand shared MC and its role in a community of inquiry.

In terms of understanding shared MC and its role in a CoI, the premise is that developing metacognitive awareness and ability is core to becoming an effective

286 Norman D. Vaughan

ELEMENTS	CATEGORIES	INDICATORS (examples only)
Social Presence	Open Communication	Risk-free expression
	Group Cohesion	Encourage collaboration
	Affective Expression	Emoticons
Cognitive Presence	Triggering Event	Sense of puzzlement
	Exploration	Information exchange
	Integration	Connecting ideas
	Resolution	Apply new ideas
Teaching Presence	Design & Organization	Setting curriculum & methods
	Facilitating Discourse	Sharing personal meaning
	Direct Instruction	Focusing discussion

FIGURE 17.4   Community of Inquiry Elements, Categories, and Indicators

inquirer. Metacognition has generally been accepted as consisting of two components—awareness of the inquiry process (monitor) and implementation strategies (regulation). Awareness allows the learner to monitor and actively manage/regulate the inquiry process. In short, metacognition awareness and implementation abilities provide the knowledge and strategies to monitor and manage effective inquiry. Most importantly, in a collaborative learning environment, awareness and implementation strategies are developed through critical discourse and the requirement of participants to explain and justify their thinking to self and others. The approach to developing a viable metacognition construct for collaborative learning environments is to subsume self and shared regulatory functions within a single construct. This shared metacognition construct (Garrison, 2017; Garrison & Akyol, 2015a, 2015b) reflects the dynamic dimensions of self- and co-regulation, each exhibiting a monitoring (awareness) and a managing (strategic action) function (Figure 17.5).

To explore the practical implications of shared MC, it is important to focus on the intersection of cognitive presence (CP) and teaching presence (TP). That begins with a consideration of TP categories (planning and organization, facilitation, and direction) as they overlap with CP operationalized through the phases of practical inquiry (triggering event, exploration, integration, and resolution). While there has been progress in defining and measuring the construct of shared MC, there has been an absence of research investigating the effective implementation of and support for this process in a blended course, which is the focus of this study (Garrison & Akyol, 2015a).

Study Context

Mount Royal University in Calgary, Alberta, Canada offers a four-year bachelor of education program. In the fall of the third year, teacher candidates are engaged

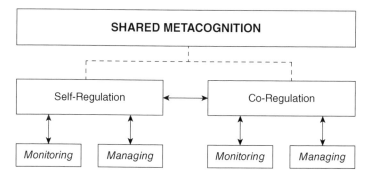

FIGURE 17.5 Shared Metacognition Construct

in a series of blended learning experiences that focus on integrating science, technology, engineering, arts, math, and Indigenous (STEAMI) education.

The semester begins with teacher candidates spending the first week in their practicum placements, helping their mentor teachers start the new school year with their K–12 students. The teacher candidates then spend one day a week in their mentor teacher's classroom, culminating in a five-week practicum experience.

On campus, the teacher candidates are engaged in a series of blended STEAMI education courses that are connected to weekly field trips. These trips include field work at the Ann and Sandy Cross Conservation Area (2020), Tim Horton Children's Ranch (The Compass, 2020), and the Telus SPARK Science Centre (2020). The teacher candidates also spend a full day teaching STEAMI lessons to children at the Nakoda Elementary School (2020) on the Stoney Nakoda First Nations Reserve.

This research study focuses on the educational technology course, which is part of the STEAMI semester. The purpose of this blended course is to provide an overview of technological influences in education. It is designed to assist prospective teachers in critically examining current and evolving applications of technology relevant to the teaching and learning process.

Research Objective

The primary objective of this research study was to investigate how a blended educational technology course for pre-service teachers can be designed, facilitated, and directed to help students develop their capacity for shared metacognition.

Methodology

An action research methodology was used for this study. This approach involved teacher candidates reflecting on how the shared metacognition construct could be developed in a blended course. The intent of this research framework was to have some practical outcome related to the lives or work of the participants, which, in this case, was the growth and development of shared metacognition for teacher candidates (Stringer, 2014).

A mixed-methods research approach guided the collection and analysis of the study data. Three sections of the educational technology course were offered in the Fall 2019 semester and the co-investigator invited the third-year teacher candidates to participate in this research study. There were a total of 80 students enrolled in the course, 70 female (88%) and 10 male (12%). Ninety percent of the students (n = 72) agreed to participate in the study, which received Mount Royal University Human Research Ethics Board (HREB) approval.

In terms of quantitative methods, the validated shared MC (Garrison & Akyol, 2015a) and CoI (Garrison, 2017) surveys were both utilized in an online format using Google Forms. The shared metacognition survey (n = 72) was deployed at the end of October, just before the teacher candidates began their five-week practicum placements. The CoI survey was administered at the end of the Fall 2019 semester in order to observe how the teacher candidates had integrated their course experiences with their practicum placements (n = 56). Descriptive statistics (frequencies, means, and standard deviations) were calculated for individual survey items using Google Spreadsheets.

With regards to qualitative methods, at the end of the Fall 2019 semester, the teacher candidates created a final blog posting, where they reflected on how they contributed to the learning of others in the course as well as what they had learned from their peers. This data was copied and pasted into a Google document, and the researchers used a constant comparative approach when reviewing the blog posts in order to identify patterns, themes, and categories of analysis that "emerged out of the data rather than being imposed on them prior to data collection and analysis" (Patton, 1990, p. 390).

Findings

The study findings regarding the development of shared metacognition in a blended course are reported using the three sub-elements or categories of the CoI's sphere of teaching presence—design, facilitation, and direction.

Design and Organization

Course design is a planning process that includes consideration of many content and process issues. The focus of the planning process for this research study was specifically on the monitoring and managing of shared metacognition.

At the beginning of the semester, the course instructor for the educational technology course had the students create an initial blog posting, where they described and shared their personal learning goals for the course as they related to the MRU BEd program's five teaching competencies (planning, facilitation, assessment, classroom environment, professional roles and responsibilities). At the

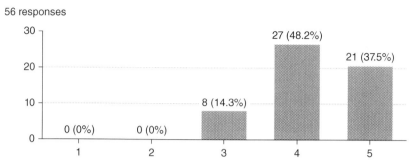

FIGURE 17.6 The Teacher Clearly Communicated Important Course Goals
Source: (CoI survey)

end of the semester, the students were required to demonstrate and describe how they had achieved these learning goals by presenting the teaching competency pages of their professional learning plan or ePortfolio.

The study participants indicated these activities were useful on a personal level, but several commented on the importance of the teacher "going over all assignments at the beginning of the semester to allow students to ask questions and also give us time to wrap our heads around the key concepts and goals of the course" (Shared MC survey participant 25). This comment was also reflected in the results from question two of the community of inquiry (CoI) survey, which asked students if their teacher clearly communicated important course goals (Figure 17.6).

The 5-point Likert-type scale for this figure ranges from strongly disagree (1) to strongly agree (5). Figure 17.6 indicates that the majority of students thought the teacher clearly communicated the course goals, but 14% of the participants were ambivalent (on the fence). Interestingly, in the final blog posting, several students identified the benefit of group work in gaining a clearer understanding of the course and assignment expectations. "It made it easier to understand the course expectations and added more perspectives as to how to approach assignments when we worked in groups" (Student blog posting 59). Another student commented that group work "ensures everyone is on the same page regarding assignment expectations" (Student blog 23).

Facilitation

Facilitation is the central activity in an educational community of inquiry for developing shared metacognition through the interactions between students and the teacher. Facilitative actions, "on the part of both the students and the instructor, create the climate, support discourse, and monitor learning. In the act of facilitation learners connect with each other, engage with the content, are cognitively present as intellectual agents, and carry out all actions central to the development and maintenance of the learning community" *(Vaughan et al., 2013, p. 46)*. In essence, the teacher is responsible for modeling the growth and development of shared metacognition in a course.

For the educational technology course, the students selected critical friends at the beginning of the semester. The role of the critical friend was to provide constructive feedback and support for all the course assignments. In addition, each of the course assignments had a group component in which students were required to work together to solve problems and test solutions related to teaching with technologies.

The majority of research participants indicated that these collaborative activities helped them get to know the other students in the course, which gave them a sense of belonging (Figure 17.7) and allowed them to feel comfortable interacting with their peers (Figure 17.8).

Highlighting the results of Figure 17.7, one student commented in her final blog posting that through group work, "we were able to gain confidence about our individual ideas with support from our peers" (Student blog 71).

Another student indicated that his high level comfort in group work contributed to "Creating stronger working connections with peers, sharing ideas and resources, and receiving critical feedback, and strategies to improve teaching and planning" (Student blog 13).

In turn, this sense of a safe learning environment allowed the students to be more willing to listen to the comments of others (Figure 17.9) as well as considering the feedback of their peers (Figure 17.10).

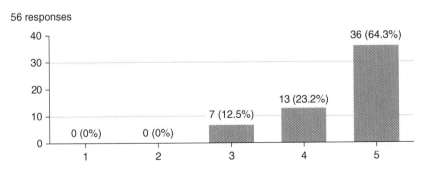

FIGURE 17.7 Getting to Know the Students in This Course Gave Me a Sense of Belonging

Source: (CoI survey)

Blended Learning and Shared Metacognition **291**

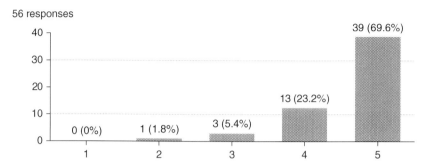

FIGURE 17.8 Comfortable Interacting with the Other Students in My Course
Source: (CoI survey)

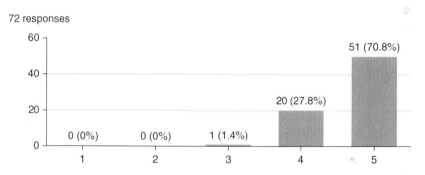

FIGURE 17.9 I Listen to the Comments of Other Students
Source: (Shared MC survey)

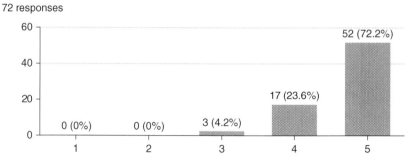

FIGURE 17.10 I Consider the Feedback from My Peers
Source: (Shared MC survey)

One participant emphasized that not only did she listen to others in the course, "I got to learn from others. I was also able to get new ideas and I was also able to share my ideas to others in my group" (Student blog 27).

Many participants in this study indicated that they had limited experience with peer feedback on assignments. For some, this requirement for all course assignments was revelational. "Working on an assignment and submitting it with zero feedback is a source of anxiety for me. However, having group members to give me constructive feedback on my assignments was the biggest advantage for me with group work" (Student blog 36).

Direct Instruction

Direct instruction is not about lecturing. Direct instruction is about ensuring the students achieve the intended learning outcomes of a course or program. It is an essential ingredient in any formal educational experience in order to help students learn how to collaboratively manage and take responsibility for their learning (shared metacognition). It has been shown that students expect structure and leadership in higher education courses, and the roles and responsibilities for direct instruction should be shared by all members of a community of inquiry (Garrison & Cleveland-Innes, 2005).

In terms of shared metacognition, some study participants indicated that they found it difficult to challenge their peers' strategies and perspectives (Figures 17.11 and 17.12).

With regards to strategies, the participants commented specifically on work ethic and quality of work. Several of the students quoted the Pareto principle (Azad, 2013), in which 20% of the group does 80% of the work "usually one or two people ended up doing the work while other group members didn't do anything" (Student blog 11). And, in terms of quality, one participant commented that "being able to trust others and their level of work is something I found difficult. I always want to try to strive for perfection (even when unattainable) so if I feel others are not as invested or do not put in as much work/effort it makes me upset" (Student blog 52).

There were several comments about the challenge of negotiating different perspectives in group work. For example, one participant stated that "Sometimes it can be difficult to cooperate with others that have different ideas and values. However, this is still a valuable experience" (Student blog 13). Another student explained how overcoming this type of challenge can be an important learning experience:

I had some group members that were quick to shut down others' ideas without backing up why. This was frustrating and at times hard to deal with, but it taught me to speak up and skills to positively work through an uncomfortable situation (Student blog 33).

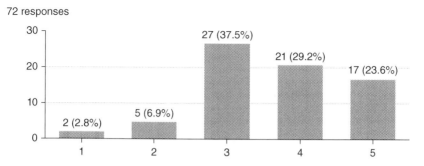

FIGURE 17.11 Challenging the Strategies of My Peers
Source: (Shared MC survey)

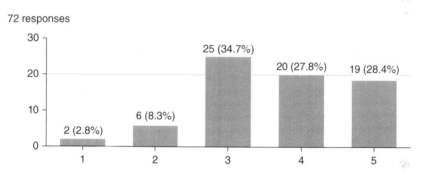

FIGURE 17.12 Challenging the Perspectives of My Peers
Source: (Shared MC survey)

Finally, students are often unwilling to disagree or challenge each other in a higher education course, especially in online discussion forums, as they do not want to offend or hurt anyone's feelings, a sense of "pathological politeness" (Garrison, 2017, p. 53). From the CoI survey results and the final blog postings, it was encouraging to see that by working in groups over the semester, the study participants became more comfortable with providing direct instruction to each other (Figure 17.13).

I got to know more students in my program and made new friendships. These friendships helped me by providing me with people I trust to go to for information. They are people that I feel comfortable sharing my ideas with and taking risks with in terms of disagreements (Student blog 47).

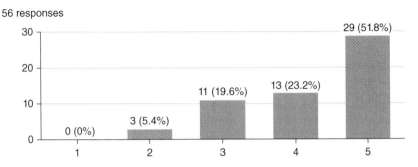

FIGURE 17.13 I Felt Comfortable Disagreeing with Other Students in This Course While Still Maintaining a Sense of Trust

Source: (CoI survey)

Another student commented that "this course helped me to formulate my teaching philosophy that knowledge is co-constructed through shared learning experiences. By working in groups, I didn't feel like I was working to build understanding alone" (Student blog 63).

Recommendations

Based on the findings from this study, a series of recommendations are made for how digital technology applications can be used to design, facilitate, and direct a blended course in higher education in order to help students develop their capacity for shared metacognition.

Design and Organization

In terms of student engagement, Littky and Grabelle (2004) emphasize the importance of establishing relevance at the beginning of a course (first R of engagement). They indicate that students should have a sense of curiosity and connectedness with the learning outcomes for the blended course. This can be achieved by having students complete an online needs assessment survey, share their relevant experiences in an online discussion forum, and create their own learning goals for the course in a blog.

Prior to the commencement of the blended course, the teacher can have students complete an anonymous needs assessment survey in which they are asked about their expectations for the course. Questions could include the following:

1. What are your goals for this course; bottom line—what do you want to "take away" from your course experience?
2. What do you expect will happen during the class sessions? What will the professor do in class, and what will you do?

3. What type of work do you expect to do outside the classroom for this course, if any?
4. How do you think your learning in this course will be assessed?
5. What type(s) of assistance with your learning do you expect to receive in this course and from whom?

This online survey can be constructed using an application such as Google Forms or SurveyMonkey. The key is to share and discuss the survey results with the students during the first class. The teacher can assign the students to small groups where they discuss the results and then share key findings with the entire class.

Also, during the first week of the course, students can be engaged in an exercise in which they each reflect back on an event that was a very powerful learning experience for them—it might or might not have been school related. The teacher can create a series of online discussion forums in the course learning management system (LMS) and then randomly assign five to six students to each forum. First, have the students share their learning experiences in their small groups and discuss why they were powerful. Second, debrief as a whole class about what makes learning experiences powerful and then, using the CoI framework, co-create a set of engagement guidelines for the course.

Finally, students can use applications such as Google Blogger and WordPress to create reflective learning blogs for the course. In their first post, students can identify their personal learning goals for the course or program. The students can then select critical friends who are responsible for providing them with constructive feedback and support on the course assignments, such as replying to blog postings.

Facilitation

The second R of engagement that Littky and Grabelle (2004) advocate for is relationships. Creating a sense of community and collaboration are key for helping students develop their capacity for shared metacognition. Unfortunately, studies indicate that many students in higher education have little formal experience working collaboratively in groups (Chang & Brickman, 2018). Thus, the teacher must model the type of engagement behaviors they expect from the students and provide opportunities for students to learn how to work successfully in groups.

For example, collaborative activities can be designed that allow students to experience all five stages of Tuckman's (1965) group development model (e.g., forming, storming, norming, performing, and adjourning). Ideally, this should be a low-stakes activity that takes place at the beginning of the semester so that students can obtain a first attempt in learning (FAIL) experience. In the case of an educational technology course, this could involve students working together collaboratively on a case study in order to come up with a solution to a school-related problem or issue (Schoology Exchange, 2017).

In addition, the participants of this study indicated that they had limited experience with the peer review process. The University of California at Los Angeles (2019) has developed a Calibrated Peer Review (CPR) tool. This web-based application allows students to learn how to provide constructive feedback to their peers. There are three components to the CPR process: student writing, calibration training, and peer review. The first phase involves students creating a written piece of work based on a topic and in a format specified by the teacher. The second phase involves calibration training. Students assess three "calibration" submissions against a detailed set of questions that address the criteria on which the assignment is based. Students individually assess each of these calibration submissions according to the questions specified by the rubric and then assign a holistic rating out of ten. Feedback at this stage is vital. If the assessments are poorly done and do not meet the teacher's expectations, the students get a second try. The quality of the assessments is taken into account in the next step, which involves the assessment of real submissions from other students. Once the deadline for calibration training has passed, each student is given anonymous submissions by three other students. They use the same rubric to assess their peers' work, this time providing comments to justify their assessment and rating. After they have completed all three, they then assess their own submissions (Likkel, 2012).

Direct Instruction

Littky and Grabelle's (2004) third R of engagement is rigor. In a higher education course, this can involve students completing a challenging problem, task, or assignment that forces them to confront different perspectives and new ways of thinking. This process involves the teacher "nudging" the students forward in their academic studies (Thaler & Sunstein, 2008). For example, students are often content to share and discuss ideas with each other but require a "gentle nudge" to integrate and apply those ideas in course assignments and everyday life.

One recommendation for direct instruction is the explicit use of Garrison et al.'s (2001) practical inquiry (PI) model for course assignments. This model is based on the cognitive presence sphere of the community of inquiry framework and involves four phases of inquiry: triggering event, exploration, integration, and resolution (Figure 17.14).

In online discussion assignments, students can use the PI model to self-code their forum posts in order to help them develop their metacognitive awareness and abilities. For example, they can label their postings as being either a triggering event, an exploration, an integration, or a resolution comment.

Another recommendation involves the use of learning contracts for group work. This can be a useful tool for helping students plan and complete collaborative inquiry-based project work. These contracts should be constructed by the students and reviewed by the teacher for constructive feedback and suggestions for modification. Both the students and the teacher should sign the final version

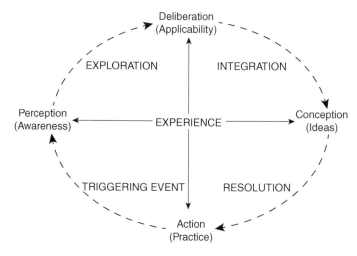

FIGURE 17.14 Practical Inquiry Model

Source: (Garrison et al., 2001)

of the learning contract. The contract then serves as an outline for the project and a tool to aid in the assessment process. Modification of the learning contract may become necessary as the learning experience progresses. Modified contracts should be approved and signed by both the students and the teacher. Failure of a student to meet her or his contract obligations may result in expulsion from the team.

Conclusion

The historical ideal of education has been to learn in collaborative communities of inquiry (Lipman, 1991). The Maori of New Zealand refer to this as the concept of *ako*, which means to both teach and learn (Alton-Lee, 2003). *Ako* recognizes the knowledge that both teachers and students bring to learning interactions, and it acknowledges the way that new knowledge and understandings can grow out of shared learning experiences. Hattie and Yates (2014) refer to this process as visible teaching and learning: "When teachers SEE learning through the eyes of their students and when students SEE themselves as their own teachers" (p. 14).

This research has demonstrated the potential of a blended approach to teaching and learning to recapture this collaborative vision for higher education. The key is to redesign our blended and online courses for active and collaborative learning experiences that enable students to take responsibility for their learning and validate their understanding through discourse and debate with their peers.

References

Alton-Lee, A. (2003). *Quality teaching for diverse students in schooling: Best evidence synthesis June 2003*. Ministry of Education.

Ann and Sandy Cross Conservation Area (2020). www.crossconservation.org/

Azad, K. (2013). Understanding the pareto principle (the 80/20 rule). https://betterexplained.com/articles/understanding-the-pareto-principle-the-8020-rule/

Bleed, R. (2001). A hybrid campus for a new millennium. *EDUCAUSE Review, 36*(1), 16–24.

Chang, Y., & Brickman, P. (2018). When group work doesn't work: Insights from students. *CBE Life Sciences Education, 17*(3), ar42. https://doi.org/10.1187/cbe.17-09-0199

Chick, N. (2013). *Metacognition*. Centre for Teaching Vanderbilt University. https://cft.vanderbilt.edu/guides-sub-pages/metacognition/

Csíkszentmihályi, M. (1990). The domain of creativity. In M. A. Runco & R. S. Albert (Eds.), *Sage focus editions, Vol. 115. Theories of creativity* (pp. 190–212). Sage Publications, Inc.

The Compass (2020). *Tim Horton's children's ranch*. https://thethcompass.com/camps/tim-horton-childrens-ranch/

Dziuban, C. D., Graham, C. R., Moskal, P. D., Norberg, A., & Sicilia, N. (2018). Blended learning: The new normal and emerging technologies. *International Journal of Educational Technology in Higher Education, 15*(3), 1–16. www.springerprofessional.de/en/blended-learning-the-new-normal-and-emerging-technologies/15469862

Dziuban, C. D., Picciano, A. G., Graham, C. R., & Moskal, P. D. (2016). *Conducting research in online and blended learning environments: New pedagogical frontiers*. Routledge.

Garnham, C., & Kaleta, R. (2002). Introduction to hybrid courses. *Teaching with Technology Today, 8*(6). www.wisconsin.edu/systemwide-it/download/ttt.zip

Garrison, D. R. (2017). *E-Learning in the 21st century: A framework for research and practice* (3rd ed.). Routledge, Falmer.

Garrison, D. R., & Akyol, Z. (2015a). Toward the development of a metacognition construct for the community of inquiry framework. *Internet and Higher Education, 24*, 66–71.

Garrison, D. R., & Akyol, Z. (2015b). Corrigendum to "toward the development of a metacognition construct for communities of inquiry." *The Internet and Higher Education, 26*, 56.

Garrison, D. R., Anderson, T., & Archer, W. (2000). Critical inquiry in a text-based environment: Computer conferencing in higher education model. *The Internet and Higher Education, 2*(2–3), 87–105.

Garrison, D. R., Anderson, T., & Archer, W. (2001). Critical thinking, cognitive presence, and computer conferencing in distance education. *American Journal of Distance Education, 15*(1), 17–23.

Garrison, D. R., & Cleveland-Innes, M. (2005). Facilitating cognitive presence in online learning: Interaction is not enough. *American Journal of Distance Education, 19*, 133–148. http://doi.org/10.1207/s15389286ajde1903_2

Garrison, D. R., & Vaughan, N. D. (2008). *Blended learning in higher education*. Jossey-Bass.

Graham, C. R. (2006). Blended learning systems: Definitions, current trends, and future directions. In C. Bonk & C. Graham (Eds), *The handbook of blended learning: Global perspectives, local designs* (pp. 3–21). Pfeiffer Publishing.

Hattie, J., & Yates, G. C. R. (2014). *Visible learning and the science of how we learn*. Routledge.

Kromydas, T. (2017). Rethinking higher education and its relationship with social inequalities: Past knowledge, present state and future potential. *Palgrave Communications, 3,* 1. www.nature.com/articles/s41599-017-0001-8#citeas

Likkel, L. (2012). Calibrated peer review: Essays increase student confidence in assessing their own writing. *Journal of College Science Teaching, 41*(3), 42–47.

Lipman, M. (1991). *Thinking in education.* Cambridge University Press.

Littky, D., & Grabelle, S. (2004). *The big picture: Education is everyone's business.* Association for Supervision and Curriculum Development.

Littlejohn, A., & Pegler, C. (2007). *Preparing for blended e-learning: Understanding blended and online learning (connecting with e-learning).* Routledge.

Mayadas, F. A., & Picciano, A. G. (2007). Blended learning and localness: The means and the end. *Journal of Asynchronous Learning Networks, 11*(1), 3–7.

Moskal, P. D., Dziuban, C. D., & Hartman, J. (2013). Blended learning: A dangerous idea? *Internet and Higher Education, 18*(3), 15–23.

Nakoda Elementary School (2020). www.nakodaschool.ca/

Norberg, A., Dziuban, C. D., & Moskal, P. D. (2011). A time-based blended learning model. *On the Horizon, 19*(3), 207–216.

Patton, M. Q. (1990). *Qualitative evaluation and research methods* (2nd ed.). Sage.

Power, M. (2008). The emergence of a blended online learning environment. *MERLOT Journal of Online Learning and Teaching, 4*(4), 503–514. http://jolt.merlot.org/vol4no4/power_1208.pdf

Regier, P. (2014, September–October). Using technology to engage the non-traditional student. *EDUCAUSE Review,* 70–88. https://er.educause.edu/articles/2014/9/using-technology-to-engage-the-nontraditional-student

Schoology Exchange (2017). *Learning from failure: 6 short EdTech case studies you need to read.* www.schoology.com/blog/learning-failure-6-short-edtech-case-studies-you-need-read

Sharpe, R., Benfield, G., Roberts, G., & Francis, R. (2006). *The undergraduate experience of blended e-learning: A review of UK literature and practice.* Higher Education Academy.

Stringer, E. T. (2014). *Action research* (3rd ed.). Sage.

Telus SPARK Science Centre (2020). www.sparkscience.ca/

Thaler, R., & Sunstein, C. (2008). *Nudge.* Penguin Books.

Tuckman, B. W. (1965). Developmental sequence in small groups. *Psychological Bulletin, 63*(6), 384–399.

University of California at Los Angeles (2019). *Calibrated peer review (CPR) tool.* http://cpr.molsci.ucla.edu/Home

Vaughan, N. D., Auger, N., Sacher, M., & Sacher, M. (2013). A blended approach to Canadian first nations education: The Sunchild e-learning community. In. L. Kyei-Blankson & E. Ntuli (Eds.), *Practical applications in blended learning environments: Experiences in K–20 education.* IGI Global.

Vaughan, N. D., Cleveland-Innes, M., & Garrison, D. R. (2013). *Teaching in blended learning environments: Creating and sustaining communities of inquiry.* Athabasca University Press. www.aupress.ca/index.php/books/120229

Williams, C. (2002). Learning on-line: A review of recent literature in a rapidly expanding field. *Journal of Further and Higher Education, 26*(3), 263–272.

Williams, J. (2003). Blending into the background. *E-Learning Age Magazine, 1.*

18

EVIDENCE-BASED BLENDED LEARNING DESIGN

A Synthesis of Findings From Four Studies

*Ron Owston, Taru Malhotra, Dennis York,
and Jirarat Sitthiworachart*

Blended learning offers many potential benefits to students, faculty, and institutions, yet developers often overlook research evidence on how blended learning programs and courses may be most effectively designed (Alammary et al., 2015; McGee, 2014). The reasons for this are varied. Individual faculty members often design their courses having little or no familiarity with the blended learning literature. Instructional designers may apply principles and procedures they use for fully face-to-face or fully online courses, without regard for the literature on the complexities of integrating the two modalities. Additionally, there is a paucity of empirical research available comparing various blended models, as most work to date focuses on comparing blended learning with traditional lectures (e.g., Means et al., 2013). For these reasons, the goal in this chapter is to synthesize design implications from four blended learning studies we conducted with data collected over three years during a major course redesign initiative. Each of these studies examined aspects of student learning and perceptions under different blended conditions.

The redesign initiative took place at a large comprehensive, urban, and diverse Canadian university. Prior to the redesign initiative, the university published a white paper citing online learning as one of several strategies that should be implemented to enhance student engagement. A working group was established to develop recommendations for online learning. The group ultimately recommended that blended learning be the focus of the online learning initiative. They adopted the former Sloan-C definition of blended learning, requiring a 30% to 79% reduction of normal face-to-face time (Allen et al., 2007). Most influential in their thinking was the work being undertaken at the University of Central Florida (UCF) (e.g., Moskal et al., 2013). The working group saw blended learning as a way to: (a) improve student learning and engagement; (b) provide a better

DOI: 10.4324/9781003037736-24

experience for commuter students, who make up the large majority of the university's student body; and (c) potentially provide better utilization of classroom space during a period of enrollment growth. To offer an incentive for faculty to participate in the redesign, a competitive fund was established and adjudicated. Successful faculty members received course redesign training, a modest research grant, and ongoing instructional and technical design assistance. The initiative involved 3,935 students and 29 courses, with each course taught by a different instructor.

The primary author was invited by the university to carry out research during project implementation. Together with colleagues, he set a research goal to attempt to understand the various conditions under which blended learning may lead to improved student learning, perceptions, and engagement. We designed four studies to examine blended learning outcomes with different student academic abilities, proportions of time online, designs, and subject areas. Our belief was that further comparative research with traditional lecture courses would not be fruitful as blended learning was becoming the "new normal" in higher education (Dziuban et al., 2013). In the near future, almost all courses will have some online components, so more helpful to course designers is research into how blended learning works under various implementations, rather than knowing whether students benefit more or less from blended learning than in-class learning.

The Four Studies

Our studies drew upon various subsets of courses and students participating in the project, depending on the research question. All 29 instructors and 2,282 students (58%) voluntarily participated. Students were given a questionnaire comprising a Likert scale and open-ended items about their perceptions of blended learning, and their course grades and grade-point averages (GPAs) were obtained from the registrar's office. A brief description of the four studies follows.

Study 1

In our first study (Owston et al., 2013), we examined the relationship between students' perceptions of their blended learning courses and satisfaction, convenience, engagement, and performance. A subset of 577 students in 11 business, health, humanities, and fine arts courses was included in this study.

Study 2

In Study 2 (Owston & York, 2018), we considered what we called the "nagging question" instructors frequently ask when developing a blended course: i.e., how much time should be spent online versus face-to-face? We studied the relationship between the proportion of time spent online in a blended course and students' perceptions and performance (N = 1,020). Courses were divided into four clusters: low blend (27% to 30% online—seven courses), medium blend (36% to 40% online—three courses), high blend (50% online—five courses), and supplemental blend (100% face-to-face lectures plus weekly online tutorial sessions that replaced compulsory face-to-face tutorials—five courses).

Study 3

For our third study (Owston et al., 2019), we compared students' perceptions of blended learning on design, interaction, learning, and satisfaction in four different blended models in large-enrollment fine arts introductory non-studio courses (N = 2,081). The models had different combinations of face-to-face lectures, online sessions, and small-group tutorials: blend CLTW (class lectures/tutorials/web-enhanced) had the regular in-class lectures and tutorials, but the course was enhanced by online discussions; blend CLOT (class lectures/online tutorials) had in-class lectures with online tutorial classes; blend OLCT (online lectures/in-class tutorials) had asynchronous online lectures with in-class tutorials; and blend CLHT (class lectures/hybrid tutorials) had in-class lectures and hybrid online/in-class tutorials.

Study 4

In our last study (Owston et al., 2020), we used the US National Science Foundation's more inclusive definition to classify courses as STEM or non-STEM (Green, 2007). This definition recognizes life sciences and some social sciences as part of STEM; hence, we included nursing, kinesiology, and some psychology as STEM courses. We compared students' perceptions and performance in six STEM and eight non-STEM courses offered in the blended format (N = 318).

Research Questions and Methodology

We reviewed our four studies, brainstorming on themes that ran through them. After categorizing the themes based on their frequency and level of importance, we developed the following three research questions for our synthesis:

1. What instructional designs tend to enhance student performance?
2. What instructional designs do students tend to prefer?
3. What instructional designs tend to engage students more?

Next, we reread the studies from the perspective of each of these questions. As we read them, we highlighted key findings, implications, and conclusions related to each question. Excerpts of the text were entered into a large working table to

Evidence-Based Blended Learning Design **303**

allow comparisons of each study's findings. At least two members of the research team independently read the studies and entered relevant text into the table. From this table, we synthesized the evidence into a narrative for each question. The findings of this synthesis for each research question follow.

Findings

Findings on Design and Performance

The focus of our first research question is on whether there are specific blended course designs in which students perform better or perceive that they perform better. There is a compelling body of research suggesting students in blended classes outperform their counterparts in traditional face-to-face lecture classes overall. Evidence of this comes from large meta-analyses (e.g., Bernard et al., 2014; Means et al., 2013; Spanjers et al., 2015) and major comparative studies (e.g., López-Pérez et al., 2011; Melton et al., 2009), as well as the ongoing collection of data on success rates at UCF (Dziuban et al., 2018). Students perceive that they learn better in blended courses than fully face-to-face ones (Melton et al., 2009; Owston et al., 2006); however, we have not found any published literature (apart from our work) that compares different blended designs with each other on actual or perceived differences in learning.

Our four studies suggest some trends about which designs are more effective and less effective than others on actual and perceived student learning. They are summarized in Table 18.1. In Study 1, we found a significant relationship between student course grades and their perceptions of learning in blended courses among first-year students ($\eta 2$ ranged from 0.66 to 0.102). This finding implied that low-performing students might not have the study skills needed to succeed in blended courses without extra academic support. A corollary is that students may have better success in blended learning in upper-level or graduate courses, where students have more developed independent study habits or self-efficacy.

TABLE 18.1 Characteristics of More and Less Effective Designs for Performance

	More Effective Designs	*Less Effective Designs*
Study 1	High achievers perceive they learn better with blended learning	Low achievers perceive they learn better in F2F
Study 2	High blend (50% online) and medium blend (36% to 40% online)	Low blend (27% to 30% online) and supplemental (100% F2F + additional online time)
Study 3	Online lectures and in-class tutorials (OLCT)	Online lectures and hybrid tutorials (CLHT)
Study 4	STEM	Non-STEM

In Study 2, we compared students' performance in courses with differing proportions of time devoted to online activity. Results showed that students in high (50% online) and medium (36% to 40% online) blends significantly outperformed those in low (27% to 30% online) and supplemental blends (where online time was in addition to regular face-to-face time) ($p < .005$). This finding implied that the advantages of blended learning might not accrue unless a substantive amount of time is spent online (i.e., from 36% to 50%).

We examined student perceptions of learning in Study 3 in four blended learning models in large-enrollment courses that had various combinations of face-to-face and online lectures and tutorial classes. Overall, courses with online lectures and in-class tutorials (blend OLCT) were the most preferred of the models studied. Blend OLCT became somewhat like a traditional course that included lecture-capture technology. Research has shown that students highly value lecture-capture courses, as they can review course content multiple times and view classes that they missed while at the same time maintaining interaction with their instructor and peers (Karnad, 2013; Soong et al., 2006; Traphagan et al., 2010). Blend OLCT could also be construed as a form of the flipped classroom, although the amount of time spent in tutorials was only one hour per week instead of the regular three hours. Courses with in-class lectures and tutorials that alternated online and face-to-face were the least preferred overall for learning (blend CLHT).

In Study 4, we compared student performance, as measured by final course grades, in six STEM and eight non-STEM blended courses. We found that STEM students outperformed non-STEM students on final course grades after adjusting for prior academic attainment using GPA as a covariate. The resulting effect size of $\eta2 = 0.37$ was relatively small yet still pedagogically meaningful. It implies that 64% of the STEM students were above the mean of the non-STEM students. This effect occurred despite the well-recognized phenomenon that students tend to be graded harder in STEM courses (Kokkelenberg & Sinha, 2010).

Findings on Design and Preference

Regarding student preferences, the focus of the second research question, our four studies showed students tend to prefer blended learning over traditional face-to-face and online learning. With this finding, together with recent studies (Marquis & Ghosh, 2017; Pechenkina & Aeschliman, 2017; Zhu, 2017), we can make a case for expanded use of blended learning to meet current students' needs and attract new students. Some of the most appealing features of blended learning are increased flexibility, reduced travel time, commuting cost savings, flexible access to course content, and intentional combination of online and face-to-face learning activities. Table 18.2 summarizes these trends.

In Study 1, high-achieving students preferred the blended mode over fully face-to-face or online learning. The high achievers also reported that they would

Evidence-Based Blended Learning Design **305**

TABLE 18.2 Characteristics of More and Less Effective Designs for Preference

	More Effective Designs	*Less Effective Designs*
Study 1	High achievers preferred blended courses (increased flexibility, reduced travel time, commuting cost savings, and access to content)	Low achievers preferred F2F
Study 2	Medium blend (36% to 40% online)	Supplemental (100% F2F + additional online time)
Study 3	Online lectures and in-class tutorials (OLCT)	Online lectures and hybrid tutorials (CLTH) and in-class learning and online tutorials (CLOT)
Study 4	Non-STEM	STEM

take a blended learning course in the future. In contrast, the low-achieving students preferred to learn in a face-to-face setting and were least likely to want to take another blended course. Our study also revealed that high achievers most preferred participating in the blended mode for lectures, discussions, and tutorials, while low achievers most preferred face-to-face formats for these activities. Moreover, we found high-achieving students preferred the flexibility afforded by blended learning more than their low-achieving counterparts ($\eta2 = .067$). Reduced travel time and increased savings of commuting expenses also appealed most to high achievers ($\eta2 = .059$).

Study 2 reveals a significant relationship between students' perceptions and the proportion of time replaced by online activities ($p < 0.001$). We found that students in the medium (36% to 40% online) and high (50% online) blends tended to have the most positive perceptions about their learning experience. The medium blend students perceived that the online and face-to-face components of the course enhanced each other significantly more than the high blend students. Noteworthy was that students in the low blend (27% to 30% online) did not rate any of the items significantly higher than students in the high or medium blends. The supplemental blend was perceived as the least attractive. This finding might have been affected by extraneous factors such as large class size, the quality of TA support, and students' level of use and comfort with internet and related technology (Alzahrani & O'Toole, 2017; Marquis & Ghosh, 2017). While Study 2 concluded that the relationship between student perceptions and the proportion of blend is not strong, some key tendencies were observed. In corroboration with other researchers (Madriz & Nocente, 2016; Ossiannilsson & Landgren, 2012), we can say that flexibility and intentional use of online and face-to-face time influence students' preferences and satisfaction with the learning process in blended environments.

In Study 3, students perceived most positively the OLCT (online lectures and in-class tutorials) blended model, followed by CLWT (in-class lectures and tutorials and web enhancement) and the least favorable, CLHT (in-class lectures and hybrid tutorials). As shown in the previous studies, flexibility and reduced travel time had a decisive role in students' preference for the blended model comprising online lectures and classroom tutorials, compared to other blended models. Students also perceived that the OLCT blended model offered an intentional mix of online and classroom activities and easily accessible learning materials. Interestingly, one of the findings showed students' positive attitudes toward the CLWT blended model were influenced by increased interaction facilitated by TAs in face-to-face tutorials with complementary online discussion forums.

In Study 4, non-STEM students rated blended learning significantly higher (than STEM students) on the intentional combination of online and face-to-face activities (with a large effect size, $\eta 2 = .088$), as well as on the opportunity of taking another blended learning course in the future ($\eta 2 = .024$). While non-STEM students were more positive in their comments (regarding online and face-to-face combination, flexibility, overall enjoyment), STEM students tended to maintain a skeptical attitude toward blended learning. These findings are in line with other research (Acosta et al., 2018; Ellis & Han, 2018) that explored students' preference for blended learning in both STEM and non-STEM disciplines. For example, students questioned the practicality/relevance of online discussions when they had to spend excessive time scrolling through discussion threads. Surprisingly, our study found no significant difference in the perceived course workload (i.e., being overwhelmed and more time and effort) in STEM and non-STEM students. This finding contradicts the results of another study focused on engineering students (Ellis & Han, 2018), which concluded students perceive a higher course workload in blended courses than those favoring face-to-face instruction.

Findings on Design and Engagement

Our third research question examined the relationship between design and engagement. Research suggests that students perform better in blended courses when they are engaged and when they get opportunities to interact with the content (S-C), with their peers (S-S), and with their instructor (S-T) (Bernard et al., 2014; Lee, 2014). Although it's difficult to measure engagement in online environments, Henrie et al. (2015) suggest that observing student interaction with the online content (S-C interaction) may help identify students who need help early on. Similarly, Vaughan (2014) suggests that student engagement directly correlates with active and collaborative strategies (S-S interaction) and interaction with faculty members (S-T interaction). To add, Manwaring et al. (2017) suggest that instructors need to plan activities for their blended courses and offer students choices to engage them better cognitively and emotionally. Instructors must design and integrate these activities and implement strategies to enhance interaction at all levels (S-C, S-S, and S-T) (Manwaring et al., 2017; Vaughan, 2014). Although it is evident that several active-learning strategies help engage students better, it is not clear what other factors one should keep in mind to enhance engagement.

All four of our studies highlight that specific designs engage students more than the others (see Table 18.3). Study 1 suggests that high-achieving students were more engaged in their blended courses than the low-achieving students ($\eta 2 = .153$). Additionally, high achievers felt that, compared to the traditional in-person courses, they interacted better with their peers, the instructor, and the course content in blended courses. In contrast, the low performers felt they specifically lacked interaction with their instructor or content in an online environment and preferred face-to-face courses instead. This discrepancy may be because high achievers took greater advantage of the opportunities afforded by blended learning, such as discussion forums, flexible study, and digital resources at their course website.

Study 2 highlights that medium and high blends (36%–50%) offer significantly higher interaction than low blends. These blends show higher forms of S-C, S-S, and S-T across face-to-face and online classes. Students in these medium and high blends felt they were more engaged and had opportunities to interact with their instructors, TAs, and peers. However, even with these blends, a few students pointed to their isolation in online spaces. An emphasis on minimizing student isolation in online spaces implies the need to focus on the design of appropriate activities. Here, activities that encourage students to interact with their peers and instructor, collaborate, problem-solve, and engage in online discussions were suggested (Owston & York, 2018).

In Study 3, students rated their blended course with in-class lectures and tutorials and web enhancement (CLTW) highest in terms of quality and quantity of S-S interaction, followed by the model with online lectures and in-class tutorials (OLCT). In-class lectures and online tutorials (CLOT) offered the least interaction and engagement, even lower than in-class lectures and hybrid tutorials (CLHT).

TABLE 18.3 Characteristics of More and Less Effective Designs for Engagement

	More Effective Designs	Less Effective Designs
Study 1	High achievers more engaged	Low achievers less engaged
Study 2	High blend (50% online) and medium blend (36% to 40% online)	Low blend (27% to 30% online), supplemental (100% F2F + additional online time)
Study 3	In-class lectures and tutorials and web enhanced (CLWT), followed by online lectures and in-class tutorials (OLCT)	In-class lectures and online tutorials (CLOT)
Study 4	Non-STEM	STEM

Study 4 shows that students in STEM courses were less satisfied than their non-STEM counterparts. Again, one of the main reasons for this dissatisfaction in STEM blended courses was the lack of interaction in the online environment. While non-STEM students enjoyed online video lectures and online discussions, STEM students found them overwhelming, "difficult to follow," "hard to pay attention [to]," and "a waste of time." Despite the higher performance, STEM students did not like the quality or the quantity of interaction in their blended courses.

Discussion and Conclusion

The purpose of this study was to synthesize the results of four separate blended learning studies we conducted to guide instructors and developers on blended course design. What is evident from our work is that no blended design is going to be universally effective across all subject areas and for all students. Instructors must be mindful of their students' needs, their academic levels, and the discipline itself they are teaching and, accordingly, customize the design of their blended course with these factors in mind. This view is consistent with Yousof et al. (2017), who found that instructors need to customize blended courses according to students' cognitive levels. It is also in accordance with Vo et al. (2020), who highlight the role of discipline on blended course design. Hence, we will discuss our results for performance, preferences, and engagement from the perspective of designing blended courses for different student characteristics and different subject areas.

When we looked at the findings for our research questions, several design trends emerged. First, courses with 36% to 50% online (medium and high blends) appear to best support student performance, preferences, and engagement overall. We believe this mixture provides a significant reduction in face-to-face time for students to be able to take advantage of the flexibility of blended learning, while at the same time retains sufficient in-person social interaction most students desire. Thus, designers might begin their planning with this split between online and in-class activities as a general rule of thumb.

A second trend is that higher-achieving students prefer blended courses and appear to be more engaged than lower-performing students. Researchers in this field (Holley & Oliver, 2010) also express concern that even though online courses are intended to include a wider range of students, they end up engaging and being more successful for mainly higher achievers. This suggests that designers (and institutional policymakers) focus their efforts more on upper-year courses, where students are more likely to have strong student skills and habits necessary to succeed in blended learning. Alternatively, if blended courses are offered at the introductory level, there should be student support programs in place to help lower-performing students develop more effective independent study skills.

Another trend is that when designing large-enrollment courses with tutorial sessions, students prefer, and they perceive to perform best with, online lectures with in-class tutorials (blend OLCT). On the other hand, students report being slightly more engaged than blend OLCT when web enhancements are made to regular in-class lectures and tutorials (blend CLTW). We suggest that further efforts be made to enhance students' engagement in courses with online lectures and in-class tutorials (OLCT), as this blend appears to offer more advantages overall. The enhancements might include building a stronger sense of community in tutorial classes (which would entail pedagogical training for TAs) and making the online portion more engaging (which may include prerecorded video lectures, interactive text and quizzes, live chats, group discussions, and group projects). This is in line with Manwaring et al. (2017), who suggest that, apart from learning activities that include active learning strategies to engage them cognitively, instructors also need to include activities that engage them socially.

Lastly, STEM students' higher performance implies designers and policymakers should focus their efforts on these disciplines if they have limited resources and need to prioritize course redesign initiatives. Vo et al. (2020) highlight the importance of instructor facilitation and feedback in STEM courses. Our findings suggest that non-STEM students view blended learning more positively and are more engaged than STEM students, which implies that efforts must be made to improve these areas in STEM courses. Possible actions include implementing online discussion forums around subject problem areas, improving instructor feedback, creating informal in-class discussion areas, and taking up in class issues raised in the online sessions and vice versa.

In conclusion, although none of the designs studied were universally effective, we suggest educators give serious attention to the model of online lectures and in-class tutorials (blend OLCT). This model may be the most viable given the COVID global pandemic as institutions are studying options to bring students back to campus and avoid large groups gathering in classrooms. Students feel they learn well with the blend OLCT model, perceive it positively, and feel engaged in courses that use this design. With this model, the instructor prepares and delivers the course content online, and TAs meet with students in small groups on campus to discuss and elaborate on lecture content and respond to student questions. The success of the model, as mentioned earlier, hinges on how well TAs are prepared to facilitate on–campus tutorial classes. Typically, TAs are assigned to tutorial classes based on their field of study without considering their preparedness to teach. Therefore, attention will need to be given to prepare TAs to successfully lead tutorial classes.

References

Acosta, M. L., Sisley, A., Ross, J., Brailsford, I., Bhargava, A., Jacobs, R., & Anstice, N. (2018). Student acceptance of e-learning methods in the laboratory class in optometry. *PLoS One*, *13*(12), e0209004. www.ncbi.nlm.nih.gov/pmc/articles/PMC6292661/

Alammary, A., Carbone, A., & Sheard, J. (2015). Identifying criteria that should be considered when deciding the proportion of online to face-to-face components of a blended course. *48th Hawaii International Conference on System Sciences*, 72–80. https://doi.org/10.1109/HICSS.2015.19

Allen, I. E., Seaman, J., & Garrett, R. (2007). *Blending in: The extent and promise of blended education in the United States*. Sloan Consortium. www.onlinelearningsurvey.com/reports/blending-in.pdf

Alzahrani, M. G., & O'Toole, J. M. (2017). The impact of internet experience and attitude on student preference for blended learning. *Journal of Curriculum and Teaching, 6*(1), 65–78. https://files.eric.ed.gov/fulltext/EJ1157440.pdf

Bernard, R. M., Borokhovski, E., Schmid, R. F., Tamim, R. M., & Abrami, P. C. (2014). A meta-analysis of blended learning and technology use in higher education: From the general to the applied. *Journal of Computing in Higher Education, 26*(1), 87–122. https://doi.org/10.1007/s12528-013-9077-3

Dziuban, C., Graham, C. R., Moskal, P., Norberg, A., & Sicilia, N. (2018). Blended learning: The new normal and emerging technologies. *International Journal of Educational Technology in Higher Education, 15*(3). https://doi.org/10.1186/s41239-017-0087-5

Dziuban, C., Moskal, P., Kramer, L., & Thompson, J. (2013). Student satisfaction with online learning in the presence of ambivalence: Looking for the will-o'-the-wisp. *Internet and Higher Education, 17*, 1–8. https://doi.org/10.1016/j.iheduc.2012.08.001

Ellis, R. A., & Han, F. (2018). Reasons why some university students avoid the online learning environment in blended courses. *Journal of Educational Multimedia and Hypermedia, 27*(2), 137–152. http://hdl.handle.net/10072/386272

Green, M. (2007). *Science and engineering degrees: 1966–2004 (NSF 07–307)*. National Science Foundation. https://cse.sc.edu/~buell/References/FederalReports/nsf07307degreesawarded.pdf

Henrie, C. R., Bodily, R., Manwaring, K. C., & Graham, C. R. (2015). Exploring intensive longitudinal measures of student engagement in blended learning. *International Review of Research in Open and Distributed Learning, 16*(3), 131–155. https://doi.org/10.19173/irrodl.v16i3.2015

Holley, D., & Oliver, M. (2010). Student engagement and blended learning: Portraits of rinks. *Computers and Education, 54*, 693–700. https://doi.org/10.1016/j.compedu.2009.08.035

Karnad, A. (2013). *Student use of recorded lectures: A report reviewing recent research into the use of lecture capture technology in higher education, and its impact on teaching methods and attendance*. http://eprints.lse.ac.uk/50929/1/Karnad_Student_use_recorded_2013_author.pdf

Kokkelenberg, E. C., & Sinha, E. (2010). Who succeeds in STEM studies? An analysis of Binghamton University undergraduate students. *Economics of Education Review, 29*(6), 935–946. https://doi.org/10.1016/j.econedurev.2010.06.016

Lee, J. S. (2014). The relationship between student engagement and academic performance: Is it myth or reality? *The Journal of Educational Research, 107*(3), 177–185. https://doi.org/10.1080/00220671.2013.807491

López-Pérez, M. V., Pérez-López, M. C., & Rodríguez-Ariza, L. (2011). Blended learning in higher education: Students' perceptions and their relation to outcomes. *Computers & Education, 56*(3), 818–826. https://doi.org/10.1016/j.compedu.2010.10.023

Madriz, F. V., & Nocente, N. (2016). Student engagement and satisfaction between different undergraduate blended learning courses. In *Proceedings of e-learn: World conference on e-learning in corporate, government, healthcare, and higher education 2016* (pp. 1443–1448).

Association for the Advancement of Computing in Education (AACE). www.learntechlib.org/j/ ELEARN/v/2016/n/1/

Manwaring, K. C., Larsen, R., Graham, C. R., Henrie, C. R., & Halverson, L. R. (2017). Investigating student engagement in blended learning settings using experience sampling and structural equation modeling. *Internet and Higher Education, 35*, 21–33. https://doi.org/10.1016/j.iheduc.2017.06.002

Marquis, G., & Ghosh, S. (2017). Student preferences for a hybrid course. *Journal of Education for Business, 92*(3), 105–113. https://doi.org/10.1080/08832323.2017.1289886

McGee, P. (2014). Blended course design: Where's the pedagogy? *International Journal of Mobile and Blended Learning, 6*(1), 33–55. Retrieved from https://eric.ed.gov/?id=EJ1108601

Means, B., Toyama, Y., Murphy, R., & Baki, M. (2013). The effectiveness of online and blended learning: A meta-analysis of the empirical literature. *Teachers College Record, 115*(3), 1–47. www.tcrecord.org/library/content.asp?contentid=16882

Melton, B. F., Bland, H. W., & Chopak-Foss, J. (2009). Achievement and satisfaction in blended learning versus traditional general health course designs. *International Journal for the Scholarship of Teaching and Learning, 3*(1), 1–13. https://digitalcommons.georgia southern.edu/cgi/viewcontent.cgi?article=1155&context=ij-sotl

Moskal, P., Dziuban, C., & Hartman, J. (2013). Blended learning: A dangerous idea? *The Internet and Higher Education, 18*, 15–23. https://doi.org/10.1016/j.iheduc.2012.12.001

Ossiannilsson, E., & Landgren, L. (2012). Quality in e-learning—a conceptual framework based on experiences from three international benchmarking projects. *Journal of Computer Assisted Learning, 28*(1), 42–51. Retrieved from www.irit.fr/recherches/ICS/projects/twintide/upload/450.pdf

Owston, R. D., Garrison, D. R., & Cook, K. (2006). Blended learning at Canadian universities: Issues and practices. In C. J. Bonk & C. Graham (Eds.), *Handbook of blended learning environments: Global perspectives, local designs* (pp. 338–350). Wiley.

Owston, R. D., & York, D. (2018). The nagging question when designing blended courses: How much time should be devoted to online activities? *Internet & Higher Education, 36*, 22–32. http://dx.doi.org/10.1016/j.iheduc.2017.09.001

Owston, R. D., York, D., & Malhotra, T. (2019). Blended learning in large enrolment courses: Student perceptions across four different instructional models. *Australasian Journal of Educational Technology, 35*(5), 29–45. Retrieved from https://eric.ed.gov/?id=EJ1235360

Owston, R. D., York, D., Malhotra, T., & Sitthiworachart, J. (2020). Blended learning in STEM and non-STEM courses: How do student performance and perceptions compare? *Online Learning Journal, 24*(3), 203–221. https://doi.org/10.24059/olj.v24i3.2151

Owston, R. D., York, D., & Murtha, S. (2013). Student perceptions and achievement in a university blended learning strategic initiative. *Internet and Higher Education, 18*, 38–46. https://doi.org/10.1016/j.iheduc.2012.12.003

Pechenkina, E., & Aeschliman, C. (2017). What do students want? Making sense of student preferences in technology-enhanced learning. *Contemporary Educational Technology, 8*(1), 26–39. https://files.eric.ed.gov/fulltext/EJ1126820.pdf

Soong, S. K. A., Chan, L. K., Cheers, C., & Hu, C. (2006). Impact of video recorded lectures among students. In H. Carter, M. Gosper, & J. Hedberg (Eds.), *Who's learning? Whose technology?* Proceedings of the 23rd Annual ASCILITE Conference. www.ascilite.org/conferences/sydney13/about/proceedings.pdf

Spanjers, I. A., Könings, K. D., Leppink, J., Verstegen, D. M., de Jong, N., Czabanowska, K., & Van Merriënboer, J. J. (2015). The promised land of blended learning: Quizzes as a moderator. *Educational Research Review, 15*, 59–74. https://doi.org/10.1016/j.edurev.2015.05.001

Traphagan, T., Kucsera, J., & Kishi, K. (2010). Impact of class lecture webcasting on attendance and learning. *Educational Technology Research and Development, 58*(1), 98–37. Retrieved from https://eric.ed.gov/?id=EJ872774

Vaughan, N. (2014). Student engagement and blended learning: Making the assessment connection. *Education Science, 4*(4), 247–264. https://doi.org/10.3390/educsci4040247

Vo, M. H., Zhu, C., & Diep, A. N. (2020). Examining blended learning implementation in hard and soft sciences: A qualitative approach. *International Journal of Research in Education and Science, 6* (2), 250–272. https://eric.ed.gov/?id=EJ1250698

Yousof, S., Yousof, R., & Md Noh, N. H. (2017). Blended learning approach for less proficient students. *Sage Open.* https://doi.org/10.1177/2158244017723051

Zhu, C. (2017). University student satisfaction and perceived effectiveness of a blended learning course. *International Journal of Learning Technology, 12*(1), 66–83. https://doi.org/10.1504/IJLT.2017.083996

SECTION VII
Science and Health Research

19

BLENDING GEOSCIENCE LABORATORY LEARNING AND UNDERGRADUATE RESEARCH WITH INTERACTIVE OPEN EDUCATIONAL RESOURCES

Juhong Christie Liu, Elizabeth Johnson, and Erik Haroldson

Introduction

Laboratory methods are fundamental components of science curriculum. Therefore, laboratory activities are a critical part of science education (Hofstein & Lunetta, 2004). These hands-on and analytical thinking activities could benefit from access to sometimes expensive instrumentation along with relevant exposition and simultaneous articulation of concepts and theories. Demonstrating procedures of properly preparing samples and operating instruments to generate useful scientific analysis takes up substantial portions of the already limited time of class sessions in traditional brick-and-mortar classrooms. When static text–based books are the only instructional materials, reviewing exposition outside classes can be challenging for students. To solve this problem, we have adopted a blended learning solution to support more effective laboratory learning activities in geosciences and related undergraduate research, developed as interactive open educational resources (OER).

Research has shown that blended learning or using online resources to guide student learning along with traditional in-class instruction has generated positive student learning outcomes (Elmer et al., 2016; Moore & Gilmartin, 2010; Sarah-Jane & Di Trapani, 2012). In particular, interactive video content integration in blended learning for science laboratory process-oriented learning has positive perception on impact of learning in early-stage studies (Schmidt-McCormack et al., 2017; Sharkey & Nurre, 2016).

When designed with engaging learning activities, OER are much sought after as a low-cost way for meeting student learning needs in laboratories, on field trips, and in undergraduate research (Robinson et al., 2014). Projects presented in this chapter have been developed on the basis of multimedia learning principles

DOI: 10.4324/9781003037736-26

and active learning strategies of guided inquiry (Blanchard et al., 2010; Clark & Mayer, 2016; Farrell et al., 1999). Two OER textbooks sponsored by National Science Foundation (NSF) and Virginia Academic Libraries Consortium (VIVA), were developed between 2016 and 2019. In the OER, HTML5-enabled interactive H5P objects and scientifically captioned videos intentionally used interactive illustration and demonstration of geoscience instrumentation and analysis with guided inquiry. The animations and videos allow larger numbers of students to review the content at their own pace, with the options of pause and replay. This detachment from traditional verbal explanation of in-person labs provided individualized flexibility for students to access learning materials. More importantly, the OER was designed to offer interactive self-assessment along with scientific exposition (Liu & Johnson, 2020).

The effectiveness of blended learning with these OER was investigated with a multi-stage mixed-methods study that began in 2017 at the primary university (PU), sponsored by NSF and VIVA, and expanded to the collaborative university (CU) in 2018. Pre- and post-test questionnaires were used to measure student knowledge and attitude changes at the beginning and end of a given semester. Class observations recorded through notes and observation photos were taken as qualitative data in the study. This chapter will inform science education from perspectives of designing, developing, and using OER and methods of blended learning in undergraduate science, technology, engineering, and mathematics (STEM) laboratory-integrated education.

Literature, Background, and Research Question

Creating engaging student learning experiences in geoscience education is uniquely challenging because of the need to blend learning of scientific theories and principles, laboratory procedures, analysis, result interpretation, and field techniques. Traditional textbooks have played a critical role in information dissemination and have provided direction for learning assessment. However, limited access to laboratory space and equipment has demonstrated a need for more explicit and illustrative instructional materials. These materials can scaffold inquiry-based approaches to the operation of and analysis with scientific instruments, along with interpreting results from acquired data, not bound by locations and access to instrumentations (Brownell et al., 2012; Cavinato, 2017; Kwanashie et al., 1989; Wainwright et al., 2004).

Shaped by technologies, learning environments have been extended beyond physical classrooms. Technologies can facilitate the provision of resources and subject-specific expertise online to support students. This allows access to learning-centered materials, search of evidence, and connection of ideas, which have been the key representations of problem-based learning (Jonassen & Rohrer-Murphy, 1999; Liaw et al., 2007). Proper use of technologies in learning requires scaffolding based on social constructivism and the learning cycle in science education (Kolb, 2014; Lawson, 1989; Marin et al., 2000). Their effectiveness requires intentionally designed learning activities that introduce the to-be-learned concepts, enabling student exploration and application through cooperative and collaborative learning with consistent self-assessment in online and in-class modalities (Blank, 2000; Estes et al., 2014; Lawson, 1989; Vaughan, 2010).

Guided inquiry initially appeared as a strategy for student learning in chemistry courses. It is an active learning strategy that provides instructional content presentation with guiding objectives, core questions, and procedural assessment so that students can focus on deep learning (Brown, 2018; Farrell et al., 1999; Purkayastha et al., 2019). Guided inquiry learning has its roots in a Piagetian model of learning and has integrated the principles and concepts of inquiry-based learning and experiential learning cycles in science and laboratory education, which has been proven effective in practice (Abdulwahed & Nagy, 2009; Freeman et al., 2014; Kolb, 2014; Piaget, 1964). Studies have also indicated that guided inquiry learning could improve student experiment design capabilities (Goodey & Talgar, 2016).

Meaningful learning is reflected with cognitive behaviors such as seeking meanings, relating ideas, use of evidence, and interest in ideas (Entwistle et al., 2000). These have been found to correlate to student perception of usefulness of learning activities, student persistence, and confidence in learning science subjects (Hanauer et al., 2016; Galloway & Bretz, 2015c). Science educators have investigated what can potentially lead to student deep learning in the constantly evolving learning environments, including the relevance of learning activities, settings that support collaboration, and methods to improve student persistence and confidence (Corwin et al., 2015; Galloway & Bretz, 2015a, 2015b, 2015c). Many studies have been conducted in various contexts and disciplines to investigate learning materials and methods and contextual factors associated with meaningful learning and student persistence in learning science (Corwin et al., 2015; Galloway & Bretz, 2015a, 2015b).

Recently, ubiquitous digital technologies and reusable instructional resources have made it possible for open educational resources (OER) to emerge at a fascinating pace in STEM education (Allen et al., 2015; Alves & Granjeiro, 2018; Harris & Schneegurt, 2016). These technology-integrated STEM OER can enable low-cost access and possibly offer interactive content presentation as well as integration with active learning strategies. Educational design research is needed to design these with optimal application of cognitive science, media production principles, and technology affordances (Gaver, 1991; McKenney & Reeves, 2019).

This study is conducted to answer the question, How can interactive open education resources (OER) be designed to affect blended learning in laboratory-based geoscience classes?

Research Design, Methods, and Context

This design-based research was initiated to develop open educational resources (OER) for geoscience laboratory-based analytical methods and microscopy for petrology and mineralogy courses. In addition to lowering the cost of textbooks, the researchers explored the adaptation of an active learning strategy known as modified guided inquiry learning into the self-assessment of learning with the online interactive OER (Bailey et al., 2012; Trevathan & Myers, 2013). Guiding objectives, core questions, and procedural assessment were developed along with the content presentation of online OER.

Research Design and Methods

The researchers in this project have investigated the pilot of online interactive OER in blended learning in the primary and collaborative universities in the Southeastern United States. Since the use of interactive OER with integration of guided inquiry learning was a novice practice in science teaching and learning, the researchers utilized an inductive approach in this design-based research. From an inductive perspective, a mixed-methods design was used in the data collection, and applied thematic analysis was conducted to interpret the meaning of the results (Creswell & Creswell, 2018; Guest et al., 2011). A mixed-methods design was adopted to conduct this design-based research through its analysis and exploration, design and construction, and evaluation and reflection stages (McKenney & Reeves, 2019). The analysis and exploration were performed, based on the synthesis of subject matter experts' reflections, to identify the needs of OER development in geoscience and investigate active learning strategies as activity design in OER. The need for low-cost textbooks was also explored through literature in OER and subject-specific pedagogy and guiding undergraduate research of the geoscience faculty on the research team (Wiley et al., 2012; Robinson et al., 2014). The following research sections focus on the design and construction of OER with guided inquiry learning and the evaluation and reflection of using these OER.

Design and Construction of OER With Active Learning Strategies

Two OER resources and one YouTube channel with Creative Commons licenses were piloted in this multi-year study, including the *Analytical Methods in Geosciences* OER textbook at https://courses.lumenlearning.com/labmethods/, *Introduction to Petrology* OER textbook at https://viva.pressbooks.pub/petrology/, and the Analytical Methods in Geosciences (AMiGEO) YouTube Channel at www.youtube.com/channel/UCyxiApPewUDARJMLI5FXHlg. Each module representing a general topic (e.g., making thin sections) was subdivided into chapters.

Laboratory Learning and Research **319**

The technological details of developing these OER textbooks have been published in Liu and Johnson (2020).

Guided inquiry was explicitly embedded into the OER modules during writing and creation of resources by following a template based on the structure of STEM process-oriented guided inquiry books (e.g., Douglas, 2014; Lantz & Cole, 2014). This template includes a list of optional or necessary skills derived from previous sections of the OER, learning objectives, and guided inquiry subsections typically focused on student interactions with one or more diagrams, videos, or readings. After exploring the resources in the subsection, students answer one or more questions (including interactive questions created using the H5P templates from h5p.org, as part of the VIVA OER publishing platform) to test their understanding of the materials. Where relevant, open-ended questions or projects are described at the end of a module or chapter. These are meant to reinforce concepts learned within the chapter.

Examples of the guided inquiry approach are provided by Module 2 of the *Introduction to Petrology* textbook, "Using the Petrographic Microscope" and chapters within this module. The module begins with a brief chapter defining a petrographic microscope and listing learning outcomes for the entire module and an interactive question about why these microscopes are still used today if the technology was largely developed 150 years ago. Links to references are provided for students to further explore the history of microscopy in the geosciences. In the second chapter, an overview of thin sections (slices of rocks mounted on glass, used in the petrographic microscope) and how thin sections are made is provided through a series of interactive diagrams, questions, and videos. The third chapter is an introduction to light and optical properties necessary to understand the mechanics of the microscope. It is not until the fourth chapter that the parts of the microscope are introduced. Students are shown a range of available microscopes and then use an interactive diagram to identify parts of the microscope. Each part or area is then explained in more detail in videos or interactive diagrams. For example, students are asked to calculate the total magnification of the field of view for different microscope objectives. At the end of the chapter, students are asked to arrange the parts of the microscope in order from lowest to highest location on the microscope to reinforce knowledge of vocabulary and the overall structure of the microscope. The fifth chapter is a troubleshooting guide, which describes commonly observed problems with using a petrographic microscope and how to solve them. This chapter includes guided inquiry scenarios of observed issues, asking students to propose tests to diagnose and fix each issue. Subsequent chapters apply the concepts of optics and microscope mechanics to identification of minerals in petrographic thin sections using different methodologies. The last chapter of the module contains two possible synthesis assignments, which pull together the combined skills and knowledge from the previous chapters. These synthesis assignments can be completed in an online or face-to-face format and can be adjusted to the needs of instructors and students.

Evaluation and Reflection Data Collection

Upon receiving institutional review board approval of the research protocol, the researchers collected quantitative and qualitative data from undergraduate students and faculty members with their informed consent. In the context of science laboratory learning, thirty-one items about perception of meaningful learning from the questionnaire of Meaningful Learning in the Laboratory Instrument (MLLI), six items about students' perception of confidence in functioning as a scientist from the College Student Persistence in the Sciences scale (PITS), and six items of encouraging collaboration and contribution from the Laboratory Course Assessment Survey (LCAS) were adopted for the pre- and post-test questionnaire in this study (Corwin et al., 2015; Galloway & Bretz, 2015a, 2015b; Hanauer et al., 2016). The pre-test also included the Pre-course Geoscience Experience Questionnaire from Koretsky et al. (2012) to understand the undergraduate student course preparation and needs. This instrument adoption, modification, and development were performed with combined expertise of geoscience laboratory education, instructional design, educational research, and evaluation.

Data were also collected through classroom observations and design documentations and logs. The STEM classroom observation checklist (Stearns et al., 2012) and Geoscience Authentic Learning Experience Questionnaire (Koretsky et al., 2012) were also utilized as validated instruments for data collection in this study.

Evaluation Context and Procedure

The two universities in this study offer undergraduate, graduate, and doctoral degrees, with undergraduate-only programs in the geosciences. The research at both locations was approved by the respective institutional review boards (IRB). The pre- and post-test questionnaires, with a web-based consent form, were deployed through an online survey platform. The surveys were sent to students in Laboratory Techniques in Geology and Introduction to Petrology at the primary university in the spring semesters of 2017, 2018, and 2019. The collaborative university studied students in a mineralogy course in the spring semester of 2019. For each study iteration, the instructors and researchers introduced the purpose of the study and explained explicitly that participation in the study would not affect student grades in the courses.

Evaluation at Primary University

The courses are typically offered once a year in the spring at the primary university, although the Introduction to Petrology course is occasionally also offered in the fall to accommodate majors. At the primary university, enrollment in the Laboratory Techniques in Geology course was limited to a maximum of 12 students, and the Introduction to Petrology course held a maximum of 21 students due to limited resources and time-intensive lab sessions requiring instructor supervision. Introduction to Petrology is a required course for a BS in geology at the primary university and enrolls sophomores, juniors, and a few seniors. The Laboratory Techniques in Geology course is an upper-level elective taken by juniors and seniors, most of whom have already completed the core Introduction to Petrology course.

In the primary university of this research study, the Introduction to Petrology course used petrographic microscopes and scanning electron microscopy (SEM) with energy-dispersive spectroscopy (EDS) as the focused instrumentation. These classes utilized lab equipment in analysis and interpretation of minerals and rocks throughout the semester, in about ten lab assignments. The Laboratory Techniques course included six modules on making thin sections, SEM, vibrational spectroscopies (Raman and FTIR), atomic absorption spectroscopy, ion chromatography, and isotope-ratioing mass spectrometry. Each module was assessed with a student report including theory, description of instrumentation, methods for operation, data collected, and interpretation of data. This study was conducted in the half semester with thin sections, SEM, and Raman/FTIR spectroscopy modules.

The Introduction to Petrology and Laboratory Techniques in Geology courses were both taught in a flipped or almost-flipped structure as blended learning. Students were expected to complete readings and interactive questions online through a learning management system (LMS) with links and embedded objects from the OER before attending face-to-face sessions. Lab or class sessions focused on answering questions about the online materials and hands-on application of the techniques on using instrumentation to collect observations and data. For the Laboratory Techniques course, students were expected to write answers to the OER embedded questions and turn them in as appendices to their final reports for each instrument module.

Evaluation at Collaborative University

At the collaborative university, the mineralogy course is required for a BS in geosciences with geology concentration and is offered on a three-semester rotation (once every three semesters) and typically enrolls 10 to 20 students but can meet the needs of more enrollment.

In the collaborative university, the study focused on petrographic microscopes and thin sections in the mineralogy course of Spring 2019; students did not access the online OER textbook chapters directly. Instead, they were given paper handouts (with electronic copies available in the course LMS) that were built by the instructor, copied directly from the OER, with minor omissions and changes such as replacement of university names.

Another pilot in the mineralogy course was to change the photo of a petrographic microscope from the OER resource to a photo of a microscope model used in the lab in the mineralogy course. The primary structure of the OER remained,

322 J. C. Liu, E. Johnson, and E. Haroldson

particularly the AMiGEO videos. Links to the videos were prompted in the course LMS. Introductory overview instructions were given by the instructor. Student-driven inquiry was afforded with the guided questions from the OER along with prompts to view the videos in order in the LMS. Students were allowed to watch the videos at their own pace, either working with classmates or alone. Student reports (assignments) from the mineralogy course were collected and graded according to a rubric (answer key). Grade marks were written on the report by hand, and scores were recorded in the course gradebook. Instructor's feedback with student reports were scanned and returned to students for their reference.

In both the primary and collaborative universities, after ensuring that no identifying marks (other than the anonymous unique IDs) were on the reports, these reports were individually scanned to PDF and then uploaded to the Open Science Framework (OSF) database, an open-access science data curation repository subscribed to by the primary university and having built-in Creative Commons license and DOI functions. OSF provided a sustainable platform for archival and data sharing among the research collaborators.

Data Analysis and Results

The pre- and post-test questionnaires were sent as links at the beginning and end of Spring 2017, 2018, and 2019 courses, respectively. The mineralogy 2019 pre-assessment was prompted the first day that AMiGEO OER resources were utilized. All the classes met in a computer lab to administer the pre-test questionnaires at these participating universities. The instructor gave students instructions on how to determine their unique ID and how to find the survey online. Then students were left alone to take the survey and meet again in the regular classroom when they had completed the survey. For the post-assessment survey, the students were directed to the availability of the survey during the instructions for the final module and asked to complete it at their leisure.

One hundred nineteen students enrolled in the Lab Methods course in the Spring 2017, 2018, and 2019 semesters, in the Introduction to Petrology Spring 2019 course, and in the mineralogy Spring 2019 course were invited to the study. Among these students, 72 students granted their consent and completed the pre-test questionnaire, yielding a response rate of 60.5%. For the post-test questionnaire, 42 completed data entry, with consent, yielding a response rate of 35.3% (see Table 19.1 for the demographic characteristics, including gender, ethnic identity, and year of college).

Perceived Knowledge and Attitudinal Changes

Students were asked to complete a pre- and post-test questionnaire prior to the use of this interactive OER textbook and at the end of its use, to measure the perceived changes in knowledge and attitude regarding geoscience lab courses

Laboratory Learning and Research **323**

TABLE 19.1 Demographic Characteristics of Participants

	Pre-questionnaire		Post-questionnaire	
	N	%	N	%
Gender				
Female	25	34.7%	19	45.2%
Male	47	65.3%	23	54.8%
Year of College				
Senior	20	27.8%	15	35.7%
Junior	45	62.5%	23	54.8%
Sophomore	6	8.3%	4	9.5%
Other	1	1.4%	0	
Ethnic Identity				
African American	1	1.4%	0	0%
Hispanic	4	5.6%	2	4.8%
Asian–American	2	2.8%	1	2.4%
White	62	86.1%	37	88.1%
Decline to reply	2	2.8%	2	4.8%

that use the OER. Descriptive analyses were conducted to compare the means between pre- and post-test results (see Table 19.2).

Because of the small sample size for the 43-item pre- and post-test questionnaire, a non-parametric statistical procedure, Mann–Whitney U test with Monte Carlo bootstrap simulation (based on 500 simulated samples) was performed to find out the statistical significance of the difference between the means of pre- and post-test results (Dwivedi et al., 2017; Gall et al., 2003). Among the questionnaire items, *When performing experiments in my Geoscience laboratory course this semester, I expect to think about what is happening at the atomic or molecular level* had post-test mean score (4.33) higher than the pre-test mean score (4.01), with U(NPre = 72, Npost = 42,) = 1,196, z = 1.993, $p < .05$.

For the items in *Rate the degree to which you agree or disagree with the following statement concerning your confidence in your abilities to function as a scientist in your area,* the following results were obtained:

> *I am confident that I can use technical science skills (use of tools instruments and techniques)*: The post-test mean score (4.31) was higher than the pre-test mean score (3.88), with U(NPre = 72, Npost = 42,) = 1,078.5, z = 2.778, $p < .05$.
>
> *I am confident that I can generate research questions to answer*: The post-test mean score (4.14) was higher than the pre-test mean score (3.89), with U(NPre = 72, Npost = 42,) = 1,192, z = 2.095, $p < .05$.

324 J. C. Liu, E. Johnson, and E. Haroldson

TABLE 19.2 Mean Score Comparison Between Pre- and Post-Test Questionnaires

When performing experiments in my Geoscience laboratory course this semester, I expect . . .

		Mean	Std. Deviation
to think about what is happening at the atomic or molecular level.	pre	4.01	0.911
	post	4.33	0.786

Rate the degree to which you agree or disagree with the following statement concerning your confidence in your abilities to function as a scientist in your area.

		Mean	Std Deviation
I am confident that I can use technical science skills (use of tools instruments and techniques).	pre	3.88	0.838
	post	4.31	0.604
I am confident that I can generate research question to answer.	pre	3.89	0.703
	post	4.14	0.814
I am confident that I can use scientific literature and reports to guide my research.	pre	4.00	0.822
	post	4.40	0.627
I am confident that I can develop theories (integrate and coordinate results from multiple studies).	pre	3.81	0.799
	post	4.19	0.671

Note: pre-test responses N = 72; post-test responses N = 42

> *I am confident that I can use scientific literature and reports to guide my research*: The post-test mean score (4.4) was higher than the pre-test mean score (4), with U(NPr e= 72, Npost = 42,) = 1,106, z = 2.565, $p < .05$.
>
> *I am confident that I can develop theories (integrate and coordinate results from multiple studies)*: The post-test mean score (4.19) was higher than the pre-test mean score (3.81), with U(NPre = 72, Npost = 42) = 1,117, z = 0.505, $p < .05$ (see Table 19.3).

The mean scores of the five items from the LCAS Collaboration six-item sub-scale were higher in post-test than the pre-test in students' responses. These were *feeling encouraged to discuss elements of my investigation with classmates or instructors* (pre = 3.63; post = 3.79), *reflect on what I was learning* (pre = 3.73; post = 3.88), *contribute my ideas and suggestions during class discussions* (pre = 3.7; post = 3.74), *help other students collect or analyze data* (pre = 3.3; post = 3.36), and *share the problems I encountered during my investigation and seek input on how to address them* (pre = 3.45; post = 3.59). No statistical significance was found with these differences (see Table 19.4).

A one-way between-subjects ANOVA was performed to compare the post-test results of the students who viewed the OER video more often (selecting strongly agree and agree) with those who did not (selecting disagree

Laboratory Learning and Research **325**

TABLE 19.3 Non-Parametric and Bootstrap Results for Pre- and Post-Test Comparison

	Mann —Whitney U	*Z*	*Asymp. Sig. (2-tailed)*	*Monte Carlo Sig. (2-tailed)*
When performing experiments in my Geoscience laboratory course this semester, I expect to think about what is happening at the atomic or molecular level.	1,196	1.993	0.046	0.036
I am confident that I can use technical science skills (use of tools instruments and techniques).	1,078.5	2.778	0.005	0.006
I am confident that I can generate research question to answer.	1,192	2.095	0.036	0.022
I am confident that I can use scientific literature and reports to guide my research.	1,106	2.565	0.01	0.008
I am confident that I can develop theories (integrate and coordinate results from multiple studies).	1,117	0.505	0.012	0.022

Note: Monte Carlo Sig.: Based on 500 sampled tables with starting seed 582839478.

TABLE 19.4 Collaboration Subscale of Laboratory Course Assessment (LCAS)

In this course, I was encouraged to . . .

		Mean	*Std. Deviation*
discuss elements of my investigation with classmates or instructors.	pre	3.63	0.745
	post	3.79	0.645
reflect on what I was learning.	pre	3.73	0.658
	post	3.88	0.395
contribute my ideas and suggestions during class discussions.	pre	3.7	0.749
	post	3.74	0.497
help other students collect or analyze data.	pre	3.3	0.968
	post	3.36	0.85
provide constructive critique to classmates and challenge each other's interpretations.	pre	3.47	0.863
	post	3.4	0.857
share the problems I encountered during my investigation and seek input on how to address them.	pre	3.59	0.807
	post	3.62	0.661

Note: pre-test responses N = 72; post-test responses N = 42

and strongly disagree). Students' perception of gaining a better understanding of conducting research with analytical instruments with views of interactive OER as the post-test results yielded statistically significant results: $F(3,41) = 5.358$, $p < .05$.

326 J. C. Liu, E. Johnson, and E. Haroldson

TABLE 19.5 Internal Reliability of Pre- and Post-questionnaires

	43-item Questionnaire	31-item MLLI	6-item LCAS	6-item PITS Confidence Scale
Cronbach's alpha	.857	.854	.834	.861

The reliability test of the three parts of the MLLI, LCAS, and PITS and the instrument as a whole in this study generated Cronbach alpha > .80 (see Table 19.5).

Proactive (and Well-Formulated) Questions From Students After Viewing Online OER

The observations in the lab revealed that students tended to ask more questions that were relevant to the operation of the instruments. Observations of the nature and content of student questions during face-to-face classes showed that students had read and interacted with the OER materials.

Adaptation to OER Development Environment

The design logs and documentation from the process of creating and implementing the OERs revealed that instructional design must look at the technology affordances with an intention and understand disciplinary-specific teaching methods and cognitive science. In the respective classes in the primary and collaborative universities, instructors adopted the OER according to their class flow and structure selectively. Another adoption reflection was about integration of interactive HTML5-based H5P objects. Through previous development of a project funded by NSF, the research team developed interactive H5P objects. The technical systems were anticipated to accommodate interactively these H5P content but had been challenging to embed, while users' feedback indicated perceived inconvenience in additional links. This experience disclosed to the researchers that using a third-party platform might trigger more cost in terms of time and resources in diagnosis for cross-system compatibility.

Discussion, Conclusion, and Scholarly Significance

The results of this study, with its pilot OER use in two universities in Laboratory Techniques, Introduction to Petrology, and mineralogy courses, indicated that statistically significant differences were found in student-perceived confidence in technical science skills and scientific research. There was a statistically significant correlation between student perception of gaining a better understanding of conducting research with analytical instruments and their view of the OER interactive content. Students perceived that collaboration in laboratory-based courses increased after the OER adoption, although with no statistical significance. With the limitation of small sample size, bootstrap simulation confirmed the statistical significance, which can possibly be confirmed as more courses adopt these OER with properly designed blended learning methods.

The primary focus of this study was not on the impact of OER in geoscience education; rather, it was intended to collect evaluative and reflective data about the design, development, and implementation of OER. These results do provide implications for (a) the cost effectiveness of using OER, "de-skilling" of content expertise so as to use OER textbooks creatively and effectively in teaching, and discipline-specific pedagogy to be integrated into these more flexibly remixable OER; (b) integration of guided inquiry learning as an active learning strategy with online components; and (c) the role of formative assessment as self-paced learning and being able to answer embedded questions (Robinson et al., 2014; Purkayastha et al., 2019).

Evidently, the free OER option saved students the cost of paying for relevant sections from multiple costly technical textbooks. Practically and pedagogically, the optimal application of these OER was found to require customized selection and modification by the geoscience faculty members from the primary and collaborative institutions. This was done to target discipline-specific skillsets, to best use the knowledge base of the instructors, and to optimally engage learning for the specific student populations.

The guided inquiry learning and self-paced formative assessment have also provided implications for effective laboratory class teaching, not attached to a physical location and not only measured by summative exams. In this study, student science learning attitude was improved with the pilot OER in a blended learning approach. Instructors perceived relevant and reliable resources outside class as references for students to review the expository content with live explanation by a scientist when instruments were not available. Process-based assessment with interactive H5P also enabled reflective learning, which has the potential to enhance higher-level thinking skills with the support and intentionally designed online part of blended learning (Bakerson et al., 2015; Soltis et al., 2015). These results have also reconfirmed the possibilities of OER impact beyond cost saving and into effectiveness of learning, as in previous studies (Martin et al., 2017; Hilton, 2016).

While this study implied possibilities of the OER design, development, and use would be optimized with solid content knowledge of the subject matter experts (geoscience faculty in both the primary and collaborative institutions), an agile and forward-thinking design perspective, in-depth understanding of technology affordances, and collaborative communication among stakeholders, it was limited by two institutions and three classes. Broader use of these OER, in the framework of RISE with the integration of usage analytics and more in-depth and constant content review and remodification, can possibly ameliorate these limitations in future OER development and application (Bodily et al., 2017).

This study has provided valuable insight and unique research procedure and results for OER design and development in STEM education. In addition, using adapted online guided inquiry learning strategies to scaffold students' inquiry in geosciences with the newly created OERs will substantially reduce the demand for equipment access during the limited seat time in laboratory courses. These also provide purposeful and interactive pre- and post-class learning materials. Along with engaging students' learning through interactive content and activities, the OER textbook will help develop sustained self-regulated learning for students of all abilities with no textbook expense. Since educational design research is associated with analysis strategies in policy analysis, field portrait, and perception poll (Mckenney & Reeves, 2019), this study can also facilitate the establishment of common languages between subject matter experts like STEM instructors, instructional designers, media producers, OER platform providers, librarians, and stakeholders in open-access policymaking.

Compliance With Ethical Standards

Ethical approval—All procedures performed in studies involving human participants were in accordance with the ethical standards as reviewed and approved by the respective institutional review boards and with the 1964 Helsinki declaration and its later amendments or comparable ethical standards.

Informed consent—Informed consent was obtained from all individual participants included in the study.

Acknowledgement

The authors gratefully acknowledge support from an NSF IUSE grant DUE-1611798 to Johnson and Liu and a Virtual Library of Virginia grant ("Creating an Interactive OER Microscopy Textbook for Petrology") to Liu and Johnson. The researchers also wish to acknowledge Dr. Jin Mao from Wilkes University for the collaboration on the research instrument development, JMU students Ceanna Adams and Mark Peale for media development, and James Madison University for the computing resource support in the VIVA project.

References

Abdulwahed, M., & Nagy, Z. K. (2009). Applying Kolb's experiential learning cycle for laboratory education. *Journal of Engineering Education, 98*(3), 283–294.

Allen, G., Guzman-Alvarez, A., Molinaro, M., & Larsen, D. (2015). Assessing the impact and efficacy of the open-access ChemWiki textbook project. *EDUCAUSE Learning Initiative Brief*, 1–8.

Alves, L. S., & Granjeiro, J. M. (2018, June). Development of digital open educational resource for metrology education. *Journal of Physics: Conference Series* (Vol. 1044, No. 1, p. 012022). IOP Publishing.

Bakerson, M., Trottier, T., & Mansfield, M. (2015). Assessment in online and blended learning environments. In S. Koc, X. Liu & P. Wachira, (Eds.). Information Age Publishing Inc. https://mafiadoc.com/assessment-in-online-and-blended-learning-_597c73591723ddb28e0735fb.html

Bailey, C. P., Minderhout, V., & Loertscher, J. (2012). Learning transferable skills in large lecture halls: Implementing a POGIL approach in biochemistry. *Biochemistry and Molecular Biology Education*, 40(1), 1–7.

Blanchard, M. R., Southerland, S. A., Osborne, J. W., Sampson, V. D., Annetta, L. A., & Granger, E. M. (2010). Is inquiry possible in light of accountability?: A quantitative comparison of the relative effectiveness of guided inquiry and verification laboratory instruction. *Science Education,* 94(4), 577–616.

Blank, L. M. (2000). A metacognitive learning cycle: A better warranty for student understanding? *Science Education*, 84(4), 486–506.

Bodily, R., Nyland, R., & Wiley, D. (2017). The RISE framework: Using learning analytics to automatically identify open educational resources for continuous improvement. *International Review of Research in Open and Distributed Learning,* 18(2), 103–122.

Brown, J. A. (2018). Producing scientific posters, using online scientific resources, improves applied scientific skills in undergraduates. *Journal of Biological Education*, 54(1), 1–11.

Brownell, S. E., Kloser, M. J., Fukami, T., & Shavelson, R. (2012). Undergraduate biology lab courses: Comparing the impact of traditionally based "cookbook" and authentic research-based courses on student lab experiences. *Journal of College Science Teaching*, 41(4), 36–45.

Cavinato, A. G. (2017). Challenges and successes in implementing active learning laboratory experiments for an undergraduate analytical chemistry course. *Analytical and Bioanalytical Chemistry*, 409(6), 1465–1470.

Clark, R. C., & Mayer, R. E. (2016). E-learning and the science of instruction: Proven guidelines for consumers and designers of multimedia learning. Hoboken, NJ: John Wiley & Sons.

Corwin, L. A., Runyon, C., Robinson, A., & Dolan, E. L. (2015). The Laboratory Course Assessment Survey: A tool to measure three dimensions of research-course design. *CBE-Life Sciences Education,* 14(ar37), 1–11. https://doi.org/10.1187/cbe.15–03–0073

Creswell, J. W., & Creswell, J. D. (2018). *Research design: Qualitative, quantitative, and mixed methods approaches*. Sage.

Douglas, E. P. (2014). *Introduction to materials science and engineering: A guided inquiry*. Pearson.

Dwivedi, A. K., Mallawaarachchi, I., & Alvarado, L. A. (2017). Analysis of small sample size studies using nonparametric bootstrap test with pooled resampling method. *Statistics in Medicine*, 36(14), 2187–2205.

Elmer, S. J., Carter, K. R., Armga, A. J., & Carter, J. R. (2016). Blended learning within an undergraduate exercise physiology laboratory. *Advances in Physiology Education*, 40(1), 64–69.

Entwistle, N., Tait, H., & McCune, V. (2000). Patterns of response to an approach to studying inventory across contrasting groups and contexts. *European Journal of Psychology of Education*, 15(1), 33–48.

Estes, M. D., Ingram, R., & Liu, J. C. (2014). A review of flipped classroom research, practice, and technologies. *International HETL Review*, *4*(7), 1–8.

Farrell, J. J., Moog, R. S., & Spencer, J. N. (1999). A guided-inquiry general chemistry course. *Journal of Chemical Education*, *76*(4), 570–574.

Freeman, S., Eddy, S. L., McDonough, M., Smith, M. K., Okoroafor, N., Jordt, H., & Wenderoth, M. P. (2014). Active learning increases student performance in science, engineering, and mathematics. *Proceedings of the National Academy of Sciences*, *111*(23), 8410–8415.

Gall, M. D., Gall, J. P., & Borg, W. R. (2003). *Educational research an introduction* (7th ed.). Pearson.

Galloway, K. R., & Bretz, S. L. (2015a). Measuring meaningful learning in the undergraduate general chemistry and organic chemistry laboratories: A longitudinal study. *Journal of Chemical Education*, *92*(12), 2019–2030.

Galloway, K. R., & Bretz, S. L. (2015b). Measuring meaningful learning in the undergraduate chemistry laboratory: A national, cross-sectional study. *Journal of Chemical Education*, *92*(12), 2006–2018.

Galloway, K. R., & Bretz, S. L. (2015c). Development of an assessment tool to measure students' meaningful learning in the undergraduate chemistry laboratory. *Journal of Chemical Education*, *92*(7), 1149–1158.

Gaver, W. W. (1991, April). Technology affordances. In *Proceedings of the SIGCHI conference on human factors in computing systems* (pp. 79–84). Association for Computing Machinery.

Goodey, N. M., & Talgar, C. P. (2016). Guided inquiry in a biochemistry laboratory course improves experimental design ability. *Chemistry Education Research and Practice*, *17*(4), 1127–1144.

Guest, G., MacQueen, K. M., & Namey, E. E. (2011). *Applied thematic analysis*. Sage.

Hanauer, D. I., Graham, M. J., & Hatfull, G. F. (2016). A Measure of College Student Persistence in the Sciences (PITS). *CBE Life Sciences Education*, *15*(ar54), 1–10. https://doi.org/ 10.1187/cbe.15–09–0185

Harris, D., & Schneegurt, M. A. (2016). The other open-access debate: Alternate educational resources need to be further developed to counteract an increasingly costly textbook burden on university students. *American Scientist*, *104*(6), 334–337.

Hilton, J. (2016). Open educational resources and college textbook choices: A review of research on efficacy and perceptions. *Educational Technology Research and Development*, *64*(4), 573–590.

Hofstein, A., & Lunetta, V. N. (2004, January). The laboratory in science education: Foundations for the twenty-first century. *Science Education*, *88*(1), 28–54.

Jonassen, D. H., & Rohrer-Murphy, L. (1999). Activity theory as a framework for designing constructivist learning environments. *Educational Technology Research and Development*, *47*(1), 61–79.

Kolb, D. A. (2014). *Experiential learning: Experience as the source of learning and development*. FT Press.

Koretsky, C. M., Petcovic, H. L., & Rowbotham, K. L. (2012). Teaching Environmental Geochemistry: An Authentic Inquiry Approach. *Journal of Geoscience Education*, *60*(4), 311–324.

Kwanashie, K. O., Amabeoku, G. J., & Auta, J. (1989). Factors modifying duration of drug action: A practical for large undergraduate classes on limited laboratory space, staff and budget. *Medical Education*, *23*(5), 409–412.

Lantz, J., & Cole, R. (2014). *Analytical chemistry: A guided inquiry approach quantitative analysis collection*. Wiley.

Lawson, A. E. (1989). A theory of instruction: Using the Learning Cycle to teach science concepts and thinking skills. *NARST Monograph, Number One*, 1989.

Liaw, S. S., Huang, H. M., & Chen, G. D. (2007). An activity-theoretical approach to investigate learners' factors toward e-learning systems. *Computers in Human Behavior, 23*(4), 1906–1920.

Liu, J. C., & Johnson, E. (2020). Instructional Development of Media-Based Science OER. *TechTrends, 64*, 439–450. https://doi.org/10.1007/s11528-020-00481-9

Marin, N., Benarroch, A., & Jiménez Gómez, E. (2000). What is the relationship between social constructivism and Piagetian constructivism? An analysis of the characteristics of the ideas within both theories. *International Journal of Science Education, 22*(3), 225–238.

Martin, M., Belikov, O., Hilton, J., Wiley, D., & Fischer, L. (2017). Analysis of student and faculty perceptions of textbook costs in higher education. *Open Praxis, 9*(1), 79–91.

McKenney, S., & Reeves, T. C. (2019). *Conducting educational design research*. Routledge.

Moore, N., & Gilmartin, M. (2010). Teaching for better learning: A blended learning pilot project with first-year geography undergraduates. *Journal of Geography in Higher Education, 34*(3), 327–344.

Piaget, J. (1964). Part I: Cognitive development in children: Piaget development and learning. *Journal of Research in Science Teaching, 2*(3), 176–186.

Purkayastha, S., Surapaneni, A. K., Maity, P., Rajapuri, A. S., & Gichoya, J. W. (2019). Critical components of formative assessment in process-oriented guided inquiry learning for online labs. *Electronic Journal of e-Learning, 17*(2), 79–92.

Robinson, T. J., Fischer, L., Wiley, D., & Hilton III, J. L. (2014). The impact of open textbooks on secondary science learning outcomes. *Educational Researcher, 43*(7), 341–351.

Sarah-Jane, G., & Di Trapani, G. (2012). A blended learning approach to laboratory preparation. *International Journal of Innovation in Science and Mathematics Education, 20*(1), 56–70.

Schmidt-McCormack, J. A., Muniz, M. N., Keuter, E. C., Shaw, S. K., & Cole, R. S. (2017). Design and implementation of instructional videos for upper-division undergraduate laboratory courses. *Chemistry Education Research and Practice, 18*(4), 749–762.

Sharkey, T. C., & Nurre, S. G. (2016). Video tutorials within an undergraduate operations research course: Student perception on their integration and creating a blended learning environment. *INFORMS Transactions on Education, 17*(1), 1–12.

Soltis, R., Verlinden, N., Kruger, N., Carroll, A., & Trumbo, T. (2015). Process-oriented guided inquiry learning strategy enhances students' higher level thinking skills in a pharmaceutical sciences course. *American Journal of Pharmaceutical Education, 79*(1), 11. https://doi.org/10.5688/ajpe79111

Stearns, L. M., Morgan, J., Capraro, M., & Capraro, R. M. (2012). A teacher observation instrument for PBL classroom instruction. *Journal of STEM Education: Innovations & Research, 13*(3), 7–16.

Trevathan, J., & Myers, T. (2013). Towards online delivery of process-oriented guided inquiry learning techniques in information technology courses. *Journal of Learning Design, 6*(2), 1–11.

Vaughan, N. D. (2010). A blended community of inquiry approach: Linking student engagement and course redesign. *The Internet and Higher Education, 13*(1–2), 60–65.

Wainwright, C., Morrell, P. D., Flick, L., & Schepige, A. (2004). Observation of reform teaching in undergraduate level mathematics and science courses. *School Science and Mathematics, 104*(7), 322–335.

Wiley, D., Hilton III, J. L., Ellington, S., & Hall, T. (2012). A preliminary examination of the cost savings and learning impacts of using open textbooks in middle and high school science classes. *International Review of Research in Open and Distributed Learning, 13*(3), 262–276.

20

STUDENT EXPERIENCES LEARNING PSYCHOMOTOR SKILLS IN A BLENDED DOCTOR OF PHYSICAL THERAPY PROGRAM

Timothy Miller and Swapna Kumar

Introduction

Graduates of physical therapist education programs must be able to competently and "safely provide evidence-based and effective physical therapy services" (American Physical Therapy Association, 2011) in today's advancing health-care environment. The responsibility of physical therapy education curricula is to meet the advances and demands of contemporary science, research, and the ever-expanding scope of clinical practice. To meet these demands, as of January 2016, the doctor of physical therapy (DPT) degree "is the required degree for all entry-level physical therapist education programs" (American Physical Therapy Association, 2011, p. 2).

DPT programs are lock-step and cohort based, with curricula averaging 115 credit hours which, depending on the curriculum, typically take two to four years to complete (Commission on Accreditation in Physical Therapy Education, 2017a). The average curricula of DPT programs comprise 80% didactic course work, ranging from the basic sciences to psychomotor skills required for clinical practice. The remaining 20% of these curricula are composed of clinical education experiences (Physical Therapist (PT) Education Overview, 2015), in which students work under the direction of a licensed physical therapist in clinical settings ranging from hospitals to skilled nursing facilities, outpatient clinics, and home health.

As of 2017, there were 243 accredited DPT programs in the United States, the overwhelming majority of which are delivered in face-to-face educational environments (Commission on Accreditation in Physical Therapy Education (CAPTE), 2017b). Expanded curricula of DPT programs, coupled with space and time limitations, has driven the consideration for contemporary, technology-based

DOI: 10.4324/9781003037736-27

334 Timothy Miller and Swapna Kumar

alternatives to face-to-face instruction to provide efficient, effective, engaging, high-quality education experiences (Adams, 2013; Boucher et al., 2013; Ford et al., 2005; Smith et al., 2006; Veneri, 2011). This chapter focuses on the design of a blended DPT program and students' perceptions of their learning in that program. The next two sections include the literature on blended learning in physical therapy education and the design of the blended DPT program. This is followed by the research design and findings, and the chapter will conclude with implications for the design of blended DPT programs.

Blended Learning in Physical Therapy Education

It is important to identify the main learning focus in physical therapy education before reviewing the literature on blended learning. Although the affective and cognitive domains of learning are accounted for in physical therapy education programs, the primary focus is the development of the psychomotor skill competency required for safe and competent clinical practice (Thoirs & Coffee, 2012). The teaching and assessment of hands-on skills are often guided by the psychomotor domain of learning (Olson, 2008) and Dawson's (1998) taxonomy of the psychomotor domain. The hierarchal learning stages of psychomotor skills are recognized as observation, trial, repetition, refinement, consolidation, and mastery (Dawson, 1998). Investigations surrounding the use of educational technology in physical therapy education literature mainly focus on teaching and learning within the psychomotor domain and sometimes the cognitive domain.

Educational technology in physical therapy education is mainly characterized by the use of online instructional videos for instructing and demonstrating psychomotor skills. Such videos are perceived as an effective solution to the challenges associated with face-to-face instruction, providing a consistent demonstration of the skills, which can be viewed, reviewed, and practiced anytime anyplace by the students (Cooper & Higgins, 2015; Ford et al., 2005; Greenberger & Dispensa, 2015; Hawk et al., 2014; Hurst, 2016; Moore & Smith, 2012; Smith et al., 2011; van Duijn et al., 2014). The review and practice of psychomotor skills that online videos provide have been found to enhance the learning of psychomotor skills (Greenberger & Dispensa, 2015; van Duijn et al., 2014). Greenberger and Dispensa (2015) investigated how students used videos for learning psychomotor skills in a physical therapy course. They found that 99% of the students (N = 254) accessed the supplemental instructional videos, which were used to prepare for practice with peers (80%) and for individual review of the material to prepare for psychomotor examinations (77%).

Blended learning has been investigated in physical therapy education courses in the last decade. Bayliss and Warden (2011), Boucher et al. (2013), and Adams (2013) investigated student performance in blended courses in which face-to-face lectures were replaced with prerecorded lectures, allowing lecture time to be replaced with student application of the material through advanced clinical problem-solving activities and psychomotor skill application and practice. Positive outcomes from blended redesigns included improved student performance on cognitive examination (Bayliss & Warden, 2011), improved student achievement indicated by higher course grades, positive student perceptions, and improved preparation for the face-to-face class time, allowing for increased practice time and application of psychomotor skills (Adams, 2013; Boucher et al., 2013). Hawk et al. (2014) replaced in-class demonstration of psychomotor skills with a digital video library of the skills to be learned in a physical therapy course. There was no difference in student performance of the psychomotor skills compared to previous face-to-face iterations of this course. The blended model allowed for face-to-face class time to be used for higher-level application (e.g., clinical problem solving) of the psychomotor skills, increased learner responsibility for skill acquisition, and increased consistent accurate reinforcement of correct performance of the skills.

Other types of blended designs were studied by Dal Bello-Haas et al. (2013), Lazinski (2017), and Rowe et al. (2013). In Lazinski's (2017) study, 75% of the course consisted of asynchronous online content such as readings, viewing instructional videos, and students sharing self-created videos performing psychomotor skills with the instructor and peers for feedback. Despite the very limited face-to-face practice of psychomotor skills, student performance on the psychomotor examination was high, and student perceptions were positive. In the Dal Bello-Haas et al. (2013) and Rowe et al. (2013) studies, the focus of the blended redesign was on the reinforcement of course content through online asynchronous activities. Both studies found that the blended redesign enhanced the learning of cognitive content and was perceived positively by the students.

Blended learning in physical therapy education is shared as an effective mode of learning in physical therapy education (Adams, 2013; Kliger & Pfeiffer, 2011; Lazinski, 2017), but most of the research is on an instructional unit or at course level, despite the recent establishment of programs in which the entire curriculum is delivered in a blended environment. Additionally, much of the focus is on the instructor side of the implementation, rather than the learner perspective of skill acquisition, strategies used, and challenges faced when learning psychomotor skills in blended environments. The purpose of this study was to explore student experiences learning psychomotor skills in a blended doctor of physical therapy (DPT) program.

Design of the Blended DPT Program

Due to the flexibility of time, access, and place that blended learning provides (Bonk & Graham, 2012; Garrison & Kanuka, 2004), the physical therapy department at a Southeastern university in the US established a blended doctor of physical therapy program in 2011, in addition to an existing face-to-face program. The impetus for creating a blended DPT program was to provide non-traditional students the opportunity to earn a DPT degree while living anywhere in the

336 Timothy Miller and Swapna Kumar

country and also working while enrolled in the program. This is in sharp contrast to face-to-face DPT programs, where students must live in close proximity to the institution and are unable to work due to the high number of credit hours per semester.

The design of the program, curriculum, and courses of the blended DPT program was informed by the community of inquiry (CoI) framework for blended learning in higher education (Garrison & Vaughan, 2008). Since an entirely blended DPT program had not previously been developed in physical therapy education, the CoI framework that comprises three core elements—social, cognitive, and teaching presence—was selected to guide development. The aim was to create a blended physical therapy program in which meaningful and collaborative educational experiences can occur through constructing knowledge between members of the learning community (Garrison & Kanuka, 2004).

All courses in the curriculum are designed with careful attention to social, cognitive, and teaching presence, with activities that ensure the students are interacting not only with each other but also with the instructor. This is seen through deliberate, open, and active instructor-to-student and student-to-student communication that facilitates social presence and teaching presence. To establish and ensure cognitive presence, students are required to engage, critically reflect, or apply course content in different ways within those interactions, both face to face and online. Furthermore, the backbone of all course planning is to design instructional content and learning activities that allow for collaborative exploration and in-depth engagement for the students to construct meaning (Garrison & Vaughan, 2008).

Program Curriculum

This DPT program delivered in a blended environment is accredited by the Commission on Accreditation in Physical Therapy Education (CAPTE), is made up of 117 credit hours, and takes four years to complete. The fall and winter semesters are each 16 weeks in duration, and the summer semester is 12 weeks. Each semester of the didactic portion of this lock-step, cohort-based curriculum is divided into monthly instructional units composed of 3.5 weeks of online content followed by a four-day (32–36 hours) on-campus face-to-face institute (Table 20.1). This cycle repeats during each monthly instructional unit of each

TABLE 20.1 Monthly Instructional Unit Design

Monthly Instructional Unit	Online	Face-to-Face Institute
Week 1	Monday–Sunday	—
Week 2	Monday–Sunday	—
Week 3	Monday–Sunday	—
Week 4	Monday–Wednesday	Thursday–Sunday

semester (Summer, Fall, Winter) throughout the year (Table 20.2). The didactic coursework begins in the summer semester of year one and concludes at the end of the summer semester in year four. By the completion of the didactic portion of the curriculum, the students have attended a total of 36 of these monthly four-day weekend institutes (Table 20.3). After the completion of the didactic portion of the curriculum, the students no longer attend any face-to-face institutes as they complete three consecutive 12-week full-time, terminal clinical experiences, leading up to graduation.

The focus of this blended curriculum design is to thoughtfully "integrate campus and online educational experience for the express purpose of enhancing the quality of the learning experience" (Garrison & Vaughan, 2008, p. 112). This thoughtful integration that leverages the advantages inherent in the blended environment allows students to "hit the ground running" when they arrive for the face-to-face portion of each course, when the time is focused on concentrated hands-on application and higher-order problem solving for the clinical decisions required for entry-level clinical practice.

Online Portion of Blend

Other than the four face-to-face days per month, the instructional content and learning activities in the blended program occur online. The design of these activities in each course is guided by the CoI. Teaching and cognitive presence are established through the instructional activities and weekly to-do-lists, while social presence is established through collaborative activities. The students work their way through the weekly content at self-selected times, completing readings and viewing screen-capture lectures such as voiced-over PowerPoint presentations as well as demonstration videos of psychomotor skills. Students are also provided

TABLE 20.2 Semester-Length and Number of Face-to-Face institutes

Semester	Number of Weeks	Number of Face-to-Face Institutes
Summer	12	3
Fall	16	4
Winter	16	4

TABLE 20.3 Face-to-Face Institutes by Year

Year in Curriculum	Number of Face-to-face Institutes
1	11
2	11
3	11
4	3

338 Timothy Miller and Swapna Kumar

weekly assignments designed to reinforce the content and, in some modules, facilitate the at-home practice of psychomotor skills. For example, as a means to stay on track with the many psychomotor skills to be learned in an instructional unit, students may be asked to share self-created videos performing a few of the many to-be-learned skills in a class-wide discussion board. These activities are designed to provide the students with an opportunity to receive feedback from peers and the instructor, as well as an opportunity to provide feedback on their peers' performance. The overall goal of these activities is to facilitate the students arrival at the face-to-face class time fully prepared to further practice, apply, and be assessed on their competency of the psychomotor skills covered in an instructional unit.

Face-to-Face Portion of Blend

At the conclusion of the online portion of each monthly instructional unit, students attend a four-day face-to-face institute. The four-day face-to-face institute consists of hands-on application, practice, and assessment of the content covered during the previous 3.5 weeks online. The activities during the face-to-face portion of the blend are designed to be a seamless extension of the CoI presences established online. In each semester, a total of three to five courses share the 32 to 36 scheduled face-to-face hours of each of the four-day institutes. For example, in a three-credit hour course with psychomotor objectives, there may only be six to ten contact hours of supervised class time for practice and application of the skills during each face-to-face institute of a semester. During this time, the students have an opportunity to engage in concentrated supervised practice of the psychomotor skills and receive direct instructor and peer feedback. Additional learning activities include the application of the skills through case studies, where the students practice the skills on their peers or instructors who pretend to have various impairments for which the psychomotor skills may need to be applied.

Psychomotor Skill Assessment

At the conclusion of the face-to-face institute, the students participate in 15-to-30-minute psychomotor (practical) examinations, in which they are assessed on their ability to demonstrate competent performance of skill(s) covered during the instructional unit. All skills in an instructional unit are fair game for examination, but due to time constraints, typically, students are assessed on only several of the many psychomotor skills covered during the instructional unit. This type of psychomotor skill assessment is not unlike face-to-face DPT or other health profession programs, where, due to time constraints, only several of the many skills covered are formally assessed.

Methods

To explore the experiences of students learning psychomotor skills in the blended DPT program, the following research questions were addressed:

1. To what extent did the program design contribute to the students' learning of psychomotor skills?
2. What strategies did the students use that facilitated their learning of psycho-motor skills?
3. What challenges did the students face learning psychomotor skills?

Research Design

To gain an in-depth understanding of student experiences learning psychomotor skills in the blended DPT program, a general qualitative approach was used. In December 2018, a purposeful sampling strategy (Creswell, 2013) was used to invite the cohort (N = 37) scheduled to graduate in May 2019 to participate in individual semi-structured interviews. Eight individuals (N = 8) from the contacted sample agreed to participate. At the time of the interviews, these individuals had completed the didactic portion of the curriculum and were completing their full-time, terminal clinical experiences.

The semi-structured interview began with each participant engaging in a cognitive think-aloud (Burbach et al., 2015; Patton, 2015) while watching a self-created video they had previously submitted during year two or three. A cognitive think-aloud was selected to help students recall their educational experiences and because of its ability to "make students' reasoning more coherent and reflective" (Ericsson & Simon, 1998, p. 183). Interview questions asked participants to share their experiences of learning psychomotor skills when not on campus, as well as the process, challenges faced, and support needed to acquire psychomotor skills throughout the blended program.

The recorded interviews were transcribed and each transcript reviewed for accuracy. The transcripts were coded using Braun and Clarke's (2006) six phases of thematic analysis: (a) becoming familiar with the data, (b) generating initial codes, (c) searching for themes, (d) reviewing themes, (e) defining and naming themes, and (f) producing the report. The goal was to provide rich, thick descriptions (Creswell, 2013) of student experiences learning psychomotor skills in the blended DPT program.

Trustworthiness (Creswell, 2013) was ensured throughout the study. Students for whom the researchers had any current grading or advising responsibilities were excluded from the contacted sample. The interview protocol underwent pilot testing and expert review. To allow for "comparability of responses" (Patton, 2015, p. 438), during data collection, the protocol was

340 Timothy Miller and Swapna Kumar

used to ask each participant the same primary questions. Following data collection, all transcripts were reviewed for accuracy and underwent member checking. Trustworthiness in data analysis was accounted for through peer coding of one of the interview transcripts. Finally, to address researcher bias that could influence the study, reflexivity and journaling were used (Creswell, 2013).

Results

In designing this inquiry, we thought we could study what the students did online or face to face and within the course versus outside the bounds of required class activities and identify the subsequent role these activities played in learning psychomotor skills. The participants, however, gave no indication that such a distinction existed. Reporting findings to the contrary require the creation of artificial separation between course activities and non-course activities, both online and face to face. The participants' perceptions of the program revealed the interconnectedness between all activities in the program, whether those took place face to face or online.

Program Design and Student Learning of Psychomotor Skills

All activities reported by the participants could be linked to and were a result of course activities. This was true regardless of official course assignments like the self-creation and sharing of videos to the course discussion board or of activities that were not course requirements, like the creation of a study guide by participants. This was also true whether the activities were delivered online and occurred during the at-home portion of the monthly instructional unit or if the activities occurred during the face-to-face institutes. In short, the data revealed that all activities related to the learning of psychomotor skills were integrally connected, reflecting that the blend of the curriculum is working as designed. The conceptualization and implementation of this blended learning environment are reflected in the findings, in which online and face-to-face activities fully support one another and are integrally connected.

For example, online activities are supplemented by face-to-face practice, and this practice is done with the use of online materials such as videos. Participants indicated that there was no separation between course and non-course activities; similarly, there was no separation between online and non-online learning. Through the purposeful blended design, the data demonstrated that all activities are integrally connected.

Students shared various strategies they used to learn psychomotor skills in the program, including viewing, creating, and sharing videos; creating study guides; working with peer groups; getting faculty feedback; and practicing.

Viewing, Creating, and Sharing Videos

Of all the strategies, watching online videos multiple times was widely shared as being the most impactful at facilitating participant learning of psychomotor skills. Participants discussed that not only did the videos provide a visual of how to properly perform the psychomotor skills, but being able to watch the videos repeatedly also facilitated their learning of the skills. Viewing the videos multiple times allowed for repeated instruction on the proper performance of psychomotor skills. In addition to watching the instructor-provided videos, several participants also watched YouTube videos. The advantage of being able to watch demonstration videos repeatedly, anytime, anyplace is well supported throughout physical therapy education research (Cooper & Higgins, 2015; Ford et al., 2005; Greenberger & Dispensa, 2015; Hawk et al., 2014; Hurst, 2016; Moore & Smith, 2012; Smith et al., 2011; van Duijn et al., 2014).

Participants were required to create videos of themselves performing psychomotor skills, share the videos with their peers, and provide feedback to each other as part of course requirements. Additionally, participants created similar videos and shared with peer study groups to provide one another feedback in the online environment. For participants, the biggest perceived advantage of creating videos was that it increased their practice of all skills. Additionally, all eight participants shared that watching their peers' videos helped their learning of psychomotor skills by allowing them to see different perspectives for performing psychomotor skills. Finally, they stated that providing one another feedback forced them to review all the psychomotor skills covered within an instructional unit.

Creating and sharing videos is a part of every course with psychomotor objectives in the program. These activities were created to establish and foster both cognitive and social presence. Creating videos allows the learners to construct and confirm meaning (Rourke et al., 2001), which in this case is psychomotor skill acquisition. Sharing the videos among peers and providing one another feedback provides an opportunity for sustained engagement and collaborative interaction among the community of learners (Garrison & Vaughan, 2008).

Creating Study Guides

Throughout each course in which the students were learning psychomotor skills, students found that the creation of study guides helped them. To create study guides, they compiled step-by-step instructions for how to perform the psychomotor skills. Some of the study guides even contained screenshot images taken from the videos for how to perform various aspects of the skills, such as hand placement or the patient's positioning. Not only did the creation of the study guides facilitate learning the skills, but participants shared that the study guides were also used to review the skills throughout the four-year program.

Working Within Peer Groups

Participants in this study consistently shared how vital peer support and constant peer communication were for learning psychomotor skills throughout the program. They created small peer study groups that they would keep in constant contact with while at a distance during the at-home portion of the monthly instructional units. Peers would communicate with one another to review and ask questions about performing psychomotor skills. Participants shared that they would receive feedback from their small groups of peers and essentially teach one another proper performance of psychomotor skills. These practices within study groups demonstrate the important role that social and cognitive presence plays in this program. Additionally, these same peer study groups would get together during the face-to-face institutes, outside scheduled class time, to practice the psychomotor skills and provide each other feedback. Participants would often get together with cohort peers who lived nearby to review and practice psychomotor skills during the at-home portion of the monthly instructional unit. Through knowledge sharing, the peer groups that interacted online and face to face provided the learners a means for collaborative sense-making opportunities as well as an avenue for deep exploration of the material, including the exchange of information, the connection of ideas, and application of solutions to problems (Garrison & Vaughan, 2008).

Getting Faculty Feedback

Much like communicating with peers, taking the initiative and time to reach out to and communicate with faculty, especially during the 3.5 weeks online, was found to facilitate learning psychomotor skills. Most of the participants shared the importance of interacting with faculty to get questions answered and to receive feedback regarding the proper performance of the psychomotor skills. Feedback is shared by Merrill (2002) as necessary for learning to occur and for facilitating problem solving and learning from mistakes by showing learners how to recognize, recover from, and eventually avoid errors. However, it is important to recognize the paradigm shift that the blended environment requires in order for the learner to receive the feedback. Students not being present with faculty members on a daily or at least a weekly basis is unique to a blended program and requires the students to take the initiative to reach out to faculty members in order to receive feedback. If they do not reach out to faculty, they miss out on the opportunity to receive feedback on questions they may have during the online 3.5 weeks of monthly instruction. This raises an important implication for blended courses or programs in which psychomotor skills are instructed. Teaching presence mainly included the design of online activities and content and face-to-face instruction in this program. This demonstrates the importance of faculty being "present" online and designing and facilitating interactions for the learners to receive feedback.

Practicing Psychomotor Skills.

Achievement of expert performance of a skill "requires engagement in deliberate practice" (Ericsson, 2004, p. S70). The importance of practice for learning psychomotor skills was shared by all participants in this study. They found that practicing on other people was best. Therefore, during the at-home portion of the monthly instructional unit, participants sought volunteers such as family members, neighbors, friends, and coworkers on whom to practice psychomotor skills. In addition to practicing on others, participants practiced the skills in a variety of creative ways, which included practicing on themselves, practicing on stuffed animals, and mirroring/mimicking the skills on an imaginary person. In addition to physically practicing the skills, some participants would mentally practice the skills through verbalizing and/or visualizing the steps required for the proper performance of the psychomotor skills. Finally, participants explained that the review and practice during the face-to-face institutes with peers played a significant role in learning psychomotor skills throughout the program. The role of practice in learning psychomotor skills is well established in motor-learning literature, which asserts increased practice time positively affects the acquisition of skills (Nicholls et al., 2016; Wulf et al., 2010).

Students' Challenges With Learning Psychomotor Skills

The blended environment also resulted in participant challenges, such as having a lack of immediate feedback, finding volunteers, and the quality of feedback provided by volunteers with no physical impairments.

Participants shared that one of the biggest challenges in a blended environment was not having instantaneous feedback from faculty when practicing the skills during the 3.5 weeks that they learned online each month. Despite having videos that demonstrated the proper performance of all psychomotor skills, not having faculty present to provide "live" feedback led to some students being unsure whether they were correctly or properly performing the skills.

A significant challenge was finding someone willing to take the time to allow the students to practice psychomotor skills. Participants shared that finding someone to practice on was a big burden when some of them lived alone or had family members unwilling to take the time to be a practice volunteer. Additionally, participants shared that the quality of feedback when practicing skills on a non-peer such as a family member or friend was also challenging. Unlike peers, participants explained, non-peer practice volunteers could not provide feedback on the accuracy of psychomotor skill performance. This is significant because the majority of participants relied heavily on practicing psychomotor skills on non-peers during the monthly online components of the program. Additionally, half the participants indicated that practicing psychomotor skills on healthy people who are not in pain and do not have physical limitations or impairments made the proper performance of the skills challenging and also made application of the skills in clinical practice difficult.

Discussion and Implications

This study demonstrated that the designed activities for learning psychomotor skills are all very connected, illustrating that the design of this blended program "works" as designed. These results demonstrate the important role cognitive, teaching, and social presence play in the learners' acquiring psychomotor skills in the blended environment, the need for increased teaching presence during the online components, and the value of the successful creation of a blended and collaborative learning environment for learning psychomotor skills.

Implications for Teaching Psychomotor Skills in Blended Environments

Based on the findings of this study. as well as prior motor-learning literature (Nicholls et al., 2016; Wulf et al., 2010), instructional design literature (Mayer, 2008; Merrill, 2002), and the community of inquiry (COI) framework for blended learning in higher education (Garrison & Kanuka, 2004; Garrison & Vaughan, 2008), implications for teaching psychomotor skills in blended environments are provided in this section:

- Encourage all students to create study guides that break down all steps of proper performance for each psychomotor skill.
- Design activities that facilitate practice as well as feedback on the performance of psychomotor skills during the online portion of the blend.
- To facilitate online feedback and discussion, create a class-wide "muddy points" discussion board for the learners to post text-based or video-based questions and the instructor to provide text-based and video-based feedback regarding psychomotor skill performance.
- Require the learners to compare and contrast the faculty-provided and the learner-created representations of the skills.
- Require the learners to write a reflection on their performance of psychomotor skills and what they have learned through watching their peers' videos.
- Due to barriers of time and access to practice volunteers, the learners may only practice skills assigned to them. Therefore, design class activities to facilitate the learners' practice of all the skills covered in an instructional unit prior to arrival at the face-to-face class time.

- If the learners have difficulty finding someone to practice on at home, encourage learners to practice on themselves, practice on an imaginary person, or practice on stuffed animals, as well as engaging in visualization and verbalization of the skills.
- Facilitate the creation of peer study groups.

Implications for Blended Programs

We also offer this guidance for other blended programs seeking to teach psychomotor skills:

- Use established blended learning frameworks such as the community of inquiry to guide the design of blended learning activities.
- Ensure that the online and face-to-face components of the program complement each other. For example, the online components should prepare students for the face-to-face components and vice-versa.
- Use a cohort-based program design to enable peer support and peer study groups that facilitate learning.
- Use evidence-based learning principles (e.g., Mayer, 2008) to guide the creation of multimedia used in the instruction of psychomotor skills.
- Design face-to-face class time for review and application of the skills, rather than initial instruction.
- Create a robust and well-organized instructional video library for the entire program/curriculum.
- Create small-group discussion boards where peer groups can demonstrate the skills, instruct one another, and provide feedback.
- Ensure the learners have indefinite access to these virtual spaces for skill assessment and self-reflection.

Conclusion

This chapter described a blended DPT program and the strategies and challenges of students learning psychomotor skills within that blended design. With blended DPT programs on the rise (Cherry & Blackinton, 2017), investigating the different types of designs in the programs and the learning of psychomotor skills by students in different programs is warranted. Comparing student experiences across blended programs could provide important insight into how student experiences, facilitating factors, and challenges faced may differ in various blended models. For example, there are now several blended DPT programs that are only two years in length, compared to the four-year blended program described in this chapter. Understanding program-level differences for students learning psychomotor skills in different blended models can provide important direction to inform which blended models may best facilitate the learning of psychomotor skills within a particular college or for a specific context.

Although blended programs in physical therapy education are rare and relatively new, this chapter provides evidence that psychomotor skills required for an entry-level, hands-on health profession can be effectively taught and learned in these educational environments. With physical therapy education being lock-step and cohort based, programs are in a unique position to take advantage of the affordances inherent in blended educational environments.

References

Adams, C. L. (2013). A comparison of student outcomes in a therapeutic modalities course based on mode of delivery: Hybrid versus traditional classroom instruction. *Journal of Physical Therapy Education, 27*(1), 20–34.

American Physical Therapy Association (2011). *Today's physical therapist: A comprehensive review of a 21st-century health care profession* (pp. 1–137). American Physical Therapy Association. www.apta.org/uploadedFiles/APTAorg/Practice_and_Patient_Care/PR_and_Marketing/Market_to_Professionals/TodaysPhysicalTherapist.pdf

Bayliss, A. J., & Warden, S. J. (2011). A hybrid model of student-centered instruction improves physical therapist student performance in cardiopulmonary practice patterns by enhancing performance in higher cognitive domains. *Journal of Physical Therapy Education, 25*(3), 14.

Bonk, C. J., & Graham, C. R. (2012). Part 1, introduction. In *Handbook of blended learning: Global perspectives, local designs* (pp. 1–21). John Wiley & Sons.

Boucher, B., Robertson, E., Wainner, R., & Sanders, B. (2013). "Flipping" Texas State University's physical therapist musculoskeletal curriculum: Implementation of a hybrid learning model. *Journal of Physical Therapy Education, 27*(3), 72.

Braun, V., & Clarke, V. (2006). Using thematic analysis in psychology. *Qualitative Research in Psychology, 3*(2), 77–101.

Burbach, B., Barnason, S., & Thompson, S. A. (2015). Using "Think Aloud" to capture clinical reasoning during patient simulation. *International Journal of Nursing Education Scholarship, 12*(1), 1–7.

Cherry, L., & Blackinton, M. (2017). Student perceptions of factors influencing success in hybrid and traditional DPT programs: A q-sort analysis. *Distance Learning, 14*(4), 37–48.

Commission on Accreditation in Physical Therapy Education (CAPTE) (Ed.). (2017a). *Fact sheet physical therapist education programs.* Commission on Accreditation in Physical Therapy Education. www.capteonline.org/uploadedFiles/CAPTEorg/About_CAPTE/Resources/Aggregate_Program_Data/AggregateProgramData_PTPrograms.pdf

Commission on Accreditation in Physical Therapy Education (CAPTE) (2017b). www.capteonline.org/home.aspx

Cooper, D., & Higgins, S. (2015). The effectiveness of online instructional videos in the acquisition and demonstration of cognitive, affective and psychomotor rehabilitation skills. *British Journal of Educational Technology, 46*(4), 768–779.

Creswell, J. W. (2013). *Qualitative inquiry & research design: Choosing among five approaches* (3rd ed.). Sage.

Dal Bello-Haas, V., Proctor, P., & Scudds, R. (2013). Comparison of knowledge and knowledge application confidence in physical therapist students completing a traditional versus blended learning professional issues course. *Journal of Physical Therapy Education*, *27*(1), 10.

Dawson, W. R. (1998). *Extensions to Bloom's taxonomy of educational objectives.* Putney Pub.

Ericsson, K. A. (2004). Deliberate practice and the acquisition and maintenance of expert performance in medicine and related domains. *Academic Medicine, 79*(Suppl.), S70–S81.

Ericsson, K. A., & Simon, H. A. (1998). How to study thinking in everyday life: Contrasting think-aloud protocols with descriptions and explanations of thinking. *Mind, Culture, and Activity, 5*(3), 178–186.

Ford, G. S., Mazzone, M. A., & Taylor, K. (2005). Effect of computer-assisted instruction versus traditional modes of instruction on student learning of musculoskeletal special tests. *Journal of Physical Therapy Education, 19*(2), 22–30.

Garrison, D. R., & Kanuka, H. (2004). Blended learning: Uncovering its transformative potential in higher education. *The Internet and Higher Education, 7*(2), 95–105.

Garrison, D. R., & Vaughan, N. D. (2008). *Blended learning in higher education: Framework, principles, and guidelines.* Jossey-Bass.

Greenberger, H. B., & Dispensa, M. (2015). Usage and perceived value of video podcasts by professional physical therapist students in learning orthopedic special tests. *Journal of Physical Therapy Education, 29*(3), 46–57.

Hawk, J., Reicherter, A. E., & Gordes, K. L. (2014). SECTIONS model: Strategizing technology-based instruction in physical therapist education. *Journal of Physical Therapy Education, 28*(1), 73–79.

Hurst, K. M. (2016). Using video podcasting to enhance the learning of clinical skills: A qualitative study of physiotherapy students' experiences. *Nurse Education Today, 45*, 206–211.

Kliger, D., & Pfeiffer, E. (2011). Engaging students in blended courses through increased technology. *Journal of Physical Therapy Education, 25*(1), 11.

Lazinski, M. J. (2017). Psychomotor skills, physical therapy, and a hybrid course: A case study. *Distance Learning, 14*(4), 23–35.

Mayer, R. E. (2008). Applying the science of learning: Evidence-based principles for the design of multimedia instruction. *American Psychologist, 63*(8), 760–769.

Merrill, M. D. (2002). First principles of instruction. *Educational Technology Research and Development, 50*(3), 43–59.

Moore, A. W., & Smith, R. A. (2012). Effects of video podcasting on psychomotor and cognitive performance, attitudes and study behaviour of student physical therapists. *Innovations in Education & Teaching International, 49*(4), 401–414.

Nicholls, D., Sweet, L., Muller, A., & Hyett, J. (2016). Teaching psychomotor skills in the twenty-first century: Revisiting and reviewing instructional approaches through the lens of contemporary literature. *Medical Teacher, 38*(10), 1056–1063.

Olson, V. D. (2008). Instruction of competent psychomotor skill. *College Teaching Methods & Styles Journal (CTMS), 4*(9), 27–30.

Patton, M. Q. (2015). *Qualitative research & evaluation methods: Integrating theory and practice* (4th ed.). Sage.

Physical Therapist (PT) Education Overview (2015). www.apta.org/PTEducation/Overview/

Rourke, L., Anderson, T., Garrison, D. R., & Archer, W. (2001). Methodological issues in the content analysis of computer conference transcripts. *International Journal of Artificial Intelligence in Education, 12*, 8–22.

Rowe, M., Bozalek, V., & Frantz, J. (2013). Using Google Drive to facilitate a blended approach to authentic learning. *British Journal of Educational Technology, 44*(4), 594–606.

Smith, A. R., Cavanaugh, C., & Moore, W. A. (2011). Instructional multimedia: An investigation of student and instructor attitudes and student study behavior. *BMC Medical Education, 11*(1).

Smith, A. R., Jones, J., Cavanaugh, C., Venn, J., & Wilson, W. (2006). Effect of interactive multimedia on basic clinical psychomotor skill performance by physical therapist students. *Journal of Physical Therapy Education, 20*(2), 61–67.

Thoirs, K., & Coffee, J. (2012). Developing the clinical psychomotor skills of musculoskeletal sonography using a multimedia DVD: A pilot study. *Australasian Journal of Educational Technology, 28*(4).

van Duijn, A. J., Swanick, K., & Donald, E. K. (2014). Student learning of cervical psychomotor skills via online video instruction versus traditional face-to-face instruction. *Journal of Physical Therapy Education, 28*(1), 94–102.

Veneri, D. (2011). The role and effectiveness of computer-assisted learning in physical therapy education: A systematic review. *Physiotherapy Theory & Practice, 27*(4), 287–298.

Wulf, G., Shea, C., & Lewthwaite, R. (2010). Motor skill learning and performance: A review of influential factors. *Medical Education, 44*(1), 75–84.

21

INTEGRATIVE BLENDED LEARNING

Theory, Disciplines, Application, Critical Thinking, and Assessment

Paige L. McDonald, Karen S. Schlumpf, Gregory C. Weaver, and Mary Corcoran

Introduction and Background

"Interdisciplinary" (Klein, 1990; Klein & Newell, 1996) has become challenging in higher education, particularly with regard to health professions education in which graduates work in teams to optimize patient health in increasingly complex contexts. Little guidance is available on how to make learning "interdisciplinary" in higher education programming, particularly about integrating various disciplinary perspectives and curricula. Additional challenges involve developing measurable competencies and encouraging innovative, collaborative models among faculty who teach different courses but have to foster knowledge integration to achieve programmatic goals.

In August 2016, the George Washington University School of Medicine and Health Sciences (GW SMHS) launched an interdisciplinary PhD in translational health sciences (THS). Designed as a blended, low-residency program of study, the curriculum integrates knowledge from multiple disciplines to develop future scholars who can enable interdisciplinary knowledge generation in future research. Within our blended model of delivery, we have flipped our class activities and adopted active, collaborative, and integrative pedagogies to accelerate knowledge application and integration. Our motto, "We do not lecture!" exemplifies the active approach to our residency weekends. We have found success with these strategies that challenge students to apply knowledge from multiple disciplines both during on-campus weekends and in final assignments. Although developed for a doctoral program, we believe this model of learning design and delivery can be applied across higher education to accelerate knowledge integration and application.

DOI: 10.4324/9781003037736-28

In this chapter, we present the rationale for our innovative model and our exploration of students' perceptions of how the model influenced their learning processes, achievement outcomes, and the process of knowledge integration during the semester of the program. This chapter presents our findings from a survey comprising Likert scale (quantitative) and open-ended (qualitative) questions administered to two cohorts of students. There is further discussion of how student responses may inform model revision and application suggestions for future research, followed by an assessment of its impact on interdisciplinary knowledge integration.

An Interdisciplinary, Blended, Low-Residency PhD

"The Doctor of Philosophy (PhD) in Translational Health Sciences (THS) is a program that strives to educate individuals capable of analyzing, synthesizing and contributing to the science of translational health sciences" ("Doctoral Handbook PhD in Translational Health Sciences," 2020). Disciplines informing the design of the program include team science, implementation science, translational research, program theory, and knowledge translation. By adopting innovative coursework and a purposively blended program structure, students were encouraged to integrate knowledge from these disciplines while conducting scientific research to generate and translate knowledge for improving health care in the population. Additionally, knowledge translation and barriers to it were incorporated into the curriculum.

The PhD in THS is a 54-credit, full-time, low-residency program delivered in a blended format. Approximately 15 students per year are admitted, and they progress through didactic programming as a cohort. The student population consists predominantly of working adults from various fields in health care and public health. Recognizing that a full-time, in-residency program would be prohibitive to the needs of young working professionals, we selected a blended, low-residency structure for greater flexibility for how and when students are required to participate.

The blended structure requires both online asynchronous sessions and face-to-face synchronous residency weekends. There are two residency weekends per semester during the program of study, each lasting two and a half days. While allowing increased access to working adults, the blended structure also enables the application of innovative pedagogies, purposefully structured to promote active and collaborative learning and knowledge integration. Within each course, we integrate "online activities with a traditional face-to-face class activities in a planned, pedagogically valuable manner while reducing face-to-face class time" (Picciano, 2009, p. 8), blending technology, media, human interactions, and learning activities. Instructional design is based on pedagogical value and potential to promote higher-order thinking and interdisciplinary knowledge integration.

Integrative Blended Learning **351**

While e-learning models that leverage internet-based technologies are relatively new to the fields of medical and health professions education, they are creating a "paradigm shift" toward more active, learner-centered pedagogies that promote self-regulation in learning while negotiating challenges of access, time, and cost (McDonald et al., in press; Myers et al., 2012; Ruiz et al., 2006; Straker et al., 2018; Wanner et al., 2019). Recent publications in these fields indicate how enhancing or blending an existing course to support the adoption of active and collaborative pedagogies can yield higher levels of learning (McDonald et al., in press; Myers et al., 2012; Ruckert et al., 2014; Straker et al., 2018). Correspondingly, when faced with the task of designing a "blend" that would promote interdisciplinary knowledge integration and self-regulation on the part of working adults, we began by considering how our structure could support the adoption of active, collaborative and integrative learning strategies. Figure 21.1 presents the model of our semester course structure with our pedagogical approach. Subsequent sections explain our semester structure, how we use Bloom's taxonomy (Anderson & Krathwohl, 2001) to guide the design of our courses and integrative activities, and our adoption of active and collaborative learning strategies to support interdisciplinary knowledge integration at higher levels of learning. An additional benefit of our approach is that it also reduces the potential workload for students within a given semester.

Course Structure and Semester Structure in Our Blended PhD

For the two years of coursework in the program, students take three three-credit courses in both the fall and spring semesters (totaling nine credit hours per semester) and two three-credit courses in the summer semester (totaling six

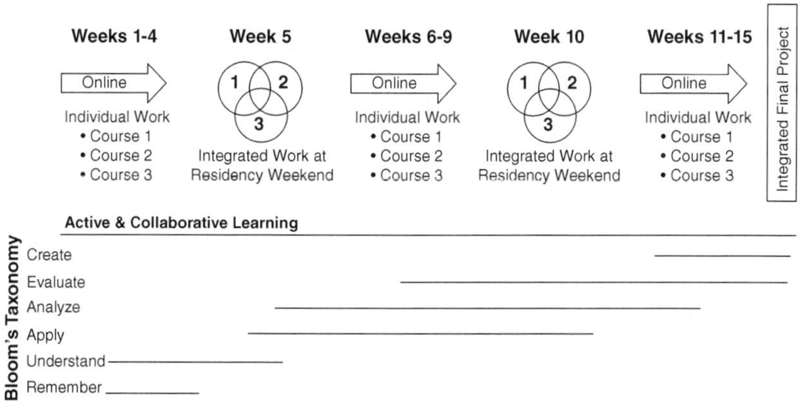

FIGURE 21.1 Blending for Integrative Learning

credit hours). Fall and spring semesters comprise 15 weeks of instruction; summer comprises 13 weeks of instruction. Figure 21.1 depicts the way in which the online and face-to-face sessions are sequenced across a 15-week semester in the program. Online instruction occurs in Weeks 1 through 4, followed by an intensive face-to-face residency in Week 5. Then online instruction occurs in Weeks 6 through 9, followed by another intensive face-to-face residency in Week 10. Weeks 11 through 15 comprise online instruction, final assignment submission, and course wrap up. During residency weekends, activities and sessions integrate content across courses in relation to semester program competencies to enhance knowledge integration and higher levels of learning.

When designing our content and delivery for both the online and face-to-face sessions within a course, we have come to consider each semester in thirds: what needs to take place in the online sessions prior to the first residency to prepare students to engage in activities, what happens online between residencies to prepare for activities in the second iteration, and what happens after the second residency to ensure students successfully demonstrate competencies and courses objectives. Next, opportunities are explored for integrative activities, particularly within residency weekend activities and end-of-course assignments.

Bloom's Taxonomy as a Semester Scaffolding Framework

Figure 21.1 indicates that Bloom's taxonomy (Anderson & Krathwohl, 2001) serves as the framework for scaffolding assignments and activities in courses and semesters (in both online and face-to-face sessions) to promote progression toward higher levels of learning and knowledge integration. Online sessions focus on materials and concepts to gain understanding and potential application (lower levels of Bloom's) prior to participation in face-to-face residency, where integrative, interactive activities focus on higher levels of learning and knowledge integration. When objectives coincide, we create one final assignment for all courses in a semester, asking students to demonstrate interdisciplinary knowledge integration.

Active and Collaborative Pedagogies for Integrative Learning

Leveraging e-learning technologies for active learning, whether in fully online, blended, or technology-enhanced courses in health professions and medical education, has yielded higher levels of learning and increased access to education (McDonald et al., in press; Myers et al., 2012; Ruckert et al., 2014; Straker et al., 2018). Correspondingly, within our PhD in THS, we have adopted a flipped pedagogical approach (McLaughlin et al., 2014) that departs from passive, lecture-based learning toward active and collaborative strategies.

Dewey (1938) proposed that with active experimentation in authentic, situated learning environments, learners could construct new meanings, learn new skills and integrate new knowledge for future application. Within this constructivist paradigm, learning represents a process necessitating both experience/action and reflection/thinking to promote the development of new mental models of skill application. Faculty must design situated learning experiences that replicate, as closely as possible, the environment in which future knowledge or skills will be applied. This allows for active engagement with the knowledge in relation to the specific context of future application. Active learning strategies can include role-playing, polling, think-pair-share groups, debates, and collaborative group problem exploration and case resolution (McDonald et al., in press; Myers et al., 2012; Ruckert et al., 2014; Straker et al., 2018).

Within the THS PhD we adopt active strategies within both the online sessions and face-to-face residency sessions. An example of active learning in an asynchronous environment is a debate contrasting the concepts of fidelity and adaptation. Debate teams form to argue the "pro" or "con" side of the statement that "Adaptation is inevitable in program theory." The teams present their arguments in a VoiceThread presentation and rebut each other using the comments feature. A judging team critiques the arguments and announces a debate winner. As this example illustrates, active engagement with course content in the online sessions focuses on promoting understanding and application of content, preparing learners for activities in residencies (such as peer critiques) incorporating evaluation, integration, and the creation of new knowledge.

As an extension of the active paradigm, collaborative learning is based on a social constructivist paradigm asserting that "cognitive development is dependent on social interaction and collaboration with more capable and knowledgeable others" (So & Brush, 2008, p. 320). The objective is to create communities of inquiry (COI) (Garrison et al., 2003; McDonald et al., in press; Straker et al., 2018). Within the cohorts, students become comfortable negotiating the meaning of challenging content with faculty and more knowledgeable peers in both online and face-to-face learning environments. The COI model proposes that collaboration in online learning communities can promote knowledge generation, application, and integration when the communities comprise social, cognitive, and teaching presence (Garrison, 2011; Garrison & Kanuka, 2004; Garrison et al., 2000, 2003). We adopt the COI model in both the online and face-to-face sessions. Social, cognitive, and faculty presence within initial online sessions of a course help build the psychological safety net that learners require to engage in meaningful negotiation of controversial and potentially unfamiliar content in subsequent collaborative activities (Straker et al., 2018; McDonald et al., in press). Collaborative activities, such as group projects that require complex problem exploration and resolution, are assigned in both the online course programming and the face-to-face residency sessions. The residency sessions, in particular, allow time for the group interaction, in which the immediacy of feedback and participant response can be critical to meaning negotiation, conflict resolution, and new knowledge generation.

While course assignments submitted to date in the program demonstrate achievement of both course level objectives and program competencies indicating the overall success of the model, we were interested in exploring students' perceptions of how this blend influenced their experiences with learning and interdisciplinary knowledge integration.

Current Research

To explore the influence of the model on students' perceived experiences about learning and interdisciplinary knowledge integration, we focused on Semester 2 in the program. In this phase, the three courses lent themselves most readily to integrative assignments and activities: in particular, to the design of a final assignment integrating content from across all three courses. Students participate in courses integrating Implementation Science and Innovation Leadership, Program Theory and Health Innovations, and Advanced Study Design for Translational Research. Table 21.1 provides the course descriptions presented

TABLE 21.1 Semester 2 Course Descriptions—PhD THS GWU

Course Title	Course Description
Implementation Science and Innovation Leadership	"This course introduces implementation science as the study of processes affecting systematic uptake of evidence into routine health care, and related outcomes of quality, cost, and effectiveness. Students study a range of influences on professional and organizational behavior essential to implementing change initiatives aligned with the needs."
Program Theory and Health Innovations	"A translational approach to practice requires health and educational innovations that are evidence based, have a theoretical foundation, and are based on strategies to support fidelity. The purpose of this course is to introduce program theory as the basis for designing health and educational innovations that can be tested using scientific methods, replicated in practice, and inform policy."
Advanced Study Design for Translation Research	"This course provides an in-depth consideration of current issues and techniques in quantitative research methods and study designs. It is intended to provide a focused understanding of designs used in translational health research, particularly quantitative approaches. The course includes a particular emphasis on measurement (health outcomes, survey and instrument design) and methods to support decision-making in health, healthcare, and health policy."

in the student handbook ("Doctoral Handbook PhD in Translational Health Sciences," 2020).

The final assignment for Semester 2 required application and integration of content from all three courses. Students were asked to identify a complex problem related to the health of a population or to a health-care system and develop an original program theory proposing a system-level innovation. The final assignment submission required students to demonstrate the integration of content from all three courses in the analysis of the complex problem, the design of the program theory for the innovation, and the design of a plan to monitor and evaluate the innovation. Residency activities prior to completion of the final assignment prepared students for success in this assignment by providing them with a safe community in which to experiment with and collaborate on various aspects of the assignment. For example, the assignment required that students apply content from their research course to design an evaluation plan for the innovation they presented in their program theory. In the second residency of the semester, students participated in an interactive workshop involving faculty from all three courses in which they designed a preliminary evaluation plan for the program they designed. During the workshop, they worked collaboratively in small groups on different aspects of the evaluation design for their individual projects. The interactive, small-group structure allowed students to actively experiment with the application of course concepts while integrating the immediate feedback of peers and, perhaps, reconsidering their approach based upon that feedback.

Because of the degree to which we were able to integrate content from all three courses in online and residency activities, we focused on this semester when exploring students' experiences about knowledge integration in relation to the application of the model. The research question guiding the exploration was "What are students' perceptions of how the application of a novel blended model in an interdisciplinary PhD program influences their learning process, learning outcomes, and interdisciplinary knowledge integration?"

Methods

In order to explore students' perceived experiences about how application of a blended model influenced their learning processes, learning outcomes, and interdisciplinary knowledge integration, we created a survey protocol to capture their assessment completing Semester 2. We administered the survey to two successive student cohorts. The students represented the third and fourth cohorts that participated in the PhD in THS, (referred to as Cohort 3 and Cohort 4). All students from both cohorts were invited to complete the anonymous survey consisting of four Likert scale questions and three open-ended prompts. Appendix A details the questions and scale adopted in the survey. The conduct of this research was deemed exempt by the GWU institutional review board.

356 McDonald, Schlumpf, Weaver, and Corcoran

Analysis and Results

Descriptive statistics (counts and frequencies) were calculated to analyze the data from the survey. Content analysis of the open-ended questions identified representative themes that appeared across the surveys, subsequently categorizing them by process, outcomes, and knowledge integration (Neuendorf, 2002). Two members of the research team applied a consensus approach for the analysis of these responses.

Quantitative Results

Seven of fifteen students from Cohort 3 completed the survey (46.7% response rate), and seven of ten students from Cohort 4 completed the survey (70% response rate) for a total N = 14 (56% response rate). The following sections detail the results from each section of the survey.

When asked whether residency weekend activities helped them learn individual course content, all students agreed (57.1%) or strongly agreed (42.9%). Students were also asked how well residency weekend activities helped them integrate knowledge from the three courses. Most agreed or strongly agreed (64.3% and 28.6%, respectively) with the statement, with one student disagreeing.

A majority of students strongly agreed (64.3%) or agreed (21.4%) that the process of completing the final semester assignment helped them understand the relationship between content in the semester courses. One student was neutral on the statement (neither agreed nor disagreed), while another disagreed.

Similarly, 64.3% of the student respondents strongly agreed that the final assignment for Semester 2 helped them integrate knowledge across the three courses for the semester. An additional 28.6% agreed, and one student neither agreed nor disagreed.

No additional comments were provided by those students who either disagreed or were neutral on survey questions, thus limiting the potential for interpreting these results.

Qualitative Findings

Active learning presented itself as a key category. A student in Cohort 4 provided their insights on the benefits of active learning for their course experience.

> I think something that rang true in these courses was the ability to learn while doing. Not sure if "action [active] learning" is the appropriate term, but I really appreciated learning while trying out the new material and applying it to a problem of my choice. This helped me to conceptualize the material in a real-life setting.

Integrated projects assisted in students' ability to understand complex course concepts, as evidenced in the following statement:

> At the beginning of the semester, I was having difficulty conceptualizing all of the different TMFs [theories, models, and frameworks] with implementation science, but by putting it into practice with the integrated projects, I had a much stronger grasp by the end of the semester.

Students reported satisfaction with the second term of the course in the way the assignments were integrated. One student stated,

> I found the integration to be successful for semester 2, I did not have the same opinion for the first semester. I believe the concepts of the first semester would have lent itself to integration, but the heavy emphasis on student teams detracted from the integration and overall learning experience.

Check-ins with the faculty also aided in the student satisfaction for the course. A student from the fourth cohort stated,

> It was a very good final assignment and the touch points throughout the semester helped greatly.

By "touch points," we concluded that the student was likely referring to a number of online and in-person active learning exercises.

Integration of course content, assignments, and projects held to aid with student satisfaction: "[The course was] well integrated. [I] really liked the final project." The integrated assignments allowed students to go deeper and present a higher quality of work for their projects, providing students with more breadth to their topics through application. One student from Cohort 4 said, "I can give more time and present more quality work." Moreover, integration allows for students to gain more connection to professional application in the classroom. A Cohort 3 student stated, "The final [was] beautifully integrated and we began to think about how validity and reliability as well as ways to manage them could be completed. The integration makes the concepts real world applicable."

Discussion and Future Research

This chapter presents an innovative model of blended learning to facilitate interdisciplinary knowledge integration and higher-order learning. Our model moves the conversation regarding blended learning beyond the confines of the physical learning space or adopted technologies. Like Norberg and colleagues, who propose a time-based redefinition of blended learning freed from the confines of the "physical teaching environments" (Norberg et al., 2011, p. 207), we propose a redefinition focused on the blending of pedagogies, disciplines, activities, and assessments. Our model allows students to engage in learning through multiple modalities, but it focuses less on the structure and more on the blend of activities and assessments required to achieve pedagogical goals.

Students' responses suggest success of the model in facilitating active learning and application of content in real-world scenarios within one semester of our program of study. Results from the Likert-scaled questions show most students agree that activities and assignments were beneficial for learning individual course content and understanding how that content was related across the semester courses. Comments from students in the open-ended section of our survey indicate metacognitive awareness of how the structure of the semester and course assignments facilitated the process of learning, in particular active engagement in the process of learning and the application of content to real-world problems. With regard to knowledge integration across the courses, all but one student agreed that the residency weekend activities and the final assignment helped them. A few comments noted how the process facilitated integration of knowledge in the final course assignment. However, there were few comments that indicated how the structure of the semester and assignment facilitated integration of knowledge while the students were in the process of learning. Correspondingly, additional research is required to query students on this aspect. Perhaps focus groups or interviews with students would allow us to delve more deeply into the structures and processes by which specific aspects of our program served as facilitators or barriers to knowledge integration.

Survey responses also indicated how application of the model in Semester 2 of our program influenced learning outcomes. In particular, students indicated that the structure of the semester facilitated a greater breadth and depth of understanding of the content in each of the courses, their integration of knowledge from the courses in the final assignment, and their self-confidence in applying the semester content in real-world scenarios. However, they also indicated how the content of the courses in this particular semester lent itself more readily to integration than the content in the previous semester. This is one of the reasons we selected this semester for our query to students. We have experienced difficulty in designing integrated final assignments for all semesters in the program, as not all the content lends itself readily to an integrated final protocol. We have designed our comprehensive exams to mirror the type of integrative assignment required in this semester. Future exploration of the efficacy of our model will involve analysis of responses to these questions for levels of integration demonstrated within a given response or knowledge artifact.

Knowledge integration is a cognitive process that can be facilitated and evaluated through learning artifacts, such as final assignments designed to integrate content across courses. However, these artifacts cannot indicate how the learning process occurred or reveal related conditions or consequences of contextual factors that influenced the process. Within our PhD in THS, we have applied a blended model for learning delivery to facilitate interdisciplinary knowledge integration. Our survey of two cohorts of students suggests that the model does facilitate active engagement with courses content, application of content in real-world scenarios (or authentic learning), and the ability to integrate content from multiple courses in a final semester assignment. However, the survey did not allow us to fully explore which aspects of the model facilitate or inhibit the process of knowledge integration for individual students. Additional methods of data collection in future research are required to fully explore this question. For example, students could be asked to complete reflective journals related to their process of knowledge integration throughout the program or within a given semester. These journals could be coded for barriers and facilitators to knowledge integration. Additionally, in-depth interviews with students could delve more deeply into which aspects of the model served as barriers or facilitators to knowledge integration. Focus groups with successive cohorts of students can help gain additional insights into the benefits of our pedagogical approach. Future research will consider how the interdisciplinary approach applied within this program relates to collaboration among faculty teams and program leadership. Research related to outcomes will also consider how interdisciplinarity is reflected in student publications.

Though this chapter focuses more heavily on students' perceptions of the model application, we would be remiss not to note the impact of model adoption on faculty. Regarding time, faculty were required to meet prior to the start of each semester to design integrated activities both for residency weekends and for final assessments. Faculty also met following each residency weekend to debrief the success of activities and to discuss potential modifications for subsequent semesters. To facilitate collaboration among faculty in the creation and administration of activities and assessments, we created shared electronic folders to house documents such as an integrated semester calendar, folders on specific residency weekend activities, and folders for assessments. Future research is required on the how adoption of the model influenced faculty time and how these structures influenced collaboration among faculty. However, it is important to note that thought must be given to the additional time and structures required for faculty collaboration.

Finally, the recent coronavirus disease 2019 (COVID-19) necessitated changes to our application of the model. Fortunately, the structures for collaboration among faculty that we had in place allowed us to work together throughout Summer 2020 to anticipate requisite changes for Fall 2020, when we were required to move toward a structure comprising asynchronous online courses and synchronous residency weekends facilitated through digital technologies. Our reliance on active and collaborative pedagogies and our familiarity with those theories assisted in any requisite redesign of activities within individual courses and across courses on residency weekends. While we are in the midst of adjusting to these changes, we have already noted that the absence of a face-to-face orientation for the newest cohort of students has influenced the social presence in Semester 1 within our courses and on residency weekends. We look forward to future research on how the recent modifications to our approach to blended during COVID-19 influence the process of learning and learning outcomes for students.

References

Anderson, L. W., & Krathwohl, D. R. (2001). *A taxonomy for learning, teaching, and assessing: A revision of Bloom's taxonomy of educational objectives*. Longman.

Dewey, J. (1938). *Experience and education*. Palgrave Macmillan.

Doctoral Handbook PhD in Translational Health Sciences (2020). https://smhs.gwu.edu/translational-health-sciences/sites/translational-health-sciences/files/THShandbook62020-ADA.pdf

Garrison, D. R. (2011). *E-learning in the 21st century*. Routledge.

Garrison, D. R., Anderson, T., & Archer, W. (2000). Critical inquiry in a text-based environment: Computer conferencing in higher education. *Internet and Higher Education, 2*, 87–105.

Garrison, D. R., Anderson, T., & Archer, W. (2003). *A theory of critical inquiry in online distance education*. Erlbaum.

Garrison, D. R., & Kanuka, H. (2004). Blended learning: Uncovering its transformative potential in higher education. *Internet and Higher Education, 7*(2), 95–105.

Klein, J. T. (1990). *Interdisciplinarity: History, theory, and practice*. Wayne State University Press.

Klein, J. T., & Newell, W. H. (1996). Advancing interdisciplinary studies. In J. G. Gaff, J. L. Ratcliff, & Associates (Eds.), *Handbook of the undergraduate curriculum: A comprehensive guide to purposes, structures, practices, and change* (pp. 393–415). Jossey-Bass.

McDonald, P. L., Straker, H. O., & Weaver, G. C. (in press). Connecting classrooms, Clinicians and community clinics through technology (C4Tech) for active and collaborative learning. *Journal of Physician Assistant Education*.

McLaughlin, J. E., Glatt, D. M. et al. (2014). The flipped classroom: A course redesign to foster learning and engagement in a health professions school. *Academic Medicine, 89*, 236–243.

Myers, J. D., Didwania, A., Shah, C., Jacobson, D. N., Ehtesham, M., & Aronowitz, P. B. (2012). E-learning-The new frontier: A report from the APDIM e-learning task force. *American Journal of Academic Medicine, 125*(12), 1234–1237.

Neuendorf, K. A. (2002). *The content analysis guidebook*. Sage.

Norberg, A., Dzuiban, C. D., & Moskal, P. D. (2011). A time-based blended learning model. *On the Horizon, 19*(3), 207–216.

Picciano, A. (2009). Blending with Purpose: The Multimodal Model. *Journal of Asynchronous Learning Networks, 13*(1), 7–18.

Ruckert, E., McDonald, P. L., Birkmeier, M., Walker, B., Cotton, L., Lyons, L., & Plack, M. (2014). Using technology to promote active and social learning experiences in health professions education. *Online Learning, 18*(4), 51–72.

Ruiz, J. G., Mintzer, M. J., & Leipzig, R. M. (2006). The impact of e-learning in medical education. *Academic Medicine, 81*(3), 207–212.

So, H., & Brush, T. A. (2008). Student perceptions of collaborative learning, social presence and satisfaction in a blended learning environment: Relationships and critical factors. *Computers & Education, 51*(1), 318–336.

Straker, H. O., McDonald, P. L., Barnett, J. S., & Collins, A. (2018). Leveraging e-learning for pedagogical innovation in PA education. *Journal of Physician Assistant Education, 29*(1), 62–66.

Wanner, G. K., Phillips, A. W., & Papanagnou, D. (2019). Assessing the use of social media in physician assistant education. *International Journal of Medical Education, 10*, 23–28.

The Future

22

EDUCATION AND BLENDED LEARNING

Some Possible Futures

Charles D. Dziuban and Anthony G. Picciano

In February 2019, an article in the *New York Times* described a global competition that hundreds of scientists enter every two years. Referred to as the "World Cup" of biochemical research, teams of scientists tackle a biological puzzle called "the protein folding problem." Essentially, they try to predict the three-dimensional shape of proteins in the human body, a problem that no one has ever been able to solve. Past winners have chipped away at it, but a solution still eludes the scientific community. In 2018, the Critical Assessment of Structure Prediction contest was not won by academics. It was won by a team at DeepMind, the artificial intelligence (AI) lab owned by Google's parent company, Alphabet, Incorporated. In describing DeepMind's accomplishment, Mohammed AlQuraishi, a biologist at the Harvard Medical School, who has dedicated his career to protein research, commented that he felt "a melancholy" after losing to DeepMind and stated that "I was surprised and deflated. They were way out in front of everyone else." He criticized big pharmaceutical companies like Merck and Novartis, as well as his academic community, for not keeping pace. "The smartest and most ambitious researchers wanting to work on protein structure will look to DeepMind for opportunities" (AlQuraishi, 2018). He urged the life-sciences community to shift its attention toward the kind of AI work practiced by DeepMind. DeepMind's victory predicted a future for biochemical research increasingly driven by machines and the people who oversee the machines. Another researcher, Derek Lowe, said: "It is not that machines are going to replace chemists. It's that the chemists who use machines will replace those that don't" (Metz, February 5, 2019). Lowe, too, was predicting that successful research was moving into a blended environment of man and AI-enhanced technology. AI development of this magnitude requires enormous amounts of data. DeepMind can lean on the massive computer data centers that underpin Google as well as many of the world's top AI researchers, who know how to get the most out of these facilities. "It allows us to be much

DOI: 10.4324/9781003037736-30

more creative, to try many more ideas, often in parallel" said Demis Hassabis, the chief executive and a co-founder of DeepMind (Metz, February 5, 2019).

Kai-Fu Lee, a former senior executive at Google and Microsoft, stated that humanity is moving toward the establishment of a "new world order" dominated by AI, cloud computing, and robotics (Lee, 2018), which will have significant ramifications for many aspects of human endeavors. How will our species respond? Lee believes that many workers will experience a "psychological loss of purpose" as AI changes the nature of their occupations (Lee, 2018, p. 21). An even more pessimistic prediction comes from Yuval Noah Harari, best-selling author of *Sapiens*, who commented that AI has the potential to create a "useless class of superfluous people" (Harari, 2017, p. 322). The term "useless class of superfluous people" surely attracts attention but may be a bit too extreme. In a later book, Harari takes a more moderate stand and discusses at length the merging of workers with large-scale integrated digital networks (Harari, 2018, p. 22). There are no firm estimates of the number of jobs in this country that will be displaced by AI and other forms of automation. While one estimate suggests 47% (Frey & Osborne, 2013), another poses 38% (Berriman & Hawksworth, 2017), and yet another puts it as low as 9% (Arntz et al., 2016). The fact is no one really knows. One aspect of this displacement is certain, and that is that many of these displaced jobs will be in white collar and professional areas such as teaching, law, and medicine, as well as the corporate sector.

One purpose of this chapter is to speculate on the future of education as online technology, including adaptive learning (also referred to as personalized learning) and analytics infused by artificial intelligence software, develop and mature. While some would argue they are different, adaptive and personalized learning are considered here as synonymous. In this final chapter, an attempt will also be made to consider the challenges for researchers who want to study about the phenomena of online and blended learning within this dynamic and changing environment. This is a risky undertaking at best since predicting the future, and in this case the evolution and growth of technology, new products, and services, is difficult. While many try to predict *what* will happen and sometimes get it right, predicting *when* something will happen is far more challenging. Online and blended learning have already advanced within education, but the most significant changes are yet to come. Evolving technologies have the potential to change the traditional roles in our schools, colleges, and universities to the point that educators will reconsider their purposes as teachers, researchers, and administrators.

The emergence in 2020 of the coronavirus pandemic reminds us just how difficult the task of predicting the future, including online technology and education, is. As mentioned in Chapter 1, the world changed as the coronavirus pandemic scourge infected tens of millions and had killed over one million of people at the time of this writing. Institutions of all types went into online mode as best they could. In education, teachers were forced to move to remote learning in a matter of days and weeks, resulting in what many consider an emerging new normal. There is a clear sense that the remote learning utilized during the pandemic will lead many education leaders and administrators to ramp up the use of online technology in all manner of instruction, research, and administration (Kelderman, 2020). Blended models especially will have a major role to play in all these activities.

The Evolving Technological Landscape

Any attempt at predicting the future should be based on calculated speculation. "What" is difficult enough, but "when" is even more difficult. Niels Bohr, the Danish physicist, was fond of saying that "prediction is very difficult, especially if it's about the future." This chapter speculates about the future of American higher education in two parts: first over the next decade or so and then in the 2030s and beyond. The latter era will see major new technological developments bringing about profound changes to our schools, colleges, and universities and presenting dilemmas for educators regarding their purpose and their role as professionals.

The next decade will see advances in the development of man-machine interfacing or the ability of digital technology to interact with and assist in human activities. Figure 22.1 provides an overview of the major technologies presently in various stages of development and evolution. Nanotechnology and quantum computing form the base for the development of man-machine interfaces such as AI, bio-sensing devices, robotics, and super-cloud computing. In the 2020s, these technologies will be more visible, but in the 2030s and beyond, they will begin to mature, integrate, and have their greatest impact. Robotics will play a major role in reshaping commercial, industrial, and manufacturing processes while bio-sensing will do the same for medical and health services. With respect to adaptive

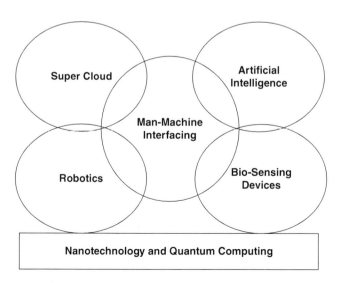

FIGURE 22.1 Technology Forces Shaping the Future of Man-Machine Interfacing

368 Charles D. Dziuban and Anthony G. Picciano

learning, the super-cloud and AI are most important and will be the focus of the remainder of this chapter.

Nanotechnology and Quantum Computing

"Nano" refers to a billionth of a meter or the width of five carbon atoms. The simplest definition of nanotechnology is technology that functions very close to the atomic level. Governments around the world have been investing billions of dollars to develop applications using it, focused on areas such as medicine, energy, materials fabrication, and consumer products. Companies such as Intel and IBM have been developing nanochip technology with the potential to change the scope of all computing and communications equipment. IBM, for instance, announced in July 2015 a prototype chip with transistors that are just seven nanometers wide, or about 1/10,000th the width of a human hair. Nanochip technology is here now and in commercial production and application. By the later 2020s, it will become a mature technology.

By the 2030s, the whole concept of the digital computer may give way to the quantum computer that operates entirely on a scale the size of atoms and smaller. Another decade or so of research and development on quantum computers may find their speed thousands of times faster than the speed of today's supercomputers. The storage capacity of such equipment will replace the gigabyte (10^9) and terabyte (10^{12}) world of today with zettabyte (10^{21}) and yottabyte (10^{24}) devices. Large-scale digitization of all the world's data will occur, with access available on mobile devices. And all this technology and computing power will eventually be less expensive than it is now. Nanotechnology and quantum computing will provide the underlying base for the development of a host of new applications using AI and super-cloud computing. The first generation of quantum computers will likely be available via the super-cloud and geared to specific applications related to large-scale, complex research in areas such as neuroscience, NASA projects, DNA, climate simulations, and machine learning.

Super-Cloud Computing and Education Resources

In 1994, a place called Futuretown was described, where, in the year 2025, people would be served by an all-inclusive Communications and Computer Services Utility (Picciano, 1994). This digital utility would provide all services related to computer, television, communications, and transaction processing, and it would be a one-stop facility for all information and entertainment services. Government, corporate America, hospitals, schools, and colleges would all use this utility for their operations. We have not quite developed this utility, but we are moving in that direction. Services provided by companies such as Optimum and Verizon already integrate data, voice, and video entertainment but do not provide for transaction processing. When this prediction was made in 1994, the internet and the World Wide Web were in the nascent stages of their development. There were few applications available other than file transfer (ftp), email, and electronic messaging. Home access was nonexistent in most parts of the country, and where it was available, users relied on slow-speed dial-up modems. While there were some limited facilities for uploading and downloading images, video was impossible due to these slow-speed connections. This began to change as higher-speed connectivity became available via cable modems, fiber optics, and digital subscriber lines (DSL) in the early 2000s. With the improvement in the speed and quality of connectivity, cloud computing or simply "the cloud" evolved, wherein users relied less on their personal computers for storing files and running programs. Cloud-computing services became readily available through major companies such as Google, Amazon, and Microsoft. Best-selling author Nicholas Carr described cloud providers as having turned data processing into utility operations that "allow vast amounts of information to be collected and processed at centralized plants" and fed into applications running on smartphones and tablets (Carr, 2014, p. 194). Essentially, cloud services can take responsibility for all file handling and storage as well as applications such as email, text messaging, and social networking. It is likely that a cloud-based database establishing a national registry of all citizens in the United States will be created similar to ones in Sweden and several other European countries. A Swedish citizen's complete medical and education information, for instance, is maintained on the national registry database. All Swedish citizens also are assigned a personal identification number (PIN) which is keyed to the national registry database. The PIN is then used for a host of services in medicine, banking, purchasing, and education. With advances in nano and quantum computing technology, cloud computing will expand significantly to the super-cloud and provide the database, communications, and computing capacity needed to perform most daily functions.

On the education front, cloud computing is just beginning to make inroads. While there has been movement to low-cloud applications such as personal email and middle-cloud applications such as course and learning management systems, mission-critical applications such as student or financial database systems are still mostly maintained locally by school districts and colleges (Green, 2015). By the end of the 2020s, it is likely that the super-cloud will have evolved to provide most digital services to all of education. By then, there will be little need for schools and colleges to maintain their own administrative databases or course/learning management systems, and the implications of cloud computing will be significant, especially for instructional course development.

First, students and faculty will be able to access large numbers of courses and course materials developed by other faculty or commercial developers. We are seeing some of this now in the open educational resources (OER) movement, but an efficient and all-inclusive file-sharing system does not presently exist. Most course materials still reside on school- or campus-based computer systems with restricted access. Furthermore, while many faculty customize materials to suit

370 Charles D. Dziuban and Anthony G. Picciano

their own courses, they are not thinking about the convenience that sharing with others would provide.

Second, the MOOC movement allowed for high investment in course development. A single course might cost $1 million or more to develop and to make available to a customer base. At most educational institutions, this type of funding and investment in course development is a rarity, but it is beginning to catch on, usually in partnership with private enterprise. Some of the materials, especially media files, are very well done and are attracting teachers who use them for their own non-MOOC courses. The MOOC courses also integrate state-of-the-art features such as adaptive/personalized learning, learning analytics, and micro assessments.

Third, adaptive learning providers and the MOOC companies before them are setting a standard for high quality course content development that may, in fact, be leading to course standardization. This is especially true for standard high school courses as well as introductory and gateway courses that make up large portions of the college curriculum. If all this course development is moved away from individual developers and instructors and onto computer facilities in the super-cloud, the ease with which faculty and students can access course material will increase tremendously. It is not unfathomable to think that there will be great pressure both inside and outside education to make use of these course materials. Policymakers who seek standards and promote common assessments will have readily accessible material in the super-cloud. Perhaps most importantly, students also will have access to these courses and materials and will be able to develop their own programs of study with or without the guidance of faculty mentors and advisors.

Artificial Intelligence and Adaptive Learning

Learning analytics software is still in its developmental stages but is gaining traction as an important facility for teaching and learning. This software increasingly depends on AI techniques that use algorithms to understand instructional processes. The software also relies on large amounts of "big" data to build a series of decision processes. Significant increases in the speed and storage capabilities of computing devices, possibly through nano- and quantum technology, will also increase the capabilities and accuracy of AI-driven learning analytics software. What is presently known as big data will be small in comparison to the "superbig" data that will be available through quantum computer systems.

AI allows learning analytics to expand in real time to support adaptive and personalized learning applications. For these applications to be successful, data must be collected for each instructional transaction that occurs in an online learning environment. Every question asked, every student response, every answer to every question on a test or other assessment is recorded and analyzed and stored for future reference. Software to grade essays and unstructured written assignments has also been evolving for several years (Markoff, April 4, 2013). While controversial, several states, such as Ohio and Utah, as well as major companies, such as the Education Testing Service and EdX, are moving to "robo-grading" and "e-rating" of essays (Smith, June 30, 2018; Ford, 2015, pp. 130–131). As a result, complete evaluations of individual students as well as entire classes are becoming more common. Alerts and recommendations can be made as instruction proceeds within a lesson, from lesson to lesson, and throughout a course. Students can receive prompts to assist in their learning, and faculty can receive prompts to assist in their teaching. By significantly increasing the speed and amount of data collection through nano- or quantum technology, the accuracy and speed of adaptive or personalized programs will be improved. Faculty will make inquiries about individual students to understand strengths and needs. They will be able to use an "electronic teaching assistant" to determine how instruction is proceeding for individual students and the class as a whole. They will be able to receive suggestions about improving instructional activities. Most AI applications in use today, and for the near future, are narrow in their application and focus on a specific activity. In the years to come, broader-purpose AI will have evolved that will be applied to a variety of activities.

Lee (2018) classifies AI into five technologically sophisticated stages as follows:

1. Internet AI—makes recommendations based on internet activity (i.e., Amazon).
2. Business AI—uses data that companies and other organizations routinely capture for commercial and procedural activities to make predictions (i.e., bank loan approval, insurance fraud, medical prognosis).
3. Perception AI—uses data from the physical world to make predictions using sensors and smart devices (i.e., weather, traffic flow, facial recognition).
4. Autonomous AI—uses all the capabilities of the previous stages plus directs and shapes the world around it (i.e., self-driving cars, assembly line production control).
5. Artificial General Intelligence—AI functions similar to the human brain and can perform any intellectual task.

The first two forms of AI are in evidence today and are utilized in adaptive learning software. The next two forms are still in their early development stages. The fifth, which is the most sophisticated form of AI, is in discussion stages, with some predicting it will be available as early as 2030 and others indicating it will not be perfected until later in the 2040s and beyond. The fact is that there are "no known algorithms for artificial general intelligence or a clear route to get there" (Lee, 2018, p. 142). However, recent advances being made with AI should not be underestimated, especially regarding algorithms that take on characteristics of machines or deep learning. Unlike many earlier forms of AI that depended on hundreds of thousands of lines of code to predict something, new advances enable AI algorithms

372 Charles D. Dziuban and Anthony G. Picciano

to learn from within themselves. Lee (2018) also cautions not to think of the development of AI as simply computer coding but rather as a new form of intellectual "electricity" that will support all forms of personal and commercial endeavors.

Steven Strogatz, professor of mathematics at Cornell University, has raised the possibility that AI has evolved to the point where it has the beginnings of insight. He described AlphaZero, a generic algorithm that mastered chess and Go with absolutely no knowledge of the games beyond their basic rules and, within a matter of hours of playing against itself, had become the best player, human or otherwise, we have ever seen. Here is an excerpt from Strogatz's essay.

> Computer chess has come a long way over the past twenty years. In 1997, I.B.M.'s chess-playing program, Deep Blue, managed to beat the reigning human world champion, Garry Kasparov, in a six-game match. In retrospect, there was little mystery in this achievement. Deep Blue could evaluate 200 million positions per second. It never got tired, never blundered in a calculation and never forgot what it had been thinking a moment earlier. For better and worse, it played like a machine, brutally and materialistically. It could out-compute Mr. Kasparov, but it couldn't outthink him. . . .
>
> These principles, which have been refined over decades of human grandmaster experience, are programmed into the engines as complex evaluation functions that indicate what to seek in a position and what to avoid: how much to value king safety, piece activity, pawn structure, control of the center, and more, and how to balance the trade-offs among them. Today's chess engines, innately oblivious to these principles, come across as brutes: tremendously fast and strong, but utterly lacking insight.
>
> All of that has changed with the rise of machine learning. By playing against itself and updating its neural network as it learned from experience, AlphaZero discovered the principles of chess on its own and quickly became the best player ever. Not only could it have easily defeated all the strongest human masters—it didn't even bother to try—it crushed Stockfish, the reigning computer world champion of chess. In a hundred-game match against a truly formidable engine, AlphaZero scored twenty-eight wins and seventy-two draws. It didn't lose a single game.
>
> Most unnerving was that AlphaZero seemed to express insight. It played like no computer ever has, intuitively and beautifully, with a romantic, attacking style. It played gambits and took risks. . . .
>
> AlphaZero won by thinking smarter, not faster; it examined only 60 thousand positions a second, compared to 60 million for Stockfish. It was wiser, knowing what to think about and what to ignore. By discovering the principles of chess on its own, AlphaZero developed a style of play that "reflects the truth" about the game rather than "the priorities and prejudices of programmers."
>
> *(Strogatz, December 28, 2018)*

Adaptive learning and analytics are already being significantly integrated with internet and business AI. The integration of learning analytics is greatly enhanced based on student responses to prompts, questions, and quizzes and, increasingly, on less-structured assessments such as essay writing. Combining these with the ongoing collection of student demographic, academic performance, and other information provides an extensive learning analytics database on which students and faculty can depend for recommendations as they proceed through a course of study. Over the next decade or so, the software supporting these types of applications will grow in sophistication, especially when integrated with super-cloud data depositories that will expand academic programs, curriculum, and course work beyond individual schools and colleges. In the 2030s and beyond, AI-based adaptive learning will come to dominate much of the instruction in all of education.

The pedagogical models being used in online education today range widely. Highly interactive models (teacher-student, student-student, student-course material) are very popular. Asynchronous (blogs, discussion boards, wikis) as well as synchronous communications (video and voice conferencing) are common. Furthermore, faculty and instructional designers integrate and blend these models to provide a variety of course activities. These models remain highly dependent on teachers to guide, direct, and facilitate instruction. They generally are not more cost efficient than traditional face-to-face instruction unless full-time teachers are replaced by contingent faculty and tutors. Recently, adaptive or personalized learning that combines programmed instruction and learning analytics is expanding and receiving a good deal of attention. Adaptive learning takes advantage of learning analytics and rudimentary AI software to monitor student progress and performance very closely and is consequently able to provide timely adjustments to the presentation of instructional material. Adaptive learning systems are also customized to the personal needs of each individual student, which is why they are frequently referred to as personalized learning systems. As described by the EDUCAUSE Learning Initiative:

> Adaptive learning is one technique for providing personalized learning, which aims to provide efficient, effective, and customized learning paths to engage each student. Adaptive learning systems use a data-driven— and, in some cases, nonlinear—approach to instruction and remediation. They dynamically adjust to student interactions and performance levels, delivering the types of content in an appropriate sequence that individual learners need at specific points in time to make progress. These systems employ algorithms, assessments, student feedback, instructor adjust-ments/interventions, and various media to deliver new learning material to students who have achieved mastery and remediation to those who have not.
>
> *(Dziuban et al., 2017)*

It should also be mentioned that adaptive learning is not brand new but can be traced back to the CAI (computer-assisted instruction) work of B.F. Skinner and Patrick Suppes in the 1950s and 1960s. However, the technology back then was very rudimentary compared to high-speed internet communications and advanced multimedia that can be delivered to homes, to businesses, and on mobile devices today.

Depending on the course design, adaptive learning can minimize the amount of interaction between the teacher and student and instead allow the software to deliver and monitor much of the course content. Learning analytics software monitors student progress and controls the pace of content delivery accordingly. Increasingly adaptive technology minimizes the faculty role in teaching and instead expands their role as tutor. The "faculty as tutor" model has been evolving as online learning has become more prevalent. Colleges with extensive experience in fully online academic programs such as Athabasca University, the University of Phoenix, and Western Governors University have promoted a model in which a master teacher administers a fixed curriculum while contingent faculty serve as guides and tutors for students. Adaptive learning programs for advanced placement and credit-recovery courses in high schools also commonly use the "teacher as tutor" model. Contingent faculty and tutors have little discretion to modify or customize the curriculum or syllabus and follow a carefully developed script. In an adaptive course, all content, assignments, and assessments are delivered by the software. The adaptive model will become more prevalent in the future and may even come to dominate much of education because of its cost-effectiveness rather than its pedagogical value. Early research does suggest, however, that student learning outcomes are comparable to other formats (Dziuban et al., 2016, 2018).

Of all the online learning models, the adaptive learning model has become the focus of a good deal of investment by corporate America and venture capital. Educational software companies such as Knewton that develop adaptive learning are raising tens of millions of investment dollars to develop new products (Wan, 2018). Knewton has partnered with Pearson and textbook companies to provide a wide range of courses and course development materials for use in higher education. The same is true at the PreK–12 level, where organizations such as APEX, ALEKS, and the Florida Virtual School offer a range of adaptive learning courses. This type of investment is not common in most traditional PreK–12 schools and colleges. To the contrary, the development of online course materials relies heavily on school-based faculty and instructional designers, many of whom have modest resources at their disposal. Eventually, the well-financed, private adaptive course developers will likely win out. While adaptive learning integrated with learning analytics is in its early stages, it will continue over the next decade to change the way most teaching and learning is conducted in education.

Enter COVID-19

COVID-19 has added an entire new dimension to the technological evolution in all aspects of our society, including education. In Spring 2020, over 90% of all courses offered in PreK–12 or postsecondary education had an online component. Faculty in all sectors converted their courses as quickly as they could to remote learning. It was a clear emergency with their own and their students' health at risk. In essence, online technology saved the semester for the education sector (Ubell, 2020). Many faculty who had never used online education or had used it modestly came to depend on it for instruction. Synchronous online communication using Zoom and other videoconferencing software became especially popular. It is likely that many faculty will continue to use online facilities in the future when the COVID-19 pandemic is over. Blended learning models especially will become more popular. At the time of this writing, it is unclear what will happen in Fall 2020 and Spring 2021, but the sense is that schools and colleges, if not already deciding to move to online instruction in some form, are developing backup plans to do so if need be should a second wave of COVID-19 develop. It is also likely that many colleges and universities will decide to operate as fully online institutions at least through Fall 2020. For example, the country's largest university system, California State University, announced that all classes would be held online in 2020–2021 (White, 2020). Other colleges and universities had already decided to move a number of their academic programs online for the foreseeable future (Kelderman, 2020).

Further Implications for the Future of Education

With the evolving technological landscape defined, it is possible to speculate how education will be broadly affected. PreK–12, which includes early childhood through secondary education, which is structurally different than higher education, will be treated separately here.

PreK–12 Education

PreK–12 education enrolls 57 million students, the vast majority of whom attend public schools governed by 13,000-plus local school districts and state bodies that provide the vast majority of funding. Approximately 11% of the students enrolled in PreK–12 education attend private schools or charter schools or are home-schooled. There are major differences among the localities and states in terms of policymaking, funding, and education requirements. Despite the advent of the "Common Core" curriculum in the past decade and a half, local school boards and states have a great deal of autonomy and develop their schools as they wish. Because PreK–12 entails such a long span of education (fifteen years from early childhood to the end of high school), issues and solutions related to the use of technology will vary depending on grade level and age of students.

In the early childhood through primary grades, schools serve a number of functions beyond instruction. Nurturing, socialization, and emotional development are as important as learning basic skills. In middle and high school, maturation and postsecondary career and education goals figure prominently into the overall education experience. Furthermore, schools are very much needed to provide safe havens for children in households where parents work. Public schools also accept all students and must be prepared to provide support and services based on a host of needs. Students who are impoverished, who do not get enough to eat, or who do not receive proper medical and health care need a community support group that a school can provide. For them, technology may be less important. Furthermore, much of the technology discussed earlier in this chapter focuses on the instructional, not the non-instructional, functions. In fact, during the coronavirus pandemic and the move to remote learning, it became clear that millions of students in inner cities as well as rural America did not own computers, and even if they did, Wi-Fi services were not always available or were very limited. Regardless, technology will play an increasing role in PreK–12 education in the years to come. Here is one possible scenario.

In 2011, Chromebooks that ran Google software for a number of applications were introduced. Schools saw Chromebooks as an inexpensive alternative to high-end tabletop and laptop computers. When Google Classroom applications were made available in 2014, PreK–12 education gravitated to Chromebooks in a major way. It is estimated that 60% of the computer devices now purchased for student use in PreK–12 schools are Chromebooks running Google Classroom. It needs to be noted that Chromebooks/Google Classroom provides mostly ancillary services, including textbook and other content materials, assignment development, tutoring, grading, and general student and teacher recordkeeping. These ancillary services have streamlined and improved communication among teachers, students, parents, and administrators and have resulted in savings, especially by providing less expensive and easily updated textbooks. Today, in 2020, Chromebooks are not used extensively to deliver courses as is typical in distance education. Google has not developed software that focuses on course delivery and instead relies on other companies to do so; however, it is likely that in the future, this will change. Adaptive or personalized learning providers will enter into agreements with Google to deliver customized courses on the Chromebook/Google Classroom platform. While some of this is already happening, over the next decade, this activity will expand significantly, especially as computer hardware advances in terms of speed and capacity and as super-cloud services become more common. This development will be most pronounced in middle school and high school, where course content focuses on specific subject matter. Basic courses in history, science, language arts, etc. will become standardized, and the Chromebook/Google Classroom platform, a tablet, or something similar

Education and Blended Learning **377**

will be the main delivery mechanism. Teacher education programs will adjust their curricula to ensure that future teachers are well trained for this environment. In fact, teachers will be trained to use this software as the main delivery vehicle for instruction in a blended learning environment as they themselves take on an enhanced tutoring support role. They will let the software diagnose learning issues and prescribe possible solutions, while they follow up to see how the students are responding and then offer additional support. For the longer term, technology in PreK–12 in the 2030s and beyond will take on a lot of the characteristics described in the next section on higher education. In fact, it is likely that many states will look at education structurally as a PreK–20 operation.

Higher Education

There are approximately 4,300 degree-granting postsecondary institutions in the United States, registering almost 18 million students. These institutions vary significantly in purpose, size, and funding sources, as noted by the Carnegie Commission on Higher Education, which lists over 30 classifications (see https://carnegieclassifications.iu.edu/classification_descriptions/basic.php). The United States Department of Education generally displays its data on postsecondary students as attending graduate, undergraduate baccalaureate, undergraduate associate, public, non-profit, and for-profit schools. Regardless of classification, all of higher education will be affected by the evolution of technology as described earlier. However, some colleges, such as for-profit institutions, may aggressively adopt the new technology more readily than others. Non-profit tuition-driven institutions may be forced to do so because of financial need and survival, while public university systems will use the technology to serve their large numbers of students. The critical question is how will the academy adapt?

Joseph E. Aoun is the president of Northeastern University and author of *Robot Proof, Higher Education in the Age of Artificial Intelligence*, in which he looks at the future of higher education and the changes that will occur as a result of digital technology and especially AI. While acknowledging American colleges and universities as among the fullest expressions of human culture ever evolved and perhaps the most effective institutions for intellectual advancement ever developed, he cautions that if they fail to respond creatively and deliberately to the technological challenges that they face, "they will wither into irrelevance" (Aoun, 2017, p. 12). In considering a future dominated by advanced technologies, educators should seek to integrate technology into a comprehensive plan that addresses other major issues that they will be facing in the not-too-distant future.

The late Clayton Christensen, Harvard Business School professor and author of *The Innovator's Dilemma*, during a speech at a higher education summit in 2017, spoke at length about disruption theory and discussed its application to colleges and universities. Higher education, he explained, was among the industries that "for several centuries was not disrupted," but "online learning has put a kink in

378 Charles D. Dziuban and Anthony G. Picciano

that" (Lederman, April 28, 2017, para. 5). He predicted that half of American universities would close or go bankrupt within 10 to 15 years. He went on to say that: "Technology itself is never the disruptor, a new business model is. But it is technology that enables the new business model to coalesce, and that's what is happening in higher education now" (Lederman, April 28, 2017, para. 6).

Drew Faust, the former president of Harvard University, in a message to the World Economic Forum in 2015, described three major forces that will shape the future of higher education:

1. the influence of technology
2. the changing shape of knowledge
3. the attempt to define the value of education

She went on to extol the facilities that digital technology and communications will provide for teaching, learning, and research. She foresees great benefits in technology's ability to reach masses of students around the globe and to quantify easily large databases for scaling-up and assessment purposes. On the other hand, she made it clear that "residential education cannot be replicated online" and stressed the importance of physical interaction and shared experiences (Picciano, 2017, p. 180).

On the nature of knowledge, she stated that the common organization of universities by academic departments may disappear because "the most significant and consequential challenges humanity faces" require investigations and solutions that are flexible and not necessarily discipline specific (Picciano, 2017, p. 180). Doctors, chemists, social scientists, and engineers will work together to solve humankind's problems.

On defining value, she notes that quantitative metrics are now evolving that can assess and demonstrate the importance of meaningful employment. She believes that higher education as well provides something very valuable: it gives people "a perspective on the meaning and purpose of their lives" and furthermore, it is not possible to quantify this type of outcome. She concluded that:

> So much of what humanity has achieved has been sparked and sustained by the research and teaching that take place every day at colleges and universities, sites of curiosity and creativity that nurture some of the finest aspirations of individuals and, in turn, improve their lives—and their livelihoods. As the landscape continues to change, we must be careful to protect the ideals at the heart of higher education, ideals that serve us all well as we work together to improve the world.
>
> *(Faust, 2015)*

While Faust presented three key elements in higher education's future, it is the interplay of these elements that will become most crucial in predicting its future.

Will technology drive the shape of knowledge and the definition of value, or will it be the other way around? Techno-centrists see technology as the driver while others who look at higher education holistically see technology as a tool serving the needs of the other elements.

Aoun, Christensen, and Faust are all respected and accomplished individuals in American higher education. In each of their predictions of the future is a role for technology to play. Aoun and Christensen have concerns about whether and if higher education can adjust and adapt to a new world order dominated by technology. Faust holds out hope that colleges will adjust and continue to function and "protect the ideals that have served us well." Most of those in higher education, and especially the faculty, like to think that Faust has it right. There will be adjustment and accommodation, and the academy will go on. However, there are dark clouds on the horizon, driven especially by financial realities as well as technological and economic competition. In addition, the academy is squarely in the crosshairs of political factions in this country and is seen as a bastion of liberal philosophy that needs to be reined in. While there is support from progressive-minded government policymakers, there is opposition from the other side of the political spectrum, where funding contraction is already in evidence.

In the United States during the past 20 years, there has been a loud, sustained call for more accountability and assessment as policymakers and the public question whether colleges and universities are as effective as they should be. The nonprofit public higher education sector, where the majority of American college students are enrolled, has seen a significant shift in funding away from government subsidy to student tuition. Contingent faculty, especially lower-paid adjuncts, now teach the majority of all postsecondary courses. It is not by accident that public higher education systems have emerged as among the most prolific in developing online education programs. They were moved to do so in order to meet student demand and also because of increasing competition from the other sectors, especially the for-profit institutions. Increasing enrollments and stagnant state government subsidies also moved many public systems to adopt online instructional technology in hopes of stabilizing costs, especially for capital and campus-building projects. In the 2020s, practically all segments of higher education (nonprofit, private, public, and for-profit) have embraced online technology as critical to their academic programs. However, what has been accomplished to date may not be enough to sustain what is coming in the years ahead. We are already seeing closures, mergers, and consolidations like never before.

The United States Education Department's National Center for Education Statistics shows that the number of colleges and universities eligible to award federal financial aid reached its peak in 2012 with 7,416 institutions. Due to closures, mergers, and consolidations, the number had declined to 6,760, or by 9%, by 2016. The vast majority of colleges that closed were in the for-profit private sector (Lederman, July 19, 2017). However, during the past several years, the nonprofit private sector and the public sector have also seen a significant number of closures. Since 2016, 170 colleges have announced closures, mergers, or consolidations. Of these, 71 were private for-profit; 63 were private nonprofit; and 36 were public colleges (Education Dive Staff, January 29, 2019). Most of the private nonprofits were small liberal arts colleges and were tuition driven, with modest endowments. The publics were mostly in the states of Georgia, Wisconsin, and Connecticut, where major restructuring of public higher education has been underway. In Wisconsin, for instance, all 13 community colleges were restructured as extension centers under the auspices of the Wisconsin system's senior colleges. In Connecticut, all 12 community colleges are in the process of being consolidated into one institution. These changes were made strictly because of existing financial exigencies. The future does not look brighter, and more governing boards in all higher education sectors will be facing serious financial pressures. Closures will be more common, and those colleges and universities that continue will have to find more cost-efficient ways of offering an education. At the time of this writing, there was great concern that the coronavirus pandemic of 2020 would accelerate the closure of many postsecondary institutions. Policymakers will look to technology to effect savings in all aspects of the higher education enterprise, including instruction, advising, counseling, administrative services, and research. It is also likely that some colleges and universities, especially those that are publicly funded, will grow significantly in terms of enrollment. An institution such as the University of Southern New Hampshire, which grew from 8,000 students in 2008 to over 122,000 by 2018 by adopting a new online education technology model, is being closely watched by educational policymakers in other states (Blumenstyk, 2018).

The critical questions to be answered by the academy are how to adapt to and address the new technologies. Full-time faculty will likely see their ranks reduced. Those who primarily teach in colleges and universities may have to adjust to a tutor role rather than developing and teaching their own content via their own pedagogical practices. Students may increasingly be allowed to select off-the-shelf courses, perhaps developed at another college, university, or private supplier. Faculty researchers may be engaged in very large-scale projects that involve multiple partners in the academy and in private industry. It is also possible that the lead researchers may be algorithms in an AI laboratory. The comments of Mohammed AlQuraishi, the biologist who, at the beginning of this chapter, had a feeling of melancholy when he saw an AI application sweep away the competition in the Critical Assessment of Structure Prediction Competition, may portend the feelings of many teaching and research faculty. Other aspects of the academy likewise will be affected by AI. Library holdings will be moved to all-electronic access, with AI speeding searches for materials and delivering same within minutes on mobile devices. Academic advisors and counselors will see their roles reduced to offering assistance only in deeply personal situations, where the human side of their work is most important. All academic advisement regarding course requirements, majors, and careers will be done via AI applications.

Administrative functions will be consolidated and centralized with super-cloud services for admissions, registration, financial aid, bursar, and purchasing. Large public university systems will see many of these services centralized and the need for presidential, vice presidential, and other administrative operations at the local campus level will be significantly reduced. The question is whether higher education can adjust to and accommodate the new world order, where technology will provide foundational services. Many educators will feel a loss of purpose in light of the fact that their expertise will be overshadowed by AI software. Younger and newer educators will take their places, accept the new order, and work within it to make it successful, but the period of transition will be tense if not painful. Educators will have no choice but to come to see technology as a primary partner in the higher education enterprise, as have counterparts in private industry (McAfee & Brynjolfsson, 2017, p. 15). As Auon, Christensen, and Faust alluded to earlier, the issue is not just that the technology changes but how people change in response to the technology. This will be higher education's challenge over the next decade and beyond.

It would be easy to dismiss negative speculation as just "crying wolf" and assume that our colleges and universities will come to weather any possible storm well. We hope that this will be the case, but it is not likely. Much of higher education, with the exception of the heavily endowed colleges, is in difficult financial times; closures, mergers, and consolidations are already happening. It is difficult to see how we will move gracefully beyond the financial exigencies already in evidence. The federal government is the one institution that might be able to ease this situation, but its debt has grown considerably in the past five years, and there does not appear to be the political wherewithal to address it. It is unlikely that the federal government will come to the rescue of higher education, especially since there will be competition from other government services such as health and social welfare. Unemployment will permeate many economic sectors. Due to the coronavirus pandemic, over 40 million Americans, or 25% of the workforce, was unemployed in the spring of 2020. In the AI arena, there will be severe competition between the United States and the People's Republic of China for dominance. Right now, seven companies are making the greatest investments in AI development (Lee, 2018, p. 91). Four (Google, Amazon, Microsoft, and Facebook) are based in this country, and three (Baidu, Alibaba, and Tencent) are based in China. The Chinese government is pouring huge amounts of capital into developing its AI capabilities and will very possibly take the lead in this area. Higher education will be directed if not forced to respond to this AI challenge. It might be beneficial for administrators, faculty, and researchers to consider how they might partner with centers of AI and adaptive learning that exist in the corporate sector (Dziuban et al., 2017). Technology companies are proliferating and generally welcome collaborators for their products and services. This was the conclusion that the biologist and chemist reached in the DeepMind vignette that opened this chapter.

Concluding Word on the Future of Education

A few years ago, a young associate professor approached us after we had given a talk about online education. Our discussion centered on the future of higher education, and she asked if we thought that in ten years she would be out of a job. Our answer to her was that she would not be displaced anytime soon, but that the way she teaches would change. We stand by that comment. Educators must be alert to new technologies, adjust to change, and adopt those that may benefit their students. These changes are best implemented through carefully planned and developed projects, programs, and initiatives, rather than by disruptive sudden upheavals. It is critical that colleges and universities be open to changing and adapting. Higher education must use technologies that are beneficial, question those that are not, but most importantly not ignore them. In addition, it would be wise for the academy to partner with those private companies that can bring financial resources and expertise to the issues that AI will usher in. The challenges are formidable. Joseph Aoun commented: "If technology can replace human beings on the job, it will. Preventing business owners from adopting a labor-saving technology would require modifying the basic incentives built into the market economy" (Aoun, 2017, p. 46).

The Future of Life Institute (2015) initiated an open letter entitled Research Priorities for Robust and Beneficial Artificial Intelligence expressing the same concerns about AI development as voiced by Aoun and others. The open letter was signed by Stephen Hawking, Elon Musk (founder of SpaceX and Tesla Motors), Steve Wozniak, (co-founder of Apple), and many of the world's top computer scientists. It also called for more dialogue among all parties involved with AI development. Their concerns should reflect the concerns of humanity over our ability to control the advancements of AI.

The future of education as laid out in the earlier paragraphs is speculation based on evolving trends in technology and how it is be used in our schools, colleges, and universities, but it is likely that something like that described here will, in fact, be the reality. In the final analysis, it may not be a question of whether all this will happen, but when. As we get from here to there, an incredibly fertile ground for research will evolve.

Blended Learning Research: The Forking Path

So far, we have addressed the potential impact of rapidly advancing global, political, economic, policy, and technology issues on the educational landscape—ones that will be inextricably connected to blended learning research. Often, however, those predictions are hampered by our tendency to overlook the past (Diamond, 2005; Banyan, 2020; Battersby, 2017), failing to recognize shifting baselines (Roberts, 2010; Soga & Gaston, 2018), and developing what Diamond (1997) termed *landscape amnesia* (Schneider et al., 2013). That is, slipping into the assumption that the way things are now should be the baseline reference point. Consider this from Roberts in his book *The Unnatural History of the Sea* (Roberts, 2010):

> A collective amnesia surrounds changes that happened more than a few decades ago, as hardly anyone reads old books or reports. People also place most trust in what they have seen for themselves, which often leads them to dismiss as far-fetched tales of giant fish or seas bursting with life from the distant, or even the recent past.
>
> *(p. 15)*

William Faulkner was credited with saying the past is current, and we should pay attention to it. However, like any proposition, there is always another side to the story. Consider this statement form Stephen Jay Gould (1996): "Most scientists don't care a fig for history. . . . [T]hey regard the past as a mere repository of error—at best a source of moral instruction in pitfalls along the paths to progress" (p. 25).

As we think about the future of blended learning research, remember that rarely will there be unanimous or even majority acceptance of the results we report or conclusions we espouse. Dialogue and disagreement fuel genuine progress. Therefore, projected futures are littered with the rhetoric of change, in which one side sees great potential while the other envisions impending disaster. For example, in the not-too-distant past, the argument about Wikipedia raged, with one cohort extoling the democratization of information and another forewarning the complete demise of information retrieval skills. Like so many others, that tumult has gone quiet.

Historical insights (DeMichele, 2020; B. Alexander, 2020; Hurston, 2018; Isenberg, 2017; Lepore, 2018; Rubenstein, 2019; Wilkerson, 2011; Momaday, 2018) should be integrated into our thinking because they become alternative and sometimes counter explanations for how we got to now (Johnson, 2015). The analogy in scientific research is that baseline data are imperative for measuring change. In order to determine what progress has been made or where an initiative such as blended learning might be going, a pre-assessment of status is necessary. When physicians assess health parameters, not only do they determine if a patient's values are in the nominal range; he or she also indexes the rate of change in that telemetry as well. This is true in education, engineering, psychological measurement, biology, physics, chemistry, and many other disciplines.

Clearly, we are experiencing a seismic shift in our thinking about how to best assess the impact of our teaching and learning in virtually all contexts (Otte, 2016). That change resonates with Thomas Khun's book *The Structure of Scientific Revolutions* (Kuhn, 2012), which exerted monumental influence on research by coining the term *paradigm shift*, which happens when what we assumed to be correct no longer explains the anomalies we observe. Presently, we are coming to terms with the fact that many of our assumptions about teaching and learning have not held up well to the test of time. Thaler (2015) reports that he spent several years writing a column entitled "Anomalies" for the *Journal of Economic Perspectives*. Just like disagreements, anomalies fuel progress in fits and starts. Hacking (2012), in writing the introduction for the 50th anniversary edition of *The Structure*, quotes Khun's opening sentence: "History if viewed as repository for more than anecdote or chronology, could produce a decisive transformation in the image of science by which we are now possessed" (p. viii).

In this world of "light speed" technological change, that sentence is even more relevant than when it was originally published.

How, then, can we make meaningful projections for effective blended learning research? Is there a protocol? Steven Johnson, in his book *Where Good Ideas Come From* (2011), provides one possibility. He cites the biologist Stuart Kaufman's notion of the adjacent possible—that is, the next reasonable step (Johnson, 2010). He describes that the possible as located right at the boundary of what is presently known, making meaningful transition attainable (Smith, 2010). The giant transformational leaps for which we yearn seem to happen rarely but develop in slow, faltering, but steady steps, much like the tortoise defeating the hare. Unfortunately, however, the adjacent possible is not as easily identifiable as we might imagine. Consider this from Robin Sloan (2012), when the protagonist, Clay, is asked to identify the adjacent possible:

> Okay: "World government . . . no cancer . . . hover-boards."
> "Go further. What's the good future after that?"
> "Spaceships. Party on Mars."
> "Further."
> "*Star Trek*. Transporters. You can go anywhere."
> "Further."
> I pause a moment, then realize: "I can't."
> We probably just imagine things based on what we already know, and we run out of analogies . . .
>
> *(p. 60)*

Given these considerations, our attempts at prediction for the future of blended learning and the research that will inform it must be considered speculation or, at best, a guess. We cannot know with certainty, but we know from decades of history that the majority of those projections will be wrong and either be discarded or modified to explain the anomalies. The only validity we can claim in this chapter is what was there at the beginning, through the good times and the bad times, and that we are here now. We have watched blended learning grow into an international phenomenon and, in some small measure, contributed to its development. Based on that history, we offer some considerations we believe will impact blended learning research in the future.

Complexity

Advancing technologies place blended learning into an increasingly complex situation. That complexity impacts research design, data analysis and interpretation at many levels. Several years ago, Jay Forrester (1961) presented a set of ground rules for operating in a complex system that have stood the test of time:

1. One can never really predict how an intervention will ripple through a complex system (Haimes, 2017; Hilpert & Marchand, 2018; O'Neil, 2017).
2. Often the outcomes will be counterintuitive (Eubanks, 2018; Haimes, 2017; Hilpert & Marchand, 2018).
3. There will always be unanticipated negative and positive side effects (Grosz, 2014; Haimes, 2017; Hilpert & Marchand, 2018).

At the time this chapter is being written (June 2020), those rules seem particularly relevant because of the COVID pandemic and the racial unrest in the United States. Perhaps both could have been predicted and possibly avoided, but they were not; therefore, we are dealing with complexities the resolution of which is much more formidable than it might have been. Taleb (2007) most likely would not call either one of those black swans—completely unpredictable—but they both show the telltale signs of retroactive explanation posited in his theory (Avishaie, 2020). That is, we developed a backfilled narrative demonstrating how the occurrence was entirely predictable. As Duncan Watts says: "Everything is Obvious Once You Know the Answer" (Watts, 2011). The reason for these missteps is due in part to an overriding characteristic of a complexity—*emergence*—meaning that the final outcomes and configuration of the system transcends the sum of its individual parts. Taleb (2018) explains it this way:

> The main idea behind complex systems is that the ensemble behaves in ways not predicted by its components. The interactions matter more than the nature of the units. Studying individual ants will almost never give us a clear indication of how an ant colony operates. For that, one needs to understand an ant colony as an ant colony, no less, no more, not a collection of ants. This is called the emergent property of the system, by which the parts and whole differ because what matters are the interactions between such parts.
>
> *(p. 69)*

Certainly, this characterizes the blended learning that responds to widely differing learning contexts interacting with the technologies and societal changes mentioned in this chapter. Understanding learning is complicated enough, but stir in the technology and society, and the situation becomes even more dynamic.

For example, each year, many scientific journals such as the *Scientific American* and the *MIT Technology Review* publish a list of the most influential technologies. The evolution is so rapid that hardly any of those technologies remain on the list from one year to the next. In conducting research, we need to understand blended learning as blended learning, not as the combination of the individual elements in its formulation. The interactions are far more important than the elements themselves. One example of this emergent thinking comes from factor analytic work, in which investigators examine some weighted combination of variables and develop a unifying construct for a particular dimension. That construct is emergent because it transcends the individual variables and encompasses them in their emergent configuration. This presents an alternative approach to meaningful research that places much more responsibility on investigators to curate their data and interpret their findings in contextually relevant ways, breaking away from what Rosling (2018) identified as the gap instinct—dividing results into two distinct categories (significant or not, for instance) and assuming that there is meaningful separation between them. Treating blended learning as a treatment effect in course mode comparison studies raises the issue of its emergent property or, more likely, its emergent properties (Dziuban et al., 2020). Blended learning carries with it other characteristics as well—diversity, for example. Page (2011) contends that diversity makes complex systems such as blended learning more robust, improving their ability to maintain functionality. He offers the example that when Europeans chose to import potatoes from South America, they primarily selected two varieties that were genetically similar. This lack of diversity fell prey to the blight parasites, whereas increased diversity could have prevented much of the problem with more resistant strains. Diversity underlies all aspects of blended learning and is evident within student types, across student types, and across student cohorts. All three variation forms impact blended research. Instructors with a modicum of experience understand the student variation within a class, across classes of the same subject, and across variant student cohorts.

The question becomes how we reframe our thinking to achieve some understanding of blended learning and not just tick off its elements. To approach this, consider adaptive learning, one of the technologies cited earlier in the chapter. This approach customizes individual student learning trajectories, depending on their baseline position and progression through the course content. No pun intended, but this process blends very nicely with the principals of blended learning because it can be tailored to individuals, then reinforced in face-to-face or other formats. A number of adaptive platforms generate large suites of real-time outcome measures. This is a tremendous resource because instructors are able to monitor not only student progress but also the rate and change of that progress. These platforms support dynamic feedback loops that can make learning autocatalytic. Complexity, diversity, and adaptiveness underlie blended learning so that it has evolved to become increasingly more important to an educational system. There are many blended learnings. They are in a state of constant change,

Education and Blended Learning **387**

responding to rapidly developing educational contexts. Researchers would be better served to stop thinking of the blended learning modality as some kind of treatment and making comparisons to other formats, such as face to face and online, avoiding the "no significant difference" studies that have not held up well (Russell, 1999). Blended learning research might be better reframed as:

1. Searching for prototypes—Finding the best example of the blended learning construct. Prototype theory suggest that there is a consensus basic-level category to which people gravitate as the most representative of objects or groups. For instance, in generational research, we portray prototype millennials in a certain specific way—the basic level. However, many who belong in this category are not a precise fit to the prototype. That doesn't mean they don't belong, but rather, they reflect the diversity within it. Prototypes are necessary for any classification research. This resonates with Kahneman's prospect theory, in which people who make decisions under risk conditions tend to use neutral reference points corresponding to basic levels (Kahneman, 2011; Lockhart et al., 2017; Margolis et al., 2017; Rosch, 1983).

2. A boundary object—Determining how blended learning holds a community of practice together and how it emerges in individual constituencies is a component of blended learning. The formation and maintenance of boundary objects is an important factor in establishing coherence in a communication network. Blended learning experiences multiple unique but complementary definitions, making it a prototype boundary object impacting how we conduct our research (Bowker & Star, 2000; Dziuban et al., 2020; Lockhart et al., 2017; Margolis et al., 2017).

3. An idealized cognitive model—Identifying what components of blended learning presumed conceived and necessary for the modality to be viable, whether they are observable or not. Idealized cognitive models are necessary for developing a working theory. Kahneman proposes two aspects of the mind—intuitive and analytic. Those two categories do not exist naturally (Kahneman, 2011). They are idealized cognitive models that he needs to develop his construct of human thought processes. Is it possible that blended learning is an idealized cognitive model? (Lakoff, 1987; Lockhart et al., 2017; Margolis et al., 2017).

Because of this, our approach to research must become emergent as well. The question of whether it is effective or not should yield to identifying which blends respond best to which learning contexts. The studies in this book confirm that contention. Blended learning research must be much more opportunistic. However, that opportunity hinges on what Setenyi (1995) defines as our inability to accumulate enough information to make conclusive decisions. Cornett (1996) formalized the notion as uncertain mediation-there is never enough data to be absolutely sure. No matter how efficient and sophisticated research becomes, it

388 Charles D. Dziuban and Anthony G. Picciano

will always demand human intervention and considered judgement if it is to have any meaningful impact on the blended learning phenomenon. Silver (2012) put it this way:

> The numbers have no way of speaking for themselves. We speak for them.
>
> *(p. 9)*

> The key to making a good forecast is not limiting yourself to quantitative information. Instead it means having a good process for weighing the information appropriately.
>
> *(p. 100)*

Reasonable findings in blended learning research likely lie in a set of if-then contingencies couched in an estimate of the chances of being wrong. Therefore, as investigators, our responsibilities have increased by an order of magnitude. But that responsibility presents us with many opportunities for our research to become much more contextual, authentic, and reflective.

The p Value

Traditionally, statistical hypothesis tests have been used to determine if research findings could be generalized beyond a particular study because the true values in populations (parameters) were unknown; investigators had to draw samples and make an estimate from them (statistics). Statistics estimate parameters; the sample mean estimates the population mean. Good samples provide accurate estimates, and biased samples are inaccurate. The dilemma in statistical research is that if the investigator knew the population value, he or she could tell immediately if the sample estimate was accurate. The Catch-22 (Heller, 1961), however, is that if the population values were known, there would be no need for the sample. Because those population values are not known, however, we endured all those statistics courses. In those classes, we learned how to do hypothesis tests by calculating sample statistics, then comparing them to predetermined percentile points in sampling distributions (we remember t, chi square and F tables)—at least the older ones in the crowd do. That procedure—a calculated value compared to the tabled one—was a test of the null (no difference) hypothesis, usually at the .05 or .01 level. What you were doing was calculating the probability, getting the sample value you had in hand if there was no difference in the population. In terms of the classic, two groups mean a comparison: How likely is the mean difference in my sample when there is no difference in the population? Investigators have been doing this for decades, with statistical significance being an important decision rule for program evaluation, funding, scientific journal publication, and, at the moment of this chapter, will be for vaccine research. However, the issues associated with these methods have not gone unnoticed by the scientific community (White et al., 2014; Van Calster et al., 2018).

Walster and Cleary (1970) demonstrated that statistical hypothesis rejection is a function of some significance level (e.g. .05 or .01), sample size, and some degree of non-nullity, a mean difference in the sample size. They demonstrated that if any two of those are selected, the third one is automatically determined. Further, they argued that most investigators arbitrarily pick .05 or .01 and collect the largest samples they can accumulate. By doing so, they lose control of how large a mean difference will be significant. They contended that if statistical significance was to be used as an effective decision rule, the investigator should make a prior judgment (emphasize judgment) about how large a difference would cause them to take action (or not), then work back to determine significance level and sample size. The sample size acts like the lens in a microscope; the more powerful the lens, the larger the object under it appears. This demonstrates the somewhat arbitrary nature of the process. The larger your sample size, the more likely you are likely to reject the null hypothesis. To demonstrate this, we encourage our readers to try a thought experiment. Google any site that does a two group mean difference test. Give one group a mean of 100 and the other a mean of 102. Select equal standard deviations of your choice. Then begin running the test with a sample size of five in each group, steadily increasing it. At first, there will be no significant differences until the sample size gets large enough to make the opposite decision. Same mean difference in each case, same standard deviation, but sample size determines whether the identical mean difference is significant or not. There should be no surprise then that many scholars have objected to this process. Thompson (1996, 2004) noted that the criticism of significance testing is long lived and suggested a series of needed reforms that would improve the research process. In his 2004 critique, he quoted Rozeboom (1997):

> Null-hypothesis significance testing is surely the most bone-headedly misguided procedure ever institutionalized in the rote training of science students. . . . It is a sociology—of—science wonderment that this statistical practice has remained so unresponsive to criticism.
>
> *(p. 335)*

This adamant statement has been supported by a number of scientists over the years. Recently, McShane et al. (2019), in their paper entitled "Abandon Statistical Significance," recommended that significance levels (p value) should not be the initial threshold consideration for the quality of research. They argued that statistical results should be considered in concert with many other factors. Taroni et al. (2016) agreed, citing the potential of simulation models enabled by high-speed computing as an augmenting factor in the determination of research quality. Thompson (2004) noted that in 1994, the American Psychological Association first addressed the issues raised by so many scientists. This led the organization to recommend that effect-size calculations accompany all statistical hypothesis tests. That proposal resonates with Walster and Cleary's (1970) recommendation that researchers first decide "How big a difference will make a difference?"

These conversations led a number of scientists (MacCoun, 2019; Brodeur et al., 2020) to identify the process of p-hacking, in which researchers manipulate their studies, knowingly or not, to achieve statistical significance, thereby increasing their chances of publication. These authors and several others concluded that this is common practice in most disciplines, predominately unrecognized by scientific journals, that leads to non-replicable results. If significance drives the data analysis process, Bill Walser would say the study should be published in the "Journal of Type One Errors." As readers of this chapter, you should recognize that we have taught you how to p-hack. Keep increasing that sample size, and eventually, you will get a statistically significant result. We guarantee it, but we strongly advise you not to be a p-hacker. This whole conversation came to a head in the journal *Nature* (Amrhein et al., 2019), where Valentin et al. and over 800 co-author scientists throughout the world were signatories of an article entitled "Retire Statistical Significance." They analyzed the results of 791 articles in five journals, finding that, mistakenly, about half those studies assumed that non-significance meant no effect. Their point was that just because investigators fail to reject the null hypotheses, that does not mean that important impacts are absent. They state: "The trouble is human and cognitive more than it is statistical: bucketing resulting into 'statistically significant and statistically nonsignificant' makes people think that the items assigned that way are categorically difference" (p. 306).

We hope our readers will recognize how this statement resonates with Rosling et al.'s (2018) gap instinct error that we pointed out earlier in this chapter. We find it interesting that so many great thinkers reach the same or similar conclusion but neither know nor even recognize each other.

The *Nature* piece concludes with this statement:

> The misuse of statistical significance has done much harm to the scientific community and those who rely on scientific advice. P values, intervals and other statistical measures have their place, but it's time for statistical significance to go.
>
> *(p. 307)*

Although statistical hypothesis testing has come under intense criticism, it can still be a useful tool in blended learning research. However, we as contemporary investigators need to give serious consideration to how and sometimes if we will incorporate that process into our work. There are times when it can be informative, but from what has developed in the conversation, it seems clear that it should not be the sole criterion for identifying viable findings. After all, the purpose of our research is to identify findings that will hold up in the larger populations that we address. Hypothesis tests have certain prerequisites if they are to be valid. The treatment must be a legitimate treatment. That is, when it is applied in various contexts, we need to have confidence that blended learning has continuity. In our opinion, the decision is questionable. Additionally, hypothesis tests should be free of confounding effects from other factors that impact the result. This is an issue for blended learning because of the impossibility of separating it from so many other aspects of the educational environment. Although these are serious issues, they do not necessarily invalidate hypothesis tests. Responsible blended learning researchers will have to pay close attention to the continuing conversation about the future and, like so many, have recommended that we use our best judgement to decide when and where this process will provide meaningful information. This conversation is likely to continue for some time, and its final resolution may well rest in the hands of uncertain mediation.

Asymmetry

Asymmetry influences much that happens in our lives. One historical example comes from the founders drafting the United States Constitution, who acceded to a 3/5 compromise that equated every five slaves to three free people to determine representation in the House of Representatives (Lepore, 2018; Forest, 2019). Another example can be found in Boghosian (2019), who indicated that in 2010, 388 individuals possessed as much wealth as the lower half of the world's population of approximately 3.5 billion people. According to him, in 2019, that number dropped to 26, confirming that inequity in the world is getting much worse. Harari (2018) is starker in his predictions, hypothesizing that unacceptable inequality will go far beyond financial implications to biological asymmetry, in which technologies that enable longer life, increased mental capacity, enhanced physical performance, and superior skill acquisition will be disproportionately available to the wealthy. Additionally, he goes on to argue that data ownership will alter the quality of life across the world because vast data stores owned by corporations (we add social media) enable big data methods to target susceptible populations with highly effective marketing strategies and political opinions. He raises disturbing questions about whether that information imbalance can be trusted. He asserts the real issue is that the exceeding wealthy few will possess power the lower classes do not and will never have. This "Matthew Effect" (Gladwell, 2011) generates circumstantial privilege for the well off. Kahneman (2011) describes this asymmetry as the endowment effect: people are more likely to retain an object they own rather than acquire that same object when they don't possess it—they want to keep what they have. Giridharadas (2018) criticizes the endowment effect, citing philanthropists and foundations that, while allegedly attempting to alleviate inequity, refuse to give up any of their power. Jack (2019) confirmed this when he cited data showing that students from families in the top 1% with incomes that exceeded $600,000 a year were 77 times more likely to attend Ivy League schools then those from families that make $30,000 a year.

Nassim Taleb, in his book *Skin in the Game* (2018), the ultimate treatise on asymmetry and inequity, addresses the 2008 financial crash with this harsh criticism:

> For instance, bank blowups came in 2008 because of the accumulation of hidden and asymmetric risks in the system: bankers, master risk transferors, could make steady money from a certain class of concealed explosive risks use academic risk models that don't work except on paper (because academics know practically nothing about risk), then invoke uncertainty after a blowup (that same unseen and unforecastable Black Swan . . .), and keep past income.
>
> *(p. 12)*

His contention is that if you don't have any skin in the game (real investment and risk), you are really not in the game because you have nothing to lose. He asserts that the most egregious asymmetry occurs where a small but wealthy and entitled elite forces its preferences and policies on the general population where the few dictate to the many—sound familiar? Later in his book, he contends that the very same mechanism of transferring risk is what impedes learning. Simply pass the responsibility for students' failure on to someone down the line. Asymmetry can be readily observed in research, including blended learning, in which academics submit scholarly papers to scientific journals knowing the chances of acceptance increase if they make the studies more complicated than necessary (Taleb, 2018). Our advice to you is that if you can't understand the article, there is probably something wrong with it.

Boghosian (2019) developed a compelling asymmetric model of free market economies by using simulated transactions among individual agents. He found that even under the circumstances of fair exchange, without corrections, resources will always gravitate from the poor to the rich. His system was based on a variant of a process called the yard sale model, in which there will be a winner and loser (Chakraborti, 2002). For example, in your yard sale, if you value your old rocking chair at $25 but someone offers you $20, and you take it, financial asymmetry occurred. The customer's resources are now worth $30—the original $25 market value plus the $5 discount—while your net worth has decreased to $20. He showed that if you simulate this asymmetry over a very large number of financial transactions, an oligarch emerges who holds the vast majority of the wealth, while the rest of the population is left with little or nothing. Although Boghosian demonstrated the asymmetry in a fair-risk economy, the process is vastly accelerated by the "Matthew effect," wealth advantage in which the well-off enjoy privileges such as superior health care, better interest rates, access to information, political influence, better financial advice, and the ability to negotiate prices, while the

Education and Blended Learning **393**

poor suffer severe disadvantages such a payday loans, no time to seek the best prices, inability to deal with bureaucracies, and the scarcity associated with poverty. Wealth advantage plays a significant role in the system's broken symmetry, and early advantages are important contributors to that imbalance. To emphasize this crippling asymmetry, he quotes James Baldwin: "Anyone who has struggled with poverty knows how extremely expensive it is to be poor" (p. 75). Boghosian (2019) adjusts the asymmetry by building a model in which wealth advantage is less than resource redistribution in the society. The result is a stable state with no oligarchies developing. However, when he used his model to analyze 14 national economies served by the Central European Bank, most of them were at the critical point for symmetry breaking. Apparently, asymmetry carries substantial momentum.

By now, we'll bet that you are asking yourself, "What does asymmetry have to do with the future of blended learning research?" Let's frame that question another way. Is blended learning a solution looking for a problem? We think not. Here is an educational asymmetry for you to consider. If a student lives in the lowest economic income quartile, the chances of him or her graduating from college are about 10% (Sherman, 2015; Cahalan et al., 2019). Put another way, the odds against are 9:1. If a student lives in the upper economic income quartile, there is an approximate 90% chance of obtaining a college degree. The odds in favor are 9:1 (Dziuban & Bush, 2020). This is the yard sale model applied to education—a very good fit. This is the problem because we are convinced that the academic talent pool in our underserved communities is as deep as in any gated neighborhood in the United States. This has been proven with clarity in the Tangelo Park Program in Orlando, Florida (n.d.), Dziuban and Bush (2020).

Mullainathan and Shafir (2013) highlight another perspective on asymmetry and its impact for opportunity and education. They use the frame "scarcity," in which needs far exceed the capacity to accommodate them. We all have experienced scarcity in one form or another. For those of us in the academy, time scarcity is well understood. However, consider students living in poverty and the unrelenting demands placed upon them. They may have to work at more than one job with uncertain and irregular hours that place excessive demands on their time, making course scheduling very difficult. If they can only attend classes part time, health care becomes an issue, as do expenses such as tuition, supplies, and textbooks. That becomes another stressor, especially if they have to wait for such things as Pell grants to arrive or, worse, take out high-interest loans because they lack the time to search for affordable financial help. Often, they have demanding family responsibilities, all of which can create transportation problems that make getting to work and school regularly and on time a daunting task.

Mullainathan and Shafir (2013) cast this as the *scarcity trap* that taxes their cognitive bandwidth. They have the academic abilities comparable to middle-class students, but the demands on their lives become a formidable barrier to their achieving academic success. The authors portray this as having no slack

394 Charles D. Dziuban and Anthony G. Picciano

(degrees of freedom), causing them to juggle their lives to the detriment of what is required by their classes.

Obvious problems develop. Work, transportation, family, and money demands pile up. If just one thing goes wrong, a secondary, unintended effect can occur— or more. A class is missed; the student is behind. The next class becomes overwhelming because of missed prerequisites—many things don't make sense. Unfortunately, if this happens more than once, dropping out can become unavoidable, causing more time and money losses. A linear class curriculum in which each class has dependencies attached to the previous session causes a ripple effect for a student coping with scarcity from which the student will be unlikely to recover.

The irony in this section is that although we have cast asymmetry as a problem that will impact blended learning research, consider that traditional universities are locked-down linear symmetric systems: syllabi, semesters, programs, years. This seems to make very little sense for students living in poverty, who have to manage the nearly overwhelming demands on their lives. In contrast, consider adaptive learning courses with modules supported by learning nodes and a go-at-your-own-pace design. An adaptive learning course can place a student at the optimal starting point, corresponding to his or her estimated competency level to help them progress at their own rate ensuring that prerequisites are met, proper knowledge levels are acquired, and concepts are reinforced, all while handing control of their learning over to them. If this is combined with a blended learning model, the reinforcement becomes even stronger. These students need asymmetry for learning, and a new direction might be the concept of asymmetric blended learning research, in which the model has a variant impact, depending on context. This thinking might reframe meaningful research into a more agile context.

"The Future Ain't What It Used to Be" —Yogi Berra

In closing this book, we butted up against scarcity. There were so many more things we wanted to say, but we ran out of chapters. Academics suffer from time scarcity, and as the deadline loomed for authors to submit their first drafts, many of them found themselves in the scarcity trap as well. They had several months to complete the work, but pressures of the pandemic consumed them, so they were forced into what Mullainathan and Shafir (2013) called tunneling—put everything else on hold, ask for an extension, and do little else but work on the chapter. The irony is that abundance (those many months) almost always leads to scarcity. In spite of those difficulties, the research in this book makes it clear that blended learning is positioned at the crossroads of educational cultures that will alter future research.

Agility and flexibility caused blended learning to develop more rapidly than any other course format. That transformed it into an educational ecosystem instead of a course modality, making any attempt to identify each and every blend rather quixotic (Picciano et al., 2010). We have followed its progression, but that only gets us from then to now. Tomorrow gets trickier because what happened in the past may not give an accurate projection of what is about to happen in the future. No flippancy intended, but it's anybody's guess. We know where blended learning started: some combination of face-to-face and online learning in a prescribed proportion. Today, that definition seems naïve. Blended learning has become the foundation of educational culture, forming one of our primary educational networks. So, as we approach the fall of 2020 with so many campuses wrestling with if and how they might bring students back, the blend-flex model became the go-to solution. Universities were built for on-campus presence, so bringing students back in small socially distanced groups gives them some measure of that experience. However, giving them the flexibility to learn remotely or online provides latitude to use instructional technologies to keep learning options responsive. Throughout this book, you can find evidence of that in higher and K–12 education, industry, adaptive learning, analytics, and other situations in which conceiving of blended learning as an ecosystem makes sense. Therefore, this format has become complex and emergent; thus, placing it in mode comparison studies makes little sense because it is tethered to almost everything in the educational environment. Therefore, our new blended research paradigm will most likely involve the scholarship of teaching and learning (SoTL) creating contextually relevant findings combined with modeling the blended ecosystem taking cause and effect off the table. M. Alexander (2020) used a similar approach when he combined trend analysis and scenario building to forecast the future of higher education. This places much more responsibility on researchers to estimate, judge, predict, explain, calculate missteps, and build feedback loops that make successive approximations to understanding. Remember, data have no voice of their own. We have to give them that voice. We have to explain why our models make sense, realizing full well that there are competitors that fit equally well, causing disagreement. The process will not be crisp but more ambiguous than the days of p values, but this is the word in which we live—increasingly complex and, at times, borderline chaotic.

Because it is an ecosystem, blended learning will merge with many aspects of education, society, and information technologies. If Floridi (2014) is correct that we are on the precipice of the infosphere (ecosystem) in which information communication technologies communicate with each other leaving us out of the loop, then we will have to monitor those goings-on for their effects on blended learning—a new research paradigm. Side effects may well arise from a number of emerging technologies we mentioned: artificial intelligence, cloud computing, robotics, quantum computing, and many others, some of which we have yet to conceive. Even the ones of which we are aware are continually evolving, so any idea of an end state is an illusion. There are others: complexity, hypothesis testing, big data, and asymmetry, all of which have undergone radical change. Our blended learning ecosystem is inundated with change agents from all sectors of

396 Charles D. Dziuban and Anthony G. Picciano

the world impacting teaching, learning, and research, but just how remains to be seen.

We can be certain, though, that meaningful blended research will be a long-haul proposition (Rosling et al., 2018; Johnson, 2015): for instance, artificial intelligence. After the initial enthusiasm, it languished in the doldrums for years until effective neural networks enabled its breakout development. From awkward, clumsy, ineffective, and patently uninteresting, we are discussing the possibility of it becoming aware. Good research is patient, sustained, careful, methodical, and filled with mistakes. Actually, there is nothing wrong with being wrong; a great deal is learned from it (Schulz, 2011). If a question is posed about what *2001: A Space Odyssey* (Clarke, 1968), (Orwell, 1950, 1984), *Brave New World* (Huxley, 2006), and *Neuromancer* (Gibson, 2000) have in common, the answer, for the most part, is that they were wrong. However, consider the monumental number of creative ideas, books, scientific literature, and inventions that have resulted from that body of work. As Richard Feynman says, "What do you care what other people think?" (Feynman, 1988). Conversely, Harari (2018) cautions that because of its influence on society, science fiction has a growing responsibility to be more accurate.

Ultimately, good research is slow and comes at a cost. Quick fixes hardly ever work. Two cases in point: Heckman (2019) and the Tangelo Park Program. Heckman published follow-up research 30 years after the Perry preschool project (Youth.gov., n.d.), showing the intergenerational impact of quality preschool education. There was improved life quality not only among the original preschoolers but also in their children. However, it took three decades to discover this. The Tangelo Park Program in Orlando (Tangelo Park Program, n.d.) has sustained educational success for 28 uninterrupted years with guaranteed funding by the Rosen Foundation working with the University of Central Florida, the Tangelo community and Orange County Public Schools. Tangelo was a dangerous place. The odds of college graduation were 9:1 against. Today those odds are 3:1 in favor (according to the National Campaign for "A Broader, Bolder Approach to Education"—see https://www.boldapproach.org/index.html). That did not happen overnight. Crime is down 78% from 1994, but in the first five years, it changed very little. Tangelo begins with schooling at two years of age and continues through college or vocational school completion. Students graduate debt free. Staying the course and long-term research were the keys. The same will be true with blended learning research.

As with so much of our work, we leave you with more questions than answers. How can we better understand learning time as a metric? Can the student voice be better integrated into blended learning? Which variables can be controlled or accounted for? How will blended learning impact the structure of colleges and universities? Can we build a student assessment model that becomes instructional? Can those assessment models be transformed from teach then test, where they are objective, non-contextual, and non-authentic, to a process that is reflective, contextual, and authentic? What will the instructor's role be in the blended eco-system? How can students be part of the instructional paradigm? Is there a proto-type blend? Can blended learning help solve the educational inequity problem? Can blended learning be functional in preschool? How will sophisticated tech-nology transform blended learning? What happens to the concept of the course in blended learning? Can blended learning transcend disciplines? Obviously, these questions are like Borges's *Garden of Forking Paths* (Borges, 1962). Each one leads to many more in a cascade of never-ending ideas. They can build their own sus-taining energy and possibly be that metaphoric perpetual motion machine. That we can't predict, but as Yogi would say, "If you come to a fork in the road—take it." Thank you for reading our book.

References

Alexander, B. (2020). *Academia next: The futures of higher education.* Johns Hopkins University Press.

Alexander, M. (2020). *The new Jim Crow: Mass incarceration in the age of colorblindness.* The New Press.

AlQuraishi, M. (2018, December 9). *AlphaFold @ CASP13: "What just happened?" Blog posting.* Retrieved February 15, 2019, from https://moalquraishi.wordpress.com/2018/12/09/alphafold-casp13-what-just-happened/

Amrhein, V., Greenland, S., & McShane, B. (2019). Comment: Retire statistical significance. *Nature, 567,* 305–307.

Aoun, R. E. (2017). *Robot proof: Higher education in the age of artificial intelligence.* The MIT Press.

Arntz, M., Gregory, T., & Zierahn, U. (May14, 2016). *The risk of automation for jobs in OECD countries: A comparative analysis.* OECD Social, Employment, and Migration Working papers, No. 189. Retrieved February 16, 2019, from www.oecd-ilibrary.org/docserver/5jlz9h56dvq7-en.pdf

Avishaie, B. (2020, April 21). The pandemic isn't a black swan but a portent of a more fragile global system. *The New Yorker.* www.newyorker.com/news/daily-comment/the-pandemic-isnt-a-black-swan-but-a-portent-of-a-more-fragile-global-system

Banyan, M. E. (2020, May 14). *Tragedy of the commons.* Retrieved June 15, 2020, from www.britannica.com/science/tragedy-of-the-commons

Battersby, S. (2017). News Feature: Can humankind escape the tragedy of the commons? *Proceedings of the National Academy of Sciences, 114*(1), 7–10.

Berriman, R., & Hawksworth, J. (2017). Will robots steal our jobs? The potential impact of automation on the UK and other major economies. *PwC.* Retrieved February 15, 2019, from www.pwc.co.uk/economic-services/ukeo/pwcukeo-section-4-automation-march-2017-v2.pdf

Blumenstyk, G. (2018, November 11). Meet the new mega university. *The Chronicle of Higher Education.* Retrieved April 27, 2019, from www.chronicle.com/article/Meet-the-New-Mega-University/245049

Boghosian, B. M. (2019). The inescapable casino. *Scientific American, 321*(5), 70–77.

Borges, J. L. (1962). *Labyrinths.* A New Directions Books.

Bowker, G. C., & Star, S. L. (2000). *Sorting things out: Classification and its consequences.* The MIT Press.

Brodeur, A., Cook, N., & Heyes, A. (2020). A Proposed Specification Check for p-Hacking. *AEA Papers and Proceedings, 110*, 66–69.

Cahalan, M., Perna, L., Wright-Kim, J., & Jiang, N. (2019). *2019 indicators of higher education equity in the United States: Historical trend report*. Pell Institute for the Study of Opportunity in Higher Education.

Carr, N. (2014). *The glass cage: Automation and us*. W. W. Norton & Company.

Chakraborti, A. (2002). Distributions of money in model markets of economy. *Saha Institute of Nuclear Physics*, 1–9.

Clarke, A. C. (1968). *2001: A space odyssey*. New American Library.

Cornett, J. W. (1996). *Uncertain mediation, unrestrained dialogue, and the role of the civics teacher: Learning about civics instruction from Hungarian educators*. Paper submitted to the Florida Law Related Education Association.

DeMichele, G. (2020). *Our bathtub wasn't in the kitchen anymore*. Book Baby.

Diamond, J. M. (1997). *Guns, germs, and steel: The fates of human societies*. W. W. Norton & Company.

Diamond, J. M. (2005). *Collapse: How societies choose to fail or succeed*. Penguin.

Dziuban, C., & Bush, M. (2020). Educational equity: A new kind of philanthropy. *EDUCAUSE Review*, 1–8.

Dziuban, C., Colm, H., Johnson, C., & Moskal, P. (2017, December 18). An adaptive learning partnership. *EDUCAUSE Review*. Retrieved April 26, 2019, from https://er.educause.edu/articles/2017/12/an-adaptive-learning-partnership

Dziuban, C., Moskal, P., & Hartman, J. (2016, September 30). Adapting to learn, learning to adapt. *ECAR Research Bulletin*. Retrieved April 26, 2019, from https://library.educause.edu/resources/2016/9/adapting-to-learn-learning-to-adapt

Dziuban, C., Moskal, P., Parker, L., Campbell, M., Colm, H., & Johnson, C. (2018, September). Adaptive learning: A stabilizing influence across disciplines and universities. *Online Learning Journal, 22* (3). Retrieved February 16, 2019, from https://olj.onlinelearningconsortium.org/index.php/olj/article/view/1465/399

Dziuban, C., Shea, P., & Moskal, P. (2020). A question of blended learning: Treatment effect or boundary object? *EDUCAUSE Review*, 1–9.

Education Dive Staff (2019, January 29). How many colleges and universities have closed since 2016? *Education Dive*. Retrieved February 19, 2019, from www.educationdive.com/news/tracker-college-and-university-closings-and-consolidation/539961/

Eubanks, V. (2018). *Automating inequality: How high-tech tools profile, police, and punish the poor*. St. Martin's Press.

Faust, D. (2015). *Three forces shaping the university of the future*. World Economic Forum. Retrieved July 9, 2015, from https://agenda.weforum.org/2015/01/three-forces-shaping-the-university-of-the-future/

Feynman, R. P. (1988). *"What do you care what other people think?": Further adventures of a curious character*. W. W. Norton & Company.

Floridi, L. (2014). *The fourth revolution: How the infosphere is reshaping human reality*. Oxford University Press.

Ford, M. (2015). *The rise of the robots: Technology and the threat of a jobless future*. Basic Books.

Forest, B. (2019). Reforming the US Senate: Original intent and representational inequality. *Political Geography, 74*, 1–3.

Forrester, J. W. (1961). *Industrial dynamics*. The MIT Press.

Frey, C. B., & Osborne, M. A. (2013, September 17). *The future of employment: How susceptible are jobs to automation*. Oxford Martin Programme on Technology and Employment.

Retrieved February 16, 2019, from www.oxfordmartin.ox.ac.uk/downloads/aca demic/The_Future_of_Employment.pdf

Future of Life Institute (2015). *Research priorities for robust and beneficial artificial intelligence: An open letter.* Retrieved August 17, 2015, from http://futureoflife.org/AI/open_letter

Gibson, W. (2000). *Neuromancer.* Ace.

Giridharadas, A. (2018). *Winners take all: The elite charade of changing the world.* Knopf.

Gladwell, M. (2011). *Outliers: The story of success.* Back Bay Books.

Gould, S. J. (1996). *The mismeasure of man.* W. W. Norton & Company.

Green, K. (2015). *The 2015 campus computing survey.* The Campus Computing Project. Retrieved November 23, 2015, from www.campuscomputing.net/item/2015-campus-computing-survey-0

Grosz, S. (2014). *The examined life: How we lose and find ourselves.* W. W. Norton & Company.

Hacking, I. (2012). Introductory essay. In *The structure of scientific revolutions* (pp. vii–xxxvii). University of Chicago Press.

Haimes, Y. Y. (2017). Risk modeling of interdependent complex systems of systems: Theory and practice. *Risk Analysis, 38(1),* 84–98.

Harari, Y. N. (2017). *Homo deus: A brief history of tomorrow.* HarperCollins Publishers.

Harari, Y. N. (2018). *21 lessons for the 21st century.* Speigel & Grau.

Heckman, J. J., & Karapakula, G. (2019). *The Perry preschoolers at late midlife: A study in design-specific inference* (No. w25888). National Bureau of Economic Research.

Heller, J. (1961). *Catch-22.* Simon & Schuster.

Hilpert, J. C., & Marchand, G. C. (2018). Complex systems research in educational psychology: Aligning theory and method. *Educational Psychologist, 53(3),* 185–202.

Hurston, Z. N. (2018). *Barracoon: The story of the last "black cargo."* Harper Collins.

Huxley, A. (2006). *Brave new world.* Harper Perennial.

Isenberg, N. (2017). *White trash: The 400-year untold history of class in America.* Penguin.

Jack, A. A. (2019). *The privileged poor: How elite colleges are failing disadvantaged students.* Harvard University Press.

Johnson, S. (2010). The genius of the tinkerer. *Wall Street Journal, 25.*

Johnson, S. (2011). *Where good ideas come from: The natural history of innovation.* Penguin.

Johnson, S. (2015). *How we got to now: Six innovations that made the modern world.* Riverhead Books.

Kahneman, D. (2011). *Thinking, fast and slow.* Farrar, Straus and Giroux.

Kelderman, E. (2020, June 1). Spurred by coronavirus, some colleges rush to move online. *The Chronicle of Higher Education.* Retrieved June 1, 2020, from www.chroni cle.com/article/Spurred-by-CoronavirusSome/248893?utm_source=at&utm_ medium=en&utm_source=Iterable&utm_medium=email&utm_campaign=campaign _1258731&cid=at&source=ams&sourceId=2343968

Kuhn, T. S. (2012). *The structure of scientific revolutions.* University of Chicago Press.

Lakoff, G. (1987). *Women, fire, and dangerous things: What categories reveal about the mind.* University of Chicago Press.

Lederman, D. (2017, April 28). *Clay Christensen, doubling down.* www.insidehighered. com/digital-learning/article/2017/04/28/clay-christensen-sticks-predictions-massive-college-closures

Lederman, D. (2017, July 19). The dulling of higher ed begins. *Inside Higher Ed.* Retrieved February 19, 2019, from www.insidehighered.com/news/2017/07/19/ number-colleges-and-universities-drops-sharply-amid-economic-turmoil

Lee, K. F. (2018). *AI super-powers: China, Silicon Valley, and the new world order.* Houghton Mifflin Harcourt.

Lepore, J. (2018). *These truths: A history of the United States.* W. W. Norton & Company.

Lockhart, J., McKee, D., & Donnelly, D. (2017). Delivering effective blended learning: Managing the dichotomy of humility and hubris in executive education. *Decision Sciences Journal of Innovative Education, 15(1),* 101–117.

MacCoun, R. (2019). p-Hacking: A strategic analysis. In L. Jussim, S. T. Stevens, & J. A. Krosnick (Eds.), *Research integrity in the behavioral sciences.* Oxford University Press, Press Forthcoming in 2020.

Margolis, A. R., Porter, A. L., & Pitterle, M. E. (2017). Best practices for use of blended learning. *American Journal of Pharmaceutical Education, 81(3),* 1–8.

Markoff, J. (2013, April 4). Essay-grading software offers professors a break. *New York Times.* Retrieved February 28, 2019, from www.nytimes.com/2013/04/05/science/new-test-for-computers-grading-essays-at-college-level.html

McAfee, A., & Brynjolfsson, E. (2017). *Harnessing our digital future: Machine platform crowd.* W. W. Norton & Company.

McShane, B. B., Gal, D., Gelman, A., Robert, C., & Tackett, J. L. (2019). Abandon statistical significance. *The American Statistician, 73(S1),* 235–245.

Metz, C. (2019, February 5). Making new drugs with a dose of artificial intelligence. *The New York Times.* Retrieved February 15, 2019, from www.nytimes.com/2019/02/05/technology/artificial-intelligence-drug-research-deepmind.html

Momaday, N. S. (2018). *House made of dawn.* Harper Perennial Modern Classics.

Mullainathan, S., & Shafir, E. (2013). *Scarcity: Why having too little means so much.* Times Books.

O'Neil, C. (2017). *Weapons of math destruction: How big data increases inequality and threatens democracy.* Broadway Books.

Orwell, G. (1950). *1984.* Penguin.

Otte, G. (2016). Technological innovation in education: What the past teaches, what the present promises. In M. Goldstein & G. Otte (Eds.), *Change we must: Deciding the future of higher education* (pp. 53–69). Rosetta Books.

Page, S. E. (2011). *Diversity and complexity.* Princeton University Press.

Picciano, A. G. (1994). *Computers in the schools: A guide to planning and administration.* Merril, Palgrave Macmillan.

Picciano, A. G. (2017). *Online education policy and practice: The past, present, and future of the digital university.* Routledge.

Picciano, T., Godambe, D., Duby, T., & Laster, S. (2010). *Ecosystems panel: Exploring world-class blended learning* [Conference Presentation]. The 7th Annual Sloan Consortium Blended Learning Conference and Workshop.

Roberts, C. (2010). *The unnatural history of the sea.* Island Press.

Rosch, E. (1983). Prototype classification and logical classification: The two systems. In E. K. Scholnick (Ed.), *New trends in conceptual representation: Challenges to Piaget's theory.* Lawrence Erlbaum Associates.

Rosling, H., Rosling, O., & Rosling Ronnlund, A. (2018). *Factfulness: Ten reasons we're wrong about the world—and why things are better than you think.* Flatiron Books.

Rozeboom, W. W. (1997). Good science is abductive, not hypothetico-deductive. In L. L. Harlow, S. A. Mulaik, & J. H. Steiger (Eds.), *What if there were no significance tests* (pp. 335–392). Erlbaum.

Rubenstein, D. M. (2019). *The American story: Conversations with master historians.* Simon & Schuster.

Russell, T. L. (1999). *The no significant difference phenomenon as reported in 355 research reports, summaries, and papers.* North Carolina State University.

Schneider, V., Leifeld, P., & Malang, T. (2013). Coping with creeping catastrophes: National political systems and the challenge of slow-moving policy problems. In Siebenhner, B., Arnold, M., Eisenack, K. & Jacob, K. H. (Eds.) *Long-term governance of social-ecological change. Series: Environmental politics* (21, pp. 221–238). Routledge.

Schulz, K. (2011). *Being wrong: Adventures in the margin of error.* Ecco.

Setenyi, J. (1995). *Teaching democracy in an unpopular democracy.* Paper presented at the What to Teach about Hungarian Democracy Conference, Kossuth Klub, Hungary.

Sherman, E. (2015). Wealthy kids 8 times more likely to graduate college than poor. *Forbes.*

Silver, N. (2012). *The signal and the noise: Why so many predictions fail—but some don't.* Penguin.

Sloan, R. (2012). *Mr. Penumbra's 24-hour bookstore.* Farrar, Straus and Giroux.

Smith, E. (2010, September 28). *The adjacent possible.* Retrieved June 15, 2020, from www.practicallyefficient.com/2010/09/28/the-adjacent-possible.html

Smith, T. (2018, June 30). More states opting to "robo-grade" student essays by computer. *NPR.* Retrieved March 3, 2019, from www.npr.org/2018/06/30/624373367/more-states-opting-to-robo-grade-student-essays-by-computer

Soga, M., & Gaston, K. J. (2018). Shifting baseline syndrome: Causes, consequences, and implications. *Frontiers in Ecology and the Environment, 16*(4), 222–230.

Strogatz, S. (2018, December 26). One giant step for a chess-playing machine. *New York Times.* Retrieved February 18, 2019, from www.nytimes.com/2018/12/26/science/chess-artificial-intelligence.html

Taleb, N. N. (2007). *The black swan: The impact of the highly improbable.* Random House Publishing Group.

Taleb, N. N. (2018). *Skin in the game: Hidden asymmetries in daily life.* Random House Publishing Group.

Tangelo Park Program (n.d.). www.tangeloparkprogram.com/about/tangelo-park-program/

Tangelo Park Program (Orlando, Florida): A Broader, Bolder Approach to Education (n.d.). *A broader, bolder approach to education.* www.boldapproach.org/index.html@p=548.html

Taroni, F., Biedermann, A., & Bozza, S. (2016). Statistical hypothesis testing and common misinterpretations: Should we abandon p-value in forensic science applications? *Forensic Science International, 259*, e32–e36.

Thaler, R. H. (2015). *Misbehaving: The making of behavioral economics.* W. W. Norton & Company.

Thompson, B. (1996). Research news and comment: AERA editorial policies regarding statistical significance testing: Three suggested reforms. *Educational Researcher, 25*(2), 26–30.

Thompson, B. (2004). The "significance" crisis in psychology and education. *The Journal of Socio-Economics, 33*(5), 607–613.

Ubell, R. (2020, May 13). How online learning kept higher ed open during the coronavirus crisis. *IEEE Spectrum.* Retrieved May 25, 2020, from https://

spectrum.ieee.org/tech-talk/at-work/education/how-online-learning-kept-higher-ed-open-during-the-coronavirus-crisis

Van Calster, B., Steyerberg, E. W., Collins, G. S., & Smits, T. (2018). Consequences of relying on statistical significance: Some illustrations. *European Journal of Clinical Investigation, 48*(5), 1–8.

Walster, G. W., & Cleary, T. A. (1970). Statistical significance as a decision rule. *Sociological Methodology, 2*, 246–254.

Wan, T. (2018, August 21). Knewton's business attracts new $25M in funding. *EdSurge. Digital Learning in Higher Ed*. Retrieved February 17, 2019, from www.edsurge.com/news/2018-08-21-knewton-s-new-business-attracts-new-25m-in-funding-but-some-things-don-t-change

Watts, D. J. (2011). *Everything is obvious: Once you know the answer*. Crown Publishing Group.

White, J. W., Rassweiler, A., Samhouri, J. F., Stier, A. C., & White, C. (2014). Ecologists should not use statistical significance tests to interpret simulation model results. *Oikos, 123*(4), 385–388.

White, T. P. (2020, May 10). *CSU Chancellor Timothy P. White's statement on Fall 2020 University operational plans*. Retrieved June 1, 2020, from https://www2.calstate.edu/csu-system/news/Pages/CSU-Chancellor-Timothy-P-Whites-Statement-on-Fall-2020-University-Operational-Plans.aspx

Wilkerson, I. (2011). *The warmth of other suns: The epic story of America's great migration*. Random House.

Youth.gov (n.d.). *Perry preschool project*. https://youth.gov/content/perry-preschool-project

Special Acknowledgement

We would like to thank Dawn, Michael, and Ali Divano for sharing some of their expertise with us for the PreK–12 portion of this chapter.

INDEX

Note: Page numbers in *italics* indicate a figure and page numbers in **bold** indicate a table on the corresponding page.

Academic Communities of Engagement (ACE) framework 8, 21, **22**; affective engagement 217, 218, 224–225; behavioral engagement 217; cognitive engagement 217, 222–224; course community peers 218, 226–227; data analysis 221; data collection 220–221; discussion 225–226; findings 221; methods 219–220; personal community peers 218, 227–228; theoretical framework 216–219, *217, 219–220*
academic success 216–219, *217, 219*
ACE framework *see* Academic Communities of Engagement (ACE) framework
achievement gaps 248
Active and Adaptive project 165; findings 167–170; method 165–166; qualitative survey 171–172
active learning 138–139, 352–353
activity mediation 273–274, *274*
activity-to-grade relationship 86, *87*
Adams, C. L. 334
adaptive instruction 24
adaptive learning 172–173, 366, 370–374, 386, 394; AI-based 373; data practices 173; faculty as partners 174; formative assessment 174–175; integration 173; research 7–8; starting small 174

Adaptive Learning Market Acceleration Program (ALMAP) initiative 164
adaptive learning system (ALS) 149; challenges 171–172; efficacy 149–150; findings 167–170; implications 158–159; integration 171; Likert-type responses 154, 167; literature review 148–149; mastery learning 159; methodology 152–154, 165–166; "not passing" grade report 166; open-ended responses 154, 167; pedagogical similarities between blended and 151–152; personalized tutoring 159; at Portland State University 165; qualitative methods 154, 157–158; quantitative methods 152–153; Realizeit platform 184–185, 188; results 154–157; self-paced learning 171; student perceptions of 164–165; and student persistence 164; student survey 166–167; study purpose 147–148; survey themes 171–172
adjacent possible notion 384
Adobe Connect 283
adult learning theory 35
adult students *see* neotraditional students
affective communication 122
affective engagement 217, 218, 224–225
agility 394

404 Index

AI *see* Artificial Intelligence (AI)
AISLE *see* Audiovisual Integration and Support for Learning Environments (AISLE)
ako (teach and learn) 297
ALEKS 374
Alexander, M. 395
Alfred P. Sloan Foundation 5
aliocentrism 88
Allen, I. E. 150
ALMAP initiative *see* Adaptive Learning Market Acceleration Program (ALMAP) initiative
AlphaZero 372
AlQuraishi, Mohammed 365, 380
ALS *see* adaptive learning system (ALS)
American Women's College, The (TAWC) 147–148
AMiGEO see *Analytical Methods in Geosciences* (AMiGEO)
Analytical Methods in Geosciences (AMiGEO) 318, 322
analytic mind 387
Anderson, Jeremy 7, 147
An, Jaesoon 7, 131
Aoun, J. E. 377, 379, 381, 382
APEX 374
Archer, M. S. 234
Armstrong, A. 36
Arnesen, Karen 8, 193
artifacts, in blended teaching 196, 198, *198*
artificial general intelligence 371
Artificial Intelligence (AI) 365–366, 370–374
asymmetry 391–394
Athabasca University 374
attitudinal changes 322–326
Audiovisual Integration and Support for Learning Environments (AISLE) 140
autonomous AI 371

Badley, G. 137
Baldwin, James 393
Barnum, K. T. 38
Baturay, M. 37, 38, 39
Bayliss, A. J. 334
Bay Path University (BPU) 147–148
Bb *see* Blackboard (Bb)
behavioral engagement 217
Belland, B. 39
Benfield, G. 272
Bergstrand, J. 141
Bernard, R. M. 14

Berra, Yogi 394–397
Bidjerano, T. 50
Biesta, G. 270, 272
big data 370
bilingual learning 248, 260
bio-sensing devices 367
BL *see* blended learning (BL)
Blackboard (Bb) 41, 74, 89, 91, 283
Bleed, Ron 282
blended learning (BL) 5; activity mediation and 272–273; boundary object 387; course delivery 150; definition 11, *13*, 15, 150, 282, 300; dissection of 270–280; diversity and 386; efficacy on student learning 151; ELL learning 249; eMAST (electronic marine acquisition seismic training) 182; engagement framework 21, **22**; future of 23–30; idealized cognitive model 387; innovation and 275–280; long-term value 187–190; *marine seismic data acquisition* case study 178–190; nature, components, and implications 11–16, **12**; online 283; pedagogical similarities between adaptive and 151–152; physical and pedagogical layers of 12–13, *13*, 15; in physical therapy education 334–335; prototypes 387; seismic crew training 180–181; self-study example 273–275; student perceptions of 300, 303, 304–305; theoretical contributions 17–23; theory development 16–17; time and process perspective 272
Blended Learning: Research Perspectives: Volume 1 5; Volume 2 5, 16
blended teaching (BT); artifacts 196, 198, *198*; competency framework 193, *195*; implementation of 132; K–12 pedagogical practices 195; rating codes for **197**
Blended Teaching Readiness Instrument 23
Bloom, B. 149, 159, 351, 351, 352
Boghosian, B. M. 391, 392, 393
Bohr, Niels 367
Borges, J. L. 397
Borup, J. 8, 194, 195, 214, 216
Bottge, B. A. 235
Boucher, B. 334
BPU *see* Bay Path University (BPU)
Bradford, George R. 8, 269
Braun, V. 339
Briggs, A. 164

Index **405**

Brigham Young University (BYU) 80
Bruner, J. 35
BT *see* blended teaching (BT)
Burkhardt, H. 16
Bushey, Heather 7, 147
Bush, M. 393
business AI 371
BYU *see* Brigham Young University (BYU)

CAI *see* computer-assisted instruction (CAI)
Calibrated Peer Review (CPR) tool 296
California State University 375
campus-based environments 283, *283*
Can Blended Learning Be Redeemed?
  (article) 11
Canvas 134, 283
CAPTE *see* Commission on Accreditation
  in Physical Therapy Education
  (CAPTE)
career-oriented program 52
Carr, Nicholas 369
CAS *see* Computer Attitudes Scale (CAS)
Center for Teaching and Learning (CTL)
  132, 138
China, capital investment for developing
  AI 381
Christensen, Clayton 377, 379, 381
Chromebooks 376
Ciabocchi, E. 104
Clarke, V. 339
Classroom Community Scale 42
Clayton Christensen Institute 196
Cleary, T. A. 389, 390
CLHT (class lectures/hybrid tutorials)
  blend 302, 304, 306
CLOT (class lectures/online tutorials)
  blend 302, 304
cloud computing 366, 369
CLTW (class lectures/tutorials/web-
  enhanced) blend 302, 304, 305–306
cognitive engagement 217, 222–224
cognitive presence, of CoI framework
  123, 284–285, *285*, **286**; exploration
  124–125; integration 125; resolution
  125–126; triggering event 124–126
Cohen, J. 42–43
CoI framework *see* Community of Inquiry
  (CoI) framework
Cole, M. 270
collaborative interactions 238–239
collaborative learning 138, 353
collaborative strategic reading (CSR) 251
collaborative web-based applications 282

Commission on Accreditation in Physical
  Therapy Education (CAPTE) 336
"Common Core" curriculum 375
communication, mediated 38
community colleges 50
Community of Inquiry (CoI) framework
  17, 21, **22**, 35–36, *36*, 353; blended
  DPT program 336, 345; coding scheme
  119, **120**; cognitive presence 123–126,
  284–285, *285*, **286**, 337; social presence
  121–123, 284–285, *285*, **286**, 337;
  teaching presence 119–121, 284–285,
  285, **286**, 337
complementary courses 74
computer-assisted instruction (CAI) 149, 374
Computer Attitudes Scale (CAS) 41
conceptual framework for learning in
  blended environments 21, **22**
Connecticut 380
constructivist paradigm 353
continuing education (CE) 140
Corcoran, Mary 9, 349
Cornett, J. W. 387
Correia, A. P. 42
course community peers 218, 226–227
course design, as learning analytics
  variable: background 74; findings
  76–86; implications 86–89; limitations
  and future work 89–90; methods and
  analysis 74–76
COVID-19 pandemic 3–4, 128, 129, 359,
  375
Cox, M. D. 118
CPM (cost per thousand) model 186
CPR tool *see* Calibrated Peer Review
  (CPR) tool
Creative Commons 317
credit attempts: hybrid ratio 58–61,
  64–68; online ratio 53–57, 61–64
Critical Assessment of Structure Prediction
  contest 365
Csikszentmihályi, M. 284
CSR *see* collaborative strategic reading
  (CSR)
CTL *see* Center for Teaching and Learning
  (CTL)

Dal Bello-Haas, V. 335
Dalton, B. 249
data collection 236, 277
data practices 195, **202**, 209, **209**; growth
  areas 203; quality practices 202–203
Davis, N. E. 42

406 Index

DeepMind 365
design fields 16
Devlin, Maura 7, 147
Dewey, J. 35, 233, 242, 353
DFW rates 77, **78**, **79**, 153–154
Diamond, J. M. 382
differentiated instruction 24
digital innovations 5
Digital Learning Collaborative 196
digital video library 335
digitized documents 131
direct instruction 120–121, 292–294, 296–297
disabled students, blended learning for: conceptual framework 232–233; data analysis 238; discussion 241–243; findings 238–241; learner agency 234; learner control 233–234; literature review 234–235; methods 235–238; purpose of study 232
discussion boards 226–227
Dispensa, M. 334
distance education 225, 269
diversity, and blended learning 386
Doctor of Philosophy (PhD), in THS 350; active and collaborative pedagogies for integrative learning 352–354; Bloom's taxonomy for scaffolding assignments 352; course and semester structure 351–352; current research 354–355; discussion and future research 357–361; methods 355; qualitative findings 356–357; quantitative results 356
Doctor of Physical Therapy (DPT) degree 8, 333; creating study guides 341; discussion 344–345; face-to-face blending 338; getting faculty feedback 342–343; implications for blended programs 345; methods 339; online blending 337–338; program curriculum 336–337; psychomotor skills 338, 340–341, 343–345; research design 339–340; results 340–345; viewing, creating and sharing videos 341; working within peer groups 342
domain-specific blended learning 24
Dottin, Raiza 8, 163
DPT degree *see* Doctor of Physical Therapy (DPT) degree
Drysdale, J. S. 18
Dubuclet, K. S. 227
Dziuban, C. D. 9, 14, 151, 154, 184, 365, 393

education, and blended learning 9, 365; adaptive learning 370–374; artificial intelligence 370–374; asymmetry 391–394; complexity 385–388; education resources 368–370; evolution after COVID-19 375; evolving technological landscapes 367–368; higher education 377–381; implications 375–381; nanotechnology 368; pre K–12 education 375–377; p value (significance levels) 388–391; quantum computing 368; research 382–384; resources 368–370; super-cloud computing 368–370
educational philosophy 233
EDUCAUSE Learning Initiative 5, 373
egocentrism 88
Ekmekci, O. 141
e-learning 182–183, 269
ELL *see* English language learners (ELL)
eMAST (electronic marine acquisition seismic training) 182
endowment effect 391
engagement 242; 3Rs of 284, 294–296; effective designs for 306–308, **307**
Engeström, Y. 274
English language learners (ELL) 235, 247; achievement gaps 248; blended learning 249; growing population of 247–248; home culture failure 248; multimodal learning 250; negative impacts of gaps 248–249; reading comprehension 250, 260; social studies learning 250–251, 255–256; strategies implemented 248; WIDA standards 253, **253**
enhanced time-based model 277, **278–279**
e-rating 371
e-textbooks 131, 134
evaluative courses 74
evidence-based blended learning: discussion 308–312; findings 303–308; four studies 301–302; research questions and methodology 302–303
evidence-based instruction 274
e-workbooks 134, 136
exploratory sources 277

face-to-face instruction 4, 157, 334, 373
face-to-face learning 37, 112, 151, 283
facilitation 121, 289–292, 295–296
faculty feedback 342–343
faculty issues 7, 21–23, **23**

Index **407**

faculty learning communities (FLC)
117; analysis 119–126; case study 118,
128; cognitive presence 123–126;
curriculum **118**; data analysis 118–119;
discussion of research questions
126–127; facilitation & management
course 118; plan & design course 118;
research questions and methodology
117–119; social presence 121–123;
students' experience 127–128; teaching
presence 119–121
FAIL experience *see* first attempt in
learning (FAIL) experience
fast-paced learning 248
Faulkner, William 383
Faust, D. 378–379, 381
Feynman, Richard 396
Field, A. 153
first attempt in learning (FAIL)
experience 295
FLC *see* faculty learning communities (FLC)
flexibility 171, 215, 394
Flipgrid 227
flipped teaching 103
Florida Virtual School 374
Floridi, L. 395
forethought 233
formative assessment, self-paced 327
Forrester, Jay 385
Francis, R. 272
Fritz, John 7, 73
Fry, R. 248
Future of Life Institute 382
Futuretown 368

Gage, K. 13
gap instinct error 386, 390
Garden of Forking Paths (Borges) 397
Garrett Dikkers, A. 227
Garrison, D. R. 37, 116, 122–123,
127–128, 137, 282–283, 284, 296, *297*
George Washington University, Translational
Health Sciences (THS) 349–361
Geoscience Authentic Learning
Experience Questionnaire 320
geoscience education, using OER 315–328
Giddens, A. 234
Ginsberg, A. P. 104
Giridharadas, A. 391
Glaser, B. G. 221
Godev, Concepcion B. 7, 131
Google Blogger 257–258, 295
Google Classroom 257, 376

Google docs 207
Google Forms 295
Google Surveys 258
Gould, Amanda 7, 147
Gould, Stephen Jay 383
Grabelle, S. 284, 294–296
Graham, C. R. 7, 8, 10, 14, 19, 98, 151,
174, 193–195, 216, 225, 233
Great Depression/New Deal content 254
Greenberger, H. B. 334
Greene, K. 194
group cohesion 123
group development stages 42
group projects 353
guided inquiry learning 226, 316–317, 327

H5P objects 316, 326, 327
Habeshaw, T. 137
Hacking, I. 384
Hale, W. 194
Halverson, L. R. 18, 137
Hanny, Courtney 8, 193
Harari, Yuval Noah 366, 391, 396
Haroldson, Erik 8, 315
Hartman, Joel 275
Hassabis, Demis 366
Hastie, M. 35
Hattie, J. 43, 297
Hawk, J. 335
Hawking, Stephen 382
Heckman, J. J. 396
Henrie, C. R. 306
high blend courses 302, 304–305
higher education 377–381
higher-level courses 77
Hindman, Lynne L. 7, 97
holistic courses 74, 273
Hrabowski, Freeman 89
hybrid courses *see* blended learning (BL)
hybrid credit attempt ratio 52, 58–61, *58,*
64–68
hybrid faculty learning community
(hybrid FLC) 97
HyFlex teaching 18–19, 105
hypothesis testing 388–390

IBM 368
ICT *see* information communications
technologies (ICT)
IHEs *see* institutions of higher education
(IHEs)
individual differentiation 248
individualized instruction 260

408 Index

Individuals with Disabilities in Education Act 235
inductive reasoning 273
informal interviews 237–238
information communications technologies (ICT) 272, 395
innovation 355; and blended learning 275–280; characteristics of 20–21; digital 5; teaching 138; technology 147
in-person courses 68, 214, 228
institutional issues 19–21, **20**
institutions of higher education (IHEs) 33
instructional design 18–19, **19**
instructor-provided videos 341
integrative blended learning 271, 349–361, *351*; active and collaborative pedagogies 352–354; Bloom's taxonomy for scaffolding assignments 352; course and semester structure 351–352; current research 354–355; discussion and future research 357–361; methods 355; qualitative findings 356–357; quantitative results 356
Intel 368
intellectual challenge 241–242
interactive e-textbooks 134
Internet AI 371
interview analysis 196, **196**
intuitive mind 387

Jack, A. A. 391
James, Scott 7, 49
Jensen, Michelle 8, 193
Johnson, Elizabeth 8, 315
Johnson, Steven 384
Joksimović, S. 38
Jung and Associates 38

K–12 blended education 8; artifacts analysis 196; data practices 195, 202–203, **202**, 209, **209**; findings 198–207; interview analysis 196–197, **196**; limitations 197–198; literature review 194–195; methods 196–198; online integration 195, 199–201, **200**, 208–209, **209**; online interaction 195, 206–208, **206**, **209**, 210; personalization 195, 203–205, **204**, 209–210, **209**; research questions 195; *see also* Academic Communities of Engagement (ACE)
Kahn, Cub 7, 97
Kahneman, D. 387, 391

Kanuka, H. 137
Kaufman, Stuart 384
Ke, F. 44
Keith-Le, J. A. 139
Khun, Thomas 383
Knewton 374
Knowles, M. 35
Koehler, M. J. 225
Kolb, D. A. 35
Koretsky, C. M. 320
Kumar, Swapna 8, 333
Kuo, Y. 39, 42

Laboratory Course Assessment Survey (LCAS) 320, 324, **325**
landscape amnesia 382–383
language ability, of ELL 248
Large Course Redesign (LCR) program 132–136
Laumakis, M. 272
Lazinski, M. J. 335
LCAS *see* Laboratory Course Assessment Survey (LCAS)
LCR program *see* Large Course Redesign (LCR) program
learner control 243
learner-learner interactions 214–215, 225
Learning Accelerator 196
learning analytics: course design variable 74–90; software 370, 373–374
learning communities 21
learning management systems (LMS) 73, 131, 283, 321, 369; Blackboard (Bb) 41, 74, 89, 91, 283; Canvas 134, 283; Moodle 134, 283; Realizeit's platform integration with 184–185
learning materials and modes 239–240
learning outcomes 90
learning theories 21
Learn Ultra 74
Leaving College (Tinto) 89
Lee, K. F. 366, 371–372
Leont'ev, Alexei 273
lesson materials and assignments 237
Likert-type responses 154, 167, 289, 358
literacy programs 209
Littky, D. 284, 294–296
Liu, Juhong Christie 8, 315
LMS *see* learning management systems (LMS)
López-Pérez, M. V. 151
low blend courses 302, 304, 305
Lowe, Derek 365

Lowenthal, P. 37
Lumley, T. 153

Malhotra, Taru 8, 300
man-machine interfaces 367, *367*
Mann-Whitney U test 323
Manwaring, K. C. 306, 309
Maori people 297
Massive Open Online Courses (MOOCs) 5, 370
mastery learning 159, 171, 205
Mathew effect 391, 392
Mayadas, A. Frank 5
MC *see* metacognition (MC)
McDonald, Paige L. 8, 349
McGee, P. 98
McShane, B. B. 389
meaningful learning 317
Meaningful Learning in the Laboratory Instrument (MLLI) 320
Means, B. 14
media, method, and modality (3Ms) of BL 11–13, **12**
medical education, technology-enhanced courses in 352
medium blend courses 302, 304, 305
Mellard, D. F. 235
Merriam, S. B. 235
Merrill, M. D. 342
metacognition (MC) 282–299; design and organization 288–289, 294–295; direct instruction 292–294, 296–297; facilitation 289–292, 295–296; findings 288–294; methodology 287–288; recommendations 294–297; research objective 287; study context 286–287; theoretical framework 284–286
Michigan Public Act 219
Miller, Timothy 8, 333
Mishra, P. 225
MIT Technology Review 386
MLLI *see* Meaningful Learning in the Laboratory Instrument (MLLI)
MMBL *see* multimodal blended learning (MMBL)
Moallem, M. 45
modified activity theory *274*, **275**, 277, *279*, *280*
modified contracts 297
Monte Carlo bootstrap simulation 323
MOOCs *see* Massive Open Online Courses (MOOCs)
Moodle 134, 283

Moore, M. G. 35, 225
Morgan, M. P. 139
Moskal, P. D. 3, 283
motivation 21, 260
Mount Royal University (MRU) 286; BEd program teaching competencies 288; Human Research Ethics Board (HREB) 288
MRU *see* Mount Royal University (MRU)
Mullainathan, S. 393, 394
multimodal blended learning (MMBL) 250, *251*; data analysis 255; data collection 255; design 260; discussion 259; ELLs benefits 260; ELLs experiences 256–259; employment of 260; interview participants 253; limitations 260; overall endorsement 259; qualitative methods 252–253; quantitative methods 252; reading comprehension 250, 260; results/findings 255–256, 259; study implementation 260–265; study treatments description 254–255; and teacher-directed (TD) schools 253–254, **254**; WIDA standards 253, **253**
Murin, A. 193
Murphy, E. 226
Musk, Elon 382

nanotechnology 367, 368
National Center for Academic Transformation (NCAT) 132, 133, 141
National Center for Education Statistics 150, 379
National Science Foundation (NSF) 316
Nature (journal) 390
NCAT *see* National Center for Academic Transformation (NCAT)
neotraditional students 34–35, 34–37; context, sample, and methods 40–42; implications and considerations 44–45; results 42–43; social presence, learning, and satisfaction 37–40; TAWD/VSSD 45–48
non-engagement 242
non-STEM courses 302, 304, 306
non-traditional students 34, 52
Norberg, A. 8, 269, 272, 277, 357
not passing (NP) rates 165, 166, 169–170
NP rates *see* not passing (NP) rates
NSF *see* National Science Foundation (NSF)
NVivo 197

410 Index

Oblinger, Diana 5
observations 237
obuchenie (training) 270
OER *see* Open Educational Resources (OER)
Office of Academic Innovation (OAI), PSU 165
Office of Distance Education 134, 136, 139–140
OLC *see* Online Learning Consortium (OLC)
OLCT (online lectures/in-class tutorials) blend 302, 304, 305, 309
Oliver, M. 11, 270
Omiteru, E. O. 164
online blended learning 269, 283; background 49–51; discussion 68–69; implications 70–72; limitations 70; methodology 51–53; results 53–68
online credit attempt ratio 52, 53–57, *54*, 61–64
online education 45, 116, 269; pedagogical models 373; perceptions and practices of 117, 119, 126, 127; student involvement 38
online integration 23, 195, 199–201, **200**, 208–209, **209**; growth areas 201; quality practices 200–201
online interaction 195, 206–208, **206**, **209**, 210; growth areas 208; quality practices 207–208
Online Learning Consortium (OLC) 3, 5–6, 11, 151
on-site facilitator 215, 219
open communication 122–123
Open Educational Resources (OER) 8, 315–316, 369; adapting to environment 326; at collaborative university 316, 321–322; context and procedure 320; cost effectiveness of 327; data analysis and results 322; design and construction of 318–319; discussion, and scholarly significance 326–328; ethical approval 328; informed consent 328; *Introduction to Petrology* course 320–321; Laboratory Course Assessment Survey (LCAS) 320, 324, **325**; *Laboratory Techniques in Geology* course 320–321; literature, background, and research question 316–317; Meaningful Learning in the Laboratory Instrument (MLLI) 320; perceived knowledge and attitudinal changes 322–326; Persistence in the

Sciences scale (PITS) 320; pre- and post-test questionnaires 323, **324**; at primary university 316, 320–321; proactive questions from students 326; reflection data collection 320; research design and methods 318
open-ended responses 154, 167
Open Science Framework (OSF) database 322
Optimum 368
Oregon State University (OSU) 97; 2016 survey 99, 103; 2019 survey 99, 103, 105; background 98; best practices 109–110; Center for Teaching and Learning 97, 104; discussion 103–106; faculty perceptions 100–101, **100**; future research 105–106; hybrid FLC participants about 101–103, **102**; institutional context 97–98; methods 98–99; online survey 111–115; results and analysis 99–103
OSF database *see* Open Science Framework (OSF) database
OSU *see* Oregon State University (OSU)
Owston, Ron 8, 300

Pace, J. R. 235
Padlet 227
Page, S. E. 386
paradigm shift 383
parent input 259
Pareto principle 292
partial dependence plots 53; hybrid students *59*, *60–61*, *65*, *66–68*; online students 54, *55*, *56–57*, *63*, *64–65*
participants 236
pathological politeness 293
Patterson, William 275
peer groups 342, 345
peer interaction 258
Penniston, Thomas 7, 73
perceived knowledge 322–326
perceived learning 38–39
perception AI 371
performance 233, 303–304, **303**
Persistence in the Sciences scale (PITS) 320
personal communication 122
personal community peers 218, 227–228
personalization 195, 203–205, **204**, 209–210, **209**; growth areas 205; quality practices 205
personalized instruction 24

Index **411**

personalized learning *see* adaptive learning
personalized tutoring 159
Pesek, J. 227
Petroleum Geo-Services (PGS): adaptive
   learning and cost effectiveness 181–185;
   hydraulic AL modules 185–187; long-
   term value 187–190; marine seismic
   data acquisition 179; offshore training
   management 178–179; seismic crew
   training 180–181; using Realizeit
   platform 184–185
PGS *see* Petroleum Geo-Services (PGS)
p-hacking 390
PhD *see* Doctor of Philosophy (PhD), in
   THS
physical therapy education: blended
   learning in 334–335; learning
   psychomotor skills 334
Piaget, J. 35
Picciano, Anthony G. 3, 9, 45, 132, 365
PI model *see* practical inquiry (PI) model
PITS *see* Persistence in the Sciences scale
   (PITS)
Portland State University (PSU) 165
Power, M. 283
practical inquiry (PI) model 296, *297*
Pre-course Geoscience Experience
   Questionnaire 320
predictive learning 187
preference, effective designs for 304–306,
   305
pre K–12 education, 375–377; *see also*
   K–12 blended education
pre-service teacher competency 194
problem-based learning 226
project-based learning 138, 226
proximal development zone 21, 217
PSU *see* Portland State University (PSU)
psychomotor skills 334; assessment 338;
   in blended teaching environments
   344–345; challenges with learning
   343–344; practicing 343; program
   design and student learning 340–341
Pulham, E. B. 194

QMCD *see* Quality Matters Course
   Development (QMCD)
Quality Matters Course Development
   (QMCD) 139–140
quantum computing 367, 368

Ragan, Larry 275
Ramani, S. 277

random forests 52–53
reading comprehension 250, 260
Realizeit platform 184–185, 188
real-time feedback 171, 172–173
reflective learning 233, 295
Reigeluth, C. 17
Reis, A. 98
relational interests 243
remote learning 375
Renfrow, Jeff 7, 33
researcher communications 238
retention rates 50
Retire Statistical Significance (article) 390
Rheingold, Howard 275
Rice, Mary Frances 8, 231, 235
Richmond, V. P. 39
Roberts, C. 383
Roberts, G. 272
Robertson, D. L. 88
Robinson, R. 174
robo-grading 371
robotics 366, 367
*Robot Proof, Higher Education in the Age of
   Artificial Intelligence* (Aoun) 377
Rodriguez, L. J. 248
Rodriquez-Manzanares, M. A. 226
Rogers, Everett 20
Rosling, H. 386, 390
Ross, B. 13
Rovai, A. P. 37, 38
Rowe, M. 335
Rozeboom, W. W. 389
Rubinstein, Sergei 273

Salami, T. O. 164
satisfaction 39–40
scarcity trap 393–394
Schlumpf, Karen S. 8, 349
Schoenfeld, A. H. 16
Scholarship of Teaching and Learning
   (SoTL) program 132, 138, 395
Schwartz, Dan 6
science and health research 8
science, technology, engineering, arts,
   math, and Indigenous (STEAMI)
   education 287
Scientific American 386
seismic crew training 180–181
self-determination 232
self-directed learning 35
self-efficacy 136
self-paced formative assessment 327
self-regulation 21, 216, 233–234, 351

412 Index

service learning 138
Setenyi, J. 387
Shafir, E. 393, 394
Sharkey, Mike 7, 73, 82
Sharpe, R. 272
Shea, P. 50
Short, Cecil R. 8, 193, 195
Short, J. 35
Silver, N. 388
Simon, Herbert 16
SIS *see* student information system (SIS)
Sitthiworachart, Jirarat 8, 300
Skibba, Karen 7, 116, 126
Skin in the Game (Taleb) 392
Skinner, B. F. 374
Sloan, Robin 384
Sloan-C BL workshops *see* Online
  Learning Consortium
small-group discussions 237–238, 345
Smith, Mark Jack 8, 178
social constructivism theories 35
social courses 74
Social Online Universal Learning (SOUL)
  147–148
social presence 37–38
social presence, of CoI framework
  284–285, *285*, **286**, 337; group
  cohesion 123; open communication
  122–123; personal/affective
  communication 122
social studies learning 250–251
Sorcinelli, M. D. 140
SoTL program *see* Scholarship of Teaching
  and Learning (SoTL) program
SOUL *see* Social Online Universal
  Learning (SOUL)
Southern New Hampshire University 3
spreaker.com 258
statistical hypothesis testing 388–390
STEAMI education *see* science,
  technology, engineering, arts, math, and
  Indigenous (STEAMI) education
Stein, J. 98
STEM courses 302, 304, 306
Stevens, M. 8, 231, 234–235, 247
Stimson, Rebecca 8, 214
Strogatz, Steven 372
structured learning 233
Structure of Scientific Revolutions, The
  (Khun) 383
student collaboration 207
student engagement 21
student information system (SIS) 152

student issues 21, **22**
student learning, Bloom's dilemma of 150
student outcomes 7
student persistence 164
student retention, and delivery modes:
  background 49–51; discussion 68–69;
  implications 70–72; limitations 70;
  methodology 51–53; results 53–68
student survey, in adaptive learning
  166–167
student-to-content interactions 306
student-to-student interactions 206,
  210, 306
student-to-teacher interactions 206, 210,
  217, 306
student work 237
study guides 341, 344
Sumler, D. 38
Sunchild E-Learning Community
  framework 283, *284*
super-cloud computing 367, 368–370
Suppes, Patrick 374
supplemental courses 74, 215, 302,
  304, 305
SurveyMonkey 295
survey responses 358
Swan, Karen 7, 49
systemocentrism 88
systems theory 20

Taleb, Nassim 392
Taleb, N. N. 385
Tangelo Park Program in Orlando 393, 396
Taroni, F. 389
TAWC *see* American Women's College,
  The (TAWC)
TAWD model *see* text-based, whole-
  group asynchronous discussion (TAWD)
  model
TD schools *see* teacher-directed (TD)
  schools
teacher-directed (TD) schools 253–254, **254**
teacher professional development 116–117
teacher support 258
teacher-to-student interactions 206, 210,
  217, 306
teaching failures 88
teaching presence, of CoI framework 337;
  design and organization 119–120, **286**,
  288–289, 294–295; direct instruction
  120–121, **286**, 292–294, 296–297;
  facilitation 121, **286**, 289–292,
  295–296

technological innovations 147
technology efficacy 41
technology-enhanced courses, in medical education 352
technology tools 257–258, 260
text-based, whole-group asynchronous discussion (TAWD) model 36–37
Thaler, R. H. 384
theoretical contributions, of blended learning 17–23; faculty issues 21–23, **23**; with good properties 17; institutional issues 19–21, **20**; instructional design issues 18–19, **19**; student issues 21, **22**
theory development, in design fields 16–17
Thompson, B. 389
Thompson, K. 172, 174
Thornton, N. 36
time-honored teaching methods 152
time scarcity 393, 394
Tinto, Vincent 89
Tough, A. 35
Trainin, G. 249
transactional distance framework 35
Trigwell, K. 11, 270, 272
t-test method 153
Tuckman, B. W. 42, 295
tunneling 394
two standard-deviation gap 149

UCF *see* University of Central Florida (UCF)
UMBC *see* University of Maryland, Baltimore County (UMBC)
UNC, Charlotte *see* University of North Carolina (UNC), Charlotte
United States Department of Education 377
United States History for Engaged Reading (USHER) curriculum 251
University of California at Los Angeles 296
University of Central Florida (UCF) 300
University of Maryland, Baltimore County (UMBC) 73–74; activity-to-grade relationship 86, *87*; College of Natural and Mathematical Sciences (CNMS) 82; course archetype sysadmin tool 74, 76–78; Division of Information Technology (DoIT) 74–75; Division of Professional Studies (DPS) 90; PIVOT (planning instructional variety in online

teaching) 90; waterfall chart 80, *81, 83–85*
University of North Carolina (UNC), Charlotte 131; Active Learning Academy 138–139; Audiovisual Integration and Support for Learning Environments (AISLE) 140; blended learning analysis 137–138; blended teaching implementation 132; Center for Teaching and Learning (CTL) 132, 138; continuing education (CE) 140; experimentation 133–136, **134–135**; beyond faculty development initiatives 140; large course redesign 132–133; Office of Distance Education 134, 136, 139–140; piloting LCR prgram 132–133; Quality Matters Course Development (QMCD) 139–140; scholarship of teaching and learning (SoTL) 132; Teaching and Learning Connections 140, 141
University of Phoenix 374
University of Southern New Hampshire 380
USHER curriculum *see* United States History for Engaged Reading (USHER) curriculum

VanLehn, K. 159
variable importance 53, **55**, 61, **62**
Vaughan, N. D. 8, 127, 128, 282–283, 306
Verizon 368
video-based, small-group synchronous discussion (VSSD) model 36–39, 41–42
videoconferencing 375
video sharing 341
Virginia Academic Libraries Consortium (VIVA) 316, 319
virtual labs 209
visible teaching 297
VitalSource 80
VIVA *see* Virginia Academic Libraries Consortium (VIVA)
Vo, M. H. 308, 309
vocabulary development 248
vocabulary knowledge 260
Voegele, Janelle D. 8, 163
VoiceThread 227
VSSD model *see* video-based, small-group synchronous discussion (VSSD) model
Vygotsky, L. 21, 35, 217, 270, 273

414 Index

Walser, Bill 390
Walster, G. W. 389, 390
Walters, Shea 8, 214
Warden, S. J. 334
waterfall chart 80, *81*, *83–85*
Watson, J. 193
Watts, Duncan 385
wealth advantage 393
Weaver, Gregory C. 8, 349
web-based technologies 282
Welch's t-test 153
Western Governors University 3, 374
Western Region University (WRU) 33
Where Good Ideas Come From (Johnson) 384
Whetten, D. 10, 17, 226
White, G. 165
Whitmer, John 7, 73
whole-class discussions 237
WIDA standards *see* World-Class
Instructional Design and Assessment
(WIDA) standards
Widmer, Maria 7, 116
Wiley, David 80

Wisconsin, university system in 380
Wladis, C. 50
Woods, R. H. 39
WordPress 295
work routines 240–241
World-Class Instructional Design and
Assessment (WIDA) standards 253, **253**
"World Cup" of biochemical research 365
Wozniak, Steve 382
WRU *see* Western Region University
(WRU)

Xie, K. 44

yard sale model 392
Yates, G. 43, 297
York, Dennis 8, 300
Yousof, S. 308
YouTube 186, 341

Zheng, Y. 136
Zirkin, B. 38
Zoom 41, 104, 283, 375

Printed in the United States
by Baker & Taylor Publisher Services